Barcelona

"All you've got to do is decide to go
and the hardest part is over.

So go!"

D0041404

THIS EDITION WRITTEN AND RESEARCHED BY

Regis St Louis,
Anna Kaminski, Vesna Maric

Contents

Left: **Seafood p131**
Barcelona's waterfront teems with restaurants serving fresh seafood

Above: **Palau de la Música Catalana p106**

Right: *Sardana* p116
Catalan folk dancing outside La Catedral

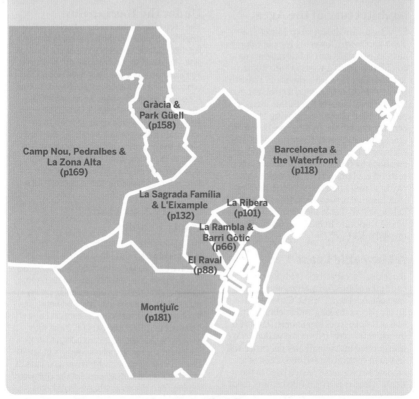

Gràcia & Park Güell (p158)

Camp Nou, Pedralbes & La Zona Alta (p169)

Barceloneta & the Waterfront (p118)

La Sagrada Família & L'Eixample (p132)

La Ribera (p101)

La Rambla & Barri Gòtic (p66)

El Raval (p88)

Montjuïc (p181)

Welcome to Barcelona

This enchanting seaside city boasts boundless culture, fabled architecture and a world-class drinking and dining scene.

Architecture of the Ages

Barcelona's architectural treasures span 2000-plus years. Towering temple columns, ancient city walls and subterranean stone corridors provide a window into Roman-era Barcino. Fast forward a thousand years to the Middle Ages by taking a stroll through the shadowy lanes of the Gothic quarter, past tranquil plazas and soaring 14th-century cathedrals. In other parts of town bloom the sculptural masterpieces of Modernisme, a mix of ingenious and whimsical creations by Gaudí and his Catalan architectural contemporaries, for which this city is so well known. Barcelona has also long inspired artists, including the likes of Salvador Dalí, Pablo Picasso and Joan Miró, whose works are in bold display in the city's myriad museums.

A Moveable Feast

Barcelona's great artistic traditions don't end at the canvas. Its masters of molecular gastronomy (Ferran Adrià, Carles Abellán et al) are part of the long and celebrated tradition of Catalan cooking. Simple, flavourful ingredients – olive oil, *jamòn,* seafood – are transformed into remarkable delicacies and served in captivating settings. Feast at an outdoor seaside table or step back to the 1920s in an art-nouveau-filled dining room.

Under the Iberian Sun

The deep blue Mediterranean beckons. Sun-drenched beaches make a fine backdrop to a jog, bike ride or leisurely stroll along the seaside – followed by a refreshing dip of course. You can also enjoy the view from out on the water while kayaking, windsurfing or taking it easy on a sunset cruise. Looming behind the city, the rolling forest-covered Collserola Hills provide a scenic setting for hiking, mountain biking or just admiring the view. Closer to the centre, hilltop Montjuïc offers endless exploring amid botanic and sculpture gardens, an old castle and first-rate museums with panoramic views at every turn.

Twenty-four Hour Party People

Barcelona's nights hold limitless possibilities. Start with sunset drinks on a hillside terrace or at a rustic beachside *chiringuito.* As darkness falls, music transforms the city: the rapid-fire rhythms of flamenco, brassy jazz spilling from basements, and hands-in-the-air indie-rock at vintage concert halls. Towards midnight the bars fill. Take your pick from old-school taverns adorned with 19th-century murals, plush lounges in lamp-lit medieval chambers or festive *cava* bars. If you're still standing at 3am, hit the clubs and explore Barcelona's unabashed wild side.

Why I Love Barcelona

By Regis St Louis, Coordinating Author

I love the sea, and taking an early-morning jog along the Mediterranean is my favourite way to start the day. I'm also a bit of a history nerd, and relish strolling the cobblestone lanes of the Gothic quarter, thinking about all the people in past centuries who walked these same streets. And then there's the food and drink – the first-rate tapas bars, the abundant and inexpensive wine, the superb and reasonably priced multicourse lunches. Add to all this Catalan creativity (Modernisme, Miró, Dalí), bohemian bars and stunning nearby getaways and you have, quite simply, one of the world's most captivating cities.

For more about our authors, see p320.

Casa Batlló by Antoni Gaudí

Barcelona's
Top 10

La Rambla *(p68)*

1 Sure it is the most touristy spot in town. But you can't come to Barcelona and not take the 1.2km stroll down the famous pedestrian boulevard that stretches toward the sea. It's pure sensory overload, with a parade of people amid open-air cafes, fragrant flower stands, a much-overlooked mosaic by Miró and the rather surreal human sculptures. If you can take your eyes off the boulevard, you'll notice key venues lining both sides of the street, including the elegant Gran Teatre del Liceu, the sprawling Mercat de la Boqueria and several major galleries.

👁 *La Rambla & Barri Gòtic*

La Sagrada Família *(p134)*

2 One of Barcelona's icons, the Modernista masterpiece remains a work in progress more than 80 years after the death of its creator, Antoni Gaudí. Fanciful and profound, inspired by nature and barely restrained by the Gothic style, Barcelona's quirky temple soars skyward with a playful majesty. Stepping through its sculpted portals is like walking into a fairy tale, where a forest of columns branch toward the ceiling and light shimmers through brilliant stained glass windows. Rich with beautifully wrought detail and packed with symbols, the basilica invites hours of contemplation.

👁 *La Sagrada Família & L'Eixample*

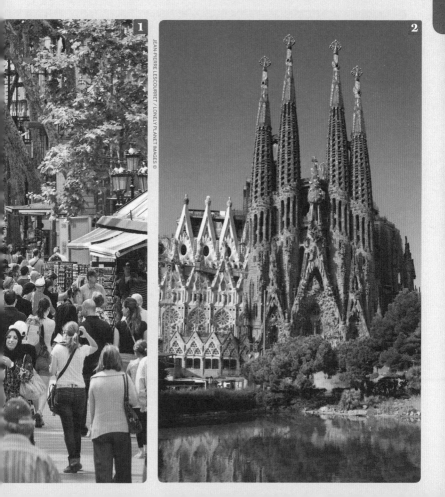

JEAN-PIERRE LESCOURRET / LONELY PLANET IMAGES ©

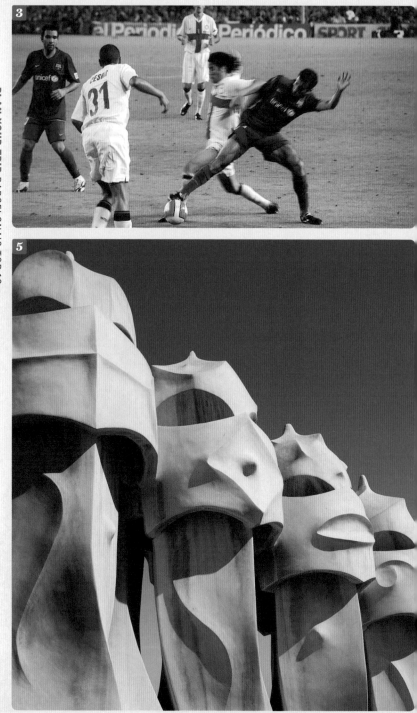

Camp Nou (p171)

3 For the sports-minded, little can compete with the spectacle of a match at FC Barcelona's massive football stadium. With a loyal fan base and an incredibly gifted team led by the likes of Lionel Messi, Camp Nou always hosts a good show – even if you can't make it to a game, it's still worth visiting. The 'Camp Nou Experience' is an interactive museum and stadium tour that takes you through the locker rooms and out onto the pitch, hallowed ground for many Catalans.

⊙ *Camp Nou, Pedralbes & La Zona Alta*

Mercat de la Boqueria (p90)

4 This temple of temptation is one of Europe's greatest permanent produce fairs. Restaurant chefs, homemakers, office workers and tourists all stroll amid the seemingly endless bounty of glistening fruits and vegetables, gleaming fish counters, dangling rolls of smoked meats, pyramids of pungent cheeses, barrels full of olives and marinated peppers, and chocolate truffles and other sweets. In the back, a handful of popular tapas bars serve up delectable morsels. There's always a line, but it's well worth the wait.

⊙ *El Raval*

La Pedrera (p139)

5 Astonishing architectural works dominate the district known as L'Eixample (the Extension), which was a blank canvas for the creation of some of Spain's finest buildings in the late 19th and early 20th centuries. La Pedrera is one of several Gaudí masterpieces on the stately Passeig de Gràcia. Here you'll find classic Gaudí flourishes: an undulating cliff-like facade, wildly sculpted wrought-iron balconies and cavern-like parabolic arches. Up on the rooftop (where summer concerts are sometimes staged), you can clamber beneath much photographed chimney pots, which stand like sentinels against the city backdrop.

⊙ *La Sagrada Família & L'Eixample*

Fundació Joan Miró (p188)

6 Picasso was born in Málaga, and Dalí hailed from Figueres, but surrealist visionary Joan Miró was a true dyed-in-the-wool *barcelonin*. As a revolutionary artist and proud Catalan, Miró etched much of his legacy on the city. The Fundació Joan Miró contains a treasure trove of his work, spanning his long and illustrious career. Footage of Miró and works by his contemporaries provide an illuminating portrait of the artist and his time. The spacious gallery is set above the city on the hills of Montjuïc, and is flanked by sculpture gardens.

◉ *Montjuïc*

Museu Picasso (p103)

7 For a portrait of the artist as a young man, head to the Museu Picasso, which showcases perhaps the world's best collection of the master's early work. Picasso lived in Barcelona between the ages of 15 and 23, and elements of the city undoubtedly influenced his work, from the dramatic, wide-eyed frescoes hanging in the Museu Nacional d'Art de Catalunya to the imaginative *trencadís*-style mosaics (pre-Cubist some say) of Gaudí. The museum's setting – inside five contiguous medieval mansions – adds to the appeal.

◉ *La Ribera*

6

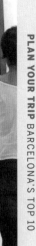

Església de Santa Maria del Mar (p105)

8 Blessed in 1384, the church of Our Lady of the Sea is one of the purest examples of Catalan Gothic architecture, generously broad and free of the baubles that characterise Gothic temples of other climes. It was raised in record time, a mere 59 years (half the time that La Sagrada Família will take), with stones painstakingly carried down from a quarry on Montjuïc. The church is remarkable for its architectural harmony and for managing to survive a devastating 11-day fire during the civil war. Live concerts and recitals are regularly staged inside the church.

◉ *La Ribera*

Museu Nacional d'Art de Catalunya *(p183)*

9 For many Catalans, Catalonia is not part of Spain but a country unto its own, with a unique and proud history. The Museu Nacional d'Art de Catalunya, encased in the grand Palau Nacional up on Montjuïc, proves the point with an impressive collection that delves into the riches of 1000 years of Catalan art. Its Romanesque frescoes, altarpieces and wood carvings – rescued from decaying churches in the Pyrenees – are truly staggering, and its collection of Gothic art gives a meaningful context to the Barri Gòtic (Gothic Quarter) down below.

◉ *Montjuïc*

La Catedral *(p71)*

10 A masterpiece of Catalan Gothic architecture, La Catedral is rightly one of the first stops on any visit to the Ciutat Vella (Old City). You can wander wide-eyed through the shadow-filled interior, with a dozen well-concealed chapels, an eerie crypt and a curious garden-style cloister that's home to 13 geese (which are deeply connected with the mythology of Barcelona's co-patron saint, Santa Eulàlia). Outside, there's always entertainment afoot, from *sardana* dancing on weekends to periodic processions and open-air markets, and street musicians are never far from the scene.

◉ *La Rambla & Barri Gòtic*

What's New

Tickets – A New Adrià Adventure

If you didn't make it to El Bulli, despair not. The Adrià brothers have opened up Tickets, a new venture that promises to keep true to their innovative spirit and blow minds and tastebuds – if you can get a table, that is. Booking is strictly online, two months in advance, so get clicking and hope for the artiest bite in town. (p193)

Palau Güell Reopens

After nearly two decades under wraps, the restored Palau Güell opened in 2011 to spectacular effect. Gaudí's early project shows the extent of his innovative genius. (p94)

Filmoteca de Catalunya

Will this be the project that finally gentrifies El Raval? The Filmoteca de Catalunya opened in February 2012 and aims to act as a cultural convergence zone. (p93)

Meet the Locals

Airbnb (www.airbnb.com) offers a fantastic new way of finding well-priced accommodation – and living as the locals do. You can rent a room in a *barcelonin*'s house, or even have an entire apartment to yourself. (p212)

Japanese Cuisine Blossoms

A number of excellent Japanese restaurants are popping up across town. Choose from sushi hotspot Koy Shunka, fantastic fusion *izakaya* Can Kenji and more. (p79, p145)

Las Arenas

Barcelona's second bullring, Las Arenas, on the busy Plaça d'Espanya, has been turned into a 5-floor shopping centre by Richard Rogers. The rooftop views are spectacular.

Museu Marítim

The wonderful Museu Marítim plans to reopen fully in 2013 – don't miss its great galleys and other seafaring wonders, and interactive displays that fascinate kids and grown-ups alike. (p120)

MIBA (Museu d'Idees i Invents de Barcelona)

This fun and educational museum, featuring original, quirky and hands-on displays, opened in 2011 in the midst of Barri Gòtic. (p75)

Disseny Hub

It's been a few years in the making, but the stunning new building of the Disseny Hub at Plaça de les Glòries is set to open in the summer of 2013. (p107)

El Paral.lel

A neighbourhood once famous as a hotspot for risque nightlife is getting its mojo back with a cluster of burlesque clubs and trendy bars.

Accessible Barcelona

Barcelona prides itself on its dedicated approach to accessibility for people with disabilities. Its adapted hotels, the Metro, Barceloneta's beaches and most museums are especially convenient. (p268)

For more recommendations and reviews, see
lonelyplanet.com/barcelona

Need to Know

Currency

The euro (€)

Language

Spanish and Catalan

Visas

Not required for US, Canadian, Australian, New Zealand or South African visitors for stays up to 90 days. European Union nationals can stay indefinitely.

Money

ATMs are widely available (La Rambla has many). Credit cards accepted in most hotels, shops and restaurants.

Mobile Phones

Local SIM cards can be used in unlocked European and Australian phones. Other phones must be set to roaming.

Time

Central European Time (GMT/UTC plus one hour).

Tourist Information

Oficina d'Informació de Turisme de Barcelona (📞 93 285 38 34; www.barcelonaturisme.com; Plaça de Catalunya 17-S; 🕗 8.30am-8.30pm; Ⓜ Catalunya) provides maps; sights information; tours, concert and events tickets; and last-minute accommodation.

Your Daily Budget

The following are average costs per day.

Budget under €50

➡ Dorm beds €15-25
➡ Set lunches from €9
➡ Free museums on Sundays

Midrange €50-200

➡ Standard double room €80-120
➡ Two-course dinner with wine for two €50
➡ Walking and guided tours €15-25

Top end over €200

➡ Boutique and luxury hotels €200 and up
➡ Multi-course meal at top restaurants per person €80
➡ Concert tickets to Palau de la Música Catalana around €50

Advance Planning

Three months before Reserve a table at a top restaurant. Buy tickets for important football matches.

One month before Check out reviews for theatre and live music and book tickets.

One week before Browse the latest nightlife listings, art exhibitions and other events to attend while in town. Reserve spa visits and organised tours.

A few days before Check the forecast on weather.com.

Websites

➡ **Lonely Planet** (www.lonelyplanet.com/spain/barcelona) Destination information, hotel bookings, traveller forum and more.

➡ **Barcelona** (www.bcn.cat/en) Town hall's official site with plenty of links.

➡ **Barcelona Turisme** (www.barcelonaturisme.com) City's official tourism website.

➡ **Le Cool** (lecool.com) Free weekly guide to what's happening in Barcelona (and other cities).

WHEN TO GO

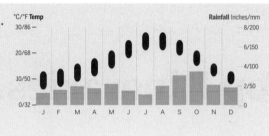

The sweltering summer (July and August) is peak tourist season: crowds swarm the city and its beaches. For pleasant weather – without the ocean dips – come in late spring (May).

Arriving in Barcelona

El Prat Airport Frequent aerobuses make the 35-minute run into town (€5.65) from 6am to 1am. Taxis cost around €25.

Estació Sants Long-distance trains arrive at this big station near the centre of town, which is linked by the Metro to other parts of the city.

Estació del Nord Barcelona's long-haul bus station is located in L'Eixample, about 1.5km northeast of Plaça de Catalunya, and is a short walk from several Metro stations.

For much more on **arrival** see p258

Getting Around

➡ **Metro** The most convenient way to get around. Trains run from 5am to midnight Sunday to Thursday, till 2am on Friday and 24 hours on Saturday. Targeta T-10 (10-ride passes) are the best value at €9.25; otherwise, it's €2 per ride.

➡ **Bus** A hop-on, hop-off Bus Turístic (p31), which leaves from Plaça de Catalunya, is handy for those wanting to see the city's highlights in one or two days.

➡ **On foot** To explore the old town, all you need is a good pair of walking shoes.

For much more on **getting around** see p262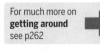

Sleeping

Barcelona has a wide range of sleeping options, from inexpensive hostels hidden in the old quarter to luxury hotels overlooking the waterfront. Good-value options include the small-scale B&B-style apartment rentals scattered around the city. Typical prices for a mid-range room for two runs from about €80 to €120 per night. Wherever you stay it's wise to book well ahead. If you plan to travel around holidays like Christmas, New Year's Eve, Easter or in the summer months, reserve a room three or four months ahead of time.

Websites

➡ **Airbnb** (www.airbnb.com) This global network has hundreds of rooms and apartments listed in Barcelona.

➡ **Oh-Barcelona** (www.oh-barcelona.com) Good-value selection of hotels, hostels and apartment rentals.

➡ **Barcelona 30** (www.barcelona30.com) Economical options for staying on a budget.

For much more on **sleeping** see p212

WHAT TO PACK

➡ Sturdy walking shoes for strolling over cobblestone lanes.

➡ A taste for seafood, *cava* (Catalan sparkling wine) and eating late at night.

➡ Sunglasses, sunscreen and a hat for defence against those Mediterranean rays.

➡ A page-turning novel set in Barcelona (try authors Manuel Vázquez Montalbán or Carlos Ruiz Zafón).

➡ A bathing suit for dips in the sea.

➡ A rain jacket or umbrella, especially for the damper months of April and November.

Top Itineraries

Day One

La Rambla & Barri Gòtic (p66)

 On day one spend the morning exploring the narrow medieval lanes of the Barri Gòtic. Have a peak inside **La Catedral** – not missing its geese-filled cloister – and stroll through the picturesque squares of **Plaça de Sant Josep Oriol** and **Plaça Reial**. Discover Barcelona's ancient roots in the fascinating **Museu d'Història de Barcelona**. Before lunch have a wander down La Rambla to take in the passing people parade.

> **Lunch** Circa-1786 Can Culleretes (p79) serves classic Catalan fare.

La Ribera (p101)

In the afternoon, wander over to La Ribera, which is packed with architectural treasures. Take a look inside the majestic **Església de Santa Maria del Mar**. At the **Museu Picasso**, beautifully set inside conjoined medieval mansions, you can spend a few hours taking in the early works of one of the great artists of the 20th century.

> **Dinner** For a seafood feast, head to unsigned El Passadís del Pep (p110).

La Ribera (p101)

Before having a late dinner (as is the custom in Spain), catch a show inside the **Palau de la Música Catalana**, one of the great Modernista masterpieces of Barcelona. Afterwards end the night with drinks at **El Xampanyet**.

Day Two

L'Eixample (p132)

 On day two start with a morning visit to **La Sagrada Família**, Gaudí's wondrous work in progress. It's worth paying a little extra for a guided tour (or audioguide) for a deeper understanding of Barcelona's most famous sight.

> **Lunch** Tapaç 24 (p145) offers gourmet tapas by celebrated chef Carles Abellán.

L'Eixample (p132)

After lunch, explore more of the great Modernista buildings by taking a stroll down L'Eixample's **Passeig de Gràcia**. Have a look at the three most famous buildings that make up **La Manzana de la Discordia**. Then visit one of Gaudí's house museums on the street – either **Casa Batlló** or **La Pedrera** further up the avenue.

> **Dinner** Experience culinary magic at L'Eixample gem Alkímia (p145).

L'Eixample (p132)

When it comes to cuisine, L'Eixample has Barcelona's biggest selection of award-winning restaurants. For an unrivalled dining experience, book a table at Jordi Vilà's much heralded **Alkímia**, where you can feast on inventive Catalan cuisine matched by first-rate Spanish wines. Afterwards, have a drink at the classy **Les Gens Que J'Aime** before moving on to the big beats at **City Hall**.

Day Three

Barceloneta & the Waterfront (p118)

 On your third day in Barcelona it's time to take in the lovely Mediterranean. Start the morning with a jog or a bike ride along the waterfront. Go from Barceloneta to Parc del Forum; beach-facing restaurants and cafes provide refreshment along the way.

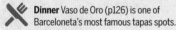 **Lunch** Seaside Can Majó (p124) serves up tasty *suquets* (seafood stews).

Barceloneta & the Waterfront (p118)

For lunch, make your way back to Barceloneta for a seafood feast. The options are bountiful, but for dining with a view, head to **Can Majó** and grab an outdoor table. Afterwards, stroll over to the **Museu d'Història de Catalunya** and peel back the centuries on an interactive journey into Catalan history.

Dinner Vaso de Oro (p126) is one of Barceloneta's most famous tapas spots.

Barceloneta & the Waterfront (p118)

In the evening there's no need to leave the edge of the sea. Have sunset drinks at one of the *chiringuitos* (beach bars), then have tapas back in Barceloneta at **Vaso de Oro** – or for something more upscale head to **Torre d'Alta Mar**. End the evening with stunning views over the sea and city from high up in the **W Hotel** at the bar **Eclipse**.

Day Four

Montjuïc (p181)

 Start the day with a scenic cable car ride up to Montjuïc, followed by a stroll past flower and sculpture gardens to the Museu Nacional d'Art de Catalunya. Take in the magnificent Romanesque frescos, vivid Gothic paintings and works by 17th-century Spanish masters.

Lunch O'Gràcia! (p164) is a charming neighbourhood spot for Catalan fare.

Gràcia (p158)

After getting a taste of Monjuïc, hop on the metro up to Gràcia and wander through its enchanting village-like streets. Cafes, bookshops and vintage shops all make for some worthwhile exploring. The bars surrounding its plazas come to life around sundown.

Dinner La Vinateria del Call (p79) is set in El Call's magical medieval streets.

Camp Nou, Pedralbes and La Zona Alta (p169)

In the evening, catch a football match at **Camp Nou**, the home of the top-ranked FC Barcelona. Amid the roar of the crowds, prepare for a serious adrenalin rush, especially if Barça is playing arch-rivals Real Madrid. If you're still going after the match, end the night over in Barri Gòtic, exploring the vibrant nightlife around Plaça Reial and along the narrow streets near Plaça George Orwell.

If You Like...

Markets

Mercat de la Boqueria One of Europe's largest food markets, with a countless array of tempting delicacies, plus tapas bars out the back. (p90)

Mercat de Sant Antoni A massive but largely tourist-free food market that also hosts a flea market on Sunday. (p42)

Mercat de Santa Caterina La Ribera's bountiful food market, with a wavy colourful roof, and archaeological fragments from the 1400s. (p108)

Els Encants Vells A sprawling flea market with plenty of treasures and trash on the edge of L'Eixample. (p154)

Mercadillo de la Plaça de Sant Josep A colourful collection of artworks sold by local artists on weekends in the Plaça de Sant Josep Oriol. (p75)

Port Antic A tiny weekend antiques market on the waterfront, at the foot of La Rambla. (p128)

Feria de Artesanía del Palau de Mar This waterfront market is a fine nautical place to browse for handicrafts and souvenirs. (p128)

Parks & Gardens

Parc de la Ciutadella Pretty landscaped grounds with dramatic fountains, curious artwork, the Catalan parliament building and a zoo. (p108)

El Raval's Moog nightclub (p98)

DIEGO LEZAMA / LONELY PLANET IMAGES ©

Park Güell A green wonderland with fine views over the city and surreal sculptural architecture courtesy of Gaudí. (p160)

Jardí Botànic One of Montjuïc's many lush gardens, full of Mediterranean flora as well as plants from similar climates. (p191)

Parc de la Creueta del Coll A family favourite near Parc Güell, with a pool, snack bar and trails. (p173)

Parc de Collserola A vast scrubby woodland with trails for bikers and runners and superb views from its hilltop location. (p174)

Jardins del Laberint d'Horta Picturesque gardens away from the city centre, with an artificial lake and waterfalls and a challenging labyrinth. (p175)

Museums

Museu d'Història de Catalunya Interactive exhibits cover 2000-plus years of Catalan history: Romans, Arabs, feudal times, the Spanish Civil War and the post-Franco era. (p121)

Museu d'Història de Barcelona Stroll over ruins of Roman-era Barcino, then see fine Catalan Gothic architecture inside a former royal palace. (p74)

Museu d'Art Contemporani de Barcelona A packed collection of 20th-century artwork in a modern Richard Meier–designed building. (p92)

Centre de Cultura Contemporània de Barcelona A must for art lovers, the CCCB hosts excellent cutting-edge exhibits. (p93)

CosmoCaixa A fun science museum that's a big hit with families – especially its re-created patch of Amazonian rainforest. (p176)

CaixaForum This art museum, housed in a Modernista building designed by Puig i Cadafalch, hosts fantastic (and free) exhibitions. (p189)

Dalí A bizarre and thought-provoking collection of sculptures and drawings by the great Catalan surrealist. (p78)

Museu-Monestir de Pedralbes A peaceful old convent with a 14th-century cloister and old-world religious artwork. (p172)

Poble Espanyol This kitschy leftover from the 1929 World Exhibition provides an overview of Spain's diverse cultures. (p190)

Museu Blau A spacious natural history and science museum with interactive exhibits and a huge animal collection – dinosaurs included. (p123)

Contemporary Architecture

Torre Agbar Jean Nouvel's striking cucumber-shaped tower dominates the new high-tech zone of 22@. (p122)

Teatre Nacional de Catalunya The design of this stately theatre is a perfect medley of Ancient Greece with high modernity. (p154)

El Fòrum A blue triangular building by Herzog & de Meuron that manages to be both organic and weirdly futuristic. (p123)

Plaça de les Glories Catalanes One of the latest projects to transform a messy urban area, with a new museum, reflecting pool and green space. (p247)

Las Arenas A remarkable conversion of bullring into shopping centre, with great views from the rooftop promenade. (p247)

For more top Barcelona spots, see the following:

➡ Visiting Modernista Buildings (32)

➡ Eating (p38)

➡ Drinking & Nightlife (p46)

➡ Gay & Lesbian Barcelona (p50)

➡ Entertainment (p52)

➡ Shopping (p54)

➡ Sports & Activities (p60)

PLAN YOUR TRIP IF YOU LIKE...

Staying Out Late

Moog A small, fun and relatively attitude-free downtown club that's a great spot for dancing. (p98)

Dietrich Gay Teatro Café One of the city's best cabarets, with drag shows most nights. (p153)

Elephant Party with the A-list crowd at this glammy mansion up in La Zona Alta. (p177)

Tinta Roja Expect live music, theatre, dancing and plenty of surprises in this colourful bohemian space. (p196)

Opium Mar A perennial club favourite for its seaside location, open-air deck and thumping dance floor. (p127)

Mirablau Well-known Mirablau, at the foot of Tibidabo, has magnificent views out over the city. (p177)

Harlem Jazz Club Hear live eclectic sounds till late in the morning at this old-school Gòtic gem. (p84)

La Confitería A fin-de-siècle mural-covered bar that was once a confectioner's shop. (p97)

Marula Cafè A small, eclectic, dance-loving space in Barri Gòtic with a serious penchant for funk and soul. (p82)

Haute Cuisine

Tickets Book well in advance to reserve a seat at Ferran Adria's newest culinary wonderland. (p193)

Cal Pep One of Barcelona's most famous tapas spots serves imaginative and mouth-watering dishes. (p112)

Torre d'Alta Mar Classic seafood dishes amid spectacular views overlooking the waterfront. (p124)

Restaurant 7 Portes An elegant art nouveau spot that's famed for its delectable paellas. (p124)

Cinc Sentits Elaborate and experimental multicourse meals have helped earn this place a Michelin star. (p148)

Pla One of the best restaurants in the Ciutat Vella, with a superb menu and a romantic medieval setting. (p79)

La Balsa Reason enough to venture out to La Zona Alta, La Balsa cooks up Catalan dishes with creative accents. (p176)

Alkímia A creative and beautifully designed place that should figure high on any visiting gourmand's list. (p145)

Cafè de l'Acadèmia An elegant spot serving delectable Catalan fare; the lunch menus are outstanding value. (p81)

Koy Shunka A hallowed space for indulging in brilliantly turned out Japanese dishes. (p79)

Fashion

La Manual Alpargatera The birthplace of espadrilles, and the world's best place to get a pair of these iconic Catalan rope-soled canvas shoes. (p87)

L'Árca de l'Àvia This atmospheric shop has an extraordinary collection of high-end vintage clothes dating back to the 1920s. (p85)

L'Illa Diagonal One of the top shopping malls for designer fashions – replete with amazing food court. (p57)

Antonio Miró Browse for haute couture at this elegant boutique and showcase for one of Barcelona's finest clothing designers. (p156)

Regia This perfumery has been around since 1928, and even has its own perfume museum on-site. (p157)

Obach This old-fashioned shop in the Barri Gòtic sells a fine array of hats for men and women. (p86)

Bagués Beautifully crafted jewellery in the architecturally stunning Casa Amatller. (p157)

FC Botiga If dressing up means sporting your team's colours, don't miss this temple to all things FC Barça. (p180)

Chocolate

Museu de la Xocolata This museum is a requisite stop for every chocolate lover. There's even a shop on-site selling the good stuff. (p109)

Cacao Sampaka One of the city's finest temples to chocolate, with a cafe where you can imbibe thick *xocolata calenta* (hot chocolate). (p155)

Escribà This Barcelona icon has two locations filled with creations that are (almost) too beautiful to eat. (p150)

Xocoa A convenient modern spot in Barri Gòtic where you can get your fix of chocolates, pastries, coffees and more. (p86)

Hofmann Pastisseria Lots of chocolate goodies, pastries and other temptations await you in this enticing shop in La Ribera. (p114)

Foix de Sarrià This brilliant pastry shop has been whipping up chocolate tortes and other finery since the 1860s. (p177)

Bubó A pastry shop and restaurant in La Ribera specialising in fantastical inventions. (p112)

Surprising Places

Museu Frederic Marès Barcelona's biggest curiosity cabinet, with a wild collection of religious sculpture, architectural fragments and 19th- and 20th-century ephemera. (p73)

Observatori Fabra Book for dinner under the stars in this Zona Alta observatory. (p175)

El Rey de la Magia A century-old magic shop full of mystery and intrigue. (p115)

Transbordador Aeri An old-fashioned cable car (with modern cables we're told) affording sublime views from its dangling trajectory. (p190)

Sinagoga Major One of Europe's oldest synagogues, this secretive place lay hidden for hundreds of years. (p77)

Bosc de les Fades Like a page torn from a fairy tale, this Barri Gòtic bar makes an enchanting setting for a drink. (p83)

Herboristeria del Rei A cinematic spice and herb shop that's been around since 1823. (p86)

Speakeasy True to its name, this well-respected Eixample restaurant lies hidden behind a cocktail bar. No passwords required. (p148)

Barcelona Pipa Club Above the Plaça Reial, this well-concealed place has long been a draw for the city's pipe smokers. (p83)

La Caseta del Migdia An outdoor bar with great views tucked amid the greenery way up on Montjuïc. (p196)

Month by Month

January

Barcelonins (people of Barcelona) head to the Pyrenees for action on the ski slopes, while others simply enjoy a bit of post-holiday downtime (school holidays run through to 8 January).

Reis/Reyes

On 5 January, the day before *Epifanía* (Epiphany), children delight in the *Cavalcada dels Reis Mags* (Parade of the Three Kings), a colourful parade of floats and music, during which countless sweets are launched from the floats into the crowds.

Festes dels Tres Tombs

In addition to live music and *gegants* (papier mâché giants worn over the shoulders of processionists), the festival dedicated to Sant Antoni features a parade of horse-drawn carts in L'Eixample near the Mercat de Sant Antoni every 17 January.

February

Often the coldest (and seemingly longest) month in Barcelona, February sees few visitors. Nonetheless, some of the first big festivals kick off, with abundant Catalan merriment amid the wintry gloom.

Carnestoltes/ Carnaval

Celebrated in February or March, this festival involves several days of fancy-dress parades and merrymaking, ending on the Tuesday before Ash Wednesday. The *Gran Rua* (Grand Parade) takes place on the Saturday evening from 5.30pm. Down in Sitges a much wilder version takes place.

Festes de Santa Eulàlia

Around 12 February this big winter fest celebrates Barcelona's first patron saint with a week of cultural events, from concerts to *castellers* (human-castle builders). See www.bcn.cat/santaeulalia for more details.

April

Spring arrives with a flourish, complete with wildflowers blooming in the countryside, Easter revelry and school holidays, although April showers can dampen spirits somewhat. Book well ahead if coming around Easter.

Día de Sant Jordi

Catalonia honours its patron saint, Sant Jordi (St George), on 23 April. Traditionally, men give women a rose and women give men a book – and La Rambla and Plaça de Sant Jaume fill with book and flower stalls.

Feria de Abril de Catalunya

Andalucía comes to the Parc del Fòrum with this

week-long southern festival featuring flamenco, a fun-fair and plenty of food and drink stalls. It kicks off in late April.

May

With sunny pleasant days and clear skies, May can be one of the best times to visit Barcelona. The city slowly gears up for summer with the opening of the *chiringuitos* (beach bars).

✺ L'Ou Com Balla

On Corpus Christi (late May or June), L'Ou com Balla ('the Dancing Egg') bobs on top of flower-festooned fountains around the city.

✺ Festa de Sant Ponç

To commemorate the patron saint of bee-keepers and herbalists, locals fill Carrer de l'Hospital in El Raval on 11 May with the chatter and bustle of a street market.

✺ Primavera Sound

For three days in late May (or early June), the Auditori Fòrum and other locations around town welcome a host of international DJs and musicians (www.primaverasound.com).

✺ Festival de Flamenco de Ciutat Vella

One of the best occasions to see great flamenco in Barcelona, this concentrated festival is held over four days at the Centre de Cultura Contemporània de Barcelona (CCCB).

June

Tourist numbers rise as Barcelona plunges into summer. Live music festivals and open-air events give the month a festive air.

✺ Festival del Grec

This eclectic program of theatre, dance and music runs for most of the summer. Performances are held all over the city, including at the Teatre Grec amphitheatre on Montjuïc, from which the festival takes its name (www.barcelonafestival.com, in Catalan).

✺ La Revetlla de Sant Joan/Verbenas de Sant Joan

The night before the Feast of St John the Baptist (24 June), the people of Barcelona hit the streets or hold parties at home to celebrate the Revetlla de Sant Joan (St John's Night).

✺ Pride Barcelona

The Barcelona Gay Pride festival is a week of celebrations held towards the end of June with a crammed program of culture and concerts, along with the traditional Gay Pride march on the last Sunday of the month (www.pridebarcelona.org, in Catalan).

☆ Sónar

Usually in mid-June, Sónar is Barcelona's celebration of electronic music and is said to be Europe's biggest such event. Locations change each year (www.sonar.es).

✺ Día de la Música

On 21 June a bevy of bands converges on Barcelona and other cities for an evening of indie music performances, usually held in Maremàgnum (www.diadelamusica.com, in Spanish).

August

The heat index soars; *barcelonins* leave the city in droves for holiday summers, as huge numbers of tourists arrive. It's a great time to hit the beach.

✺ Festa Major de Gràcia

Locals compete for the most elaborately decorated street in this popular week-long Gràcia festival held around 15 August. People pour in to listen to bands in the streets and squares, fuel on snacks and drink at countless street stands (www.festamajordegracia.org, in Catalan).

✺ Festa Major de Sants

The district of Sants launches its own week-long version of decorated mayhem, held around 24 August, hot on the heels of Gràcia's (www.festamajordesants.net, in Catalan).

✺ Festes de Sant Roc

For four days in mid-August, Plaça Nova in the Barri Gòtic becomes the scene of parades, the *correfoc* (fire run), a market, traditional music and magic shows for kids.

September

After a month off, *barcelonins* return to work. Temperatures stay warm through September, making for fine beach days.

✺ Diada Nacional de Catalunya

Catalonia's national day curiously commemorates

(Top) *Castellers* (human-castle builders) celebrate Festes de la Mercè in Plaça de Sant Jaume

(Bottom) *Barcelonins* light candles during the pre-Christmas Fira de Santa Llúcia

Barcelona's surrender on 11 September 1714 to the Bourbon monarchy of Spain, at the conclusion of the War of the Spanish Succession.

🎆 Festes de la Mercè

Barcelona's co-patron saint is celebrated with fervour in this massive four-day fest. The city stages sporting events, free concerts and street performers galore (www.bcn.cat/merce).

🎆 Mostra de Vins i Caves de Catalunya

Cava (sparkling Catalan wine) flows at this expo, usually held at Maremàgnum over four days towards the end of September.

🎆 Festa Major de la Barceloneta

Barcelona's other big September celebration honours Sant Miquel on 29 September. It lasts about a week and involves plenty of dancing and drinking, especially on the beach.

December

Barcelonins gear up for Christmas and the city is festooned with colourful decorations. Relatively few visitors arrive – at least until Christmas, when the city fills with holidaying out-of-towners.

🎁 Fira de Santa Llúcia

Held from early December to Christmas, this holiday fair features a market with hundreds of stalls selling all manner of Christmas decorations and gifts – including the infamous Catalan nativity scene character, the *caganer* (the crapper).

With Kids

Barcelona is a great city for older kids and teens – the Catalan attitude means they are included in many seemingly adult activities, like eating late meals at bars or restaurants. Babies will love the warm Mediterranean culture, and toddlers will be showered with attention.

KRZYSZTOF DYDYNSKI / LONELY PLANET IMAGES ©

El Gat de Raval by Fernando Botero

Dining Out With Kids

Barcelona – and Spain in general – is super friendly when it comes to eating with children. Locals take their kids out all the time and don't worry too much about keeping them up late, so going out to eat or to sip a beer on a terrace on a late summer evening needn't mean leaving children with minders – and they're bound to strike up a friendship or two! Spanish kids tend to eat the Mediterranean offerings enjoyed by their parents, but many restaurants have children's menus that serve up burgers, pizzas, tomato-sauce pasta and the like. Good local – and child-proof – options commonly found on tapas menus are the *tortilla de patatas* (potato omelette) or *croquetas de jamón* (croquettes with ham).

Best Kid Friendly Eateries

La Nena (p164)

Fantastic for chocolate and all manner of sweet things, this cafe has a play area and toys and books in a corner.

Fastvínic (p148)

Great for an off-peak lunch or quick dinner, while the kids entertain themselves by drawing on the glass wall.

Granja Viader (p94)

No kid will be left unimpressed – and without a buzz! – by the thick hot chocolate here.

Best Parks

Parc de la Ciutadella (p108)

It's got a zoo, a pond and a playground that gets a bunch of fun toys out after 4pm; it's also a great place to meet other parents.

Parc d'Atraccions (p174)

This fabulous funfair on top of mount Tibidabo is excellent for adrenaline-loving kids and grown-ups.

Parc de la Creueta del Coll (p173)

Excellent for its splashing pool, swings and snack bar.

Font Màgica (p190)

The light show is guaranteed to make the little ones shout 'Again!'

Parc de Collserola (p174)

A huge park in the hills that's welcome to families for its verdancy.

Best Kid-Friendly Museums

CosmoCaixa (p176)

A fantastic science museum whose interactive displays fascinate kids of all ages.

MIBA (Museu d'Idees i Invents de Barcelona, p75)

The Museum of Inventions and Ideas is great for toddlers or teens thanks to its fun, wide-ranging and interactive displays.

Museu de la Xocolata (p109)

It's all about chocolate – need we say more? Don't miss the chocolate-model-making sessions for kids.

Zoo de Barcelona (p109)

All the animals you can think of are in this relatively small space: yawning hippos, spluttering elephants and frowning gorillas. The big cats are here too, and the monkeys.

L'Aquàrium (p121)

This a fantastic aquarium, one of Europe's largest, with tank after tank of glimmering, colourful fish.

Poble Espanyol (p190)

Kids and parents can enjoy going through a mini Spain together; there are also special kid-oriented games and quests.

Best Ways to See the City

By Bike

Barcelona has tons of outlets that hire bicycles with little child-carrying trolleys in the front (p263).

On Segway

Parents and older kids and teens can mount these futuristic-looking vehicles and scoot around town (p31).

NEED TO KNOW

➡ Get a babysitter at **5 Serveis** (www.5serveis.com) or **Tender Loving Canguros** (www.tlcanguros.com).

➡ Nappies, dummies, creams and formula can be bought at any of the city's many pharmacies. Nappies are cheaper in supermarkets.

➡ Make sure you have your child's **EHIC card** (www.applyehic.org) before you travel within the EU.

➡ Barcelona's accessible Metro system is great for families with buggies. Be mindful of your bags though – pickpockets on the Metro like to target distracted parents.

➡ The narrow streets of the Ciutat Vella, with their unpredictable traffic and abundance of dog poo, are less buggy-friendly than the rest of Barcelona.

By Bus

Barcelona's bus tours are great for older kids – hop on and climb up to the open top floor to see the views (p264).

By Cable Car

Travel to Montjuïc from Barceloneta beach through the air. The Transbordador Aeri is bound to be loved by all ages (p122).

Best Shopping With Kids

Imaginarium

This international chain, with shops dotted around Barcelona (and Spain), sells toys and clothes. Some branches have a cafe for babies and kids (www.imaginarium.ie).

Ivo & Co.

The perfect place to buy vintage designer clothes and wooden toys for your tots (www.ivoandco.com).

Costura (p100)

For those who fancy making their kids' clothes, this gorgeous shop sells fabrics, patterns and all the sewing kits you need. Or you can just buy something ready-made.

Like a Local

Whether you're a frequent visitor or a first-timer, taking a local approach when it comes to eating, drinking and other amusements offers a rewarding way to experience the city.

Tapas bar at Mercat de la Boqueria (p90)

When to Dine

In Barcelona, and elsewhere in Spain, meal times run late. Most restaurants don't open for dinner until 8.30pm or 9pm and close at midnight or 1am; peak dining time is around 10pm. Locals commonly have lunch around 2 to 4pm. This is followed by a nice long siesta (a loll on the beach or in one of the parks is a fine choice when the weather is pleasant). Locals aren't big on breakfast – a croissant and a *cortado* (espresso with milk) is a typical way to start the day.

Water & Wine

Lunch or dinner, wine is always a fine idea, according to most *barcelonins*. Luckily, many restaurants offer *menú del día* (menu of the day, or fixed price) lunches that include a glass of red or white. If you become a regular, waiters may give you complementary refills or even leave the bottle. Of course, you can also opt for another drink. A word on water: no one drinks it straight from the tap (taste it and you'll know why). Order *agua mineral,* either *con gas* (bubbly) or *sin gas* (still).

Tapas

When hunger pains arrive in the afternoon or early evening, locals head out for a pre-dinner *tapa*. This means visiting the local favourite for a bite of anchovies, sausage, squid, wild mushrooms, roasted peppers or dozens of other tempting morsels. Wine, *cava* (sparkling wine) or beer all make fine accompaniments. Many tapas spots are quite lively stand-around-the-bar affairs. When it's time for a change of scenery, *barcelonins* might make their way to dinner or just move on to another tapas bar and skip the sit-down formality altogether.

Local Meal Spots

La Rambla is fine for a stroll, but no local would eat there. The same holds for Carrer Ferran and other tourist-packed streets in Barri Gòtic. The Gòtic does, however, have some local-favoured gems, particularly on the narrow lanes of the east side, closer to Via Laietana. For an authentic dining experience, browse the streets of El Born, Barceloneta, El Raval and Gràcia.

Weekends

Many *barcelonins* head out of town on the weekends. That could mean skiing in the Pyrenees in the winter, or heading up the Costa Brava in the summer. Those that stick around might hit up flea markets or produce markets, head to the beach, or have an outing in the park. The parks are liveliest on weekends, when local musicians, picnickers and pop-up markets add to the city's relaxed air. Culture-craving locals might hit an art opening, see a rep film (CCCB is a good place for a wide range of cultural fare) or catch a concert.

The Sunday Feast

Sunday is typically the most peaceful day for Catalans, and a fine occasion for gathering with family or friends over a big meal. Lunch is the main event, and many restaurants prepare Sunday-only specials. Lots of places close on Sunday nights too, so it's worth lingering over a long multi-course meal – a rich paella in Barceloneta followed by a long leisurely stroll along the waterfront is always a hit.

Festivals & Other Events

One of the best ways to join in for local amusement is to come for one of the city's big festivals (p21). During the summer (June–August), Musica als Parcs features 30 or so open-air concerts held from June to August at a dozen parks in Barcelona, and free concerts are held at various venues around the city. Stop in at a tourist office for the latest schedule.

Local Listings

If you can read some Spanish, browse the latest art openings, film screenings, concerts and other events in the Guia del Ocio (www.guiadelocio.com), Time Out Barcelona (www.timeout.cat, in Catalan) or daily pa-

PLAN YOUR TRIP LIKE A LOCAL

NEED TO KNOW
➡ **Spotted by Locals** (www.spotted bylocals.com/barcelona) Up-to-date reviews of favourite spots – restaurants, bars, cinemas, galleries and more. All are written by local residents and include a mix of new and classic places.

➡ **Living Barcelona** (http://barce lona.bligoo.es, in Spanish) Reviews on intriguing restaurants, bars, cafes and shops in Spanish.

➡ **Barcelona Sights** (http://barcelo nasights.blogspot.com) Keeps an eye on upcoming events.

➡ **Oh-Barcelona** (www.oh-barce lona.com/en/blog) This apartment-rental site also lists upcoming events and tips for weekend getaways.

➡ **Barça Central** (http://barca central.com) The latest news about FC Barça.

pers like La Vanguardia (www.lavanguardia. com) and El Pais (www.elpais.com). Friday papers list the weekend's events (most with pull-out supplements), and are often worth a read even if your Spanish is limited.

Football

FC Barcelona plays a prominent role in the city's imagination. Heading to a match at Camp Nou (p180) is the best way to catch a bit of Barcelona fever, but watching it onscreen at a tavern can be just as much fun depending on the crowd. For the most fervent fan base, head to Barceloneta, El Raval, Gracia or Sarria, where you'll find lively spots to catch a game.

Daily journal Marca (www.marca.com, in Spanish) has the latest on sporting news.

Sardana

On weekends (6pm on Saturday and noon on Sunday), aficionados of the traditional Catalan folk dance *sardana* gather in front of La Catedral for group dancing to a live 10-piece band.

For Free

With a bit of planning, you'll find Barcelona surprisingly affordable. Many museums offer free days, and some of the best ways to experience the city don't cost a penny – hanging out on the beach, exploring fascinating neighbourhoods and parks, and drinking in the views from hilltop heights.

CaixaForum

GUY MOBERLY / LONELY PLANET IMAGES ©

Walking Tours

Taking a self-guided walking tour (p30) is a great free way to enjoy some of the city's architectural treasures. Highlights include Park Güell (p160), La Sagrada Família (p134), Palau de la Música (p106) and the many buildings in L'Eixample. Several companies also offer pay-what-you-wish walking tours. Runner Bean Tours (p30) offers two different itineraries daily, exploring the Ciutat Vella and the Modernista architecture of L'Eixample.

Picnics

You can eat very well on a budget if you stick to set menus at lunchtime. For even less, you can put together a picnic of fresh fruits, cheese, smoked meats and other goodies purchased at local markets. Prices are a bit higher at La Boqueria (p90). You'll find better deals and an equally staggering selection at the Mercat de Sant Antoni (p42), on the western edge of El Raval. La Ribera also has the handy Mercat de Santa Caterina (p108). Barceloneta and the other beaches are good places for a picnic. For more shade and seclusion – and pretty views – head up to Montjuïc.

Museums

Entry to some sights is free on occasion, most commonly on the first Sunday of the month, while quite a few attractions are free from 3pm to 8pm on Sundays. Others are always free. The ones listed on the following page are most likely to attract your attention.

Alternatively, one combined €7 ticket, which has no expiry date, can be used to visit all the components of the Museu d'Història de Barcelona. The main centre is the Plaça del Rei complex, where you can discover parts of Roman and medieval Barcelona. The ticket also includes the Museu-Monestir de Pedralbes (p172), the Centre d'Interpretació in Park Güell (p160), civil-war air raid shelter Refugi 307 (p193), Via Sepulcral Romana (p78) and Domus Romana (p78).

Festivals

Another appealing budget option is to plan a trip around a festival (p21). Barcelona's best fests never charge admission and you can catch free concerts and other live entertainment, and eat and drink at street stalls for very little.

Concerts

From June to August, Barcelona hosts Música als Parcs (Music in the Parks), a series of open-air concerts held in different parks and green spaces around the city. Over 40 different concerts feature classical, blues and jazz groups. Popular venues include Parc de la Ciutadella (p108), Parc de Joan Miró (p192) and Parc Turó (Av de Pau Casals 19, Sant Gervasi). Stop in at the tourist office or go online (www.bcn.cat) for a schedule.

Dance

Dance-lovers visiting in early July shouldn't miss the five-day **Dies de Dansa** (www.mataro.com), featuring a wide variety of day and night performances – all free – held at venues like the Centre de Cultura Contemporània de Barcelona (p93), Fundació Joan Miró (p188) and Macba (Museu d'Art Contemporani de Barcelona p92).

Other Events

Another great free event in July is Montjuïc de Nit (www.bcn.cat/cultura/montjuicnit), which features one night of free music, dance, theatre and cinema, plus free admission to museums (open till 1am) up on Montjuïc. If you're around on Earth Day (21 & 22 April), be mindful that the Fira de la Terra has free performances, exhibits, food stalls and workshops with an earth-first focus.

FREE MUSEUMS

Free Always
➡ CaixaForum (p189)
➡ Castell de Montjuïc (p189)
➡ Centre d'Art Santa Mònica (p69)
➡ Església de Sant Pau (p93)
➡ Església de Santa Maria del Mar (p105)
➡ Església de Santa Maria del Pi (p75)
➡ Estadi Olímpic (p190)
➡ Fundació Joan Brossa (p144)
➡ Museu de Carrosses Fúnebres (p145)
➡ Museu d'Història de la Immigració de Catalunya (p122)
➡ Palau del Lloctinent (p73)
➡ Park Güell (p160)
➡ Temple Romà d'August (p78)
➡ Universitat de Barcelona (p142)

Free on the First Sunday of the Month
➡ Museu d'Història de Catalunya (p121)
➡ Museu Etnològic (p191)
➡ Museu Barbier-Mueller d'Art Pre-Colombí (p107)
➡ Museu Nacional d'Art de Catalunya (p183)
➡ Museu Picasso (p103)
➡ Palau Güell (p94)
➡ Palau Reial de Pedralbes (p173)

Free at Other Times
➡ La Catedral (p71) From 8am to 12.45pm and 5.15pm to 8pm Monday to Saturday.
➡ Jardí Botànic (p191) On the last Sunday of the month.
➡ Jardins del Laberint d'Horta (p175) On Wednesdays and Sundays.
➡ Museu de la Música (p143) From 3pm to 8pm on Sundays.
➡ Museu d'Història de Barcelona (p74) From 4pm to 8pm on the first Saturday of the month.
➡ Museu Marítim (p120) From 3pm to 8pm on Sundays.

Guided Tours & Walks

There are many ways to get a more in-depth look at the city, whether on a specialised walking tour through the Ciutat Vella, on a bicycle excursion around the centre or on a hop on, hop off bus tour all across town.

Bike tour on Plaça del Rei

KRZYSZTOF DYDYNSKI / LONELY PLANET IMAGES ©

Walking Tours

The Oficina d'Informació de Turisme de Barcelona organises a series of guided walking tours (p157). One explores Barri Gòtic; another follows in Picasso's footsteps and winds up at the Museu Picasso, to which entry is included in the price; and a third takes in the main jewels of Modernisme. It also offers a 'gourmet' tour of traditional purveyors of fine foodstuffs across the Ciutat Vella (Old City). Stop by the tourist office, go online or call for the latest schedule. All tours last two hours and start at the tourist office.

More specialised tours are also bookable through the tourist office. Themes include running, shopping, literary Barcelona, film tours, birdwatching and the civil war.

Barcelona Metro Walks (http://bcnshop. barcelonaturisme.com) consists of seven self-guided routes across the city, combining use of the Metro and other public transport as well as stretches on foot. Tourist information points at Plaça de Catalunya (p267) and Plaça de Sant Jaume (p267) sell the €13 package, which includes a walks guide, 2-day transport pass and map.

My Favourite Things (☑63 726 54 05; www.myft.net; tours €26-32) offers tours for no more than 10 participants based on numerous themes: anything from design to food. Other activities include flamenco and salsa classes and bicycle rides in and out of Barcelona. Meeting points vary, so phone ahead or check the website for more information.

Runner Bean Tours (☑63 610 87 76; www.runnerbeantours.com; ☉11am year-round & 4.30pm Apr-Sep) comprises several daily thematic tours. It's a pay-what-you-wish tour, with a collection taken at the end for the guide. The Old City tour explores the Roman and medieval history of Barcleona, visiting highlights in the Ciutat Vella (Barri Gòtic, El Raval and La Ribera). The Gaudí tour takes in the great works of Modernista Barcelona. It involves two trips on the Metro. Both tours depart at 11am from Plaça Reial (and also at 4.30pm from April through September) and last for about 2 and a half hours. It's wise to book ahead, as tour numbers are limited. Runner Beans also runs a Kids and Family Walking Tour; check the website for departure times and to book a spot.

Scooter & Go-Cart Tours

Barcelona Scooter (Map p302; ☑93 221 40 70) offers a three-hour tour around the city by scooter (€50) in conjunction with the city tourism office. Departure is from the Cooltra rental outlet at 3.30pm on Thursdays and 10.30am on Saturdays.

Barcelona Segway Fun (Map p292; ☑67 048 40 00; www.barcelonasegwayfun.com) offers urban and even country tours on two-wheel people-movers! A 90-minute tour costs €45 and leaves from Plaça San Just in Barri Gòtic at 12.30pm daily. Two-hour tours also depart from here (10am and 5pm, €57).

GoCar (Map p300; ☑90 230 13 33; www. gocartours.es; Carrer de Freixures 23bis; per hr/ day €35/€99) has GPS-guided 'cars' (actually two-seat, three-wheel mopeds) that allow you to tour around town, park where motorbikes are allowed and listen to commentaries on major sites as you go. The GPS system makes it virtually impossible to get lost.

Trixi Tours

These three-wheeled cycle taxis (Map p292; ☑93 268 21 05; www.trixi.info; Plaça dels Traginers 4) operate around the Ciutat Vella, the waterfront and the city centre (noon to 8pm daily between March and November). They can take two passengers on guided tours costing €15/25/45/65/150 for 30-minute/1-

BICYCLE TOURS

Barcelona is awash with companies offering bicycle tours. Tours typically take two to four hours and generally stick to La Sagrada Família, the Ciutat Vella and the beaches. Operators include the following:

➡ **Bike Tours Barcelona** (☑93 268 21 05; www.bicicletabarcelona.com; Carrer de l'Esparteria 3; Ⓜ Barceloneta; tours €22)

➡ **Barcelona by Bike** (☑93 268 81 07; www.barcelonabybike.com; Carrer de la Marina 13; Ⓜ Ciutadella Vila Olímpica; tours €22)

➡ **CicloTour** (☑93 317 19 70; www. barcelonaciclotour.com/eng; Carrer dels Tallers 45; Ⓜ Catalunya; tours €21)

➡ **BarcelonaBiking.com** (p263)

NEIGHBOURHOOD TOURS

For more self-guided tours in this guide, see the following sections:

➡ Barri Gòtic (p80)

➡ El Raval (p95)

➡ La Ribera (p111)

➡ Barceloneta & the Waterfront (cycling tour, p125)

➡ L'Eixample (p146)

➡ Gràcia (p163)

➡ Montjuïc (p195)

hour/2-hour/3-hour/8-hour tours. You can find them in front of La Catedral.

Bus Tours

Bus Turístic (☑93 285 38 32; www.barcelona turisme.com; 1 day €24/14 adult/child, 2 days €31/18 adult/child; ☉9am-8pm, 7pm in winter; every 5-25 minutes) is a hop on, hop off service that stops at virtually all of the city's main sights. Audioguides (in 10 languages) provide running commentary on the 44 stops on the three different circuits. The service operates from Plaça de Catalunya and Plaça del Porta de la Pau.

Tickets are available online and on the buses, and allow unlimited travel over one day or two consecutive days.

The two key routes take about two hours each; the blue route runs past La Pedrera on Passeig de Gràcia and takes in La Sagrada Família, Park Güell and much of La Zona Alta (including Pedralbes and Camp Nou). The red route also runs up Passeig de Gràcia and takes in Port Vell, Port Olímpic and Montjuïc. The third (green route), from Port Olímpic to the Fòrum, runs from April to September and takes 40 minutes. Other private companies run similar services.

Barcelona Guide Bureau places professional guides at the disposal of groups for tailor-made tours of the city. Several languages are catered for. It also offers a series of daily tours, from a six-hour exploration of Barcelona (adult/child €66/35 departing at 9am) to a trip to Montserrat, leaving Barcelona at 3pm and lasting about four hours (adult/child €45/20).

Tours are also available by boat (p129) and even helicopter (p263).

Steps leading up the Sala Hipóstila (Doric Temple), Park Güell

⊙ Visiting Modernista Buildings

With hundreds of photogenic buildings scattered around town, Barcelona can present a daunting challenge to those seeking a grand overview of its Modernista masterpieces. What follows is a practical guide to getting the most out of a visit to this incredible city. For more on the story of Gaudí, his contemporaries and Modernista architecture, see (p241).

Casa Batlló by Antoni Gaudí

Keys to Modernisme

Barcelona's Modernista buildings arose during La Renaixença, a period of great artistic and political fervor that was deeply connected to Catalan identity, and transformed early-20th-century Barcelona into a showcase for avant-garde architecture. Aiming to establish a new Catalan archetype, Gaudí and other visionary architects drew inspiration from the past, using elements from the Spanish vernacular – shapes, details and brickwork reminiscent of Islamic, Gothic and Renaissance designs. The Modernistas also revived traditional artisan trades, which you can see in the exquisite stonework and stained-glass windows, and in their artful use of wrought iron, ceramics and mosaic tiles. Nature was celebrated and imitated to perfection in Gaudí's organic forms: leaning tree-like columns, walls that undulate like the sea, and the use of native plants as decorative elements. Inside these buildings, the artistry and imaginative design continues; for a deeper appreciation of how it all works as a whole, visitors will want to spend ample time both inside and out.

Walking vs Metro

Modernista sites in L'Eixample and the Ciutat Vella are best visited on foot. To visit La Sagrada Família or Park Güell, however, you'll need to take the Metro – unless you're up for a long and time-consuming walk.

NEED TO KNOW

Organised Tours

A number of companies offer Modernista walking tours:

Barcelona Walking Tours (p157) has a Modernista tour that leaves daily from the tourist office on Plaça de Catalunya and takes in some of the great Modernista buildings of L'Eixample.

Runner Bean Tours (p30) has a daily tour devoted specifically to Gaudí. It's conducted mostly on foot with two short jaunts by Metro.

Barcelona has several other guided tour options, including by bus, bicycle and scooter (p31).

Ruta del Modernisme

Aficionados of Barcelona's Modernista heritage should consider the **Ruta del Modernisme** (www.rutadelmodernisme. com) pack. For €12 you receive a guide to 115 Modernista buildings great and small, a map and discounts of up to 50% on the main Modernista sights in Barcelona, as well as some in other municipalities around Catalonia. The discounts are valid for a year. For €18 you get another guide and map, Sortim, which leads you to bars and restaurants located in Modernista buildings around the city. The proceeds of these packs go to the maintenance and refurbishment of Modernista buildings.

The Ruta del Modernisme guide (in various languages) is available in bookstores. You can then take it to one of three Centres del Modernisme to obtain the discount cards, or you can buy the lot at those centres. The most accessible and likely to be open centre is Plaça de Catalunya's main tourist office (p267).

How Much Time

It's impossible to see all the major sites in one day, although you can see some of the highlights on a packed day or two of sightseeing. To avoid architecture fatigue, you might prefer to spread your visits out on three or four half-days, mixing Modernisme with museum-going, downtime on the beach, and other sightseeing.

(Above) Casa Batlló, known to locals as *casa dels ossos* (house of bones) or *casa del drac* (house of the dragon)

(Left) Gaudí's Salamander sculpture at Park Güell, incorporating the Catalan mosaic style of *trencadís*

Modernista Buildings

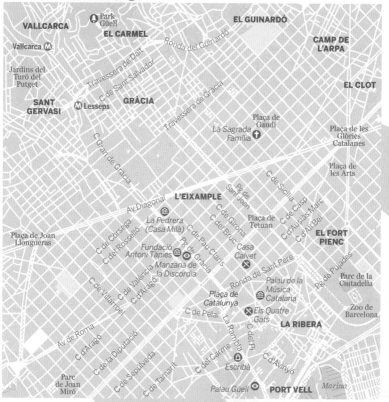

Where to Start

L'EIXAMPLE

Plaça de Catalunya is a fine entry point to the Modernista gems of L'Eixample, with a stroll up the scenic Passeig de Gràcia past many fine architectural works. You could spend a full day visiting the mansion-museums here, and dipping on and off the avenue, between Plaça de Catalunya and Plaça de Joan Carles I (about nine blocks northwest).

If time is limited, head to the Passeig de Gràcia Metro stop, just steps from three of the finest buildings on the avenue. Here you can see three magnificent buildings – Casa Batlló (p140), Casa Amatller (p141) and Casa Lleó Morera (p142) – each an individual masterpiece designed by different architects and embodying a radically varied perspective on the Modernista experience. These three buildings by Gaudí, Puig i Cadafalch and Domènech i Montaner all lie on one block and together comprise the Manzana de la Discordia (Block of Discord, p140).

PARK GÜELL

Park Güell provides a fascinating counterpoint to the more urban setting of L'Eixample. Here, architecture interacts in unusual ways with the hilly landscape to create a fairytale-like wonderland. Aside from mosaic-covered walls and sculptures, a cavernous space of leaning tree-like columns and a fantastic much-photographed lizard (or dragon), Park Güell is also home to the **Casa-Museu Gaudí** (www.casamuseugaudi.org; adult/senior & student €5.50/4.50; ☉10am-8pm), where Gaudí lived for 20 years; it's packed with some of his thought-provoking designs.

LA SAGRADA FAMÍLIA

It's a long walk (2km) from the Plaça de Catalunya up to the Basilica, so it's worth hopping on the Metro to save your stamina (which will come in handy inside the massive church). Allow several hours to adequately explore the site inside and out. You can buy your tickets online and avoid having to wait in line (though you'll need access to a printer to print out your tickets).

CIUTAT VELLA

Not all the Modernista buildings are in L'Eixample. El Raval has one striking Gaudí work, the Palau Güell (p94), while Barri Gòtic is home to the intriguing Casa Martí, better known for the restaurant Els Quatre Gats (p37), and La Ribera has the stunning Palau de la Música Catalana (p106). It's possible to see them all on a leisurely half-day stroll between the three neighbourhoods.

When to Go

Mornings are the best time to visit these sites, both to beat the crowds, and for optimal light if you're taking pictures. Prepare for long lines at La Sagrada Família – if possible, avoid going on weekends when lines are longest.

Audioguides

Audioguides are offered at most major sites for a few extra euros, and provide more in-depth information about the building's unique design, as well as background information on its architect and era. Specialised guidebooks to the most important architectural sites are also available at many of the museum bookstores.

Suggested Routes
A MORNING OF MODERNISME

Start the day off with pastries and coffee at the Modernista gem Escribà (Map p292). From there walk a few blocks south and down Carrer Nou de Rambla to visit the recently restored Palau Güell (p94), one of Gaudí's early masterpieces. Afterwards take the Metro up to Passeig de Gràcia and have a look at the so-called Manzana de la Discordia – Casa Batlló (p140), Casa Amatller (p141) and Casa Lleó Morera (p142) – deciding for yourself who among Gaudí, Puig i Cadafalch and Domènech i Montaner has created the most successful work of art. Afterwards, stroll up Passeig de Gràcia, a true architectural showcase, and end your tour at Gaudí's La Pedrera (p139).

RICHARD CUMMINS / LONELY PLANET IMAGES ©

Casa Amatller by Josep Puig i Cadafalch

Stained-glass ceiling at the Palau de la Música Catalana by Lluís Domènech i Montaner

A DAY OF MODERNISME

For a full day of exploration, continue on from La Pedrera and treat yourself to lunch at first-rate restaurant Casa Calvet (p147, reserve ahead), set inside one of Gaudí's classic buildings. After dining, head up to La Sagrada Família (p134) for a tour of one of the world's most dynamic ecclesiastical designs. Afterwards, make your way up to Park Güell (p160) for an afternoon stroll through the eye-catching park. Next head back down to the Ciutat Vella for a concert inside the luminescent Palau de la Música Catalana (p106, buying tickets in advance is recommended). There's an onsite cafe if you need a bite before the show. Afterwards, stroll over to **Els Quatre Gats** (Map p292; ☎93 302 41 40; Carrer de Montsió 3; meals €30; ⊗8am-2am; ⓂUrquinaona) for a nightcap (or a meal) inside a whimsical building designed by Puig i Cadafalch.

Quimet i Quimet tapas bar (p193), El Poble Sec

 **Eating**

Barcelona has a celebrated food scene fuelled by a combination of world-class chefs, imaginative recipes and magnificent ingredients fresh from farms and the sea. Catalan culinary masterminds like Ferran Adrià and Carles Abellán have become international icons, reinventing the world of haute cuisine, while classic old-world Catalan recipes continue to earn accolades in dining rooms and tapas bars across the city.

Diners in Plaça Reial

New Catalan Cuisine

Since the closing of the El Bulli – widely hailed as one of the world's best restaurants – in 2011, Ferran Adrià, along with his brother Albert, has turned his focus to Barcelona, with the opening of the tapas bars Tickets and 41-degrees. Like El Bulli, there's plenty of imagination among deconstructed dishes like liquid olives, 'air baguettes' (made with Iberian ham) and parmesan ice cream. For more on the new Catalan cuisine, better known as *nueva cocina española*, see p253.

Other great chefs who've followed on the heels of Adrià continue to redefine contemporary cuisine. The Michelin-starred chef Carles Abellán, at Tapaç 24, playfully reinterprets traditional tapas with dishes like the bite-sized mini-pizza sashimi with tuna; *melón con jamón*, a millefeuille of layered carmelised Iberian ham and thinly slice melon; oxtail with cauliflower puree; and an ever-changing parade of other mouth-watering bites.

Another star of the Catalan cooking scene is Jordi Vilà, who continues to wow diners at Alkímia with reinvented Catalan classics. The Roca brothers, famed for their two Michelin-star restaurant El Cellar de Can Roca in Girona, have brought culinary high-art to Moo, operating out of the Hotel Omm. Other major players on the Catalan dining scene are Fermi Puig, head chef at the five-star Hotel Majestic; Xavier Pellicer at ABaC Barcelona; and Sergi Arola, who's in charge of the kitchen at Hotel Arts.

NEED TO KNOW

Price Ranges

In our listings, we've used the following price codes to represent the cost of a main course:

€	less than 10
€€	10 to 20
€€€	over 20

Opening Hours

Most restaurants open from 1 to 4pm and from 8.30pm to midnight.

Reservations

➡ At midrange restaurants and simpler taverns you can usually turn up and find a spot without booking ahead.

➡ At high-end restaurants, and for dinner especially, it is safer to make a booking. Thursday to Saturday nights are especially busy.

Tipping

A service charge is often, but not always, included in the bill. Catalans and other Spaniards are not overwhelming tippers. If you are particularly happy, 5% to 10% on top is generally fine.

Menú del Dia

The *menú del día*, a full set meal with water and wine (and usually with several meal options), is a great way to cap prices at lunchtime. They start from around €8 to €10 and can move as high as €25 for more elaborate offerings.

Menú de Degustación

At high-end restaurants you can occasionally opt for a *menú de degustación*, a tasting menu involving samples of different dishes. This can be a great way to get a broader view of what the restaurant does and has the advantage of coming at a fixed price.

Dress Code

Barcelonins tend toward informal but stylish wear when eating out, whether at festive tapas bars or mid-range restaurants. Although there are no strict dress codes, locals dress up a bit more for the finer dining rooms: skirts or dresses for ladies, button-downs and slacks or designer jeans for the gents (sports jackets are optional; ties are a rarity).

(Above) Biscuits and cakes on display in a shop window

(Left) Tapas

Classic Catalan Cuisine

Traditional Catalan recipes showcase the great produce of the Mediterranean: fish, prawns, cuttlefish, clams, pork, rabbit, game, first-rate olive oil, peppers and loads of garlic. Classic dishes also feature unusual pairings: cuttlefish with chickpeas, cured pork with caviar, rabbit with prawns, goose with pears.

SAUCES

The essence of Catalan food lies in its sauces for meat and fish. There are five main types: *sofregit* (fried onion, tomato and garlic), *samfaina* or *chanfaina* (*sofregit* plus red pepper and aubergine or courgette), *picada* (based on ground almonds, usually with garlic, parsley, pine nuts or hazelnuts, and sometimes breadcrumbs), *allioli* (pounded garlic with olive oil, sometimes with egg yolk added to make more of a mayonnaise) and *romesco* (an almond, red pepper, tomato, olive oil, garlic and vinegar sauce, used especially with *calçots*).

PAELLA & FIDEUÀ

Arròs a la cassola or *arròs a la catalana* is the moniker given to Catalan paella. It's cooked in an earthenware pot without saffron, whereas *arròs negre* is rice cooked in squid ink – much tastier than it sounds. *Fideuà* is similar to paella, but uses vermicelli noodles rather than rice. It usually comes with a little side dish of *allioli*.

CALÇOTS

Catalans are passionate about *calçots* (large, sweet spring onions), which are barbecued over hot coals, dipped in tangy *romesco* sauce and eaten voraciously when in season (between January and March). *Calçots* are usually a first course, followed by copious meat and sausage dishes.

Classic Catalan Dishes

STARTERS

Amanida catalana (Catalan salad) Almost any mix of lettuce, olives, tomatoes, hard-boiled eggs, onions, chicory, celery, green peppers and garlic, with tuna (almost always canned), ham or sausage, and either mayonnaise or an oil and vinegar dressing.

Calçots amb romesco Sweet and juicy spring onions cooked up on a barbecue.

Escalivada Red peppers and aubergines (sometimes onions and tomatoes too), grilled, cooled, peeled, sliced and served with an olive oil, salt and garlic dressing.

Esqueixada Salad of *bacallà*/*bacalao* (shredded salted cod) with tomatoes, red peppers, onions, white beans, olives, olive oil and vinegar.

Pintxos Basque-style tapas, often served with a toothpick.

MAIN COURSES

Arròs a la cassola/arroz a la catalana Catalan paella, cooked without saffron.

Arròs negre Rice cooked in black cuttlefish ink.

Bacallà a la llauna Salted cod baked in tomato, garlic, parsley, paprika and wine.

Botifarra amb mongetes Pork sausage with fried white beans.

Cargols/Caracoles Snails, often stewed with *conill*/*conejo* (rabbit) and chilli.

Escudella A meat sausage and vegetable stew, the sauce of which is mixed with noodles or rice and served as a soup. The rest is served as a main course and is known as *card d'olla*. It is generally only available in winter.

Fideuà Similar to paella but with vermicelli noodles as the base. It is usually served with tomato and meat and/or sausage or fish; there is also a cuttlefish-ink version. *Fideuà* is most often accompanied by a little side dish of *allioli* (pounded garlic with olive oil) that you can mix in as you wish.

Fricandó Pork and vegetable stew.

TOP TAPAS PLATES

If you opt for *tapes*/tapas, it is handy to identify some of the common items:

➡ **boquerons/boquerones** white anchovies in vinegar – delicious and tangy

➡ **mandonguilles/albóndigas** meatballs

➡ **pebrots/pimientos de Padrón** little green peppers from Galicia, some of which are hot

➡ **patates braves/patatas bravas** potato chunks bathed in a slightly spicy tomato sauce, sometimes mixed with mayonnaise

➡ **gambes/gambas** prawns, either done *al all/al ajillo* (with garlic) or *a la plantxa/plancha* (grilled)

➡ **chipirons/chipirones** baby squid

➡ **calamars/calamares a la Romana** deep-fried calamari rings

Sarsuela/zarzuela Mixed seafood cooked in *sofregit* (fried onion, tomato and garlic sauce) with seasonings.

Suquet de peix Fish and potato hotpot.

Truita de botifarra Sausage omelette, a Catalan version of the famous Spanish *tortilla*.

DESSERTS
Crema catalana A cream custard with a crisp burnt-sugar coating.

Mel i mató Honey and fresh cream cheese.

Music A serving of dried fruits and nuts, sometimes mixed with ice cream or a sweetish cream cheese and served with a glass of muscatel.

Food Markets

Barcelona has some fantastic food markets. Foodies will enjoy the sounds, smells and most importantly tastes of the Mercat de la Boqueria (p90). This is probably Spain's biggest and best market, and it's conveniently located just off La Rambla. Here you can find temptations of all sorts, from plump fruits and veggies, freshly squeezed juices, artisanal cheeses, smoked meats, seafood and pastries. The best feature: an array of tapas bars and food stalls in the back where you can sample amazingly fresh dishes cooked up to perfection.

La Boqueria is not the only food market in Barcelona. Most *barris* host their own markets, which are generally much smaller affairs and relatively tourist-free. Some other great market options are **Mercat de Sant Antoni** (Map p306; Carrer de Mallorca 157; ⏱7am-8.30pm; ⓂHospital Clínic), Mercat de Santa Caterina (p108), **Mercat del Ninot** (Map p310; Carrer de Mallorca 157; ⓂHospital Clínic), **Mercat de la Llibertat** (Map p312; Plaça de la Llibertat; ⓇFGC Gràcia) and **Mercat de l'Abaceria** (Map p310; Travessera de Gràcia 186; ⓂFontana).

Eating by Neighbourhood

Gràcia & Park Güell
Hip and characterful tapas bars and taverns
(p162)

Camp Nou, Pedralbes & La Zona Alta
Culinary gems well worth the trip
(p175)

La Sagrada Família & L'Eixample
Some of Barcelona's best restaurants
(p145)

La Ribera
Atmospheric and avant-garde restaurants
(p110)

Plaça de Catalunya

Port Olímpic

Barceloneta & the Waterfront
Top choice for seafood and paella
(p124)

El Raval
Classic, budget and artful newcomers
(p93)

La Rambla & Barri Gòtic
Both touristy and well-respected eateries
(p79)

Port Vell

Mediterranean Sea

Montjuïc
Sparse but good selections
(p193)

Seafood platter at Los Caracoles (p81)

Ordering Tapas

Often much more fun than a full sit-down meal is snacking on bite-sized goodies known as *tapes*, or tapas. Too many travellers miss out on the joys of tapas because, unless you speak Spanish, ordering can seem like one of the dark arts of Spanish etiquette. Fear not – it's not as difficult as it first appears.

Tapas are always taken with a drink and often while standing or sitting at the bar. (In some bars you'll also get a small free *tapa* when you buy a drink.) Ordering tapas generally works like this: you take your seat at the bar or one of the cafe-style tables usually on hand, order drinks (try the slightly fizzy white wine, *txacolí*) and ask for a plate. Many of the tapas are *montaditos* (a sort of canapé), which can range from a creamy Roquefort cheese and walnut combination to a chunk of spicy sausage. They all come with toothpicks. These facilitate their consumption, but

serve another important purpose too: when you're ready to leave, the toothpicks are counted up and the bill presented.

While a *tapa* is a tiny serving, if you particularly like something you can have a *ración* (rations; large tapas servings) or *media ración* (half-rations; medium tapas servings). Remember, however, that two or three *raciónes* can easily constitute a full meal; the *media ración* is a good choice if you want to experience a broader range of tastes.

In addition to the plates displayed on the bar, some tapas venues will also offer hot dishes fresh from the kitchen. The bar staff will typically go around the bar and see if anyone is interested. If you see something you like, take it! Other places only bring out hot plates when ordered. Have a look at the menu, which might be a posted chalkboard listing the day's specials. If you can't choose, ask for *la especialidad de la casa* (the house specialty), and it's hard to go wrong.

Lonely Planet's Top Choices

Tickets (p193) The celebrated new restaurant by Ferran Adrià, showcasing Barcelona's best *nueva cocina española*.

Alkímia (p145) Magnificent Catalan cuisine by Michelin-starred Jordi Vilà.

Koy Shunka (p79) Mouthwatering avant-garde Japanese fare, probably Barcelona's best.

Tapaç 24 (p145) Innovative chef Carles Abellàn creates some of Barcelona's best tapas.

Pla (p79) Delectable fare in a candle-lit medieval dining room.

Casa Delfin (p110) Heavenly Mediterranean fare served in atmospheric La Ribera.

Best by Budget

€

Can Maño (p126)

Sureny (p164)

La Llar de Foc (p165)

Bitácora (p126)

La Cova Fumada (p124)

Envalira (p165)

€€

Cafe de l'Academia (p81)

La Vinateria dell Call (p79)

Cal Pep (p112)

Botafumeiro (p162)

La Molina (p175)

Bar Pinotxo (p94)

€€€

El Passadís del Pep (p110)

Restaurant Evo (p194)

Torre d'Alta Mar (p124)

Hofmann (p176)

Can Travi Nou (p177)

Best for Tapas

Bar Pinotxo (p94)

La Cova Fumada (p124)

Vaso de Oro (p126)

Cata 1.81 (p147)

Taktika Berri (p148)

Quimet i Quimet (p193)

Cal Pep (p112)

Bodega Sepúlveda (p149)

Best for Catalan

Sureny (p164)

El Glop (p165)

La Molina (p175)

Via Veneto (p175)

Envalira (p165)

Restaurant Roig Robí (p164)

Best for Nueva Cocina Española

Tickets (p193)

Alkímia (p145)

Cinc Sentits (p148)

Best for Basque

Ipar-Txoko (p164)

Taktika Berri (p148)

Zarautz (p196)

Best for Architecture

Casa Calvet (p147)

El Asador de Aranda (p177)

Best Cafes

Liadísimo (p176)

Lilipep (p112)

La Nena (p164)

Cosmo (p151)

La Clandestina (p83)

Čaj Chai (p82)

Caelum (p82)

Best for Fusion

Pla (p79)

Con Gracia (p164)

Can Kenji (p145)

Best for Vegetarians

Cereria (p81)

Himali (p165)

Amaltea (p149)

Organic (p96)

Sesamo (p96)

Best for Carnivores

Bilbao (p164)

Patagonia (p147)

El Asador de Aranda (p177)

Best for Late-Night Eating

Dos Trece (p97)

Elisabets (p96)

El Glop (p165)

Best for Chocolate-Lovers

La Nena (p164)

Xocoa (p86)

Cacao Sampaka (p155)

Museu de la Xocolata (p109)

Granja Viader (p94)

Best for Old-World Ambience

Can Culleretes (p79)
Els Quatre Gats (p37)
Ca L'Isidre (p94)
Casa Leopoldo (p94)

Best for Picnics

Mercat de la Boqueria (p90)
La Llavor Dels Orígens (p112)
Joan Murrià (p156)
Mauri (p150)
Casa Gispert (p114)

Best for Views

Torre d'Alta Mar (p124)
Miramar (p196)
Xiringuito D'Escribà (p126)
Can Majó (p124)

Best for Market Dining

Bar Joan (p113)
Bar Pinotxo (p94)

Best for Brunch

Milk (p82)
Dos Trece (p97)

Best for Romantic Dining

La Vinateria dell Call (p79)
Pla de la Garsa (p112)
Alba Granados (p148)
Pla (p79)
Casa Calvet (p147)

Best for Food & Wine

La Vinateria dell Call (p79)
Cata 1.81 (p147)
Terrabacus (p148)
La Panxa Del Bisbe (p165)

Best for Historic Atmosphere

Casa Leopoldo (p94)
Can Travi Nou (p177)
Barramòn (p194)
Restaurant 7 Portes (p124)

Best for Lunch Specials

Cafè de l'Acadèmia (p81)
O'Gràcia! (p164)
Casa Amalia (p147)
En Aparté (p112)

Best for Desserts

Foix de Sarrià (p177)
Bubó (p112)
Mandarosso Pastis (p112)
Olivia (p97)
Escribà (p81)
Caelum (p82)

Best Pre- or Post-Museum Dining

Museu d'Historia de Catalunya (p121)
Pla dels Àngels (p96)
Museu Nacional d'Art de Catalunya (p184)

Best for Seafood

Restaurant 7 Portes (p124)
El Cangrejo Loco (p126)
Bar Celta (p81)
Els Pescadors (p126)
Can Majó (p124)
Can Ros (p124)

Best for Latin American

El Rincón Maya (p149)
Patagonia (p147)
Cantina Machito (p166)

Best for Mediterranean

Noti (p145)
La Balsa (p176)
Hofmann (p176)
Embat (p147)
O'Gràcia! (p164)

Best for Italian

Lac Majùr (p165)
Melton (p148)
Xemei (p194)
Le Cucine Mandarosso (p110)
Monty Café (p166)
Tantarantana (p112)

Best for Portuguese

A Casa Portuguesa (p168)
Cerveseria Brassia Gallega (p149)
Bar Celta (p81)
Botafumeiro (p162)

Drinking & Nightlife

Barcelona is a nightlife-lovers' town, with an enticing spread of candlelit wine bars, old-school taverns, stylish lounges and kaleidoscopic nightclubs where the party continues until daybreak. For something a little more sedate, the city's atmospheric cafes and teahouses make a fine retreat when the skies turn grey.

Bars & Lounges

Barcelona has a dizzying assortment of bars where you can start – or end – the night. The atmosphere varies tremendously – candelit, mural-covered chambers in the medieval quarter, antique-filled converted storefronts and buzzing Modernista spaces are all part of the scene. Of course, where to go depends as much on the crowd as it does on ambience – here you'll find a quick rundown of the drinking scene by neighbourhood in the city.

Wherever you end up, keep in mind that eating and drinking go hand in hand in Barcelona (as in other parts of Spain), and some of the liveliest bars serve up as much tapas as they do alcohol.

Wine & Cava Bars

A growing number of wine bars scattered around the city provide a showcase for the great produce from Spain and beyond. Vine-minded spots like tapas restaurant Cata 1.81 (p147) serve a huge selection of wines by the glass, with a particular focus on stellar new vintages. A big part of the experience is having a few bites while you drink. Expect sharing plates, platters of cheese and charcuterie and plenty of tapas.

Cava bars tend to be more about the festive ambience than the actual drinking of *cava* (p254), a sparkling white or rosé, most of which is produced in Catalonia's Penedès region. At the more famous *cava* bars you'll have to nudge your way through the garrulous crowds and enjoy your bubbly standing up. Two of the most celebrated *cava* bars are El Xampanyet (p113) in La Ribera and Xampanyeria Can Paixano (p126) in Barceloneta.

Rooftop & Hotel Bars

Barcelona has a handful of rooftop bars that provide an enchanting view over the city. Depending on the neighbourhood, the vista may take in the rooftops of the old city, the curving beachfront or the entire expanse of the city centre with the Collserola Hills and Tibidabo in the distance. Most of these drinking spots are perched atop high-end hotels, but are not solely the domain of visiting foreigners. An increasing number of style-minded *barcelonins* (people of Barcelona) are drawn to these spaces. Late in the evening you'll find a mostly local crowd.

A few top picks:

➡ **B-Lounge** (p216) Boasts dramatic 360-degree views from its rooftop terrace; its location in Raval makes it a good place to start off the night before heading to nearby clubs.

➡ **La Isabala** (p215) On the 7th floor terrace of Hotel 1898, this handsomely designed summertime spot is a peaceful oasis from the Rambla down below.

➡ **Eclipse Lounge** (p217) Not a rooftop bar, but high up nonetheless on the 26th floor of the waterfront hotel W Barcelona, with panoramic views and a loungelike atmosphere with DJs, fancy cocktails and an A-list crowd.

➡ **Angels & Kings** (p218) On the 6th floor of Hotel ME, this open-air nightspot has a large terrace with swimming pool, fine views and festive ambience.

➡ **Mirablau** (p177) This open-air spot at the foot of Tibidabo is a city icon, famous for its unrivalled view over the city.

Beach Bars

During the summer, small wooden beach bars, affectionately known as *chiringuitos,* open up all along the strand, from Barceloneta all the way up to Platja de la Nova Mar Bella. Here you can dip your toes in the sand and nurse a cocktail while watching the city at play against the backdrop of deep blue Mediterranean. Ambient grooves add to the laid-back environment.

One of the liveliest beachside bars lies northeast of the city on Cavaió beach in Arenys de Mar (accessible from Barcelona by train). **Lasal** (www.lasal.com) hosts topnotch DJs and has a tropical-themed party atmosphere. It opens from mid-May to September.

Clubs

Barcelona's *discotecas* (clubs) are at their best from Thursday to Saturday. Indeed, many open only on these nights. A surprising variety of spots lurk in the labyrinth of the Ciutat Vella, ranging from plush former dance halls to grungy subterranean venues that fill to capacity.

Along the waterfront it's another story. At Port Olímpic sun-scorched crowds of visiting yachties mix it up with tourists and a few locals at noisy, back-to-back dance bars right on the waterfront. The best spots are over on the Barceloneta side.

A sprinkling of well-known clubs is spread over the classy parts of town, in L'Eixample and La Zona Alta. As a rule of thumb they attract a beautiful crowd.

STREETS & PLAZAS TO BAR-HOP

➜ **Plaça Reial**, Barri Gòtic

➜ **Carrer dels Escudellers**, Barri Gòtic

➜ **Carrer de Joaquín Costa**, El Raval

➜ **Carrer Nou de la Rambla**, El Raval

➜ **Carrer de Santa Mònica**, El Raval

➜ **Platja de la Barceloneta**, Barceloneta

➜ **Carrer d'Aribau**, L'Eixample

➜ **Plaça del Sol**, Gràcia

➜ **Plaça de la Revolucion de Septembre de 1868**, Gràcia

➜ **Plaça de la Vila de Gracia**, Gràcia

NEED TO KNOW

Opening Hours

➜ **Bars** Typically open around 6pm and close at 2am (3am on weekends).

➜ **Clubs** Open from midnight until 6am, Thursday to Saturday.

➜ **Beach Bars** 10am to midnight (later on weekends) from April to October.

When to Go

➜ Bars get lively after 11pm or midnight.

➜ Clubs get underway around 2am.

Getting In

Cover charges range from nothing to over €20 (often less if you go early). The admission price usually includes your first drink. Bouncers have the last say on dress code and your eligibility to enter. If you're in a big group, break into smaller groups.

Guides for the Latest Nightlife

➜ **Guia del Ocio** (www.guiadelociobcn.com)

➜ **Go Mag** (www.go-mag.com)

➜ **Metropolitan** (www.barcelona-metropolitan.com)

➜ **Barcelonarocks.com** (www.barcelonarocks.com)

➜ **Clubbingspain.com** (www.clubbingspain.com)

Drinking Glossary

Coffee

➜ *cafe con leche:* half coffee, half milk

➜ *cafe solo:* a short black or espresso

➜ *cortado:* a short black with a little milk

Beer

➜ *cerveza:* beer

➜ *caña:* a small draught beer

➜ *tubo:* a large draught beer

➜ *jarra:* a stein of beer (sometimes a pint)

➜ *quinto:* a 200ml bottle

➜ *tercio*: a 300ml bottle

➜ *clara:* a shandy – a beer with a hefty dash of lemonade (or lemon Fanta)

Wine

➜ *vino de la casa:* house wine

➜ *txakolin:* lightly sparkling white wine from the Basque country

Drinking by Neighbourhood

Gràcia & Park Güell
Young hipster crowd
(p166)

**Camp Nou, Pedralbes
& La Zona Alta**
High-end nightclubs
(p177)

**La Sagrada Família
& L'Eixample**
Student bars, tiny
lounges, gay clubs
(p150)

La Ribera
Cava and wine
bars, lounges
(p113)

*Plaça de
Catalunya*

*Port
Olímpic*

El Raval
Bohemian bars,
small clubs
(p97)

**La Rambla &
Barri Gòtic**
Packed with bars, cafes,
outdoor spots, clubs
(p82)

**Barceloneta &
the Waterfront**
Neighbourhood taverns,
seaside bars, touristy clubs
(p126)

*Port
Vell*

*Mediterranean
Sea*

Montjuïc
Art-minded bars, clubs, open-air spots
(p196)

Cafes

The cafe scene in Barcelona is incredibly vibrant and makes a great setting for an afternoon pick-me-up. You'll find charming teashops hidden on the narrow lanes of Barri Gòtic, bohemian hang-outs in El Raval, hipster haunts in L'Eixample and Modernista gems on La Rambla. While coffee, tea or perhaps *xocolata calenta* (hot chocolate) are the main attractions, most places also serve snacks, and some serve beer, wine and sometimes cocktails.

Lonely Planet's Top Choices

Les Gens Que J'Aime (p153) Stylish but unpretentious gem in L'Eixample.

Terrazza (p196) Summertime open-air dancing and revelry in the Poble Espanyol complex.

La Caseta del Migdia (p196) An open-air charmer, hidden in the thickets of Montjuïc.

Monvínic (p150) Enchanting setting amid one of Spain's best wine bars.

Elephant (p177) Painfully hip nightclub in a Zona Alta mansion

Best for Wine-Lovers

La Vinya del Senyor (p113)

La Baignoire (p166)

Premier (p152)

Best for Absinthe

Bar Marsella (p99)

Absenta (p127)

Best for Beer

La Cerveteca (p82)

Café de l'Opera (p83)

Best for House-Made Vermouth

La Confitería (p97)

Absenta (p127)

Best for Cocktails

Dry Martini (p151)

Gimlet (p113)

Boadas (p98)

Best for Modernista Decor

Bar Muy Buenas (p97)

Casa Almirall (p98)

London Bar (p98)

El Paraigua (p83)

Café de l'Opera (p83)

Best for Old-World Ambience

Raïm (p166)

Bar Marsella (p99)

La Confitería (p97)

Bar Pastís (p97)

Bar Muy Buenas (p97)

Best for Medieval Ambience

La Fianna (p113)

Dusk (p82)

Best for Dancing

Marula Cafè (p82)

Jamboree (p84)

Razzmatazz (p127)

Mirablau (p177)

Sutton The Club (p178)

CDLC (p127)

City Hall (p152)

Best Bohemian Hang-outs

Ké? (p127)

Oviso (p82)

Absenta (p127)

Best for Rock-Lovers

Alfa (p166)

Musical Maria (p166)

Noise i Art (p167)

Garaje Hermético (p153)

Best for Style Mavens

Otto Zutz (p178)

33|45 (p97)

Shôko (p127)

Best Beachfront Settings

Santa Marta (p127)

Shôko (p127)

Opium Mar (p127)

Best Student Hang-outs

Le Journal (p166)

Mediterráneo (p151)

Betty Ford (p98)

Negroni (p97)

Best for Funhouse Atmosphere

La Fira (p151)

Museum (p151)

Bosc de les Fades (p83)

Tinta Roja (p196)

Best Late Cafes

Cosmo (p151)

Cafè de l'Ópera (p83)

La Clandestina (p83)

Salterio (p83)

Čaj Chai (p82)

Caffè San Marco (p177)

★ Gay & Lesbian Barcelona

Barcelona has a vibrant gay and lesbian scene, with a fine array of restaurants, bars and clubs in the area known as the 'Gaixample' (a clever conjoining of Gay and L'Eixample), an area about five to six blocks southwest of Passeig de Gràcia around Carrer del Consell de Cent.

Local Attitudes

Despite fierce opposition from the Catholic church, Spain legalised same-sex marriage in 2005. It became the fourth country in the world to do so. A poll just prior to the legislation found that over 60% of Spaniards favoured the legalisation of same-sex marriage. Gay and lesbian married couples can also adopt children.

As a rule, Barcelona is pretty tolerant and the sight of gay couples arm in arm is generally unlikely to raise eyebrows.

Bars

Befitting a diverse city of its size, the bar scene offers plenty of variety, with stylish cocktail bars, leather bars, bear bars, easygoing pubs and theme bars (with drag shows and other events) all part of the mix.

Clubs

As with all clubs in town, things don't get going until well into the early morning (around 2am). The bigger and better known clubs like Metro (p152), one of Barcelona's pioneers in the gay club scene, host topnotch DJs, multiple bars, a dark room, drag shows and other amusements. Keep in mind that most of the clubs open only from Thursday to Saturday nights.

The Lesbian Scene

The lesbian bar scene is a little sparse compared to the gay scene, with more places catering to a mixed gay-lesbian crowd (and a few straights thrown in) than an exclusively lesbian clientele. The one place that's proudly lesbian is Aire (p152), which should be a requisite stop for every nightlife-loving lesbian visiting the city. Some nominally straight bars and clubs host periodic lesbian parties. Keep an eye out for party flyers in shops and bars in the Gaixample for the latest.

Special Events

The gay and lesbian community from Barcelona and beyond take centre stage during the annual **Pride Barcelona** (www.pride barcelona.org). The weeklong event takes place in late June and features concerts, campy drag shows, film screenings, art shows and open-air dance parties – complete with lots and lots of foam. It culminates with a festive parade along Carrer de Sepúlveda and ends at the Plaça d'Espanya where the big events are held.

Also of note is the **Barcelona International Gay and Lesbian Film Festival** (www.barcelonafilmfestival.org) held from late October to early November, with most of the screenings held at the Filmoteca de Catalunya (p93). Film lovers might also be able to catch a bit of the **Sitges Film Festival** (sitgesfilmfestival.com), which happens just prior in early October.

Sitges: Catalonia's Gay Capital

Barcelona has a busy gay scene, but Spain's gay capital is the saucily hedonistic Sitges (p207), a major destination on the international gay party circuit. The gay community there takes a leading role in the wild Carnaval celebrations in February/March.

Lonely Planet's Top Choices

Metro (p153) The city's finest (and longest-running) gay club.

Dietrich Gay Teatro Café (p153) Always a fun scene with nightly drag shows.

Hotel Axel (p221) Stylish gay boutique hotel in the heart of Gaixample.

Aire (p152) Barcelona's best lesbian bar, with a fab dance floor.

Best Gay Stays

Hotel California (p221)

Casa de Billy Barcelona (p221)

Best Gay Clubs

Arena Madre (p152)

La Base (p152)

Best Laid-Back Gay Bars

Átame (p151)

La Chapelle (p151)

Museum (p151)

Punto BCN (p152)

Dacksy (p151)

Best Leather Bar

New Chaps (p153)

Best Bear Bar

Bacon Bear (p151)

Best Mixed Clubs

Arena Classic (p152)

Terrazza (p196)

Best Gay-Friendly Beaches

Platja de la Mar Bella (p121)

Platja de Sant Miquel (Map p302)

Best Gay-Themed Shops

Nosotraos (p157)

Cómplices (p86)

NEED TO KNOW

Gay Organisations

➡ **Casal Lambda** (☎93 319 55 50; www.lambdaweb.org; Carrer de Verdaguer i Callís 10; Ⓜ Urquinaona) A GLBT social, cultural and information centre in La Ribera.

➡ **Coordinadora Gai-Lesbiana Barcelona** (☎93 298 00 29; www.cogailes.org; Carrer de Violant d'Hongria 156; Ⓜ Plaça del Centre) The city's main coordinating body for GLBT groups.

➡ Ca la Dona (p268) hosts some lesbian groups, and also runs the lesbian information line **Línia Rosa** (☎90 060 16 01).

Useful Websites

➡ **Gay Apartments Barcelona** (www.gayapartmentbarcelona.com) Aside from the holiday-rent apartment listings, this site has information on saunas, shops, restaurants and more.

➡ **Nois** (www.revistanois.com) Free magazine with up-to-date listings.

➡ **60by80** (www.60by80.com) An excellent gay travellers' website. Click on Barcelona under City guides and take it from there.

➡ **VisitBarcelonaGay.com** (www.visitbarcelonagay.com) Everything from fetish sections to saunas and accommodation tips.

➡ **GaySitges** (www.gaysitges.com) A site dedicated to this gay-friendly coastal town.

⭐ Entertainment

Barcelona teems with stages hosting all manner of entertainment: underground cabaret, comic opera, high drama. Dance companies are thick on the ground and popular local theatre companies, when not touring the rest of Spain, keep folks strapped to their seats.

Classical Music & Opera

Barcelona is blessed with a fine line-up of theatres for grand performances of classical music, opera and more. Its two historic – and iconic – music houses are the Gran Teatre del Liceu (p84) and the Palau de la Música Catalana (p113).

Dance

Some fine local contemporary dance companies, along with international visiting companies from time to time, maintain a fairly busy performance program across town. Look for leaflets at Palau de la Virreina (p69) and watch theatre listings. For ballet and other big spectacles, you need to wait for acts to arrive from abroad.

FLAMENCO

Seeing good performances of this essentially Andalucian dance and music is not easy. The few *tablaos* are touristy and often tacky. You can catch flamenco on Friday nights at the Jazz Sí Club (p99); also watch out for big name performers at the Palau de la Música Catalana (p113). The **Festival de Flamenco de Ciutat Vella** (http://ciutatflamenco.com) is on in May. A series of concerts between from mid-February and April comprises the **De Cajón Festival Flamenco** (www.the project.es, in Spanish).

SARDANA

In Barcelona the best chance you have of seeing people dancing the *sardana* is either at noon on Sunday or 6pm on Saturday in front of La Catedral. It is occasionally performed in Plaça de Sant Jaume too. For more information, contact the **Agrupació Cultural Folclòrica de Barcelona** (☑93 315 14 96). You can also see the dance during some of the city's festivals.

Theatre

Most local theatre is performed in Catalan or Spanish. The monthly guide *Teatre BCN* can be picked up at the Palau de la Virreina (p69).

Cinemas

Outdoor cinema screens are set up in summer at or near the Castell de Montjuïc and in the Fòrum. Foreign films with subtitles and original soundtracks are marked 'VO' *(versió original)* in movie listings.

Entertainment by Neighbourhood

⇒ **La Rambla & Barri Gòtic** This is where you'll find the Gran Teatre de Liceu and the weekly *sardana* dances.

⇒ **El Raval** Great for theatre, jazz and flamenco on Friday nights at the Jazz Sí Club.

⇒ **La Ribera** The eclectic and spectacular Palau de la Música Catalana is here.

⇒ **Montjuïc** This is where you'll find the Palau de la Virreina and occasional starlit film screenings on Montjuïc.

Lonely Planet's Top Choices

Palau de la Música Catalana (p113) This glittering Modernista gem, the city's traditional home for classical and choral music, is a multi-sensory delight.

Gran Teatre del Liceu (p84) 19-century style meets cutting-edge acoustics at Barcelona's premier opera house.

Filmoteca de Catalunya (p93) This new arts centre, almost a decade in the making, comprises a film archive, a bookshop, a cafe, offices and a dedicated space for exhibitions.

Cangrejo (p99) Glorious cabaret kitsch with cult *barcelonin* drag star Carman Mairena.

Best for Theatre

Teatre Nou Tantarantana (p99)

Teatre Romea (p99)

Teatreneu (p167)

Sala Beckett (p167)

Best for Off-Beat Shows

Teatre Llantiol (p99)

Sala Apolo (p197)

Dietrich Gay Teatro Café (p153)

Best for Jazz

Harlem Jazz Club (p84)

Jazz Sí Club (p99)

Jamboree (p84)

Bel-Luna Jazz Club (p153)

Best for Flamenco

Jazz Sí Club (p99)

Tablao Nervión (p114)

Sala Tarantos (p85)

Best Performing Arts Centres

Filmoteca de Catalunya (p93)

Centre de Cultura Contemporània de Barcelona (p93)

Teatre Nacional de Catalunya (p154)

Best for Live Bands

Heliogàbal (p167)

Elèctric Bar (p167)

Sala Apolo (p197)

Sidecar Factory Club (p84)

Best Cinemas

Verdi (p167)

Casablanca Kaplan (p167)

Méliès Cinemes (p154)

Yelmo Cines Icària (p128)

Best for Classical Music

Palau Robert (p154)

L'Auditori (p153)

L'Ateneu (p84)

PLAN YOUR TRIP ENTERTAINMENT

NEED TO KNOW

Tickets

➡ The easiest way to get hold of tickets (*entradas*) for most venues throughout the city is through the Caixa de Catalunya's **Tel-Entrada** service (www.telendra.com) or **ServiCaixa** (www.servicaixa.com). With the latter, you can pick up tickets purchased online at selected La Caixa bank's ServiCaixa ATMs.

➡ For exhibitions and other free activities, check out www.forfree.cat.

Listings

➡ The Palau de la Virreina's (p69) Arts Information Office has oodles of information on theatre, opera, classical music and more.

➡ The **Guía del Ocio** (www.guiadelociobcn.es, in Spanish; €1) has ample listings for all forms of entertainment.

➡ The monthly *Informatiu Musical* leaflet has the best coverage of classical music. You can pick it up at tourist offices and the Palau de la Virreina.

Coquette (p114)

Shopping

If your doctor has prescribed an intense round of retail therapy to deal with the blues, then Barcelona is the place. Across Ciutat Vella (Barri Gòtic, El Raval and La Ribera), L'Eixample and Gràcia is spread a thick mantle of boutiques, historic shops, original one-off stores, gourmet corners, wine dens and more designer labels than you can shake your gold card at. You name it, you'll find it here.

Herboristeria del Rei (p86)

Design

Whether you are looking for homewares, gifts or decoration, you'll quickly realise that Barcelona is a style city. This much is clear from its flagship design stores like Vinçon and Cubiña – and even the souvenirs have flair. High-end design shops are best found in L'Eixample and El Born, while arty places are scattered around El Raval, where you'll find anything from quirky furniture to homewares with a difference.

Boutique Barcelona

The heart of Barri Gòtic has always been busy with small-scale merchants, but the area has come crackling to life since the mid-1990s. Some of the most curious old stores, such as purveyors of hats and candles, lurk in the narrow lanes around Plaça de Sant Jaume. The once-seedy Carrer d'Avinyó has become a minor young-fashion boulevard. Antique stores line Carrer de la Palla and Carrer dels Banys Nous.

La Ribera is nothing less than a gourmand's delight. Great old stores and some finger-licking newbies deal in specialty foodstuffs, like coffee, chocolate and cheese. Amid such wonderful aromas, a crop of fashion and design stores caters to the multitude of yuppies in the *barri*.

Gràcia is also full of quirky little shops. In particular, check out Carrer de Verdi for anything from clothes to bric a brac.

El Raval is fantastic for unique boutiques and artists selling their own creations - from fashion, to prints, food and bric a brac.

NEED TO KNOW

Where To Go

For high fashion, design, jewellery and department stores, the principal shopping axis starts on Plaça de Catalunya, proceeds up Passeig de Gràcia and turns left into Avinguda Diagonal, along which it extends as far as Plaça de la Reina Maria Cristina. The densely packed section between Plaça de Francesc Macià and Plaça de la Reina Maria Cristina is an especially good hunting ground.

Business Hours

➡ In general, shops are open between 9am or 10am and 1.30pm or 2pm and then again from around 4pm or 4.30pm to 8pm or 8.30pm Monday to Friday. Many shops keep the same hours on Saturday, although some don't bother with the evening session.

➡ Large supermarkets, malls and department stores such as El Corte Inglés stay open all day from Monday to Saturday, between about 10am and 10pm.

➡ Many fashion boutiques, design stores and the like open from about 10am to 8pm Monday to Saturday.

➡ A few shops open on Sundays and holidays, and the number increases in the run up to key consumer holiday periods.

Sale Time

The winter sales start shortly after Reis (6 January) and, depending on the store, can go on well into February. The summer sales start in July, with stores trying to entice locals to part with one last wad of euros before they flood out of the city on holiday in August. Some shops prolong their sales to the end of August.

High Street Chains & Department Stores

Everyone knows that across Europe (and further afield), Spain's chains rule the high street. This is the home of the ubiquitous Zara, Mango, Pull and Bear, Bershka, Massimo Dutti, Zara Home (in fact, all owned by one company, Inditex) – and sure enough, you'll find all of them dotted around Barcelona. Women's underwear is

(Above) Vintage treasure troves abound in El Raval

(Left) El Ingenio (p86)

stylish and affordable at Oysho and Women's Secret, while UK hits like Topshop and Topman also feature off La Ramba de Catalunya.

The best, most all-encompassing department store is El Corte Inglés – an enormous fortress-like main branch towers over Plaça Catalunya. It covers everything from books, music and food, to fashion, jewellery, kids' clothes, technology and homewares. There are smaller branches across town. FNAC is another biggie that serves the same purpose as El Corte Inglés, though it's a touch more modern.

Vintage Fashion

El Raval is best for vintage fashion. You'll discover old-time stores that are irresistible to browsers, and a colourful array of affordable, mostly second-hand clothes boutiques. The central axis here is Carrer de la Riera Baixa, which plays host to everything from '70s threads to military cast-offs. Carrer dels Tallers is also attracting a growing number of clothing and shoe stores (although CDs remain its core business). Art galleries, designer outlets and quality bookstores all huddle together along the streets running east of Macba towards La Rambla.

Designers

The heart of L'Eixample, bisected by Passeig de Gràcia, is known as the Quadrat d'Or (Golden Square) and is jammed with all sorts of glittering shops. Passeig de Gràcia is a bit of a who's who of international shopping – you'll find Spain's own high-end designers like Loewe on Passeig de Gràcia, along with Armani, Chanel, Gucci, Burberry and the rest.

El Born, particularly Carrer del Rec, is big on stocking cool designers like Isabel Marant, Marni, Chloé, or Hoss Intropia, in small, clean-line boutiques. Some Barcelona-based designs are also sold here. This is a great area if you have money to spend and hours to browse beautiful boutiques.

Markets

Barcelona's food markets are some of the best in Europe – just think of the inviting, glistening, aromatic and voluptuous offerings to be savoured in Mercat de la Boqueria (p90) or **Mercat de Santa Caterina** (Map p300; Avinguda de Francesc Cambó;

Ⓜ Jaume I) – but every neighbourhood has its own central market, full of seasonal offers.

Several flea markets, like Els Encants Vell (p154), offer opportunities to browse and enjoy the local buzz, and perhaps even find a good bargain.

Shopping Strips

➡ **Avinguda del Portal de l'Àngel** With El Corte Inglés leading the way, this broad pedestrian avenue is lined with everything from shoe shops to patisseries, and feeds into Carrer dels Boters and Carrer de la Portaferrissa, characterised by stores offering light-hearted costume jewellery and young streetwear.

➡ **Avinguda Diagonal** The boulevard is loaded with international fashion names, department stores and design boutiques, suitably interspersed with eateries to allow weary shoppers to take a load off.

➡ **Carrer d'Avinyó** Once a fairly squalid old-town road (where Picasso and his friends used to frequent houses of ill repute), Carrer d'Avinyó has morphed into a dynamic young fashion street.

SHOPPING MALLS

Barcelona has no shortage of shopping malls. One of the first to arrive was **L'Illa Diagonal** (Map p316; ☑ 93 444 00 00; www.lilla.com; Avinguda Diagonal 549; ⏱ 10am-9.30pm Mon-Sat; Ⓜ Maria Cristina), designed by star Spanish architect Rafael Moneo. The **Centre Comercial Diagonal Mar** (Map p304; ☑ 902 530300; www.diagonalmar.com; Avinguda Diagonal 3; Ⓜ El Maresme Fòrum) by the sea is one of the latest additions.

The city's other emporia include **Centre Comercial de les Glòries** (Map p304; ☑ 93 486 04 04; www.lesglories.com; Gran Via de les Corts Catalanes; Ⓜ Glòries), in the former Olivetti factory; **Heron City** (☑ 902 401144; www.heroncitybarcelona.com; Passeig de Rio de Janeiro 42; Ⓜ Fabra i Puig), just off Avinguda Meridiana, about 4km north of Plaça de les Glòries Catalanes; and the **Centre Comercial Gran Via 2** (☑ 902 301444; www.granvia2.com; Gran Via de les Corts Catalanes 75; Ⓡ FGC Ildefons Cerdà) in L'Hospitalet de Llobregat.

Hat shop in Barri Gòtic

➡ **Carrer de la Riera Baixa** The place to look for pre-loved threads.

➡ **Carrer del Petritxol** Best for chocolate shops and art.

➡ **Carrer del Consell de Cent** The heart of the private art-gallery scene in Barcelona, between Passeig de Gràcia and Carrer de Muntaner.

➡ **Carrer del Rec** Another threads street, this one-time stream is lined with bright and cool boutiques. Check out Carrer del Bonaire and Carrer de l'Esparteria too. You'll find discount outlets and original local designers.

➡ **Carrer dels Banys Nous** Along with nearby Carrer de la Palla, this is the place to look for antiques.

➡ **Passeig de Gràcia** This is the premier shopping boulevard, chic with a capital 'C', but mostly given over to big name international brands.

➡ **Rambla de Catalunya** A prettier boulevard than Passeig de Gràcia, Rambla de Catalunya is peppered with all sorts of shops. Stop for a coffee on the central pedestrian strip along the way.

Shopping by Neighbourhood

➡ **Barri Gòtic & La Rambla** Excellent for all kinds of retail – boutiques, design and souvenirs.

➡ **El Raval** Here is a cluster of independent stores – vintage fashion and all kinds of original and arty shops –and the iconic Mercat de la Boqueria.

➡ **La Ribera** El Born is the place for cool designer boutiques that sell high-end fashion and excellent food shops for the gourmet traveller.

➡ **Port Vell & Barceloneta** A few massive malls and little markets can be found around Barceloneta.

➡ **L'Eixample** High-end heartstoppers, dazzling jewellery and high-street chains find home along the wealthy streets of L'Eixample.

➡ **Gràcia** Dotted with fantastic little shops that sell anything from vintage cameras to unique fashion and food.

➡ **La Zona Alta** This is the city's Beverly Hills, so expect high prices and bijou boutiques.

Lonely Planet's Top Choices

Vinçon (p154) The Barcelona design icon sells furniture and homewares to die for.

Mercat de la Boqueria (p90) Stock up on budget delicacies amid one of Europe's most vibrant food markets.

Vila Viniteca (p114) Oenophiles unite at this wonderful wine shop.

Coquette (p114) Simple and beautiful designer clothes for women.

A Casa Portuguesa (p168) Food, wine and glorious cakes from Portugal.

Best for Design & Craft

Cubiña (p155)
Costura (p100)
Fantastik (p100)
Teranyina (p100)

Best for Fashion

Antonio Miró (p156)
Farrutx (p157)

Loewe (p156)
Bagués (p157)

Best Markets

Mercat de Santa Caterina (p108)
Els Encants Vells (p154)
El Bulevard dels Antiquaris (p154)

Best Kept Secrets

El Rey De La Magia (p115)
Herboristeria Del Rei (p86)
La Portorriqueña (p100)
Sala Parés (p85)
El Ingenio (p86)
Taller de Marionetas Travi (p85)

Best for Food & Wine

Casa Gispert (p114)
Vila Viniteca (p114)
Barcelona Reykjavik (p100)
Caelum (p82)

Best for Books

Casa del Llibre (p155)
Ras (p100)
Come In (p155)
Laie (p155)
Hibernian (p168)

Best for Vintage

L'Arca de l'Àviva (p85)
El Bulevard dels Antiquaris (p154)
Els Encants Vells (p154)
Port Antic (p128)

Best for Shoes

La Manual Alpargatera (p87)
Nu Sabates (p115)
Camper (p157)
Farrutx (p157)

Best for Accessories

Obach (p86)
Sergio Aranda (p157)
Espacio de Creadores (p86)
La Roca Village (p156)

Sports & Activities

The Mediterranean oceanfront and rambling hilly park overlooking the city make fine settings for a bit of outdoor activity beneath the (generally) sunny skies of Barcelona. For a break from museum-hopping and overindulging at tapas bars, Barcelona has the antidote – running, swimming, cycling or simply pumping fists in the air at a never-dull FC Barça match.

Football

Football in Barcelona has the aura of religion. For much of the city's population, support of FC Barça is an article of faith. But the city has another hardy (if less illustrious) side, RCD Espanyol. FC Barça is traditionally associated with the Catalans and even Catalan nationalism, while Espanyol is often identified with Spanish immigrants from other parts of the country.

Cycling

Barcelona's long enticing seafront makes a fine setting for a ride and the bike lane separate from traffic and pedestrians ensures you can get going at a good clip (though you'll have to move slowly at peak times, like on summer weekends). The city itself has over 180km of bike lanes, including along major streets like Passatge de Sant Joan, Consell de Cent, Av Diagonal and Ronda de Sant Pau/Comte d'Urgell. Avid mountain bikers will want to make their way up to the vast Parc de Collserola (p174) with rambling trails on a wooded massif overlooking the city. There are also several options available for bike tours (p31) and hire (p263).

Running

The waterfront esplanade and beaches are all perfect for an early morning run, before the crowds come out. Locals with serious running credentials take to Parc de Collserola, which is laced with trails. Among the best is the Carretera de les Aigües, a 9km-long track from Tibidabo to the suburb of Sant Just Desvern, with superb views over the city. More convenient are the gardens and parkland of Montjuïc.

Swimming

If you like swimming in the sea, head to the beaches north of Platja Nova Icària (p121), which are cleaner than those nearer the port. Barcelona also has some great lap-swimming options, including several waterfront sports centres (p129) and the ex-Olympic **Piscines Bernat Picornell** (Map p318; www.picornell. cat; Avinguda de l'Estadi 30-38; adult/child €9.65/5.95; ☺6.45am-midnight Mon-Fri, 7am-9pm Sat, 7.30am-4pm Sun; ☐50, 61 or 193).

Spas & Relaxation

A day at the spa can be a fantastic way to recharge after a few days exploring, or perhaps a few nights on the town. The best spas, like **Aire de Barcelona** (Map p300; ☎90 255 57 89; www.airedebarcelona.com; Passeig de Picasso 22; ⓂArc de Triomf; treatments €28-125), come replete with candlelit anterooms and sumptuous baths and steamrooms. Most high-end hotels have spas, though the more charming options are scattered around town.

SWIMMING AU NATUREL

In addition to the ill-defined nudists' strip at the southwest end of Platja de la Mar Bella and the predominantly gay strip at Platja de Sant Miquel, you can also get it all off year-round at the Piscines Bernat Picornell. On Saturday nights between 9pm and 11pm, the pool (with access to sauna and steam bath) is open only to nudists. On Sundays between October and May, the indoor pool opens for nudists only from 4.15pm to 6pm.

Lonely Planet's Top Choices

Camp Nou (p171) See a match at the world famous football stadium.

Aire de Barcelona (p60) A beautiful Banys Àrabs–style spa in a historic setting in El Born.

Platja de Sant Sebastià (Map p302) The starting point for a scenic run or cycle along the waterfront.

Piscines Bernat Picornell (p60) A truly Olympian setting for a swim.

Best Places for a Run or Bike-ride

Montjuïc (p186)

Parc de Collserola (p174)

The waterfront promenade (p125)

Best Spas

Rituels d'Orient (p180)

Aqua Urban Spa (p168)

Flotarium (p168)

Best Walking Tours

Old City Tour by Runner Bean Tours (p30)

Modernisme Tour by Oficina d'Informació de Turisme de Barcelona (p30)

Picasso Tour by Oficina d'Informació de Turisme de Barcelona (p30)

Gourmet Tour by Oficina d'Informació de Turisme de Barcelona (p30)

Barcelona Metro Walks (self-guided, p30)

Best Tours

Bicycle tours (p31)

Excursion boat tours (p129)

BCN Skytour (helicopter tours, p263)

Trixi ('cycle-taxi' tours, p31)

Barcelona Segway Fun (p31)

NEED TO KNOW

FC Tickets

Tickets to FC Barcelona matches are available at Camp Nou (p171), as well as through the **Servi-Caixa** (www.servicaixa.com) ticketing service. Tickets can cost anything from €35 to upwards of €200, depending on the seat and match. The ticket windows open on Saturday morning and in the afternoon until the game starts. If the match is on Sunday, it opens Saturday morning only and then on Sunday until the match starts. Usually tickets are not available for matches with Real Madrid.

You will almost definitely find scalpers lurking near the ticket windows. They are often club members and can sometimes get you in at a significant reduction. Don't pay until you are safely seated.

If you can't make it to see Barça play, a trip to Camp Nou's multimedia museum (p171), replete with a tour of the locker rooms and the field, is a fine back-up option.

Aquatic Sports

The sunny Mediterranean beckons! For a short jaunt out on the water, you can join one of several excursion boats (p129) that head out from the foot of La Rambla. For a more hands-on option, the Base Nautica Municipal (p129) offers instruction in sailing, kayaking and windsurfing.

Explore Barcelona

BARCELONA'S
TOP SIGHTS

Neighbourhoods at a Glance

❶ La Rambla & Barri Gòtic (p66)

La Rambla, Barcelona's most famous pedestrian strip, is always a hive of activity with buskers and peddlers, tourists and con artists (watch out!) mingling amid the sunlit cafes and shops on the boulevard. The adjoining Barri Gòtic is packed with historical treasures – relics of ancient Rome, 14th-century Gothic churches and atmospheric cobblestone lanes lined with shops, bars and restaurants.

❷ El Raval (p88)

The once down-and-out district of El Raval is still seedy in parts, though it has seen remarkable rejuvenation in recent years, with the addition of cutting-edge museums and cultural centres, including the Richard Meier–designed Museu d'Art Contemporani

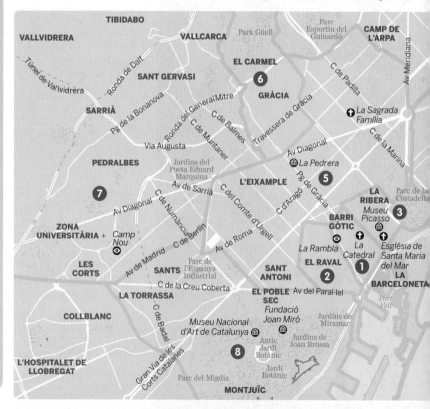

de Barcelona. Other highlights include El Raval's bohemian nightlife and the sprawling culinary delights at Mercat de la Boqueria.

③ La Ribera (p101)

This medieval quarter has a little of everything, from high-end shopping to some of Barcelona's liveliest tapas bars. Key sights include the supurb Museu Picasso, Gothic church Santa Maria del Mar and Modernista concert hall Palau de la Música Catalana. For a bit of fresh air, locals head to the manicured gardens of Parc de la Ciutadella.

④ Barceloneta & the Waterfront (p118)

The formerly industrial waterfront has experienced a dramatic transformation in the last three decades, with sparkling beaches and seaside bars and restaurants, elegant

sculptures, a 4.5km-long boardwalk, ultra-modern high-rises and yacht-filled marinas. Your gateway to the Mediterranean is the gridlike neighbourhood of Barceloneta, an old-fashioned fishing quarter full of traditional seafood eateries.

⑤ La Sagrada Família & L'Eixample (p132)

The elegant, if traffic-filled, district of L'Eixample is a showcase for Modernista architecture, including Gaudí's unfinished masterpiece, La Sagrada Família. Here is a celebrated dining scene, with high-end boutiques and wildly diverse nightlife: university party spots, gilded cocktail lounges and the buzzing gay club scene of the 'Gaixample' are all part of the mix.

⑥ Gràcia & Park Güell (p158)

Gràcia was an independent town until the 1890s. Its narrow lanes and picturesque plazas still have a villagelike feel, and it has long been a magnet to a young, hip, largely international crowd. Here you'll find well-worn cafes and bars, vintage shops, and a smattering of multicultural eateries. On a hill to the north lies the outdoor Modernista storybook of Park Güell, yet another captivating work by Gaudí.

⑦ Camp Nou, Pedralbes & La Zona Alta (p169)

Several of Barcelona's most sacred sights nestle inside the huge expanse beyond L'Eixample. One is the peaceful monastery of Pedralbes; the other is the great shrine to Catalan football, Camp Nou. Other attractions include the amusement park and great views atop Tibidabo, the hilly trails of Parc de Collserola, and CosmoCaixa, the city's best science museum.

⑧ Montjuïc (p181)

The hillside overlooking Barcelona's port has some of the city's finest art collections: the Museu Nacional d'Art de Catalunya, the Fundació Joan Miró and CaixaForum. Other galleries, gardens and an imposing castle form part of the scenery – which, incidentally, offers great views over the city.

La Rambla & Barri Gòtic

Neighbourhood Top Five

1 Taking in Barcelona's liveliest street scene along **La Rambla** (p68), with its human statues, open-air eateries, flower stalls and saunterers from every corner of the globe.

2 Exploring the hidden nooks and crannies of the magnificent Gothic masterpiece of **La Catedral** (p71).

3 Walking amid the ruins of Roman-era Barcino at the **Museu d'Història de Barcelona** (p74).

4 Ogling the strange and wondrous collections at the **Museu Frederic Marès** (p73).

5 Enjoying an alfresco meal or a drink in the picturesque **Plaça Reial** (p76).

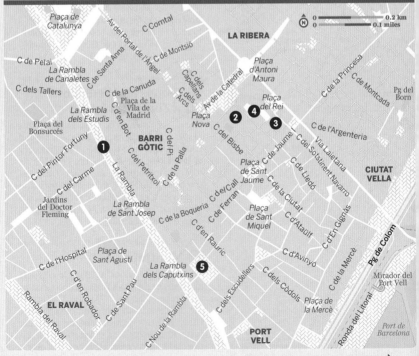

For more detail of this area, see Map p292 ➡

Explore: La Rambla & Barri Gòtic

La Rambla is Spain's most talked-about boulevard. It packs a lot of colour into a short walk, with flower stands, historic buildings, overpriced beers and tourist tat, and a ceaseless parade of humanity. Once a sewage ditch on the edge of the medieval city, it still marks the southwest flank of Barri Gòtic, the nucleus of old Barcelona.

Worthwhile tourist attractions line both sides of La Rambla, but the promenade is more about strolling the boulevard than ticking off sights. Come in the early morning to see it at its most peaceful, then return in the afternoon for the circus parade in all its colourful unruliness.

You could easily spend a week exploring the Barri Gòtic without leaving its medieval streets. The tangle of narrow lanes and tranquil plazas conceals some of the city's most atmospheric shops, restaurants, cafes and bars. There are swarms of tourists afoot – and some overpriced restaurants to avoid – but the Gòtic rewards the urban explorer.

Wandering without an itinerary is a delight, though you won't want to miss La Catedral and the smattering of Roman ruins inside the Museu d'Història de Barcelona. Another highlight is lingering over coffee or an alfresco meal at one of Barri Gòtic's many outdoor plazas.

By night, Barri Gòtic transforms into a mazelike collection of bars and clubs concealed in daylight. The streets around Plaça Reial and Plaça de George Orwell (also known as Plaça del Trippy) are good places to bar-hop, though you'll find nightspots all over the neighbourhood. A mostly local crowd takes over later in the night.

Local Life

➡ **Folk Dancing** Although it's mostly old-timers dancing the *sardana*, a new youthful wave now enjoys this traditional Catalan dance. Join in at 6pm on Saturday and noon on Sunday in front of La Catedral (p71).

➡ **Hang-outs** Head to the southeast corner of Barri Gòtic for bohemian Bootleg (p82) and Clandestina (p83). Čaj Chai (p82) is also a much-loved meeting spot.

➡ **Bar-hopping** Plaça Reial, Plaça de George Orwell and the narrow lanes between the two are the best spots to take in the local Gòtic nightlife (p82).

Getting There & Away

➡ **Metro** Key stops on La Rambla include Catalunya, Liceu and Drassanes; Jaume I and Urquinaona are best for Barri Gòtic's east side.

➡ **Bus** Airport and night buses commute from Plaça de Catalunya.

➡ **Taxi** Hail taxies on La Rambla or Plaça de Catalunya.

Lonely Planet's Top Tip

For the best-value dining, plan to at least have a big meal at lunchtime. Many restaurants in the Barri Gòtic offer three-course meals for €10 to €12, including wine.

✖ Best Places to Eat

➡ Pla (p79)

➡ La Vinateria dell Call (p79)

➡ Koy Shunka (p79)

➡ Can Culleretes (p79)

➡ Cafè de l'Acadèmia (p81)

For reviews, see p79 ➡

☕ Best Places to Drink

➡ Oviso (p82)

➡ La Cerveteca (p82)

➡ Čaj Chai (p82)

➡ Marula Cafè (p82)

➡ Polaroid (p82)

For reviews, see p82 ➡

◉ Best Historical Treasures

➡ Temple Romà d'August (p78)

➡ Via Sepulcral Romana (p78)

➡ Sinagoga Major (p77)

➡ Domus Romana (p78)

For reviews, see p73 ➡

TOP SIGHTS
LA RAMBLA

Flanked by narrow traffic lanes and plane trees, the middle of La Rambla is a broad pedestrian boulevard, crowded every day until the wee hours with a cross-section of *barcelonins* (people of Barcelona) and out-of-towners. Dotted with cafes, restaurants, kiosks and news-stands, and enlivened by buskers, pavement artists, mimes and living statues, La Rambla rarely allows a dull moment.

It takes its name from a seasonal stream (*raml* in Arabic) that once ran here. From the early Middle Ages on, it was better known as the *Cagalell* (Stream of Shit) and lay outside the city walls until the 14th century. from the 16th to the early 19th centuries monastic buildings were built here, as were mansions of the well-to-do. Unofficially, La Rambla is divided into five sections, which explains why many know it as Las Ramblas.

DON'T MISS...

➡ Palau de la Virreina
➡ Centre d'Art Santa Mònica
➡ Església de Betlem
➡ Palau Moja
➡ Mosaïc de Miró

PRACTICALITIES

➡ Map p292
➡ MCatalunya, Liceu or Drassanes

La Rambla de Canaletes

The section of La Rambla north of Plaça de Catalunya is named after the **Font de Canaletes** (Map p292), an inconspicuous turn-of-the-20th-century drinking fountain, the water of which supposedly emerges from what were once known as the springs of Canaletes. It used to be said that *barcelonins* 'drank the waters of Les Canaletes'. Nowadays, people claim that anyone who drinks from the fountain will return to Barcelona, which is not such a bad prospect. Delirious football fans gather here to celebrate whenever the main home side, FC Barcelona, wins a cup or the league premiership.

A block east along Carrer de la Canuda is Plaça de la Vila de Madrid, with a sunken garden where Roman tombs lie exposed in the Via Sepulcral Romana (p78).

La Rambla dels Estudis

La Rambla dels Estudis, from Carrer de la Canuda running south to Carrer de la Portaferrissa, was formerly home to a twittering bird market, which closed in 2010 after 150 years operation.

Església de Betlem

Just north of Carrer del Carme, this **church** (Map p292) was constructed in baroque style for the Jesuits in the late 17th and early 18th centuries to replace an earlier church destroyed by fire in 1671. Fire was a bit of a theme for this site: the church was once considered the most splendid of Barcelona's few baroque offerings, but leftist arsonists torched it in 1936.

Palau Moja

Looming over the eastern side of La Rambla, **Palau Moja** (Map p292) is a rare example of a more pure neoclassical pile. Its clean, classical lines are best appreciated from across La Rambla. It houses government offices and the Generalitat's bookshop – a fine place to browse for coffee table tomes on Catalan art and architecture, though most titles are in Catalan.

La Rambla de Sant Josep

From Carrer de la Portaferrissa to Placa de la Boqueria, what is officially called La Rambla de Sant Josep (named after a now nonexistent monastery) is lined with flower stalls, which give it the alternative name La Rambla de les Flors. This stretch also contains the scurrilous Museu de l'Eròtica (p78).

Palau de la Virreina

The **Palau de la Virreina** (Map p292) is a grand 18th-century rococo mansion (with some neoclassical elements) that houses a municipal arts-and-entertainment information and ticket office. More importantly, it's home to the **Centre de la Imatge** (Map p292; ☑93 316 10 00; www.bcn.cat/virreinacen tredelaimatge; 99 Palau de la Virreina), which has rotating photography exhibits. Admission prices and opening hours vary.

Just south of the Palau, in El Raval, is the **Mercat de la Boqueria** (p90), one of the best-stocked and most colourful produce markets in Europe.

Mosaïc de Miró

At Plaça de la Boqueria, where four side streets meet just north of Liceu Metro station, you can walk all over a Miró – the colourful **mosaic** (Map p292) in the pavement. Miró chose this site as it's near the house where he was born on the Passatge del Crèdit. The mosaic's bold colors and vivid swirling forms are instantly recognisable to Miró fans, though plenty of tourists stroll right over it without realising it. You'll find the artist's signature on a tile near the bottom of the work.

La Rambla dels Caputxins

La Rambla dels Caputxins, named after a now non-existent monastery, runs from Plaça de la Boqueria to Carrer dels Escudellers. The latter street is named after the potters' guild, founded in the 13th century, the members of which lived and worked here. On the western side of La Rambla is the Gran Teatre del Liceu (p76); to the southeast is the entrance to the palm-shaded Plaça Reial (p76). Below this point La Rambla gets seedier, with the occasional strip club and peep show.

La Rambla de Santa Mònica

The final stretch of La Rambla widens out to approach the Mirador de Colom (p76) overlooking Port Vell. La Rambla here is named after the Convent de Santa Mònica, which once stood on the western flank of the street and has since been converted into the **Centre d'Art Santa Mònica** (Map p292; ☑93 567 11 10; www.artssantamonica.cat; La Rambla de Santa Mònica 7; admission free; ⓘ11am-9pm Tue-Sun & holidays; Ⓜ Drassanes), a cultural centre that mostly exhibits modern multimedia installations.

DINING & DRINKING ON LA RAMBLA

You can grab ice cream, cold drinks and snacks on La Rambla, but for something more substantial skip the chaotic restaurants on the boulevard and try one of these:

➡ **Bosc de les Fades** (p83) – a whimsical drinking spot straight out of Alice in Wonderland.

➡ **Café de l'Òpera** (p83) – elegant art nouveau cafe across from the Gran Teatre del Liceu.

➡ **Plaça Reial** (p76) – for a sit-down meal, your best local bet is at one of the many restaurants ringing this plaza.

In *Homage to Catalonia*, Orwell vividly described La Rambla gripped by revolutionary fervour in the early days of the civil war. 'Down the Ramblas, the wide central artery of the town where crowds of people streamed constantly to and fro, the loud-speakers were bellowing revolutionary songs all day and far into the night...'

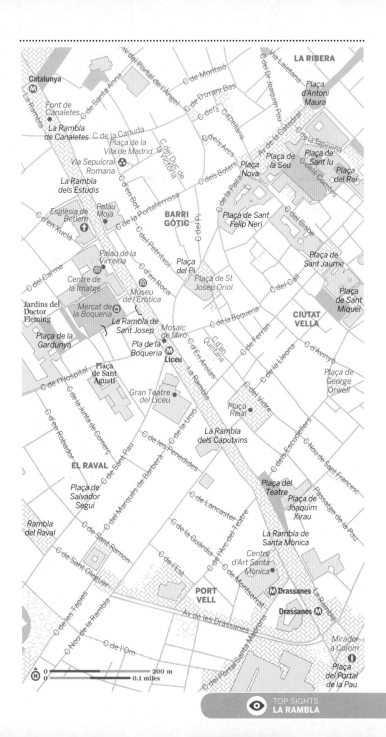

TOP SIGHTS
LA CATEDRAL & AROUND

Approached from the broad Avinguda de la Catedral, Barcelona's central place of worship presents a magnificent image. The richly decorated main (northwest) facade, laced with gargoyles and the stone intricacies you would expect of northern European Gothic, sets it quite apart from other churches in Barcelona. The facade was actually added in 1870 (and is receiving a serious round of restoration), although it is based on a 1408 design. The rest of the building was built between 1298 and 1460. The other facades are sparse in decoration, and the octagonal, flat-roofed towers are a clear reminder that, even here, Catalan Gothic architectural principles prevailed.

The Interior

The interior is a broad, soaring space divided into a central nave and two aisles by lines of elegant, slim pillars. The cathedral was one of the few churches in Barcelona spared by the anarchists in the civil war, so its ornamentation, never overly lavish, is intact.

Coro

In the middle of the central nave is the late-14th-century, exquisitely sculpted timber *coro* (choir stalls). The coats of arms on the stalls belong to members of the Barcelona chapter of the Order of the Golden Fleece. Emperor Carlos V presided over the order's meeting here in 1519.

DON'T MISS...

➡ The *claustre* and its 13 geese
➡ Views from the roof
➡ The crypt
➡ The *coro*

PRACTICALITIES

➡ Map p292
➡ ☎93 342 82 60
➡ www.website.es/catedralbcn
➡ Plaça de la Seu
➡ admission free, special visit €5, coro admission €2.20, Sala Capitular admission €2
➡ ⊙8am-12.45pm & 5.15-8pm Mon-Sat, special visit 1-5pm Mon-Sat, 2-5pm Sun & holidays, Sala Capitular 10am-12.15pm & 5.15-7pm Mon-Sat, 10am-12.45pm & 5.15-7pm Sun
➡ ⓜJaume I

In the first chapel on the right from the northwest entrance, the main crucifixion figure above the altar is Sant Crist de Lepant. It is said Don Juan's flagship bore it into battle at Lepanto and that the figure acquired its odd stance by dodging an incoming cannonball. Left from the main entrance is the baptismal font where, according to one story, six North American Indians brought to Europe by Columbus after his first voyage of accidental discovery were bathed in holy water.

Crypt

A broad staircase before the main altar leads you down to the crypt, which contains the tomb of Santa Eulàlia, one of Barcelona's two patron saints.

The Roof

For a bird's-eye view (mind the poop) of medieval Barcelona, visit the cathedral's roof and tower by taking the lift (€2.20) from the Capella de les Animes del Purgatori near the northeast transept.

Claustre

From the southwest transept, exit by the partly Romanesque door (one of the few remnants of the present church's predecessor) to the leafy *claustre* (cloister), with its fountains and flock of 13 geese. The geese supposedly represent the age of Santa Eulàlia at the time of her martyrdom and have, generation after generation, been squawking here since medieval days. They make fine watchdogs! One of the cloister chapels commemorates 930 priests, monks and nuns martyred during the civil war.

In the northwest corner of the cloister is the Gothic **Capella de Santa Llúcia** (Map p292), one of the few reminders of Romanesque Barcelona.

Casa de L'Ardiaca

Upon exiting the Capella de Santa Llúcia, wander across the lane into the 16th-century Casa de L'Ardiaca, which houses the city's archives. Stroll around the supremely serene courtyard, cooled by trees and a fountain; it was renovated by Lluís Domènech i Montaner in 1902, when the building was owned by the lawyers' college. Domènech i Montaner also designed the postal slot, which is adorned with swallows and a tortoise, said to represent the swiftness of truth and the plodding pace of justice. There are remnants of some stout Roman wall in here. Upstairs, you can look down into the courtyard and across to La Catedral.

Palau Episcopal

Across Carrer del Bisbe is the 17th-century **Palau Episcopal** (Map p292; Palau del Bisbat; Bishop's Palace). Virtually nothing remains of the original 13th-century structure. The Roman city's northwest gate stood here and you can see the lower segments of the Roman towers that stood on either side of the gate at the base of the Palau Episcopal and Casa de L'Ardiaca. In fact, the lower part of the entire northwest wall of the Casa de L'Ardiaca is of Roman origin – you can also make out part of the first arch of a Roman aqueduct.

TOP SIGHTS
MUSEU FREDERIC MARÈS

One of the wildest collections of historical curios lies inside this vast medieval complex, once part of the royal palace of the counts of Barcelona. A rather worn coat of arms on the wall indicates that it was also, for a while, the seat of the Spanish Inquisition in Barcelona.

Frederic Marès i Deulovol (1893–1991) was a rich sculptor, traveller and obsessive collector. He specialised in medieval Spanish **sculpture**, huge quantities of which are displayed in the basement and on the ground and 1st floors – including some lovely polychrome wooden sculptures of the Crucifixion and the Virgin. Among the most eye-catching pieces is a reconstructed Romanesque doorway with four arches, taken from a 13th-century country church in the Aragonese province of Huesca.

The top two floors comprise **'the collector's cabinet'**, a mind-boggling array of knick-knacks: medieval weaponry, finely carved pipes, delicate ladies' fans, intricate 'floral' displays made of seashells and 19th-century daguerreotypes and photographs. A room that once served as Marès' **study** and library is now crammed with sculpture. The shady courtyard houses a pleasant summer **cafe** (Cafè de l'Estiu) that's well worth a visit after browsing the collections.

DON'T MISS...

➡ Displays from the collector's cabinet
➡ Sculptures on the 1st floor
➡ Marès' study
➡ The courtyard cafe

PRACTICALITIES

➡ Map p292
➡ ☑93 256 35 00
➡ www.museumares.bcn.es
➡ Plaça de Sant Iu 5
➡ admission €4.20, after 3pm Sun & 1st Sun of month free
➡ ⊙10am-7pm Tue-Sat, 11am-8pm Sun
➡ Ⓜ Jaume I

LA RAMBLA & BARRI GÒTIC MUSEU FREDERIC MARÈS

SIGHTS

LA RAMBLA   STREET
See p68.

LA CATEDRAL   CHURCH
See p71.

FREE PALAU DEL LLOCTINENT   HISTORIC SITE
Map p292 (Carrer dels Comtes; ⊙10am-7pm; Ⓜ Jaume I) Gracefully restored in 2006, this converted 16th-century palace has a peaceful courtyard worth wandering through. Have a look upwards from the main staircase to admire the extraordinary timber *artesonado* (Mudéjar wooden ceiling with interlaced beams leaving a pattern of spaces for decoration), which is constructed to appear as the upturned hull of a boat. It was done in the 16th century by Antoni Carbonell. Exhibitions, usually related in some way to the archives, are sometimes staged.

Next to the Plaça del Rei, the *palau* (palace) was built in the 1550s as the residence of the Spanish *lloctinent* (viceroy) of Catalonia and later converted into a convent. From 1853 it housed the Arxiu de la Corona d'Aragón, a unique archive with documents detailing the history of the Crown of Aragón and Catalonia, starting in the 12th century and reaching to the 20th.

MUSEU DIOCESÀ   MUSEUM
Map p292 (Casa de la Pia Almoina; ☑93 315 22 13; www.arqbcn.org; Avinguda de la Catedral 4; adult/child €6/3; ⊙10am-2pm & 5-8pm Tue-Sat, 11am-2pm Sun; Ⓜ Jaume I) Barcelona's Roman walls ran across present-day Plaça de la Seu into what subsequently became the Casa de la Pia Almoina. The city's main centre of charity was located here in the

---

LOCAL KNOWLEDGE

GRAFFITI ARTIST

Across Plaça Nova from La Catedral your eye may be caught by child-like scribblings on the facade of the **Col.legi de Arquitectes** (Architectural College, Map p292). It is, in fact, a giant contribution by Picasso from 1962. The artwork, which represents Mediterranean festivals, was much ridiculed by the local press when it was unveiled.

TOP SIGHTS
MUSEU D'HISTÒRIA DE BARCELONA

One of Barcelona's most fascinating museums takes you back through the centuries to the very foundations of Roman Barcino. You'll stroll amid extensive ruins of the town that flourished here following its founding by Emperor Augustus around 10 BC.

Below ground is a remarkable walk through about 4 sq km of excavated Roman and Visigothic Barcelona. After the display on the typical Roman *domus* (villa), you reach a **public laundry**; outside in the street were containers for people to urinate into, as the urine was used as disinfectant. You pass dyeing shops, a public cold-water bath and shops dedicated to the making of *garum* (a fish sauce enjoyed across the Roman Empire), a 6th-century church and **wine-making stores**.

Ramparts then wind upward, past remains of the gated patio of a Roman house, the medieval Palau Epis-copal (Bishops' Palace) and into two broad vaulted halls with **displays on medieval Barcelona**. The finale is the **Saló del Tinell**, the royal palace banqueting hall and a fine example of Catalan Gothic (built 1359–70). It was here that Fernando and Isabel heard Columbus' first reports of the New World.

DON'T MISS...

- ➡ Public laundry
- ➡ Wine-making stores
- ➡ Saló del Tinell
- ➡ Medieval Barcelona

PRACTICALITIES

- ➡ Map p292
- ➡ ☏93 256 21 00
- ➡ www.museuhisto ria.bcn.cat
- ➡ Plaça del Rei
- ➡ adult/child €7/free
- ➡ ◷10am-7pm Tue-Sat, 10am-8pm Sun
- ➡ Ⓜ Jaume I

11th century, although the much-crumbled remains of the present building date back to the 15th century. Today it houses the Diocesan Museum, which has a small exhibit on Antoni Gaudí (including a fascinating documentary on his life and philosophy) on the top floor. There's also a sparse collection of medieval religious art usually supplemented by a temporary exhibition or two.

PLAÇA DE SANT JAUME
PLAZA

Map p292 (Ⓜ Jaume I) In the 2000 or so years since the Romans settled here, the area around this square (often remodelled), which started life as the forum, has been the focus of Barcelona's civic life. Facing each other across it are the Palau de la Generalitat (seat of Catalonia's regional government) on the north side and the Ajuntament (town hall) to the south. Behind the Ajuntament rise the awful town hall offices built in the 1970s over Plaça de Sant Miquel. Opposite is a rare 15th-century gem, Casa Centelles, on the corner of Baixada de Sant Miquel. You can wander into the fine Gothic-Renaissance courtyard if the gates are open.

AJUNTAMENT
ARCHITECTURE

Map p292 (☏93 402 70 00; www.bcn.cat; Plaça de Sant Jaume; ◷10.30am-1.30pm Sun; Ⓜ Liceu or Jaume I) The Ajuntament, otherwise known as the Casa de la Ciutat, has been the seat of power for centuries. The Consell de Cent (the city's ruling council) first sat here in the 14th century, but the building has lamentably undergone many changes since the days of Barcelona's Gothic-era splendour.

Only the original, now disused, entrance on Carrer de la Ciutat retains its Gothic ornament. The main 19th-century neoclassical facade on the square is a charmless riposte to the Palau de la Generalitat. Inside, the Saló de Cent is the hall in which the town council once held its plenary sessions. The broad vaulting is pure Catalan Gothic and the *artesonado* demonstrates fine work. In fact, much of what you see is comparatively recent. The building was badly damaged in a bombardment in 1842 and has been repaired and tampered with repeatedly. The wooden neo-Gothic seating was added at the beginning of the 20th century, as was the grand alabaster retablo (retable, or altarpiece) at the back. To the right you enter the small Saló de la Reina

Regente, built in 1860, where the Ajuntament now sits. To the left of the Saló de Cent is the Saló de les Croniques – the murals here recount Catalan exploits in Greece and the Near East in Catalonia's empire-building days.

PALAU DE LA GENERALITAT   PALACE

Map p292 (www.gencat.cat; Plaça de Sant Jaune; MLiceu or Jaume I) Founded in the early 15th century, the Palau de la Generalitat is open on limited occasions only (the second and fourth weekends of the month, plus open-door days). The most impressive of the ceremonial halls is the **Saló de Sant Jordi**, named after St George, the region's patron saint. At any time, however, you can admire the original Gothic main entrance on Carrer del Bisbe. To join weekend visits, book on the website.

Marc Safont designed the original Gothic main entrance on Carrer del Bisbe. The modern main entrance on Plaça de Sant Jaume is a late-Renaissance job with neo-classical leanings. If you wander by in the evening, squint up through the windows into the Saló de Sant Jordi (Hall of St George) and you will get some idea of the sumptuousness of the interior.

If you do get inside, you're in for a treat. The usual entrance is from Carrer de Sant Sever. The first rooms you pass through are characterised by low vaulted ceilings. From here you head upstairs to the raised courtyard known as the Pati dels Tarongers, a modest Gothic orangery (opened about once a month for concert performances of the palace's chimes). The 16th-century Sala Daurada i de Sessions, one of the rooms leading off the patio, is a splendid meeting hall lit up by huge chandeliers. Still more imposing is the Renaissance Saló de Sant Jordi, the murals of which were added last century – many an occasion of pomp and circumstance takes place here. Finally, you descend the staircase of the Gothic Pati Central to leave by what was, in the beginning, the building's main entrance.

MIBA (MUSEU D'IDEES I INVENTS DE BARCELONA)   MUSEUM

Map p292 (Museum of Ideas and Inventions; ☏93 332 79 30; www.mibamuseum.com; Carrer de la Ciutat 7; adult/child €7/5; ◷10am-7pm Tue-Sat, to 2pm Sun; MJaume I) New in 2011, this museum has a fascinating collection of curiosities from the world of both brilliant and bizarre inventions: mops with

ⓘ ROMAN WALLS

From Plaça del Rei it's worth taking a detour northeast to see the two best surviving stretches of Barcelona's Roman walls, which once boasted 78 towers (as much a matter of prestige as of defence). **One wall** (Map p292) is on the southwest side of Plaça Ramon de Berenguer Gran, with the **Capella Reial de Santa Àgata** (Map p292) atop. The square itself is dominated by a statue of count-king Ramon de Berenguer Gran done by Josep Llimona in 1880. The **other wall** (Map p292) is a little further south, by the northern end of Carrer del Sotstinent Navarro. The Romans built and reinforced these walls in the 3rd and 4th centuries AD, after the first attacks by Germanic tribes from the north.

microphones on the handle (so you can sing while you work), a seat for inserting suppositories, mugs with biscuit storage, wristbands that measure UV rays and eyeglasses adjustable to any prescription. There are also metal slides between floors (who needs the stairs?) and some rather creatively configured toilets.

PLAÇA DE SANT JOSEP ORIOL   PLAZA

Map p292 (MLiceu) This small plaza is the prettiest in the Barri Gòtic. Its bars and cafes attract buskers and artists and make it a lively place to hang out. It is surrounded by quaint streets, many dotted with appealing cafes, restaurants and shops.

Looming over the square is the flank of the **Església de Santa Maria del Pi** (Map p292; ◷9.30am-1pm & 5-8.30pm; MLiceu), a Gothic church built in the 14th to 16th centuries. The bulk of it was completed in 1320–91. With its 10m diameter, the beautiful rose window above its entrance on Plaça del Pi is claimed by some to be the world's biggest. The interior of the church was gutted when leftists ransacked it in the opening months of the civil war in 1936 and most of the stained glass is modern. Perhaps one happy result of the fire was the destruction of the 19th-century neo-Gothic seating, which therefore had to be replaced by the 18th-century baroque original.

The third chapel on the left is dedicated to Sant Josep Oriol, who was parish priest here from 1687 to 1702. The chapel has a map showing the places in the church where he worked numerous miracles (he was canonised in 1909). According to legend, a 10th-century fisherman discovered an image of the Virgin Mary in a *pi* (pine tree) that he was intent on cutting down to build a boat. Struck by the vision, he instead built a little chapel, later to be succeeded by this Gothic church. A pine still grows in the square.

PLAÇA REIAL   PLAZA

Map p292 (MLiceu) One of the most photogenic squares in Barcelona, the Plaça Reial is a delightful retreat from the traffic and pedestrian mobs on the nearby Rambla. Numerous eateries, bars and nightspots lie beneath the arcades of 19th-century neoclassical buildings, with a buzz of activity at all hours.

It was created on the site of a convent, one of several destroyed along La Rambla (the strip was teeming with religious institutions) in the wake of the Spain-wide disentailment laws that stripped the Church of much of its property. The lamp posts by the central fountain are Antoni Gaudí's first known works in the city.

The southern half of the Barri Gòtic is imbued with the memory of Picasso, who lived as a teenager with his family in Carrer de la Mercè, had his first studio in Carrer de la Plata and was a regular visitor to a brothel at Carrer d'Avinyó 27. That experience may have inspired his 1907 painting *Les Demoiselles d'Avignon*.

GRAN TEATRE DEL LICEU   ARCHITECTURE

(☑93 485 99 14; www.liceubarcelona.com; La Rambla dels Caputxins 51-59; ⊘guided tour 10am, unguided visits 11.30am, noon, 12.30pm & 1pm; MLiceu) If you can't catch a night at the opera, you can still have a look around one of Europe's greatest opera houses, known to locals as the Liceu. Smaller than Milan's La Scala but bigger than Venice's La Fenice, it can seat up to 2300 people in its grand horseshoe auditorium.

Built in 1847, the Liceu launched such Catalan stars as Josep (aka José) Carreras and Montserrat Caballé. Fire virtually destroyed it in 1994, but city authorities were quick to get it back into operation. Carefully reconstructing the 19th-century auditorium and installing the latest in theatre technology, technicians brought the Liceu back to life in October 1999. You can take a 20-minute quick turn around the main public areas of the theatre or join a one-hour guided tour.

On the guided tour you are taken to the grand foyer, with its thick pillars and sumptuous chandeliers, and then up the marble staircase to the Saló dels Miralls (Hall of Mirrors). These both survived the 1994 fire and the latter was traditionally where theatregoers mingled during intermission. With mirrors, ceiling frescoes, fluted columns and high-and-mighty phrases in praise of the arts, it all exudes a typically neobaroque richness worthy of its 19th-century patrons. You are then led up to the 4th-floor stalls to admire the theatre itself.

The tour also takes in a collection of Modernista art, El Cercle del Liceu, which contains works by Ramon Casas. It is possible to book special tours, one that is similar to the guided tour described but including a half-hour music recital on the Saló dels Miralls. The other tour penetrates the inner workings of the stage and backstage work areas.

The financial crisis has had its effect on the arts throughout Spain, and the Liceu has had its own stand-off with the government due to the budget cuts announced in early 2012. The Liceu's director general, Joan Francesco Marco, threatened closures of the house for two months in the spring and summer of 2012, triggering wide criticism in the local press and proposed staff strikes. Labor unions' negotiations have paused the Liceu's crisis for the time being by trying to close the €3.7 million funding gap; it remains to be seen how the Liceu's funding is managed in the years to come.

MIRADOR DE COLOM   VIEWPOINT

Map p302 (☑93 302 52 24; Plaça del Portal de la Pau; lift adult/child €4/3; ⊘8.30am-8.30pm; MDrassanes) High above the swirl of traffic on the roundabout below, Columbus keeps permanent watch, pointing vaguely out to the Mediterranean. Built for the Universal Exhibition in 1888, the monument allows you to zip up 60m in the lift for bird's-eye views back up La Rambla and across the ports of Barcelona.

It was in Barcelona that Columbus allegedly gave the delighted Catholic monarchs a report of his first discoveries in the Americas after his voyage in 1492. In the 19th century it was popularly believed here that Columbus was one of Barcelona's most illustrious sons. Some historians still make that claim.

ESGLÉSIA DE SANTS JUST I PASTOR CHURCH

Map p292 (📞93 301 74 33; www.basilicasantjust. cat; Plaça de Sant Just 5; ⏱11am-2pm & 5.30-8pm Mon-Sat, 10am-1pm Sun; Ⓜ Liceu or Jaume I) This somewhat neglected, single-nave church, with chapels on either side of the buttressing, was built in 1342 in Catalan Gothic style on what is reputedly the site of the oldest parish church in Barcelona. Inside you can admire some fine stained-glass windows. In front of it, in a pretty little square that was used as a set (a smelly Parisian marketplace) in 2006 for *Perfume: The Story of a Murderer,* is what is claimed to be the city's oldest Gothic fountain.

On the morning of 11 September 1924, Antoni Gaudí was arrested as he attempted to enter the church from this square to attend Mass. In those days of the dictatorship of General Primo de Rivera, it took little to ruffle official feathers, and Gaudí's refusal to speak Spanish (Castilian) to the overbearing Guardia Civil officers who had stopped him earned him the better part of a day in the cells until a friend came to bail him out.

FREE CENTRE D'INTERPRETACIÓ DEL CALL HISTORIC SITE

Map p292 (📞93 256 21 22; www.museuhistoria. bcn.cat; Placeta de Manuel Ribé; ⏱11am-2pm Tue-Fri, to 7pm Sat & Sun; Ⓜ Jaume I or Liceu) Once a 14th-century house of the Jewish weaver Jucef Bonhiac, this small visitors centre is dedicated to the history of Barcelona's Jewish quarter, the Call. Glass sections in the ground floor allow you to inspect Mr Bonhiac's former wells and storage space. The house, also known as the Casa de l'Alquimista (Alchemist's House), hosts a modest display of Jewish artefacts, including ceramics excavated in the area of the Call, along with explanations and maps of the one-time Jewish quarter.

The area between Carrer dels Banys Nous and Plaça de Sant Jaume was the heart of the city's medieval Jewish quarter, or Call Major, until a bloody pogrom in the 14th century drove out most of the Jews living here. The subsequent expulsion of all Jews in the country in the 15th century put an end to the Jewish presence in Barcelona. The Call Menor extended across the modern Carrer de Ferran as far as Baixada de Sant Miquel and Carrer d'en Rauric. The present Església de Sant Jaume on Carrer de Ferran was built on the site of a synagogue.

EL CALL

One of our favourite places to wander in the Ciutat Vella (Old City) is El Call (pronounced 'kye'), which is the name of the medieval Jewish quarter that flourished here until a tragic pogrom in the 14th century. Today its narrow lanes hide some surprising sites (including an ancient synagogue unearthed in the 1990s and the fragments of a women's bathhouse discovered inside the basement of the cafe Caelum). Some of the old town's most unusual shops are here, selling exquisite antiques, handmade leather products, even kosher wine. Its well-concealed dining rooms and candelit bars and cafes make a fine destination in the evening.

El Call (which probably derives from the Hebrew word 'kahal', meaning 'community') is a tiny area, and a little tricky to find. The boundaries are roughly Carrer del Call, Carrer dels Banys Nous, Baixada de Santa Eulalia and Carrer de Sant Honorat.

Even before the pograms of 1391, Jews in Barcelona were not exactly privileged citizens. As in many medieval centres, they were obliged to wear a special identifying mark on their garments and had trouble getting permission to expand their ghetto as the Call's population increased (as many as 4000 people were crammed into the tiny streets of the Call Major).

SINAGOGA MAJOR SYNAGOGUE

Map p292 (📞93 317 07 90; www.calldebarcelona. org; Carrer de Marlet 5; admission by suggested donation €2.50; ⏱10.30am-6.30pm Mon-Fri, to 2.30pm Sat & Sun; Ⓜ Liceu) When an Argentine investor bought a run-down electrician's store with an eye to converting it into central Barcelona's umpteenth bar, he could hardly have known he had stumbled onto the remains of what could be the city's main medieval synagogue (some historians cast doubt on the claim). A guide will explain what is thought to be the significance of the site in various languages.

Fragments of medieval and Roman-era walls remain in the small vaulted space that you enter from the street. Also remaining are tanners' wells installed in the 15th century. The second chamber has been spruced up for use as a synagogue. A remnant of late-Roman-era wall here, given its orientation facing Jerusalem, has led some to speculate that there was a synagogue here even in Roman times. There were four synagogues in the medieval city, but after the pogroms of 1391, this one (assuming it was the Sinagoga Major) was Christianised by the placing of an effigy of St Dominic on the building.

FREE TEMPLE ROMÀ D'AUGUST   RUIN

Map p292 (Carrer del Paradis; ⊙10am-8pm Tue-Sun; MJaume I) Opposite the southeast end of La Catedral, narrow Carrer del Paradis leads towards Plaça de Sant Jaume. Inside No 10, itself an intriguing building with Gothic and baroque touches, are four columns and the architrave of Barcelona's main Roman temple, dedicated to Caesar Augustus and built to worship his imperial highness in the 1st century AD.

You are now standing on the highest point of Roman Barcino, Mont Tàber (a grand total of 16.9m, unlikely to induce altitude sickness). You may well find the door open outside the listed hours. Just pop in.

VIA SEPULCRAL ROMANA ARCHAEOLOGICAL SITE

Map p292 (☎93 256 21 00; www.museuhistoria. bcn.cat; Plaça de la Vila de Madrid; admission €2; ⊙11am-2pm Tue-Fri, to 7pm Sat & Sun; MCatalunya) Along Carrer de la Canuda, a block east of the top end of La Rambla, is a sunken garden where a series of Roman tombs lies exposed. The burial ground stretches along either side of the road that led northwest out of Barcelona's Roman predecessor, Barcino. Roman law forbade burial within city limits and so everyone, the great and humble, were generally buried along roads leading out of cities. A smallish display in Spanish and Catalan by the tombs explores the Roman road and highway system, burial and funerary rites and customs. A few bits of pottery (including a burial amphora with the skeleton of a three-year-old Roman child) accompany the display.

DOMUS ROMANA   ARCHAEOLOGICAL SITE

Map p292 (☎93 256 21 00; www.museuhisto ria.bcn.cat; Carrer de la Fruita 2; admission €2; ⊙10am-2pm Sat & Sun; MLiceu) The remains of a Roman domus (town house) have been unearthed and opened to the public. The house (and vestiges of three small shops) lay close to the Roman forum, and the owners were clearly well off. Apart from getting something of an idea of daily Roman life through these remains, the location also contains six medieval grain silos installed at the time the Jewish quarter, the Call, was located in this area. The whole is housed in the mid-19th-century Casa Morell. So, in an unusual mix, one gets a glimpse of three distinct periods of history in the same spot.

MUSEU DE L'ERÒTICA   MUSEUM

Map p292 (Erotica Museum; ☎93 318 98 65; www. erotica-museum.com; La Rambla de Sant Josep 96; admission €9; ⊙10am-8pm; MLiceu) Observe what naughtiness people have been getting up to since ancient times, with historical relics like Indian bas-reliefs showing various aspects of tantric love, 18th-century wood carvings depicting Kama Sutra positions, Japanese porcelain porn and African fornication carvings. Despite the premise, overall it's a rather buttoned-up affair, and probably not worth the high admission price (despite the free drink).

MUSEU DE CERA   MUSEUM

Map p292 (☎93 317 26 49; www.museocerabcn. com; Passatge de la Banca 7; adult/child €15/9; ⊙10am-10pm daily Jun-Sep, 10am-1.30pm & 4-7.30pm Mon-Fri, 11am-2pm & 4.30-8.30pm Sat, Sun & holidays Oct-May; MDrassanes) Inside this late-19th-century building you can stand, sit and lounge about with 300 wax figures. Frankenstein is here, along with Luke Skywalker, Hitler, Mussolini, Che Guevara, Fidel Castro, General Franco and head of the former Catalan government-in-exile Josep Taradellas. Kids may get a kick out of the museum, but the price tag is steep for often poorly executed representations.

ESGLÉSIA DE LA MERCÈ   CHURCH

Map p292 (Plaça de la Mercè; MDrassanes) Raised in the 1760s on the site of its Gothic predecessor, the baroque Església de la Mercè is home to Barcelona's most celebrated patron saint. It was badly damaged during the civil war, but what remains is quite a curiosity. The baroque facade facing the square contrasts with the Renaissance flank along Carrer Ample. The latter was actually moved here from another nearby church that was subsequently destroyed in the 1870s.

DALÍ   MUSEUM

Map p292 (Museo Real Círculo Artístico de Barcelona; ☎93 318 17 74; www.daliabarcelona.com; Carrer dels Arcs 5; adult/child €10/7; ⊙10am-10pm; MLiceu) One of the best things about this collection is its superb location in the Royal Art Circle building just near La Catedral.

This somewhat hyped display offers 60-odd little-known sculptures by Salvador Dalí, a man who was largely renowned for his paintings. Documents, sketches and photos by and of the artist complete the picture. If you can't visit his museum-mausoleum in Figueres, this is no substitute, but does provide some clues to the life and work of the mustachioed maestro.

MUSEU DEL CALÇAT   MUSEUM

Map p292 (Footwear Museum; ☑93 301 45 33; Plaça de Sant Felip Neri 5; admission €2.50; ☉11am-2pm Tue-Sun; Ⓜ Jaume I) This obscure museum is home to everything from Egyptian sandals to dainty ladies' shoes of the 18th century. The museum and cobblers' guild, which has its roots in the city's medieval past, were moved here shortly after the civil war.

 EATING

First things first: skip the strip. La Rambla is fine for people-watching, but no great shakes for the palate. Instead venture off into the streets that wind into Barri Gòtic, and your belly (and wallet) will be eternally grateful. Inside the medieval labyrinth, choices abound. If you had to pinpoint any one area, it would be the eastern half of the *barri* (neighbourhood) near Via Laietana on the narrow streets above the cathedral (around Carrer de les Magdalenes) and between Plaça de Sant Jaume and the waterfront. Here you'll find a huddle of old-time tapas bars as well as innovative newcomers. All are laden with atmosphere.

TOP CHOICE **KOY SHUNKA**   JAPANESE €€€

Map p292 (☑93 412 79 39; www.koyshunka.com; Carrer de Copons 7; multicourse menus €72-108; ☉lunch Tue-Sun, dinner Tue-Sat; Ⓜ Urquinaona) Down a narrow lane north of La Catedral, Koy Shunka opens a portal to exquisite dishes from the East – mouthwatering sushi, sashimi, seared Wagyu beef and flavour-rich seaweed salads are served alongside inventive cooked fushion dishes like *almejas finas al vapor con sake* (steamed clams with sake) or *tempura de vieira y lagostino con setas de japonesas* (tempura of scallops and king prawns with Japanese mushrooms). Don't miss the house specialty of *toro* (tender tuna belly).

🛈

MANIC MONDAYS

Many attractions shut their doors on Monday, but there are plenty of exceptions. Among the more enticing ones:
➡ Gran Teatre del Liceu (p76)
➡ La Catedral (p71)
➡ Museu de l'Eròtica (p78)
➡ Museu de Cera (p78)
➡ Dalí (p78)
➡ Sinagoga Major (p77)

Most diners sit at the large wraparound counter, where you can watch the culinary wizardry in action. Set multicourse menus are pricey but well worth it for those seeking a truly extraordinary dining experience.

TOP CHOICE **PLA**   FUSION €€

Map p292 (☑93 412 65 52; www.elpla.cat; Carrer de la Bellafila 5; mains €18-24; ☉dinner daily; 🖋; Ⓜ Jaume I) One of Barri Gòtic's long-standing favourites, Pla is a stylish, romantically lit medieval den (with a huge stone arch) where the cooks churn out such temptations as oxtail braised in red wine, seared tuna with roasted aubergine, and 'Thaistyle' monkfish with prawns, lemongrass and apple foam. It has a tasting menu for €36 from Sunday to Thursday.

LA VINATERIA DEL CALL   SPANISH €€

Map p292 (☑93 302 60 92; http://lavinateriadel call.com; Carrer de Sant Domènec del Call 9; small plates €7-11; ☉dinner; Ⓜ Jaume I) In a magical setting in the former Jewish quarter, this tiny jewelbox of a restaurant serves up tasty Iberian dishes including Galician octopus, cider-cooked chorizo and the Catalan *escalivada* (roasted peppers, aubergine and onions) with anchovies. Portions are small and made for sharing, and there's a good and affordable selection of wines.

CAN CULLERETES   CATALAN €€

Map p292 (☑93 317 30 22; Carrer Quintana 5; mains €8-14; ☉lunch & dinner Tue-Sat, lunch Sun; Ⓜ Liceu) Founded in 1786, Barcelona's oldest restaurant is still going strong, with tourists and locals flocking to enjoy its rambling interior, old-fashioned tile-filled decor, and enormous helpings of traditional Catalan food. The multicourse lunch specials (€12.80) are a good value.

START **LA CATEDRAL**
END **PLAÇA DEL REI**
DISTANCE 1.5KM
DURATION 1½ HOURS

Neighbourhood Walk
Hidden Treasures in the Barri Gòtic

This scenic walk through the Barri Gòtic will take you back in time, from the early days of Roman-era Barcino through to the medieval era.

Before entering the cathedral, have look at ❶ **three Picasso friezes** (p73) on the building facing the square. After noting his signature style, wander through ❷ **La Catedral** (p71); don't miss the cloister with its flock of 13 geese.

Leaving the cathedral, enter the former gates of the ancient fortified city and turn right into ❸ **Plaça de Sant Felip Neri**. Note the shrapnel-scarred walls of the old church, damaged by pro-Francist bombers in 1939. A plaque commemorates the victims (mostly children) of the bombing.

Head out of the square and turn right. On this narrow lane you'll spot ❹ **a small statue of Santa Eulàlia**, one of Barcelona's patron saints, who suffered various tortures during her martyrdom.

Make your way west to the looming 14th-century ❺ **Església de Sant Maria del Pi**, which is famed for its magnificent rose window.

Follow the curving road and zigzag down to ❻ **Plaça Reial** (p76), one of Barcelona's prettiest squares. Flanking the fountain are lamp posts designed by Antoni Gaudí.

Stroll up to Carrer de la Boqueria and turn left on Carrer de Sant Domènec del Call. This leads into the district of El Call, once the heart of the medieval Jewish quarter, until the bloody pogrom of 1391. The ❼ **Sinagoga Major** (p77), one of Europe's oldest, was discovered in 1996.

Head across Plaça de Sant Jaume and turn left after Carrer del Bisbe. You'll soon pass the entrance to the remnants of a ❽ **Roman Temple**, with four columns hidden in a small courtyard.

The final stop is ❾ **Plaça del Rei**, a picturesque plaza where Fernando and Isabel received Columbus following his first New World voyage. The former palace today houses a superb history museum, with significant Roman ruins underground.

CAFÈ DE L'ACADÈMIA
CATALAN €€

Map p292 (☑93 319 82 53; Carrer de Lledó 1; mains €13-17; ⊘Mon-Fri; ⓂJaume I) Expect a mix of traditional dishes with the occasional creative twist. At lunchtime, local Ajuntament (town hall) office workers pounce on the *menú del día* (set menu; €14, or €10 at the bar). In the evening it is rather more romantic, as low lighting emphasises the intimacy of the timber ceiling and wooden decor. Offerings range from *chuletón* (huge T-bone steak) for two to *guatlla farcida de foie d'ànec i botifarra amb salsa de ceps* (quail stuffed with duck foie gras and sausage with a mushroom sauce).

CERERÍA
VEGETARIAN €€

Map p292 (☑93 301 85 10; Baixada de Sant Miquel 3; mains €9-16; ⊘dinner Mon-Sat; 🛜🍽; ⓂJaume I) Black-and-white marble floors, a smattering of old wooden tables and ramshackle displays of instruments (most made onsite) lend a certain bohemian charm to this small vegetarian restaurant. The pizzas are delicious here, and feature organic ingredients – as do the flavourful galettes, dessert crêpes and bountiful salads. There are some fine vegan options to be had here, too.

CERVECERÍA TALLER DE TAPAS
SPANISH €€

Map p292 (☑93 481 62 33; Carrer Comtal 28; mains €8-15; ⊘10am-midnight Mon-Sat, from noon Sun; ⓂUrquinaona) Amid white stone walls and beneath a beamed ceiling, this buzzing easygoing place serves a broad selection of tapas as well as changing daily specials like *cochinillo* (roast suckling pig). A smattering of beers from across the globe – Leffe Blond, Guinness, Brahma (Brazil) and Sol (Mexico) – add to the appeal.

BUN BO
VIETNAMESE €

Map p292 (☑93 301 13 78; Carrer dels Sagristans; mains €7-11; ⊘1pm-midnight; ⓂJaume I) Tucked away on a tiny plaza near the cathedral, Bun Bo serves up hearty bowls of *pho* (noodle soup with beef or chicken), *bánh xèo* (savoury pancakes) and other Vietnamese classics. You can dine outside under shaded chrome tables or amid the flamboyant interior, complete with paper lanterns, oversized photos of Halong Bay and a precariously perched cyclo taxi. Bun Bo also features a good line in cocktails and lunch specials.

LA PLATA
TAPAS €

Map p292 (Carrer de la Mercè 28; tapas around €3.50; ⊘9am-3pm & 6pm-late Mon-Sat; ⓂJaume I) La Plata, hidden down a narrow lane near the waterfront, is a humble but well-loved *bodega* that serves just three plates: *pescadito frito* (small fried sardines), *butifarra* (sausage) and tomato salad. Add to this the drinkable, affordable wines (€1 per glass) and you have the makings of a fine pre-dinner tapas spot.

AGUT
CATALAN €€

Map p292 (www.restaurantagut.com; Carrer d'en Gignàs 16; mains €16-25; ⊘lunch & dinner Tue-Sat, lunch Sun; ⓂDrassanes) This classic Catalan eatery lies deep in the Gothic labyrinth. A series of cosy dining areas is connected by broad arches while, high up, the walls are tightly lined by artworks. There's art in what the kitchen serves up, too, from the oak-grilled meat to a succulent variety of seafood offerings, like the *cassoleta de rap a l'all cremat amb cloïsses* (monkfish with browned garlic and clams).

LOS CARACOLES
SPANISH €€€

Map p292 (☑93 301 20 41; www.los-caracoles. es; Carrer dels Escudellers 14; mains €13-32; ⓂDrassanes) Currently run by the fifth generation of the Bofarull family, 'The Snails' started life as a tavern in 1835 and is one of Barcelona's best-known, if somewhat touristy, restaurants. Several interlocking rooms (consider asking for the small medieval-looking banquet room) have centuries of history seemingly greased into the tables and garlic-clad walls. This could even distract you from the rotisserie chickens and snails that are the house specialities.

BAR CELTA
GALICIAN €

Map p292 (Carrer de la Mercè 16; tapas €3-6; ⊘noon-midnight Tue-Sun; ⓂDrassanes) This bright, rambunctious tapas bar specialises in *pulpo* (octopus) and other creature of the sea like *navajas* (razor clams). And it does a good job too: even the most discriminating of Galician natives give this spot the thumbs up. Take a seat at the zinc bar, order a bottle of Ribeiro – here served the traditional Galician way, in little white ceramic cups, or *tazas* – and tuck into your hearty seafood *raciones* (larger portions of tapas dishes).

CAELUM
CAFE €

Map p292 (☑93 302 69 93; Carrer de la Palla 8; snacks €2-4; ☺10.30am-8.30pm Mon-Thu, 10.30am-11.30pm Fri & Sat, 11.30am-9pm Sun; Ⓜ Liceu) Centuries of heavenly gastronomic tradition from across Spain are concentrated in this exquisite medieval space in the heart of the city. Sweets (such as the irresistible marzipan from Toledo) made by nuns in convents across the country make their way to this den of delicacies. There's a shop adjoining the pretty cafe where you can buy goodies to take home; there's also an atmospheric underground chamber where you can secret yourself for tea and pastries from 3.30pm to closing time.

MILK
BRUNCH €

Map p292 (www.milkbarcelona.com; Carrer d'en Gignàs 21; mains €9-10; ☺10am-4pm & 6.30-11.30pm ; Ⓜ Jaume I) Also known to many as a cool cocktail spot, the Irish-run Milk's key role for Barcelona night owls is providing morning-after brunches (served till 4pm). Avoid direct sunlight and tuck into pancakes, eggs Benedict and other hangover dishes in a small but cosy setting.

🍷 DRINKING & NIGHTLIFE

OVISO
BAR

Map p292 (Carrer d'Arai 5; ☺10am-2am; Ⓜ Liceu) Oviso is a popular budget-friendly restaurant with outdoor tables on the plaza, but it shows its true bohemian colours by night, with a wildly mixed crowd, a rock-and-roll vibe and a two-room fin-de-siècle interior plastered with curious murals – geese taking flight, leaping dolphins and blue peacocks framing a bright red wall.

LA CERVETECA
BAR

Map p292 (Carrer de Gignàs 25; ☺4-10pm Mon-Thu, 1-11pm Fri & Sat, 1-10pm Sun; Ⓜ Jaume I) An unmissable stop for beer lovers, La Cerveteca serves an impressive variety of global craft brews. In addition to scores of bottled brews, there's a frequent rotation of what's on draught. Recent hits include Taras Boulba (a Belgian pale ale), Hell (a German lager) and Spaceman IPA (from the USA). The medieval walls and standing cask tables (with a few seats in back) are a fine setting for an early evening pick-me-up.

ČAJ CHAI
CAFE

Map p292 (☑93 301 95 92; Carrer de Sant Domènec del Call 12; ☺3-10pm Mon, 10.30am-10pm Tue-Sun; Ⓜ Jaume I) Inspired by Prague's bohemian tearooms, this bright and buzzing cafe in the heart of the old Jewish quarter is a tea connoisseur's paradise. Čaj Chai stocks over 100 teas from China, India, Korea, Japan, Nepal, Morocco and beyond. It's a much-loved local haunt.

MARULA CAFÈ
BAR

Map p292 (www.marulacafe.com; Carrer dels Escudellers 49; ☺11pm-5am; Ⓜ Liceu) A fantastic funk find in the heart of the Barri Gòtic, Marula will transport you to the 1970s and the best in funk and soul. James Brown fans will think they've died and gone to heaven. It's not, however, a monothematic place and occasionally the DJs slip in other tunes, from breakbeat to house. Samba and other Brazilian dance sounds also penetrate here.

POLAROID
BAR

Map p292 (Carrer dels Còdols 29; ☺7pm-2.30am; Ⓜ Drassanes) True to name, Polaroid is a blast from the past with its VHS tapes mounted on the walls, old film posters, comic-book-covered tables, action-figure displays and other kitschy decor. Not surprisingly, it draws a fun, unpretentious crowd who come for cheap cañas (draught beer; €2), good mojitos and free popcorn.

BOOTLEG
BAR

Map p292 (Carrer de Lledó 5; ☺9.30am-12.30am Sun-Thu, to 2am Fri & Sat; Ⓜ Jaume I) One of a growing number of enticing cafe-bars along this street, Bootleg is a warmly lit, split-level spot with a stylish but unpretentious crowd (equal parts expat and barcelonín) that come for good conversation, fairly priced drinks and snacks with a soundtrack of ambient electronica.

DUSK
LOUNGE

Map p292 (Carrer de la Mercè 23; ☺6pm-2.30am; Ⓜ Drassanes) Tucked away on an atmospheric lane in the Gothic quarter, Dusk teeters between rowdy bar and intimate cocktail lounge. It has various rooms with low lighting, age-old brick walls and comfy couches framed by red curtains but it also shows sports on a big-screen TV. It's a mostly foreign crowd swilling cocktails and nibbling on tapas.

BOSC DE LES FADES
LOUNGE

Map p292 (Passatage de la Banca 5; ☺10am-1am; **M**Drassanes) True to name, the 'Forest of the Faeries' offers a whimsical retreat from the busy Ramblas nearby. Lounge chairs and lamplit tables are scattered beneath an indoor forest complete with trickling fountain and grotto. It's an intriguing spot for a few cocktails to start off the night.

BARCELONA PIPA CLUB
BAR

Map p292 (✆93 302 47 32; www.bpipaclub.com; Plaça Reial 3; ☺10pm-4am; **M**Liceu) This pipe smokers' club is like an apartment, with all sorts of interconnecting rooms and knick-knacks – notably the pipes after which the place is named. Buzz at the door and head two floors up.

BLONDIE
BAR

Map p292 (www.blondie-bcn.com; Carrer d'en Roca 14; ☺8pm-2am; **M**Liceu) Long a dark little dive that had slowly sunk into oblivion, this Italian-run bar now has a strong local following who come for new wave hits from the '80s. There's also subtle, multicoloured lighting, black-and-white tile walls, Estrella Galicia beer (the country's crispest lager) and something of a conspiratorial air.

EL PARAIGUA
BAR

Map p292 (✆93 302 11 31; www.elparaigua.com; Carrer del Pas de l'Ensenyança 2; ☺10am-midnight Mon-Wed, 11am-2am Thu-Sat; **M**Liceu) A tiny chocolate box of dark tinted Modernisme, the 'Umbrella' has been serving up drinks since the 1960s. The turn-of-the-20th-century decor was transferred here from a shop knocked down elsewhere in the district and cobbled back together to create this cosy locale.

Take a trip in time from Modernisme to medieval by heading downstairs to the brick and stone basement bar area. Amid 11th-century walls, DJs spin on Thursdays (from 10pm) and live bands – funk, soul, rock, blues – hold court on Fridays and Saturdays (from 11.30pm).

MANCHESTER
BAR

Map p292 (www.manchesterbar.com; Carrer de Milans 5; ☺7pm-2.30am; **M**Liceu) A drinking den that has undergone several transformations down the years now treats you to the sounds of great Manchester bands, from the Chemical Brothers to Oasis, but probably not the Hollies. It has a pleasing rough-and-tumble feel, with tables jammed in every which way.

SINATRA
BAR

Map p292 (✆93 412 52 79; Carrer de les Heures 4-10; ☺6pm-2.30am Sun-Thu, to 3am Fri & Sat; **M**Liceu) Around 11pm from Wednesday to Saturday, this popular restaurant transforms into a lively nightspot, with DJs spinning a mixed bag (house music, old-school jazz, '80s) to a largely foreign crowd. The deco interior adds a classy element to the ambience, and cocktails are first rate.

CAFÈ DE L'ÒPERA
CAFE

Map p292 (✆93 317 75 85; www.cafeoperabcn.com; La Rambla 74; ☺8.30am-2.30am; **M**Liceu) Opposite the Gran Teatre del Liceu is La Rambla's most intriguing cafe. Operating since 1929, it is pleasant enough for an early evening libation or coffee and croissants. Head upstairs for an elevated seat above the busy boulevard. Can you be tempted by the *cafè de l'Òpera* (coffee with chocolate mousse)?

LA CLANDESTINA
CAFE

Map p292 (✆93 319 05 33; Baixada de Viladecols 2; ☺10am-10pm Sun-Thu, to midnight Fri & Sat; 🛜; **M**Jaume I) Opt for tea, Turkish coffee, mango lassi or a Middle Eastern *narghile* (the most elaborate way to smoke). Like other cafes and bars nearby, Clandestina sports a bohemian ambience with colour-saturated walls, black cats milling about and a changing display of local artwork for sale. There's also beer and wine on hand.

SALTERIO
CAFE

Map p292 (Carrer de Sant Domènec del Call 4; ☺2pm-1am Mon-Sat; **M**Jaume I) A wonderfully atmospheric spot tucked down a tiny lane in the Call, Salterio serves refreshing teas, Turkish coffee and snacks amid stone walls, incense and ambient Middle Eastern music. Try the mint tea, which is filled with real mint, as good as in Morocco.

BLVD
CLUB

Map p292 (✆93 301 62 89; www.boulevardculture club.com; La Rambla 27; ☺midnight-6am Wed-Sat; **M**Drassanes) Flanked by striptease bars (in the true spirit of the lower Rambla's old days), this place has undergone countless reincarnations. The culture in this club is what a long line-up of DJs brings to the (turn)table. With three different dance spaces, one of them upstairs, it has a deliciously tacky feel, pumping out anything from 1980s hits to house music (especially on Saturdays in the main room). There's no particular dress code.

KARMA
CLUB

Map p292 (☎93 302 56 80; www.karmadisco. com; Plaça Reial 10; ☺midnight-5.30am Tue-Sun; MLiceu) During the week Karma plays good, mainstream indie music, while on weekends the DJs spin anything from rock to disco. A golden oldie in Barcelona, tunnel-shaped Karma is small and becomes quite tightly packed (claustrophobic for some) with a good-natured crowd of locals and out-of-towners.

LA MACARENA
CLUB

Map p292 (☎637 416647; www.macarenaclub. com; Carrer Nou de Sant Francesc 5; ☺midnight-5am; MDrassanes) You simply won't believe this was once a tile-lined Andalucian flamenco musos' bar. Now it is a dark dance space, of the kind where it is possible to sit at the bar, meet people around you and then stand up for a bit of a shake to the DJ's electro and house offerings, all within a couple of square metres.

 **ENTERTAINMENT**

HARLEM JAZZ CLUB
LIVE MUSIC

Map p292 (☎93 310 07 55; www.harlemjazzclub. es; Carrer de la Comtessa de Sobradiel 8; admission €6-15; ☺8pm-4am Tue-Thu & Sun, to 5am Fri & Sat; MDrassanes) This narrow, old-town dive is one of the best spots in town for jazz. Every now and then it mixes it up with a little Latin, blues or African rhythms. It attracts a mixed crowd who maintain a respectful silence during the acts. Usually there are two sessions with different musos each night. Get in early if you want a seat in front of the stage.

JAMBOREE
LIVE MUSIC

Map p292 (☎93 319 17 89; www.masimas.com/ jamboree; Plaça Reial 17; admission €8-13; ☺8pm-6am; MLiceu) Since long before Franco bit the dust, Jamboree had been bringing joy to the jivers of Barcelona, with headline jazz and blues acts of the calibre of Chet Baker and Ella Fitzgerald. Nowadays two concerts are held most nights (at 8pm and 10pm), after which Jamboree morphs into a DJ-spinning club at midnight: sounds

under the low arches range from hip hop through funk to R&B. WTF jam sessions are held Mondays (entrance a mere €4).

SIDECAR FACTORY CLUB
LIVE MUSIC

Map p292 (☎93 302 15 86; www.sidecarfactory club.com; Plaça Reial 7; admission €8-18; ☺10pm-5am Mon-Sat; MLiceu) With its entrance on Plaça Reial, you can come here for a meal before midnight or a few drinks at ground level (which closes by 3am at the latest), or descend into the red-tinged, brick-vaulted bowels for live music most nights. Just about anything goes here, from UK indie through to country punk, but rock and pop lead the way. Most shows start around 10pm. DJs take over at 12.30am to keep things going.

CONCERT DE CARILLÓ
LIVE MUSIC

Map p292 (www.gencat.net/presidencia/carillo, in Spanish; Palau de la Generalitat, Plaça de Sant Jaume; ☺noon 1st Sun of month Oct-Jul, 9pm various days Jul; MJaume I) Some 5000kg of bronze in 49 bells (better known as a carillon) swings into action for free monthly 'concerts' in the seat of the Catalan government, allowing spectators a rare chance to get inside. In the pretty Gothic Pati dels Tarongers, an internal terrace lined with orange trees at the heart of the building, the audience is treated to a midday performance of just about anything, from classical through bossa nova.

L'ATENEU
CLASSICAL MUSIC

Map p292 (☎93 343 21 61; www.masimas.com/ fundacio; Carrer de la Canuda 6; admission €12-15; MCatalunya) For intense 30-minute sessions of chamber music, pay a visit to this hallowed academic institution-cum-club. Concerts are typically held Fridays, Saturdays and Sundays at 6pm, 7pm and 8pm.

GRAN TEATRE DEL LICEU
THEATRE, LIVE MUSIC

Map p292 (☎93 485 99 00; www.liceubarcelona. com; La Rambla dels Caputxins 51-59; ☺box office 1.30-8pm Mon-Fri & 1hr before show Sat & Sun; MLiceu) Barcelona's grand old opera house, restored after fire in 1994, is one of the most technologically advanced theatres in the world. To take up a seat in the grand auditorium – returned to its 19th-century glory but with the very latest in acoustic accoutrements – is to be transported to another age. Tickets can cost anything from €8 for a cheap seat behind a pillar to €194 for a well-positioned night at the opera.

THE FURIOUS FURA DELS BAUS

Keep your eyes peeled for any of the eccentric (if not downright crazed) performances of Barcelona's **La Fura dels Baus** (www.lafura.com) theatre group. It has won worldwide acclaim for its brand of startling, often acrobatic, theatre in which the audience is frequently dragged into the chaos. The company grew out of Barcelona's street-theatre culture in the late 1970s and, although it has grown in technical prowess and received great international acclaim, it has not abandoned the rough-and-ready edge of street performances.

SALA TARANTOS   FLAMENCO

Map p292 (☑93 319 17 89; www.masimas.net; Plaça Reial 17; admission from €7; ⊙shows 8.30pm, 9.30pm & 10.30pm; ⓂLiceu) Since 1963, this basement locale has been the stage for up-and-coming flamenco groups performing in Barcelona. These days Tarantos has become a mostly tourist-centric affair, with half-hour shows held three times a night. Still, it's a good introduction to flamenco, and not a bad setting for a drink.

TABLAO CORDOBÉS   FLAMENCO

Map p292 (☑93 317 57 11; www.tablaocordobes. com; La Rambla 35; show €39, with dinner €62-70; ⊙shows 8.15pm, 10pm & 11.30pm; ⓂLiceu) This *tablao* (restaurant where flamenco is performed) is typical of its genre and has been in business since 1970. Artists perform on a tiny hardwood stage with a vaulted backdrop that is supposed to make us think of Granada's El Alhambra. Generally, tourists book for the dinner and show, although you can skip the food and just come along for the performance (about 1¼ hours). Some great names have come through here, so it is not always cheese.

🔒 SHOPPING

A handful of interesting shops dots La Rambla, but the real fun starts inside the labyrinth. Young fashion on Carrer d'Avinyó, a mixed bag on Avinguda del Portal de l'Àngel, some cute old shops on Carrer de la Dagueria and lots of exploring in tight old lanes awaits.

TALLER DE MARIONETAS TRAVI   TOYS

Map p292 (☑93 412 66 92; Carrer de n'Amargós 4; ⊙noon-9pm Mon-Sat; ⓂUrquinaona) Opened in the 1970s, this atmospheric shop sells beautifully handcrafted marionettes. Don Quixote, Sancho and other iconic Spanish figures are on hand, as well as unusual works from other parts of the world – including rare Sicilian puppets and pieces from Myanmar (Burma), Indonesia and other parts. Most are made from wood or papier mâché and have fully articulated parts. Best of all, you can have a puppet made in your own likeness (prices from €300). Bring a photo and stop in for details.

L'ARCA DE L'ÀVIA   VINTAGE, CLOTHING

Map p292 (☑93 302 15 98; Carrer dels Banys Nous 20; ⓂLiceu) Grandma's chest is indeed full of extraordinary remembrances from the past, including 18th-century embroidered silk vests, elaborate silk kimonos and wedding dresses and shawls from the 1920s. Owing to its incredible collection, it has provided clothing for films including *Titanic*, *Talk to Her* and *Perfume*.

SALA PARÉS   ARTS & CRAFTS

Map p292 (☑93 318 70 20; www.salapares.com; Carrer del Petritxol 5; ⊙4-8pm Mon, 10.30am-2pm & 4.30-8pm Tue-Sat; ⓂLiceu) Picasso had works on sale here a century ago in what is one of the city's most venerable and still-dynamic private galleries. In business since 1877, the gallery has maintained its position as one of the city's leading purveyors of Catalan art – with works from the 19th century to the present.

PAPABUBBLE   FOOD

Map p292 (☑93 268 86 25; www.papabubble.com; Carrer Ample 28; ⓂLiceu) It feels like a step into another era in this candy store, where they make up pots of rainbow-coloured boiled lollies, just like some of us remember from corner-store days as kids. Watch the sticky sweets being made before your eyes. For all its apparent timelessness, this is a relatively new venture. Started by Australians in Barcelona, this sweet reminiscence now has shops in Amsterdam, New York and a handful of other cities.

CERERIA SUBIRÀ
HOMEWARES

Map p292 (☎93 315 26 06; Baixada de la Llibreteria 7; Ⓜ Jaume I) Even if you're not interested in myriad mounds of colourful wax, pop in just so you've been to the oldest shop in Barcelona. Cereria Subirà has been churning out candles since 1761 and at this address since the 19th century; the interior has a voluptuous, baroque quality.

XOCOA
FOOD

Map p292 (☎93 301 11 97; www.xocoa-bcn. com; Carrer del Petritxol 11-13; Ⓜ Liceu) Tucked along cafe- and boutique-lined Carrer de Petritxol, this den of dental devilry displays ranks and ranks of original chocolate bars, chocolates stuffed with sweet stuff, gooey pastries and more. It has over a dozen other branches scattered about town.

GOTHAM
HOMEWARES

Map p292 (☎93 412 46 47; www.gotham-bcn.com; Carrer de Cervantes 7; ⓧ11am-2pm & 5-8pm Mon-Fri; Ⓜ Jaume I) Retro design lovers will fall hard for this captivating store with its mid-century chrome lamps, sleek Danish modern furnishings and geometric home decorative items. Objects date from the 1930s to the 1970s, and if those elk horns don't fit in your suitcase, you can always opt for one of Gotham's iconic T-shirts.

ESPACIO DE CREADORES
FASHION

Map p292 (☎93 318 03 31; Carrer Comtal 22; Ⓜ Catalunya) This outlet store, featuring a broad selection of cut-price women's fashion and accessories by a long list of Spanish and some international designers, claims to slash original prices by up to 70%.

URBANA
FASHION

Map p292 (☎93 269 09 20; Carrer d'Avinyó 46; ⓧ11am-9pm Mon-Sat; Ⓜ Liceu) Colourful, fun city clothes, shoes and accessories await boys and girls in this easygoing store with Basque Country origins. It offers a variety of eye-catching apparel, like graphic T-shirts for men by Supremebeing, floral dresses by Yumi and stylish hats by Atlantis.

CÓMPLICES
BOOKS

Map p292 (Carrer de Cervantes 4; Ⓜ Jaume I) One of the most extensive gay and lesbian bookstores in the city has a mix of lowbrow erotica – DVDs, magazines, graphic novels – as well as more intellectually stimulating reading. It's a welcoming place for all ages and orientations.

FC BOTIGA
SOUVENIRS

Map p292 (☎93 269 15 32; Carrer de Jaume I, 18; ⓧ10am-9pm; Ⓜ Jaume I) Need a Lionel Messi football jersey, a blue and burgundy ball, or any other soccer paraphernalia pertaining to what many locals consider the greatest team in the world? This is a convenient spot to load up without traipsing to the stadium.

HERBORISTERIA DEL REI
SPECIALTY

Map p292 (☎93 318 05 12; www.herboristeriadel rei.blogspot.com; Carrer del Vidre 1; ⓧ4-8pm Tue-Fri, 10am-8pm Sat; Ⓜ Liceu) Once patronised by Queen Isabel II, this timeless corner store flogs all sorts of weird and wonderful herbs, spices and medicinal plants. It's been doing so since 1823 and the decor has barely changed since the 1860s. However, some of the products have, and you'll find anything from fragrant soaps to massage oil nowadays. Film director Tom Tykwer shot scenes of *Perfume: The Story of a Murderer* here.

LE BOUDOIR
ACCESSORIES

Map p292 (☎93 302 52 81; www.leboudoir.net; Carrer de la Canuda 21; Ⓜ Catalunya) Need to spice up the bedroom situation? Take a stroll around this sensual shop, where anything from lacy, racy underwear to exuberant sex toys is available. Crystal-covered handcuffs might be fun, or perhaps a bit of slap and tickle with a whip and mask?

EL INGENIO
SPECIALTY

Map p292 (☎93 317 71 38; www.el-ingenio.com; Carrer d'en Rauric 6; Ⓜ Liceu) In this whimsical fantasy store you will discover giant Carnaval masks, costumes, theatrical accessories and other fun things. You can pick up some elegant Venetian masks, flamenco costumes, gorilla heads, yo-yos, kazoos, unicycles and other novelty items.

OBACH
ACCESSORIES

Map p292 (☎93 318 40 94; Carrer del Call 2; Ⓜ Liceu) Since 1924 this store in the heart of El Call (the former Jewish quarter) has been purveying all manner of headgear. You'll find Kangol mohair berets, hipsterish short-brimmed hats, fedoras, elegant straw sun hats and a full-colour spectrum of *barrets* (berets).

CASA BEETHOVEN
MUSIC

Map p292 (☎93 301 48 26; La Rambla de Sant Josep 97; Ⓜ Liceu) This isn't any old sheet-music shop. In business since 1880, Casa

Beethoven's customers have included Montserrat Caballé, Josep Carreras and Plácido Domingo. It keeps up with the times, however, and you're as likely to find music by Metallica as by Mozart. On Saturdays small concerts are sometimes held.

LA MANUAL ALPARGATERA   SHOES
Map p292 (☑93 301 01 72; http://homepage.mac.com/manualp; Carrer d'Avinyó 7; Ⓜ Liceu)

Everyone from Salvador Dalí to Jean Paul Gaultier has ordered a pair of *espadrilles* (rope-soled canvas shoes or sandals) from this famous store, which is the birthplace of the iconic footware. The shop was founded just after the Spanish Civil War, though the roots of the simple shoe design date back thousands of years.

El Raval

Neighbourhood Top Five

1 Shopping and browsing at the buzzing and beautiful **Mercat de la Boqueria** (p90), and eating at one of the lively market bars.

2 Exploring the **Antic Hospital de la Santa Creu** (p91) and relaxing with a coffee in its courtyard cafe.

3 Getting to know the art collection at **Macba** (p92) and watching the skaters out the front.

4 Having a glass of cloudy absinthe in one of **Raval's historic bars** (p98).

5 Walking around the artfully restored **Palau Güell** (p94).

For more detail of this area, see Map p296 ➡

Explore El Raval

Long one of the most rough-and-tumble parts of Barcelona, El Raval is now so hip in a grungy, inner-city way that *barcelonins* have even invented a verb for rambling around El Raval: *ravalejar*.

The northern half of El Raval is the best place to start your ramble. Spend a day wandering along the art-shop-filled Carrer del Pintor Fortuny, lunching in the colourful Mercat de la Boqueria (p90), and dedicate a few hours to the fascinating Macba (p92). Join the youthful set of hedonists on La Rambla del Raval's cluster of bars.

Night-time is El Raval's forte, and not only because of all the illicit activities taking place under the shroud of darkness. This is where you will find some of the more eccentric, trendy and downright ancient bars and clubs. The better part of Universitat de Barcelona's faculties, with some 6000 students, fill the bars and clubs along Carrer de Valldonzella and Carrer de Joaquín Costa.

The area between Carrer de l'Hospital and the waterfront – also known as Barri Xino – is where El Raval retains its dodgy flavour of yore. Beware of boozy middle-of-the-night ramblings here, since the area around Carrer de Sant Pau remains a haunt of junkies and dealers. Carrer de Sant Ramon is particularly busy with prostitutes. The city's central cinema archive, Filmoteca de Catalunya (p93), recently relocated to the area bounded by the Rambla del Raval and Carrer de Sant Pau in an attempt at changing the face of this part of town. Barring the dodginess, don't miss this part of El Raval – several fine old bars (p98) have stood the test of time.

If you're curious about the fabric of life of multicultural Raval, take an afternoon to stroll along Carrer de l'Hospital. Fridays see the street fill with Muslims for the week's main prayers at the local mosque; numerous halal butcher shops, cafes and barbers' shops cater to the area's large Pakistani and North African population.

Local Life

➡ **Market Lunch** Don't miss La Boqueria's food. Either self-cater or let the local chefs ply you with delicacies.

➡ **Art Shops** El Raval is Barcelona's artiest *barri* (neighbourhood), so make sure you explore the art galleries and craft shops (p100) for local talent.

➡ **Sugar Rush** Locals swear that some of the best chocolate in town is to be had at Granja Viader (p94).

Getting There & Away

➡ **Underground Rail** El Raval is encircled by three Metro lines: 1, 2 and 3. The Línia 3 stop at Liceu is a convenient exit point.

Lonely Planet's Top Tip

For a spot of sun away from the noisy El Raval streets, head for the garden cafe at the **Antic Hospital de la Santa Creu** (p91).

✕ Best Places to Eat

➡ Bar Pinotxo (p94)
➡ Ca L'Isidre (p94)
➡ Casa Leopoldo (p94)
➡ Granja Viader (p94)
➡ Elisabets (p96)

For reviews, see p93 ➡

☕ Best Places to Drink

➡ Bar La Concha (p97)
➡ 33|45 (p97)
➡ La Confitería (p97)
➡ Negroni (p97)

For reviews, see p97 ➡

🔒 Best Arts & Crafts Shops

➡ Costura (p100)
➡ Fantastik (p100)
➡ Teranyina (p100)

For reviews, see p100 ➡

EL RAVAL

TOP SIGHTS
MERCAT DE LA BOQUERIA

One of the greatest sound, smell and colour sensations in Europe is Barcelona's most central produce market, the Mercat de la Boqueria. It spills over with all the rich and varied colour of plentiful fruit and vegetable stands, seemingly limitless varieties of sea critters, sausages, cheeses, meat (including the finest Jabugo ham) and sweets.

According to some chronicles, there has been a market in this place since 1217. As much as it has become a modern-day attraction, this has always been the place where locals have come to shop.

Between the 15th and 18th centuries a pig market known as Mercat de la Palla (Straw Market) stood on this spot; it was considered part of a bigger market that extended to the Plaça del Pi. What we now know as La Boqueria didn't come to exist until the 19th century, when the local authorities decided to build a structure that would house fishmongers and butchers, as well as fruit and vegetable sellers. The iron Modernista gate was constructed in 1914.

Many of Barcelona's top restaurateurs buy their produce here, although nowadays it's no easy task getting past the seething crowds of tourists to snare the slippery slab of sole, or the tempting piece of *queso de cabra* (goat's cheese).

La Boqueria is dotted with half a dozen or so unassuming places to eat, and eat well. It's worth trying some of Catalonia's gastronomical specialities, like *bacallà salat* (dried salted cod), usually served in an *esqueixada*, a tomato, onion and black olive salad, topped with the dried cod; *calçots* (a cross between a leek and an onion), which are grilled and eaten as a messy whole; *cargols* (snails), a Catalan staple best eaten baked *(a la llauna)*; *peus de porc* (pork trotters), often stewed with snails; or *percebes*, a particular type of shell that looks like witch fingers, which are much loved across Spain and eaten with a garlic and parsley sauce.

DON'T MISS...

➡ Digging into local specialties at a food stall

➡ Picking up fresh produce for a beach picnic

PRACTICALITIES

➡ ☎93 412 13 15

➡ www.boqueria.info

➡ La Rambla 91

➡ ⊙8am-8.30pm Mon-Sat

➡ Ⓜ Liceu

TOP SIGHTS
ANTIC HOSPITAL DE LA SANTA CREU

Behind the Mercat de la Boqueria (p90) stands what was, in the 15th century, the city's main hospital. The restored Antic Hospital de la Santa Creu (Former Holy Cross Hospital) today houses the Biblioteca de Catalunya (Library of Catalonia), as well as the Institut d'Estudis Catalans (Institute for Catalan Studies).

The Library

The hospital, which was begun in 1401 and functioned until the 1930s, was considered one of the best in Europe in its medieval heyday. Entering from Carrer de l'Hospital, you find yourself in a delightfully bedraggled **courtyard garden** that is home to the homeless, students on a study break and a cheerful bar-cafe. Off the garden lies the entrance to the prestigious Massana conservatorium and, up a sweep of stairs, the **library** (Map p296; admission free; ⊗9am-8pm Mon-Fri, 9am-2pm Sat; ⓂLiceu). The library is the single most complete collection of documents (estimated at around three million) tracing the region's long history. You can freely visit the most impressive part, the grand reading rooms beneath broad Gothic stone arches, where you can also see temporary displays of anything from old records to medieval monastic hymnals.

The former hospital's Gothic chapel, **La Capella** (Map p296; ☎93 442 71 71; www.bcn.cat/lacapella; admission free; ⊗noon-2pm & 4-8pm Tue-Sat, 11am-2pm Sun & holidays; ⓂLiceu), is worth poking your nose into for the frequent temporary exhibitions.

Otherwise, it is possible to join a tour on 23 April (Sant Jordi) and one day late in September (the date changes), when the entire building throws itself open for guided visits.

The guided visit takes you through the library's public areas and others usually closed to the public, such as the Museu del Llibre Frederic Marès, a former private ward in the hospital, whose bright tile decoration of the stations of the cross was done in the 17th century. Marès donated 1500 documents and books to the library, some of which are on display. He also sculpted medallions of great figures of Catalan culture. Antoni Gaudí wound up in the Via Crucis ward in 1926 after being run over by a tram; he died here.

The Institute

Approaching the complex down a narrow lane from Carrer del Carme or from Jardins del Doctor Fleming (the little park with swings), you arrive at the entrance to the **institute** (Map p296; ⓂLiceu), which sometimes opens its doors for expositions. If it's open, wander into what was the 17th-century Casa de Convalescència de Sant Pau, which housed recovering patients from the hospital. At first, it hosted just seven men and five women. By the end of the 17th century, there were 200 beds and 400 mattresses and patients received meat and desserts (which is more than many might have hoped for outside). The hospice operated until the early 20th century. The building, which centres on a cloister, is richly decorated with ceramics (especially the entrance vestibule). In the centre of the cloister you'll find a statue of St Paul, after whom the house is named. Situated up on the 1st floor at the far end is what was once an orange garden, now named after the Catalan novelist Mercè Rodoreda.

DON'T MISS...

➡ The reading rooms and its temporary displays
➡ The courtyard garden
➡ The 17th-century Casa de Convalescència de Sant Pau
➡ The site's Gothic chapel, La Capella

PRACTICALITIES

➡ Map p296
➡ ☎93 270 23 00
➡ www.bnc.cat
➡ Carrer de l'Hospital 56
➡ ⓂLiceu

TOP SIGHTS
MACBA

Designed by Richard Meier and opened in 1995, Macba (Museu d'Art Contemporani de Barcelona) has become the city's foremost contemporary art centre, with captivating exhibitions for the serious art lover. The permanent collection is on the ground floor and dedicates itself to Spanish and Catalan art from the second half of the 20th century, with works by Antoni Tàpies, Joan Brossa and Miquel Barceló, among others, though international artists, such as Paul Klee, Bruce Nauman and John Cage, are also represented.

The gallery, across two floors, is dedicated to temporary visiting exhibitions that are almost always challenging and intriguing. Macba's philosophy is to do away with the old model of a museum where an artwork is a spectacle and to create a space where art can be viewed critically, so the exhibitions are usually tied in with talks and events. If you're after some serious brain candy, Macba is your place.

Across the main skateboard-infested square, the renovated 400-year-old Convent dels Àngels houses **La Capella Macba** (Map p296; Plaça dels Àngels; MUniversitat), where the Macba regularly rotates selections from its permanent collection. The Gothic framework of the one-time convent-church remains intact.

The library and auditorium stage regular concerts, talks and events, all of which are either reasonably priced or free. The extensive art bookshop is fantastic for both stocking up on art and art theory books, as well as quirky gifts and small design objects.

DON'T MISS...

➡ The permanent collection of 20th-century Spanish and Catalan art

➡ La Capella Macba

➡ The fascinating temporary exhibitions

PRACTICALITIES

➡ Map p296

➡ ☑93 412 08 10

➡ www.macba.cat

➡ Plaça dels Àngels 1

➡ adult/concession €7.50/6

➡ ⊘11am-8pm Mon & Wed, to midnight Thu & Fri, 10am-8pm Sat, 10am-3pm Sun & holidays

➡ MUniversitat

⊙ SIGHTS

MERCAT DE LA BOQUERIA MARKET
See p90.

**ANTIC HOSPITAL DE LA
SANTA CREU** HISTORIC BUILDING
See p91.

MACBA MUSEUM
See p92.

**TOP CHOICE FILMOTECA DE
CATALUNYA** ARTS CENTRE
Map p296 (✆93 567 10 70; www.filmoteca.
cat; Plaça Salvador Seguí 1-9; tickets from €2-4;
⊙8am-10pm; MLiceu) After almost a decade
in planning, the Filmoteca de Catalunya
moved into this modern 6000-sq-metre
building in March 2012. It's a glass, metal
and concrete beast that hulks in the midst
of the dodgiest Raval – the square is frequented by prostitutes day and night – but
the building's interior shouts revival, with
light and space, wall-to-wall windows, skylights and glass panels that let the sun in
through in bold Catalan reds and yellows.

In addition to two cinema screens total-
ing 555 seats, the new Filmoteca comprises
a film library, a bookshop, a cafe, offices
and a dedicated space for exhibitions. This
is mainly a film archive space, though,
which is being hailed as the marker of a
cultural turning point for its new neighbourhood. The Filmoteca's screenings and
exhibitions for 2012 include exploring the
work of filmmakers such as Bigas Lunas
and Jacques Tourneur.

**CENTRE DE CULTURA CONTEMPORÀNIA
DE BARCELONA** CULTURAL BUILDING
Map p296 (CCCB; ✆93 306 41 00; www.cccb.
org; Carrer de Montalegre 5; 2 exhibitions adult/
child under 16yr/senior & student €6/free/4.50,

1 exhibition €5/free/3, free Wed, 8-10pm Thu,
3-8pm Sun; ⊙11am-8pm Tue, Wed & Fri-Sun,
11am-10pm Thu; MUniversitat) A complex of
auditoriums, exhibition spaces and conference halls opened here in 1994 in what had
been an 18th-century hospice, the Casa de
la Caritat. The courtyard, with a vast glass
wall on one side, is spectacular. With 4500
sq metres of exhibition space in four separate areas, the centre hosts a constantly
changing program of exhibitions, film cy-
cles and other events.

ESGLÉSIA DE SANT PAU CHURCH
Map p296 (Carrer de Sant Pau 101; ⊙cloister
10am-1pm & 4-7pm Mon-Sat; MParal.lel) The
best example of Romanesque architecture
in the city is the dainty little cloister of this
church. Set in a somewhat dusty garden,
the 12th-century church also boasts some
Visigothic sculptural detail on the main
entrance.

✗ EATING

**For contrast alone, El Raval is possibly
the most interesting part of the old
town. Timeless classics of Barcelona's
dining scene are scattered across what
was long the old city's poorest *barri*.
Since the late 1990s, battalions of hip
new eateries and artsy restaurants can
be found in the area around Macba.
Some of the cheapest eats in town,
full of character, lurk along El Raval's
streets. You'll find most of these
neighbourhood gems north of Carrer de
Sant Pau towards Carrer de Pelai, and
scattered around the the university and
Ronda de Sant Antoni.**

EL RAVAL SIGHTS

REVIVING EL RAVAL

The Filmoteca de Catalunya's relocation to the Raval from the neighbourhood of
Sarrià is part of 'Raval Revival', an ongoing project to set up the neighbourhood as
one of Spain's most influential cultural centres. As part of the project, representatives from Macba, the Gran Teatre del Liceu, the Centre de Cultura Contemporània
de Barcelona, the Biblioteca de Catalunya, Arts Santa Mònica, the Virreina Centre de
la Imatge, the Institut d'Estudis Catalans and the Filmoteca de Catalunya meet three
times a year with the aim of creating a cultural network with the Raval as its nucleus.
The project will see cinema take a leading role in these multimedia creations – one
example is the Filmoteca de Catalunya's restoration of Fritz Lang's silent film *The
Nibelungs*, which commissioned an original score from the Liceu orchestra.

TOP SIGHTS
PALAU GÜELL

This extraordinary mansion, one of few major Modernista buildings raised in Ciutat Vella, was finally reopened in its entirety in May 2010 after nearly 20 years under refurbishment. It's a magnificent example of the early days of Gaudí's fevered architectural imagination, and gives an insight into its maker's prodigious genius.

Gaudí built the palace just off La Rambla in the late 1880s for his wealthy and faithful patron, the industrialist Eusebi Güell. Although a little sombre compared with some of his later whims, it is still a riot of styles (Gothic, Islamic, art nouveau). After the civil war the police occupied it and tortured political prisoners in the basement. The building was then abandoned, this leading to its long-term disrepair.

Up two floors are the main hall and its annexes; central to the structure is the magnificent music room with its rebuilt organ that is played during opening hours. The hall is a parabolic pyramid – each wall an arch stretching up three floors and coming together to form a dome. The family rooms are sometimes labyrinthine, sometimes grand stained-glass affairs. The roof is a mad tumult of tiled mosaics and even fanciful chimney pots. The audio guide, included in the entry price, is worth getting for its photo and music illustrations of the Güell family's life.

DON'T MISS...

➡ The music room
➡ The family rooms
➡ The tiled roof

PRACTICALITIES

➡ Map p296
➡ ☎93 317 39 74
➡ www.palauguell.cat, in Spanish
➡ Carrer Nou de la Rambla 3-5
➡ adult/concession €10/8
➡ ⊙10am-8pm daily Apr-Sep, 10am-5.30pm Oct-Mar
➡ Ⓜ Drassanes

TOP CHOICE BAR PINOTXO
TAPAS €€

Map p296 (Mercat de la Boqueria; meals €20; ⊙6am-5pm Mon-Sat Sep-Jul; ⓂLiceu) Bar Pinotxo is arguably La Boqueria's, and even Barcelona's, best tapas bar. It sits among the half-dozen or so informal eateries within the market, and the popular owner, Juanito, might serve up chickpeas with a sweet sauce of pine nuts and raisins, a fantastically soft mix of potato and spinach sprinkled with coarse salt, baby soft baby squid with cannellini beans, or a quivering cube of caramel sweet pork belly.

TOP CHOICE CA L'ISIDRE
CATALAN €€€

Map p296 (☎93 441 11 39; www.calisidre.com; Carrer de les Flors 12; mains €20-70; ⊙Mon-Sat, closed Easter & 3 weeks in Aug; ⓂParal.lel) Lurking in an unappealing backstreet off El Raval, Ca L'Isidre is an old-world gem. Immaculately kept dining areas stretch away from the entrance, dominated by warm timber and tiles. The menu is a work of art in itself - try artichoke hearts stuffed with mushrooms and foie gras, tuna steak with a tomato coulis or lamb's brains with black butter. King Juan Carlos and superchef Ferran Adrià love it.

CASA LEOPOLDO
CATALAN €€€

Map p296 (☎93 441 30 14; www.casaleopoldo.com; Carrer de Sant Rafael 24; meals €50; fixed menu €25 lunch & dinner Tue & Thu, lunch only Wed; ⊙lunch & dinner Tue-Sat, lunch Sun Sep-Jul; ⓂLiceu) Long hidden in the slum alleys of El Raval, this was writer Manuel Vázquez Montalbán's favourite restaurant. Several rambling dining areas in this 1929 classic have magnificent tiled walls and exposed beam ceilings. The mostly seafood menu is extensive and the wine list strong. The excellent value fixed menu, called Menú de la Fonda, includes all of the house classics.

GRANJA VIADER
CAFE €

Map p296 (☎93 318 34 86; www.granjaviader.cat; Carrer d'en Xuclà 4; ⊙9am-1.45pm & 5-8.45pm Tue-Sat, 5-8.45pm Mon; ⓂLiceu) For more than a century, people have flocked down this alley to get to the cups of homemade hot chocolate and whipped cream (ask for a *suís*) ladled out in this classic Catalan-style milk bar cum deli. The Viader clan invented Cacaolat, a forerunner of kids' powdered-chocolate beverages. The interior is delightfully vintage and the atmosphere always upbeat.

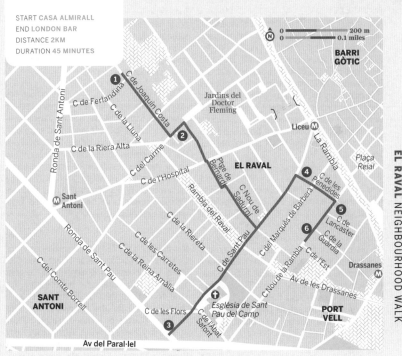

EL RAVAL NEIGHBOURHOOD WALK

Neighbourhood Walk
Modernista Wining & Dining in El Raval

Long run by the Almirall family that opened it in the mid-19th century, the corner tavern **1 Casa Almirall** (p98) on Carrer de Joaquín Costa preserves much of its Modernista decor, especially in the picture windows opening on to the street, and the counter and display cabinet.

You'll recognise similarly sinuous curves as you enter **2 Bar Muy Buenas** (p97) on Carrer del Carme. Opened as a milk bar in the late 19th century, it retains much of its original decoration. It's a welcoming, cosy spot for a tipple and snacks.

On Carrer de Sant Pau, past the Romanesque church, drop by **3 La Confitería** (p97), once a barbers' shop and then a long-time confectioner's. It was lovingly restored for its reconversion into a bar in 1998. Most of the elements, including facade, bar counter and cabinets, are the real deal.

The **4 Hotel España** (p216) is known above all for its dining rooms, part of the 1903 design by Domènech i Montaner. The Sala Arnau (Arnau Room) features a

magnificent alabaster fireplace designed by Eusebi Arnau. Moderately priced traditional Catalan fare is served.

While wandering around El Raval, you should not miss its Modernista star, one of Gaudí's earlier big commissions. **5 Palau Güell** (p94) is a remarkable building recently renovated to perfection. If you're passing by at night while doing a round of the bars, make a note to return here by day.

A classic of Barcelona nightlife for over a century, the **6 London Bar** (p98) displays Modernista decor and is run by the family of the waiter who founded it in 1910. In its heyday it stayed open 24 hours a day and attracted the likes of Pablo Picasso and Joan Miró for countless swift beers.

ELISABETS
CATALAN €

Map p296 (☑93 317 58 26; Carrer d'Elisabets 2-4; mains €7-9; ☉Mon-Sat Sep-Jul; ⓂCatalunya) This unassuming restaurant is popular for no-nonsense local fare. The walls are lined with old radio sets and the *menú del día* (set menu; €10.75) varies daily. If you prefer *a la carta*, try the *ragú de jabalí* (wild boar stew) and finish with *mel i mató* (a Catalan dessert made from cheese and honey). Those with a post-midnight hunger on Friday nights can probably get a meal here as late as 1am.

PLA DELS ÀNGELS
MEDITERRANEAN €

Map p296 (☑93 329 40 47; www.semproniana. net; Carrer Ferlandina 23; set lunch/dinner €10/15, meals €20; ☉1.30-4pm & 9-11.30pm daily; ⓂUniversitat) Just next door to Macba, this is a suitably colourful and lively little bistro with brightly painted walls and tightly squeezed tables in the back room. More space (but less cuteness) is to be had in the bar area, at the front. The cooking is Catalan-French and Italian, and can be quite quirky, with salads like mango, tofu, mint and oregano, and pear, chestnut and pine nut soup.

SESAMO
VEGETARIAN €

Map p296 (☑93 441 64 11; www.sesamo-bcn. com, in Spanish; Carrer de Sant Antoni Abat 52; set lunch €7 ☉lunch & dinner Mon, Tue & Thu-Sat, lunch Sun; ⓂSant Antoni) For 'food without beasts', this relaxed corner eatery attracts all sorts. Drop by for juices and pastries at breakfast, a three-course set lunch or dinner. Wafting electronica is almost soothing and nice touches include the home-baked bread and cakes.

RESTAURANT EL CAFETÍ
CATALAN €€

Map p296 (☑93 329 24 19; www.elcafeti.com; Passatge de Bernardí; mains €8-15, menú del día €12; ☉lunch & dinner Tue-Sat, lunch Sun; ⓂLiceu) This diminutive eatery is filled with antique furniture and offers traditional local cooking, with one or two unorthodox variations. Paella and other rice dishes dominate. It is down an arcade just off Carrer de Sant Rafael.

BIBLIOTECA
MEDITERRANEAN €€€

Map p296 (☑93 412 62 21; www.bibliotecarestaurant.cat; Carrer de la Junta de Comerç 28; meals €35-40; ☉dinner Mon-Fri, lunch & dinner Sat; ⓂLiceu) Exposed-brick and creamy-white decor dominate in the 'Library', where the food represents a broad sweep across Spain, with careful creative touches and a good wine list. A good sample is *bacallà confitat amb suc d'escamarlans i llegums de temporada* (pickled salted cod with crayfish juice and seasonal vegetables).

CAN LLUÍS
CATALAN €€€

Map p296 (Carrer de la Cera 49; meals €30-35; ☉Mon-Sat Sep-Jul; ⓂSant Antoni) Three generations have kept this spick and span old-time classic in business since 1929. Beneath the olive-green beams in the back dining room you can see the spot where an anarchist's bomb went off in 1946, killing the then owner. Expect fresh fish and seafood. The *llenguado* (sole) is oven cooked with whisky and raisins.

EN VILLE
FRENCH €€

Map p296 (☑933 02 84 67; www.envillebarcelona. es; Carrer del Doctor del Dou 14; set lunch €10, mains €10-12; ☉lunch & dinner; ⓂUniversitat) You'll want to come here more for the divine decor than the standard food, though the €10 menú del día is great value, with its large platter of seafood, ample salads and large glasses of wine. Turning up early for lunch is advised to beat the queues at the door, though. Admire the fragrant bouquets on the tables, the paintings on the walls and the antique details all around.

MAMA I TECA
CATALAN €

Map p296 (☑93 441 33 35; Carrer de la Lluna 4; mains €8-10; ☉lunch & dinner Sun-Mon & Wed-Fri, dinner Sat; ⓂSant Antoni) Mama i Teca, a tiny place with half a dozen tables, is more a lifestyle than a restaurant. The setting is a multicultural and often rowdy street deep in El Raval. Locals drop in and hang about for a drink, and diners are treated to Catalan treats served without rush. How about cod deep fried in olive oil with garlic and red pepper, or a juicy sirloin steak?

ORGANIC
VEGETARIAN €

Map p296 (www.antoniaorganickitchen.com; Carrer de la Junta de Comerç 11; mains €5-8; ☉12.45pm-midnight; ⓂLiceu) As you wander into this sprawling vegetarian spot, to the left is the open kitchen, where you choose from a limited range of options that change from day to day. Servings are generous and imaginative. The salad buffet is copious and desserts are good. The set lunch costs €9.50 plus drinks.

DOS TRECE
INTERNATIONAL €

Map p296 (☎93 301 73 06; www.dostrece. net; Carrer Carme 40; set lunch €11; mains €8; ☺10am-2am Mon-Thu, 10am-3am Fri-Sun; Ⓜ Universitat) A good place for eating and drinking, Dos Trece is perfect for late night bites and Sunday brunches (beware: the eggs Benedict goes fast!). In the evenings you can order a burger or choose from the eclectic menu, and stick around for drinks in the lively atmosphere.

OLIVIA
CAFE €

Map p296 (☎93 318 63 80; Carrer Pintor Fortuny 22; cakes from €3; ☺9am-9pm Mon-Sat, 10am-9pm Sun Oct-May. 9am-9pm Mon-Sat Jun-Sep; 🛜; Ⓜ Catalunya) A relaxed little cafe on a quiet El Raval street, Olivia makes excellent cake (carrot, pineapple, you name it) and good coffee. The shop-window seating is perfect for watching (which can be an activity in itself in rampant El Raval), the decor is simple and minimal with a single row of wooden tables and there is always good jazz playing in the background.

🍷 DRINKING & 🍸 NIGHTLIFE

Bars and clubs have been opening up along the long, slummy alleys of Raval for the last two decades, making this one of the edgiest areas of town to go out. You'll find supertrendy places alongside some great old harbour-style taverns that still thrive – there are joints that have been the hang-outs of the city's bohemia since Picasso's times. The lower end of El Raval has a long history of dodginess and the area around Carrer de Sant Pau retains its edgy feel: drug dealers, pickpockets and prostitutes mingle with the streams of nocturnal hedonists. Keep your wits about you if walking around here late at night.

BAR LA CONCHA
BAR

Map p296 (Carrer de la Guàrdia 14; ☺5pm-3am; Ⓜ Drassanes) This place is dedicated to the worshipping of the actress Sara Montiel: the entire bar is covered with over 250 photos of the sultry star. Born in 1928, Montiel bared all on the silver screen in an era that condemned nudity to shameful brazenness – hence 'la concha' can be read as a sly

salute to female genitalia (it's a word commonly used in the Spanish slang).

La Concha used to be a largely gay and transvestite haunt, but anyone is welcome and bound to have fun – especially when the drag queens come out to play. The music ranges from *paso dobles* (a kind of lively ballroom dance music) to Spanish retro pop.

LA CONFITERÍA
BAR

Map p296 (Carrer de Sant Pau 128; ☺11am-2am; Ⓜ Paral.lel) This is a trip into the 19th century. Until the 1980s it was a confectioner's shop, and although the original cabinets are now lined with booze, the look of the place has barely changed in its conversion into a laid-back bar. A quiet enough spot for a house *vermut* (€3; add your own soda) in the early evening, it fills with theatregoers and local partiers later at night.

33|45
BAR

Map p296 (Carrer Joaquín Costa 4; ☺10am-1:30am Mon-Thu, 10am-3am Fri & Sat, 10am-midnight Sun; Ⓜ Universitat) This super-trendy cocktail bar, on the nightlife-laden Joaquín Costa street, has excellent *mojitos* – even pink strawberry ones! – and a fashionable crowd. The main area has DJ music and lots of excited noise making, while the back room is scattered with sofas and armchairs for a post-dancing slump.

NEGRONI
COCKTAIL BAR

Map p296 (Carrer de Joaquín Costa 46; ☺7pm-2am Mon-Thu, 7pm-3am Fri & Sat; Ⓜ Liceu) Good things come in small packages and this teeny cocktail bar confirms the rule. The black and beige decor lures in a largely student set to try out the bar's cocktails, among them the flagship Negroni, a Florentine invention with one part Campari, one part gin and one part sweet vermouth.

BAR MUY BUENAS
BAR

Map p296 (Carrer del Carme 63; ☺9am-2am Mon-Thu, 9am-3am Fri & Sat, 7pm-2am Sun; Ⓜ Liceu) This bar started life as a late-19th-century corner store. The Modernista decor and relaxed company make this a great spot for a quiet *mojito*. You may catch a little live music or even a poetry reading, and can nibble on a limited menu of Middle Eastern titbits.

BAR PASTÍS
BAR

Map p296 (☎93 318 79 80; www.barpastis.com; Carrer de Santa Mònica 4; ☺7.30pm-2am Sun-Fri, 7.30pm-3am Sat; Ⓜ Drassanes) A French

EL RAVAL DRINKING & NIGHTLIFE

LOCAL KNOWLEDGE

RAVAL'S HISTORIC BARS

⇒ London Bar (p98)

⇒ Bar Marsella (p99)

⇒ La Confitería (p97)

⇒ Bar Muy Buenas (p97)

⇒ Casa Almirall (p98)

cabaret theme (with lots of Piaf in the background) dominates this tiny, cluttered classic. It's been going, on and off, since the end of WWII. You'll need to be in here before 9pm to have a hope of sitting, getting near the bar or anything much else. On some nights it features live acts, usually performing French chansons.

BETTY FORD
BAR

Map p296 (✐93 304 13 68; Carrer de Joaquín Costa 56; ◷6pm-1.30am Sun & Mon, 2pm-1.30am Tue-Thu, 2pm-2.30am Fri & Sat; MUniversitat) This enticing corner bar is one of several good stops along the studenty run of Carrer de Joaquín Costa. It does some nice cocktails and the place fills with an even mix of locals and foreigners, generally not much over 30. They cook up some decent burgers, too.

MARMALADE
BAR

Map p296 (www.marmaladebarcelona.com; Carrer de la Riera Alta 4-6; ◷7pm-3am; MSant Antoni) From the street you can see the golden hues of the backlit bar way down the end of a long lounge-lined passageway. To the left of the bar by a bare brick wall is a pool table, popular but somehow out of place in this chic, ill-lit chill den (with attached restaurant). Happy hour (cocktails for €4) is from 7pm to 9pm.

LONDON BAR
BAR

Map p296 (Carrer Nou de la Rambla 34-36; ◷7.30pm-4am Tue-Sun; MLiceu) Open since 1909, this Modernista bar started as a hang-out for circus hands and was later frequented by the likes of Picasso, Miró and Hemingway. Today, it fills to the brim with punters at the long front bar and rickety old tables. On occasion, you can attend concerts at the small stage right up the back.

BARRAVAL
BAR

Map p296 (✐93 329 82 77; Carrer de l'Hospital 104; ◷7pm-2.30am Tue-Thu, 7pm-5am Fri, noon-5am Sat, noon-5pm Sun; MLiceu) With its designer looks, greys, black and subtle lighting, this is a hard-to-categorise, all-in-one evening-out location split over two floors. Mediterranean fusion dishes reign in the early evening as people crowd in for dinner. From 11pm, DJs fill the air with jazz, funk, R&B, soul and Latin sounds.

BOADAS
COCKTAIL BAR

Map p296 (Carrer dels Tallers 1; ◷noon-2am Mon-Thu, noon-3am Fri & Sat; MCatalunya) One of the city's oldest cocktail bars, Boadas is famed for its daiquiris. The bow-tied waiters have been serving up unique drinkable creations since Miguel Boadas opened it in 1933. Miró and Hemingway drank here. Miguel was born in Havana, where he was the first barman at the immortal La Floridita.

CASA ALMIRALL
BAR

Map p296 (Carrer de Joaquín Costa 33; ◷5.30pm-2.30am Sun-Thu, 7pm-3am Fri & Sat; MUniversitat) In business since the 1860s, this unchanged corner bar is dark and intriguing, with Modernista decor and a mixed clientele. There are some great original pieces in here, like the marble counter, and the cast-iron statue of the muse of the Universal Exposition, held in Barcelona in 1888.

KENTUCKY
BAR

Map p296 (Carrer de l'Arc del Teatre 11; ◷10pm-3am Tue-Sat; MLiceu) A haunt of visiting US Navy boys, this exercise in smoke-filled Americana kitsch is the perfect way to finish an evening – if you can squeeze in. All sorts of odd bods from the *barri* and beyond gather here. An institution in the wee hours, this place often stays open as late as 5am.

MOOG
CLUB

Map p296 (www.masimas.com/moog; Carrer de l'Arc del Teatre 3; admission €10; ◷midnight-5am; MDrassanes) This fun and minuscule club is a standing favourite with the downtown crowd. In the main dance area, DJs dish out house, techno and electro, while upstairs you can groove to a nice blend of indie and occasional classic-pop throwbacks.

ZENTRAUS
CLUB

Map p296 (Rambla del Raval 41; ◷11pm-3am; MLiceu) Get down into this cheerfully bump-and-grind, semisubterranean dance club. Drum 'n' bass earlier in the week rises to a deep house crescendo on Saturdays, and drops back into a mellow mix on Sundays. It puts on food, too. Only problem is it closes just when you're getting into the swing.

⭐ ENTERTAINMENT

CANGREJO
GAY CLUB

Map p296 (📞93 301 29 78; Carrer de Montserrat 9; ⏰9.30pm-1am Sun, Wed & Thu, 9.30pm-3am Fri & Sat; Ⓜ Drassanes) This altar to kitsch, a dingy dance hall that has transgressed since the 1920s, is run by the luminous underground cabaret figure of Carmen Mairena and exudes a gorgeously tacky feel, especially with the midnight drag shows on Friday and Saturday. Due to its popularity with tourists, getting in is all but impossible unless you turn up early.

JAZZ SÍ CLUB
LIVE MUSIC

Map p296 (📞93 329 00 20; www.tallerdemusics. com; Carrer de Requesens 2; admission €8, drink included; ⏰6-11pm; Ⓜ Sant Antoni) A cramped little bar run by the Taller de Músics (Musicians' Workshop) serves as the stage for a varied program of jazz through to some good flamenco (Friday nights). Thursday night is Cuban night, Sunday is rock and the rest are devoted to jazz and/or blues sessions. Concerts start around 9pm but the jam sessions can get going as early as 6.30pm.

ROBADORS 23
LIVE MUSIC

Map p296 (Carrer d'en Robador 23; admission €2-3; ⏰8pm-2am; Ⓜ Liceu) On what remains a classic dodgy El Raval street, where a hardy band of streetwalkers, junkies and other misfits hang out in spite of all the work being carried out to gentrify the area, a narrow little bar has made a name for itself with its Wednesday night gigs. Jazz is the name of the game and the free concerts start at 8.30pm.

TEATRE GOYA
THEATRE

Map p296 (📞93 343 53 23; www.teatregoya.cat; Carrer de Joaquín Costa 68; admission €23-30; ⏰box office 5.30pm to start of show; Ⓜ Sant Antoni) A classic stage that long had its shutters down, the Goya was reopened to much fanfare in 2009. The program is generally mid- to highbrow, complementing partner theatre Teatre Romea. Among the first pieces shown (in Catalan), were Oscar Wilde's *An Ideal Husband* and David Mamet's *November*.

TEATRE LLANTIOL
THEATRE

Map p296 (📞93 329 90 09; www.llantiol.com; Carrer de la Riereta 7; admission €6-10; Ⓜ Sant Antoni) At this curious place in El Raval all sorts of odd stuff, from concerts and ballads to magic shows, is staged. On Saturday nights at 12.30am there is a regular cabaret-variety slot, a bit of a throwback to another era. About once a month you can see stand-up comedy in English here, too. Check out the **Giggling Guiri** (www. comedyinspain.com) – *guiri* is a slang word for foreigner – program for upcoming acts, mostly from the UK.

TEATRE NOU TANTARANTANA
THEATRE

Map p296 (📞93 441 70 22; www.tantarantana. com; Carrer de les Flors 22; ⏰box office 1hr before show; Ⓜ Paral.lel) Apart from staging all sorts of contemporary and experimental drama (anything from Harold Pinter to local creations), this cosy theatre also has a kids' program. These shows tend to start at 6pm (noon on Sundays). The adult theatre productions are at 9pm Wednesday to Saturday, and 7pm Sunday.

TEATRE ROMEA
THEATRE

Map p296 (📞93 301 55 04; www.teatreromea. com; Carrer de l'Hospital 51; admission €17-28; ⏰box office 4.30pm to start of show Wed-Sun; Ⓜ Liceu) Deep in El Raval, this 19th-century theatre was resurrected at the end of the 1990s and is one of the city's key stages for quality drama. It usually fills up for a broad range of interesting plays, often classics with a contemporary flavour, in Catalan and Spanish.

THE GREEN FAIRY

Bar Marsella (Map p296; Carrer de Sant Pau 65; ⏰10pm-2am Mon-Thu, 10pm-3am Fri & Sat; Ⓜ Liceu) has been in business since 1820, and has served the likes of Hemingway, who was known to slump here over an *absenta* (absinthe). The bar still specialises in absinthe, a drink to be treated with respect. Your glass comes with a lump of sugar, a fork and a little bottle of mineral water. Hold the sugar on the fork, over your glass, and drip the water onto the sugar so that it dissolves into the absinthe, which turns yellow. The result should give you a warm glow.

EL RAVAL ENTERTAINMENT

🛍 SHOPPING

The area boasts a handful of art galleries around Macba, along with a burgeoning secondhand and vintage clothes scene on Carrer de la Riera Baixa. Carrer dels Tallers is one of the city's main music strips.

TOP CHOICE RAS
BOOKS

Map p296 (www.rasbcn.com; Carrer del Doctor del Dou 10; ⊘noon-8pm Tue-Sat; MUniversitat) This is an amalgam of bookshop and gallery space that hosts exhibitions by experimental local and international artists, all the while offering beautifully designed photography, architecture and art books. It's one of those places that you will love to spend an hour or two in, browsing and reading the books and seeing the art on display.

TOP CHOICE BARCELONA REYKJAVIK
FOOD

Map p296 (www.barcelonareykjavik.com; Carrer Doctor del Dou 12; ⊘9am-9pm Mon-Sat, 10.30am-3pm Sunday; MCatalunya) Bread lovers, rejoice! Well, technically, you're never out of good bread in Barcelona, what with the ubiquitous baguette, but you'll be hard pressed to find bread *this* good anywhere in town. All loaves are made using organic flour – spelt, wholemeal, mixed cereals and so on – and sourdough yeast. The bakery also produces excellent pastry. Two more shops can be found in El Born and Gràcia.

TOP CHOICE COSTURA
ARTS & CRAFTS

Map p296 (www.costuratienda.com; Carrer Doctor del Dou 4; ⊘10am-2pm & 4-9pm Mon-Sat; MCatalunya) This is a treat of a shop – a tiny space that is a mix of a haberdashery, atelier and shop that dedicates itself to the craft of sewing children's clothes. It sells ready-made clothes and patterns (both child and adult sizes) for blouses, shirts, dresses, trousers and shorts, and stocks gorgeous fabrics. The friendly owners also organise sewing workshops (ask in store for details).

FANTASTIK
ARTS & CRAFTS

Map p296 (www.fantastik.es; Carrer de Joaquín Costa 62 ; ⊘11am-2pm & 4-9pm Mon-Thu, 11am-9pm Fri & Sat, closed Sun; MUniversitat) Over 400 products – including a Mexican skull rattle, robot moon explorer from China or recycled plastic zebras from South Africa – can be found in this bright shop that sources its items from Mexico, India, Bulgaria, Russia, Senegal and 20 other countries. It's a perfect place to buy all the things you don't need but can't live without.

LA PORTORRIQUEÑA
COFFEE

Map p296 (Carrer d'en Xuclà 25; MCatalunya) Coffee beans from around the world, freshly ground before your eyes, has been the winning formula in this store since 1902. It also offers all sorts of chocolate goodies. The street is good for little old-fashioned food boutiques.

HOLALA! PLAZA
FASHION

Map p296 (Plaça de Castella 2; MUniversitat) Backing on to Carrer de Valldonzella, where it boasts an exhibition space (Gallery) for temporary art displays, this Ibiza import is inspired by that island's long established (and somewhat commercialised) hippie tradition. Vintage clothes are the name of the game, along with an eclectic program of exhibitions and activities.

CASTELLÓ
MUSIC

Map p296 (Carrer dels Tallers 3 & 7; MCatalunya) These two stores are part of a large family business that has been going since 1935 and that is said to account for a fifth of the retail record business in Catalonia.

TERANYINA
ARTS & CRAFTS

Map p296 (Carrer del Notariat 10; MCatalunya) Artist Teresa Rosa Aguayo runs this textile workshop in the heart of the artsy bit of El Raval. You can join courses at the loom, admire some of the rugs and other works that Teresa has created and, of course, buy them.

La Ribera

Neighbourhood Top Five

1 Admiring the simplicity and beauty of the Gothic **Església de Santa Maria del Mar** (p105)

2 Being introduced to the origins of Picasso's genius at the fascinating **Museu Picasso** (p103)

3 Enjoying a show and the Modernista interior at the **Palau de la Música Catalana** (p106)

4 Taking in the marvelous ancient-Latin-American art at the **Museu Barbier-Mueller d'Art Pre-Colombí** (p107)

5 Putting your feet up and your bum down on the grass at **Parc de la Ciutadella** (p108)

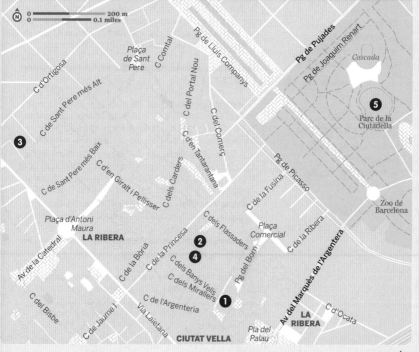

For more detail of this area, see Map p300 ➡

Lonely Planet's Top Tip

Getting around all of Barcelona's museums can be anything but cheap, so take advantage of free Sundays (p29), when entry into many of the city's museum will cost you zilch!

 ## Best Places to Eat

➡ Casa Delfin (p110)

➡ Le Cucine Mandarosso (p110)

➡ El Passadís Del Pep (p110)

➡ Cal Pep (p112)

➡ En Aparte (p112)

For reviews, see p110 ➡

Best Places to Drink

➡ Mudanzas (p113)

➡ La Vinya del Senyor (p113)

➡ Gimlet (p113)

➡ El Xampanyet (p113)

➡ Miramelindo (p113)

For reviews, see p113 ➡

Best for Architecture

➡ Església de Santa Maria del Mar (p105)

➡ Palau de la Música Catalana (p106)

➡ Carrer de Montcada (p107)

For reviews, see p107 ➡

LA RIBERA

Explore: La Ribera

La Ribera widely refers to the entire area covered by the city council's rather long-winded appellation of Sant Pere, Santa Caterina i la Ribera. The gentrified area south of Carrer de la Princesa is generally known as El Born, after busy, bar-lined Passeig del Born. This area should be your first port of call, specifically a stroll down the Carrer de Montcada, a street rich in Gothic and baroque mansions as well as the city's major museums – the Museu Picasso, Museu Barbier-Mueller d'Art Pre-Colombí and part of the Disseny Hub, and many art galleries and shops.

Passeig del Born was Barcelona's main square from the 13th to the 18th centuries. It still has an air of excitement around it – it's lined with bars, cafes and restaurants, and the streets that cross this short drag are packed with some impressive (quite high-end) shopping. The area is best explored day and night – it's a heterodox cosmopolitan jumble in a magnificent medieval setting.

Northwest of Carrer de la Princesa, the area's physiognomy changes. A mess of untidy streets wiggles northwards around the striking modern reincarnation of the Mercat de Santa Caterina and on towards the Modernista Palau de la Música Catalana. Little by little, some outstanding eating and drinking options have opened up in these narrow, winding streets.

Via Laietana, a rumbling fuel-fumed thoroughfare, marks the southwest side of La Ribera, while the Parc de la Ciutadella closes off its northeastern flank. The park is a rare green space in central Barcelona, and densely packed considering its size – you can lounge on its stretches of grass, sit by the grand fountain or visit the zoo.

Local Life

➡ **Market Secrets** Locals get their eggs at the Mercat de Santa Caterina (p108), where, in season, stallholders 'flavour' their eggs by stacking them up and placing truffles among them. They are divine when soft-boiled.

➡ **A Slice of Culture** Join the largely local clientele for a weekend lunchtime classical concert at the Palau de la Música Catalana (p106). Take advantage of the natural daylight to see the beautiful interior of the main hall.

➡ **Barcelona Style** Join the beautiful *barcelonins* and shop in some of the city's best fashion boutiques (p114).

Getting There & Away

➡ **Metro** Línia 4 coasts down the southwest flank of La Ribera, stopping at Urquinaona, Jaume I and Barceloneta. Línia 1 also stops nearby, at Urquinaona and Arc de Triomf (the nearest stop for the Parc de la Ciutadella).

TOP SIGHTS
MUSEU PICASSO

The setting alone, in five contiguous medieval stone mansions, makes the Museu Picasso unique (and worth the probable queues). The pretty courtyards, galleries and staircases preserved in the first three of these buildings are as delightful as the collection inside.

The Early Years

This collection concentrates on the artist's formative years, yet there is enough material from subsequent periods to give you a thorough impression of the man's versatility and genius. Above all, you come away feeling that Picasso was the true original, always one step ahead of himself (let alone anyone else) in his search for new forms of expression.

The collection includes more than 3500 artworks, larely pre-1904, which is apt considering that the artist spent his formative creative years in Barcelona. Allegedly it was Picasso himself who proposed the museum's creation, to his friend and personal secretary Jaume Sabartés, a Barcelona native, in 1960. Three years later, the 'Sabartés Collection' was opened, since a museum bearing Picasso's name would have been met with censorship – Picasso's opposition to the Franco regime was well known. The Museu Picasso we see today opened in 1983, and gradually expanded with donations from Salvador Dalí and Sebastià Junyer Vidal, among others, though most artworks were bequeathed by Picasso himself. His widow, Jacqueline Roque, also donated 41 ceramic pieces and the *Woman With Bonnet* painting after Picasso's death.

DON'T MISS

➡ *Retrato de la Tía Pepa*
➡ *Ciència i Caritat*
➡ *Terrats de Barcelona*
➡ *El Foll*
➡ *Las Meninas*

PRACTICALITIES

➡ Map p300
➡ 93 256 30 00
➡ www.museu picasso.bcn.es
➡ Carrer de Montcada 15-23
➡ adult/student/ senior & child under 16yr €11/6/free, 3-8pm Sun & 1st Sun of month free
➡ ◷10am-8pm Tue-Sun & holidays
➡ Ⓜ Jaume I

The permanent collection is housed in Palau Aguilar, Palau del Baró de Castellet and Palau Meca, all dating to the 14th century. The 18th-century Casa Mauri, built over medieval remains (even some Roman leftovers have been identified), and the adjacent 14th-century Palau Finestres accommodate temporary exhibitions.

The last rooms contain engravings and some 40 ceramic pieces completed throughout the latter years of his unceasingly creative life. You'll see plates and bowls decorated with simple, single-line drawings of fish, owls and other animal shapes, typical for Picasso's daubing on clay.

The Collection

A visit starts with sketches and oils from Picasso's earliest years in Málaga and La Coruña – around 1893–95. Some of his self-portraits and the portraits of his father, which date from 1896, are evidence enough of his precocious talent. *Retrato de la Tía Pepa* (Portrait of Aunt Pepa), done in Málaga in 1896, shows the incredible maturity of his brushstrokes and his ability to portray character – at the tender age of 15! Picasso painted the enormous *Ciència i Caritat* (Science and Charity) in the same year. His ingeniousness extends to his models too, with his father standing in for the doctor, and a beggar whom he hired off the street along with her offspring modeling the sick woman and the child.

In rooms 5–7 paintings from his first Paris sojourn hang, while room 8 is dedicated to the first significant new stage in his development, the Blue Period. *Woman with Bonnet* is an important work from this period, depicting a captive from the Saint-Lazare women's prison and veneral disease hospital which Picasso visited when in Paris – this also sets up the theme of Picasso's fascination with those inhabiting the down-and-out layers of society.

His nocturnal blue-tinted views of *Terrats de Barcelona* (Roofs of Barcelona) and *El Foll* (The Madman) are cold and cheerless, yet somehow alive. *Terrats de Barcelona* was painted in 1903, during his second stint at the 17 Carrer de la Riera Sant Joan street studio – he painted the city rooftops frequently, from different perspectives, in this period. Picasso also did many drawings of beggars, the blind and the impoverished elderly throughout 1903 and 1904 – *El Foll* is one of the most impressive from those series.

A few cubist paintings pop up in rooms 10 and 11; check out the *Glass and Tobacco Packet* still-life painting, a beautiful and simple work. Picasso started to experiment with still life in 1924 – something he'd done before but had not taken to as seriously as he would from here on.

Las Meninas through the Prism of Picasso

From 1954 to 1962 Picasso was obsessed with the idea of researching and 'rediscovering' the greats, in particular Velázquez. In 1957 he created a series of renditions of the latter's masterpiece *Las Meninas,* now displayed in rooms 12–15. It is as though Picasso has looked at the original Velázquez painting through a prism reflecting all the styles he had worked through until then, creating his own masterpiece in the process. This is a wonderful opportunity to see *Las Meninas* in its entirety in this beautiful space.

TOP SIGHTS
MUSEU PICASSO

ESGLÉSIA DE SANTA MARIA DEL MAR

At the southwest end of Passeig del Born stands the apse of Barcelona's finest Catalan Gothic church, Santa Maria del Mar (Our Lady of the Sea). Built in the 14th century with record-breaking alacrity for the time (it took just 54 years), the church is remarkable for its architectural harmony and simplicity.

The People's Church

Its construction started in 1329, with Berenguer de Montagut and Ramon Despuig the architects in charge. During construction, the city's *bastaixos* (porters) spent a day each week carrying the stone required to build the church on their backs from royal quarries in Montjuïc. Their memory lives on in reliefs of them in the main doors and stone carvings elsewhere in the church. The walls, side chapels and facades were finished by 1350 and the entire structure was completed in 1383.

The Interior

The exterior gives an impression of sternness, and the narrow streets surrounding it are restrictive and claustrophobic. It may come as a (pleasant) surprise then to find a spacious and light interior – the central nave and two flanking aisles separated by slender octagonal pillars give an enormous sense of lateral space.

The interior is almost devoid of imagery of the sort to be found in Barcelona's other large Gothic churches, but Santa Maria was lacking in superfluous decoration even before anarchists gutted it in 1909 and 1936. Keep an eye out for **music recitals**, often baroque and classical.

DON'T MISS

➡ The church's architects in memorial stone relief

➡ A live-music performance

PRACTICALITIES

➡ Map p300

➡ ☎ 93 319 05 16

➡ Plaça de Santa Maria del Mar

➡ ⏰ 9am-1.30pm & 4.30-8pm

➡ Ⓜ Jaume I

TOP SIGHTS
PALAU DE LA MÚSICA CATALANA

NEIL SETCHFIELD / LONELY PLANET IMAGES ©

This concert hall is a high point of Barcelona's Modernista architecture: a series of crescendos in tile, brick, sculpted stone and stained glass. Built by Domènech i Montaner between 1905 and 1908 for the Orfeo Català musical society, it was conceived as a temple for the Catalan Renaixença (Renaissance). The *palau* (palace) was built with the help of some of the best Catalan artisans of the time, in the cloister of the former Convent de Sant Francesc, and since 1990 it has undergone several major changes.

The Facade

The *palau,* like a peacock, shows off much of its splendour on the outside. Take in the principal facade with its mosaics, floral capitals and the sculpture cluster representing Catalan popular music.

The Interior

Wander inside the foyer and restaurant areas to admire the spangled, tiled **pillars**. Best of all, however, is the richly colourful **auditorium** upstairs, with its ceiling of blue-and-gold stained glass and shimmering skylight that looks like a giant, crystalline, downward-thrusting nipple. Above a bust of Beethoven on the stage towers a wind-blown sculpture of Wagner's Valkyries (Wagner was top of the Barcelona charts at the time it was created). This can only be savoured on a guided tour or by attending a **performance** – either is highly recommended. Tour tickets can be bought as much as a week in advance by phone or online. Space is limited to a maximum of 55 people.

DON'T MISS

- ➡ The principal facade's mosaics and columns
- ➡ The foyer and restaurant's pillars
- ➡ The auditorium
- ➡ A performance – day or night!

PRACTICALITIES

- ➡ Map p300
- ➡ ☏ 902 475485
- ➡ www.palaumusica.org
- ➡ Carrer de Sant Francesc de Paula 2
- ➡ adult/child/student & EU senior €15/free/€7.50
- ➡ ⏱ 50min tours every 30 minutes 10am-6pm Easter week & Aug, 10am-3.30pm Sep-Jul
- ➡ Ⓜ Urquinaona

⊙ SIGHTS

MUSEU PICASSO MUSEUM
See p103.

**ESGLÉSIA DE SANTA
MARIA DEL MAR** CHURCH
See p105.

**PALAU DE LA
MÚSICA CATALANA** ARCHITECTURE
See p106.

CARRER DE MONTCADA STREET
(ⓂJaume I) An early example of town planning, this medieval high street was driven towards the sea from the road that in the 12th century led northeast from the city walls. It was the city's snootiest address for the merchant classes. The bulk of the great mansions that remain today mostly date to the 14th and 15th centuries.

This area was the commercial heartland of medieval Barcelona. Five of the mansions on the east side of the street have been linked to house the Museu Picasso (p103). Across the road, others house the Museu Barbier-Mueller d'Art Pre-Colombí (p107) and the Disseny Hub (p107). Several other mansions on this street are commercial art galleries where you're welcome to browse. The biggest, at No 25, is the local branch of the prestigious Parisian Galeria Maeght (p114) in the 16th-century Palau dels Cervelló. If you promise to drink, you can sip wine or cocktails (both rather expensive) inside the baroque courtyard of the originally medieval **Palau de Dalmases** (Map p300; ☑93 310 06 73; ☺8pm-2am Tue-Sat, 6-10pm Sun; ⓂJaume I) at No 20 while listening to baroque music or operatic snippets (a peek inside isn't allowed without a definitive commitment to consume when you enter!).

At the corner of Carrer dels Corders and the northern end of the street, just beyond the 19th-century Carrer de la Princesa, stands a much-meddled-with Romanesque chapel, the **Capella d'en Marcús** (Map p300), once a wayfarers' stop on the road northeast out of medieval Barcelona.

**MUSEU BARBIER-MUELLER
D'ART PRE-COLOMBÍ** MUSEUM
Map p300 (☑93 310 45 16; www.barbier-mueller.ch; Carrer de Montcada 14; adult/child under 16yr/senior & student €3.50/free/1.70, 1st Sun of month free; ☺11am-7pm Tue-Fri, 10am-7pm Sat, 10am-3pm Sun & holidays; ⓂJaume I) The wonderfully illuminated artefacts inside the medieval Palau Nadal are part of the treasure trove of pre-Columbian art collected by Swiss businessman Josef Mueller (who died in 1977) and his son-in-law Jean-Paul Barbier, who directs the Musée Barbier-Mueller in Geneva. Together, the two museums form one of the most prestigious collections of such art in the world.

In blacked-out rooms, the beautifully spotlit artefacts stand out as if on stage. South American gold jewellery introduces the collection, followed by rooms containing ceramics, jewellery, statues, textiles and other objects. Every year or two, the composition of the exhibition is altered, with pieces moved around between Barcelona and Geneva and items displayed on loan from other collections. It's one of the most enchanting museums in town.

DISSENY HUB MUSEUM
Map p300 (☑93 256 23 00; www.dhub-bcn.cat; Carrer de Montcada 12; adult/child under 16yr/senior & student €5/free/3, 3-8pm Sun free; ☺11am-7pm Tue-Sat, to 8pm Sun, to 3pm holidays; ⓂJaume I) The 13th-century Palau dels Marquesos de L022 (which underwent repeated alterations into the 18th century) is temporary home to part of the city's Disseny (Design) Hub collection of applied arts – this is where it has its temporary exhibitions, study galleries and activities.

Often the exhibition on the ground floor is free, while the more extensive 1st-floor exhibition is what you pay for (admission includes entry to both locations). The permanent collections of Disseny are housed in the Palau Reial de Pedralbes and the new building, scheduled for completion in 2013, will be in Plaça de les Glòries. The building's courtyard, with its cafe-restaurant, makes a delightful stop.

OLD FLAME

Opposite Església de Santa Maria del Mar's southern flank, an eternal flame burns brightly over an apparently anonymous sunken square. This was once El Fossar de les Moreres (The Mulberry Cemetery), the site of a Roman cemetery. It's also where Catalan resistance fighters were buried after the Siege of Barcelona ended in defeat in September 1714.

LA RIBERA SIGHTS

LOCAL KNOWLEDGE

PALAU DE LA MÚSICA CATALANA THROUGH THE AGES

The original Modernista creation, now a World Heritage Site, did not meet with universal approval in its day. The doyen of Catalan literature, Josep Pla, did not hesitate to condemn it as 'horrible', but few share his sentiments today. Domènech i Montaner himself was also in a huff. He failed to attend the opening ceremony in response to unsettled bills.

The palau was at the centre of a fraud scandal from 2009 to 2012, as its president, Felix Millet, who subsequently resigned, admitted to having syphoned off millions of euros of its funds. He and his partner were ordered to repay the embezzled money to the palau in March 2012.

MERCAT DE SANTA CATERINA   MARKET

Map p300 (⌖93 319 17 40; www.mercatsanta caterina.net; Avinguda de Francesc Cambó 16; ⏲7.30am-2pm Mon, to 3.30pm Tue, Wed & Sat, to 8.30pm Thu & Fri; MJaume I) Come shopping for your tomatoes at this extraordinary-looking produce market, built by Enric Miralles and Benedetta Tagliabue to replace its 19th-century predecessor. Finished in 2005, it is distinguished by its kaleidoscopic and weirdly wavy roof, held up above the bustling produce stands, restaurants, cafes and bars by twisting slender branches of what look like grey steel trees.

The multicoloured ceramic roof (with a ceiling made of warm, light timber) recalls the Modernista tradition of *trencadís* decoration (a type of mosaic, such as that in Park Güell). Indeed, its curvy design, like a series of Mediterranean rollers, seems to plunge back into an era when Barcelona's architects were limited only by their (vivid) imagination. The market roof bares an uncanny resemblance to that of the Escoles de Gaudí at La Sagrada Família.

The market's 1848 predecessor had been built over the remains of the demolished 15th-century Gothic Monestir de Santa Caterina, a powerful Dominican monastery. The **Espai Santa Caterina** (Map p300; admission free; ⏲8.30am-2pm Mon-Wed & Sat, to 8pm Thu & Fri), a small section of the church foundations, is glassed over in one corner as an archaeological reminder.

PARC DE LA CIUTADELLA   PARK

Map p300 (Passeig de Picasso; ⏲8am-6pm Nov-Feb, to 8pm Oct & Mar, to 9pm Apr-Sep; MArc de Triomf) Come for a stroll, a picnic, a visit to the zoo or to inspect Catalonia's regional parliament, but don't miss a visit to this, the most central green lung in the city. Parc de la Ciutadella is perfect for winding down.

After the War of the Spanish Succession, Felipe V razed a swath of La Ribera to build a huge fortress (La Ciutadella), designed to keep watch over Barcelona. It became a loathed symbol of everything Catalans hated about Madrid and the Bourbon kings, and was later used as a political prison. Only in 1869 did the central government allow its demolition, after which the site was turned into a park and used for the Universal Exhibition of 1888.

The monumental **cascada** (waterfall, Map p300) near the Passeig de Pujades park entrance, created between 1875 and 1881 by Josep Fontserè with the help of an enthusiastic young Gaudí, is a dramatic combination of statuary, rugged rocks, greenery and thundering water. All of it perfectly artificial! Nearby, hire a rowing boat to paddle about the small lake.

To the southeast, in what might be seen as an exercise in black humour, the fort's former arsenal now houses the **Parlament de Catalunya** (Map p300; www.parlament.cat; ⏲guided tours from 10am-1pm Sat & Sun, plus holidays). You can join free guided tours, in Catalan and Spanish (Castilian) only, on Saturdays and Sundays. The building is open for independent visiting on 11 September from 10am to 7pm. The most interesting stops are the sweeping Escala d'Honor (Stairway of Honour) and the several solemn halls that lead to the Saló de Sessions, the semicircular auditorium where parliament sits. At the centre of the garden in front of the *parlament* is a statue of a seemingly heartbroken woman, *Desconsol* (Distress; 1907), by Josep Llimona.

The Passeig de Picasso side of the park is lined by several buildings constructed for the Universal Exhibition. The medieval-looking caprice at the top end is the most engaging. Known as the **Castell dels Tres Dragons** (Castle of the Three Dragons, Map p300), it long housed the Museu de Zoologia, which is now closed. Domènech i Montaner put the 'castle's' trimmings on a pioneering steel frame. The coats of arms are all invented and the whole building exudes a teasing, playful air. It was used as a cafe-restaurant during the Universal Exhibition of 1888.

To the south is **L'Hivernacle** (Map p300), an arboretum or miniature botanical garden. Next come the former **Museu de Geologia** (Map p300) and **L'Umbracle** (Map p300), another arboretum. On Passeig de Picasso itself is Antoni Tàpies' typically impenetrable **Homenatge a Picasso** (Map p300). Water runs down the panes of a glass box full of bits of old furniture and steel girders.

Northwest of the park, Passeig de Lluís Companys is capped by the Modernista **Arc de Triomf** (Map p300; Passeig de Lluís Companys; Ⓜ Arc de Triomf), designed by Josep Vilaseca as the principal exhibition entrance, with unusual, Islamic-style brickwork. Josep Llimona did the main reliefs. Just what the triumph was eludes us, especially since the exhibition itself was a commercial failure. It is perhaps best thought of as a bricks-and-mortar embodiment of the city's general fin de siècle feel-good factor.

ZOO DE BARCELONA   ZOO

Map p300 (Ⓣ902 457545; www.zoobarcelona. com; Passeig de Picasso & Carrer de Wellington; adult/child under 3yr/senior/child 3-12yr €17/ free/8.90/10.20; ⊙10am-7pm Jun-Sep, to 6pm mid-Mar–May & Oct, to 5pm Nov–mid-Mar; Ⓜ Barceloneta) The zoo is a great day out for kids, with 7500 critters that range from geckos to gorillas – there are more than 400 species, plus picnic areas dotted all around. A new site being built on the coast of El Fòrum northeast of the city centre will ease the currently slightly crowded space.

MUSEU DE LA XOCOLATA   MUSEUM

Map p300 (Ⓣ93 268 78 78; www.museuxocolata. cat; Plaça de Pons i Clerch; adult/child under 7yr/ senior & student €4.30/free/3.65; ⊙10am-7pm Mon-Sat, to 3pm Sun & holidays; Ⓜ Jaume I) Chocoholics have a hard time containing themselves in this museum dedicated to the fundamental foodstuff – especially when the entry ticket is a chocolate bar! Expect to learn about chocolate mainly via the tastebuds – the informative side is a patchy mix of legend and history here.

A little salivation for sweet tooths is inevitable, as the museum sits in part of the **former Convent de Sant Agustí** (Map p300). The displays themselves trace the origins of chocolate, its arrival in Europe and the many myths and images associated with it. Among the informative stuff (with panels in various languages) and machinery used in the production of chocolate are choc models of buildings such as La Sagrada Família, along with various characters, local and international. It's all enough to have you making for the nearest sweet shop, but you don't have to – plenty of chocolate is sold right here! Kids and grown-ups can join guided tours or take part in chocolate-making and tasting sessions, especially on weekends.

Under the Gothic arches of what remains of the convent's one-time cloister is a pleasant cafe-bar, the **Bar del Convent** (Map p300; ⊙10am-9pm Mon-Thu, 11am-11pm Fri, 1pm-midnight Sat) – particularly good for people with children. Kids often play football in the cloister grounds. You enter at Carrer del Comerç 36.

ARXIU FOTOGRÀFIC
DE BARCELONA   GALLERY

Map p300 (Ⓣ93 256 34 20; www.bcn.cat/arxiu/ fotografic; Plaça de Pons i Clerch; admission free; ⊙10am-7pm Mon-Sat; Ⓜ Jaume I) On the 2nd floor of the former Convent de Sant Agustí is the modest exhibition space of this city photo archive. Photos on show are generally related to the city, as the photo collection is principally devoted to that theme, from the late 19th century until the late 20th century.

A wonderful recent exhibition by the US photographer Mark Klett displayed 're-photographed' Barcelona cityscapes from Montjuïc.

MUSEU DEL REI DE LA MAGIA   MUSEUM

Map p300 (Ⓣ93 319 73 93; www.elreydelamagia. com; Carrer de l'Oli 6; admission with/without show €12/5; ⊙6-8pm Thu, with show 6pm Sat & noon Sun; Ⓜ Jaume I) This museum is a timeless curio. It is the scene of magic shows, home (upstairs) to collections of material that hark back to the 19th-century origins of the shop (everything from old posters and books for learning tricks to magic wands and trick cards) and the place for budding magicians of all ages to enrol in courses. Seeing is believing.

The museum is run by the same people who have the nearby magic shop (p115) on Carrer de la Princesa.

ESGLÉSIA DE SANT PERE DE
LES PUELLES   CHURCH

Map p300 (Plaça de Sant Pere; admission free; Ⓜ Arc de Triomf) Not a great deal remains of the original church or convent that stood here since early medieval times. The church's pre-Romanesque Greek-cross floor plan survives, as do some Corinthian columns beneath the 12th-century dome and a much-damaged Renaissance vault leading into a side chapel.

It was around this church that settlement began in La Ribera. In 985, a Muslim raiding force under Al-Mansur attacked Barcelona and largely destroyed the convent, killing or capturing the nuns.

MERCAT DEL BORN
MARKET

Map p300 (Plaça Comercial; ⓂBarceloneta) Excavation in 2001 at the former Mercat del Born, a late-19th-century produce market built of iron and glass, unearthed great chunks of one of the districts flattened to make way for the much-hated Ciutadella. Historians found intact streets and the remains of houses, dating as far back as the 15th century.

Excitement was such that plans to locate a new city library in the long-disused market were dropped. Instead, the site will become a museum and cultural centre – the projected date is still undecided.

CASA LLOTJA DE MAR
ARCHITECTURE

Map p300 (☎902 44 84 48; www.casallotja.com; Passieg d'Isabel II, 1; ⓂBarceloneta) The centrepiece of the city's medieval stock exchange (more affectionately known as La Llotja) is the fine Gothic Saló de Contractacions (Transaction Hall), built in the 14th century. Pablo Picasso and Joan Miró attended the art school that was housed in the Saló dels Cònsols from 1849.

These and five other halls were encased in a neoclassical shell in the 18th century. The stock exchange was in action until well into the 20th century and the building remains in the hands of the city's chamber of commerce. Occasionally it opens the doors to the public but the rooms are more generally hired out for events.

✖ EATING

If you'd mentioned El Born (El Borne in Spanish) in the early 1990s, you wouldn't have raised much interest. Now the area is peppered with bars, dance dives, groovy designer stores and restaurants. El Born is where Barcelona is truly cooking – avant-garde chefs and fusion masters have zeroed in on this southern corner of La Ribera to conduct their culinary experiments. If you don't want to play such wild games, there's plenty of the traditional stuff to choose from, too.

TOP CHOICE CASA DELFÍN
CATALAN €

Map p300 (Passeig del Born 36; mains €4-12; ⊙noon-1am; ⓂBarceloneta) One of Barcelona's culinary delights, Casa Delfín is everything you dream of when you think of Catalan (and Mediterranean) cooking. Start with the tangy and sweet *calçots* (a cross between a leek and an onion; February and March only) or salt-strewn *padron* peppers, moving on to grilled sardines specked with parsley, then tackle the meaty monkfish roasted in white wine and garlic.

Or tease some mussels and clams out of their shells, all the while crunching on the Catalan *coca* flatbread – done here to perfection and smeared with tomatoes and olive oil. For the finale, choose the Eton Mess (the English owner Kate's only tribute to her homeland) – but keep in mind that the long glass of mashed-up cream, meringue and berries will sweeten two or three.

LE CUCINE MANDAROSSO
ITALIAN €

Map p300 (☎932 69 07 80; www.lecucinemandarosso.com; Carrer Verdaguer i Callis 4; mains €8, lunch menu €10; ⊙lunch & dinner; ⓂUrquinaona) What a treat it is to discover the world of Mandarosso. This is comfort food done to perfection – the menu changes daily, with only six mains to choose from, five of which are pasta, and one vegetable, fish or meat. The antipasti can be vegetables, or fresh cheese, such as the wonderfully creamy *burrata* (fresh cheese made from mozzarella and cream), buffalo-milk mozzarella, or smoked scamorza and provola cheese.

Combine a good pasta dish – the 'al forno' (baked) options are outstanding with a green salad, and follow up with the homemade cakes. More can be had at Mandarosso Pastis (p112), around the corner. The fresh produce is bought daily from the Santa Caterina market, and the rest is imported from Italy. The €10 lunch menu is exceptionally good value. Book in advance for dinner.

EL PASSADÍS DEL PEP
SEAFOOD €€

Map p300 (☎93 310 10 21; www.passadis.com; Pla del Palau 2; mains €15-20; ⊙lunch & dinner Tue-Sat, dinner Mon Sep-Jul; ⓂBarceloneta) There's no sign, but locals know where to head for a seafood feast. They say the restaurant's raw materials are delivered daily from fishing ports along the Catalan coast. There is no menu – what's on offer depends on what

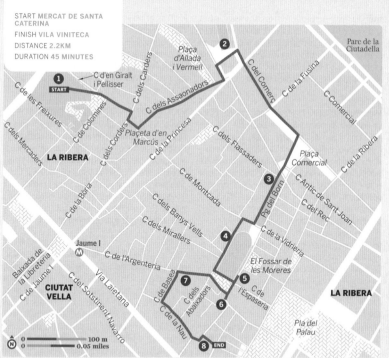

Neighbourhood Walk
A Foodie's Feast in La Ribera

A foodie will be beguiled beautifully by the choice in La Ribera. Begin in the modern version of a 19th-century market, **1 Mercat de Santa Caterina** (p108). A close rival to La Boqueria, its stands overflow with fish, cold meats, cheeses, countless varieties of olives, olive-oil and vinegar specialist Olisoliva, bar-eateries and a good restaurant.

Barcelona is awash in specialist chocolate stores, whether traditional *granjas* (milk bars) for enjoying thick hot chocolate with a pastry or modern dens of chocolate iniquity. Where better to get introduced to the history behind this seductive food than the **2 Museu de la Xocolata** (p109)?

If you haven't had your chocolate cravings satisfied at the museum, head on to **3 Hofmann Pastisseria** (p114) and choose from gourmet chocolate bars and all sorts of sweet goodies in jars.

The incredibly atmospheric 19th-century **4 Casa Gispert** (p114) wouldn't be out of place in a Tim Burton movie. The wooden shelves groan under jars of dried fruit, honeyed hazelnuts and fragrant pine nuts.

On the opposite side of the square you'll find the most startling array of sausages – the *botifarra* being the quintessential Catalan sausage – and all sorts of other gourmet goodies on offer at **5 La Botifarreria** (p114).

If there is such a thing as chic cake, it is made at **6 Bubó** (p112). Little shiny squares of chocolate are dotted with rubylike raspberries and pistachio jewels.

Coffee lovers will cherish **7 El Magnífico** (p114), with its range of fine coffees from around the world. This is a Barcelona institution. Head up to Carrer de l'Argenteria and follow your nose.

No food experience is complete without wine. To investigate some of the enormous variety of Catalan and Spanish drops, explore **8 Vila Viniteca** (p114). The store has many international wines on hand and also occasionally hosts tasting events.

the sea has surrendered on the day – but you can count on something along the lines of fresh seafood and/or fish, a bit of *jamón* (cured ham), tomato bread and grilled vegetables. Just head down the long, ill-lit corridor and entrust yourself to their care.

CAL PEP
TAPAS €€

Map p300 (☑93 310 79 61; www.calpep.com; Plaça de les Olles 8; mains €8-18; ⊙lunch Tue-Sat, dinner Mon-Fri Sep-Jul; MBarceloneta) It's getting a foot in the door here that's the problem – there can be queues around the square with people trying to get in. And if you want one of the five tables out the back, you'll need to call ahead. Most people are happy elbowing their way to the bar for some of the tastiest gourmet seafood tapas in town.

Pep recommends *cloïsses amb pernil* (clams and ham) or the *trifàsic* (combo of calamari, whitebait and prawns). Its other pièce de résistance is a super smooth *tortilla de patatas* (Spanish omelette) and tuna tartare.

EN APARTÉ
FRENCH €

Map p300 (☑932 69 13 36; www.enaparte.es; Carrer Lluis el Piados 2; mains €8-10; MArc de Triomph or Urquinaona) A great low-key place to eat good-quality French food, just off the quiet Plaça de Sant Pere. The restaurant is small but spacious, with sewing-machine tables and vintage details, and floor-to-ceiling windows that bring in some wonderful early-afternoon sunlight.

The lunchtime menu (€11) is excellent, offering a salad (beetroot and apple and walnut), and a quiche or a vegetable dish such as stuffed peppers with a potato gratin.

TANTARANTANA
MEDITERRANEAN €

Map p300 (☑93 268 24 10; Carrer d'en Tantarantana 24; mains €6-7; ⊙dinner Mon-Sat; MJaume I) Surrounded as it is by the furiously fashionable front-line nuclei of *nueva cocina española* – the new Spanish cuisine – this spot is a refreshing contrast. There is something comforting about the old-style marble-top tables, upon which you can sample simple but well-prepared dishes such as risotto or grilled tuna served with vegetables and ginger. It attracts a 30-something crowd who enjoy the outdoor seating in summer.

PLA DE LA GARSA
CATALAN €€

Map p300 (☑933 15 24 13; www.pladelagarsa.com; Carrer dels Assaonadors 13; mains €10; ⊙dinner; MJaume I) This 17th-century house is the ideal location for a romantic candlelit dinner. Timber beams, anarchically scattered tables and soft ambient music combine to make an enchanting setting over two floors for traditional, hearty Catalan cooking, with dishes such as *timbal de botifarra negra* (a black pudding dish with mushrooms).

MANDAROSSO PASTIS
CAFE, PASTELERÍA €

Map p300 (☑933 19 05 02; www.lecucinemandarosso.com; Carrer General Alvarez de Castro 5-7; ⊙8am-9pm Tue-Sat, 9am-2pm Sun, closed Mon; MUrquinaona) Little sister to Le Cucine Mandarosso (p110), this is its cake-focused cafe. The place is tiny, with two small tables and one wooden communal table, a little record player that blasts old hits, and the glowing cake counter. It also serves breakfast.

BUBÓ
PASTELERÍA, RISTORANTE €

Map p300 (☑93 268 72 24; www.bubo.ws; Carrer de les Caputxes 6 & 10; ⊙4pm-midnight Mon, 10am-midnight Tue-Thu & Sun, 10am-2am Fri & Sat; MBarceloneta) Carles Mampel is a sweet artist, literally. It is difficult to walk by his bar and pastry shop without taking a seat outside to try one of his fantasy-laden creations. Try saying no to a mousse of *gianduia* (a dark hazelnut cream) with mango cream, caramelised hazelnuts with spices, and a hazelnut biscuit.

LILIPEP
CAFE €

Map p300 (☑933 10 66 97; Carrer del Pou de la Cadena 8; ⊙10am-10pm Tue-Thu, to midnight Fri-Sun; ☎✐; MJaume I) If you're in need of a break from sightseeing or indeed a little drink with a *tapa* (included!), head for this German-Catalan concoction, hidden in a little side street off the Carrer de la Princesa. Help yourself to the books as you have your coffee and check out what the next live performance might be. There are vegetarian and meat-based dishes, and Lilipep also does hearty German breakfasts.

LA LLAVOR DELS ORÍGENS
CATALAN €

Map p300 (www.lallavordelsorigens.com; Carrer de la Vidrieria 6-8; mains €8-10; ⊙12.30pm-12.30am; MJaume I) In this treasure chest of Catalan regional products, the shop shelves groan under the weight of bottles and packets of goodies. It also has a long menu of smallish dishes, such as *sopa de carbassa i castanyes* (pumpkin and chestnut soup) or *mandonguilles amb albergìnies* (rissoles with aubergine), that you can mix and match over wine by the glass.

BAR JOAN
CATALAN €

Map p300 (☎93 310 61 50; Mercat de Santa Caterina; menú del día €11; ☺lunch Mon-Sat; ⓜJaume I) Along with the popular Cuines de Santa Caterina, there are a couple of bar-eateries in the Mercat de Santa Caterina. Bar Joan is known especially to locals for its *arròs negre* (cuttlefish-ink rice) on Tuesdays at lunchtime. It's a simple spot, but it always fills up with hungry passers-by, black rice or no black rice.

🍺 DRINKING & NIGHTLIFE

Countless bars dot the elongated Passeig del Born and the web of streets winding off it and around the Església de Santa Maria del Mar – the area has an ebullient party feel.

MUDANZAS
BAR

Map p300 (☎93 319 11 37; Carrer de la Vidrieria 15; ☺10am-2.30am; ⓜJaume I) This was one of the first bars to get things into gear in El Born and it still attracts a faithful crowd. It's a straightforward place for a beer, a chat and perhaps a sandwich. Oh, and it has a nice line of Italian grappas.

LA VINYA DEL SENYOR
WINE BAR

Map p300 (Plaça de Santa Maria del Mar 5; ☺noon-1am Tue-Sun; ⓜJaume I) Relax on the *terrassa*, which lies in the shadow of Església de Santa Maria del Mar, or crowd inside at the tiny bar. The wine list is as long as *War and Peace* and there's a table upstairs for those who opt to sample by the bottle rather than the glass.

GIMLET
COCKTAIL BAR

Map p300 (Carrer del Rec 24; cocktails €10; ☺10pm-3am; ⓜJaume I) Transport yourself to a Humphrey Bogart movie. White-jacketed bar staff with all the appropriate aplomb will whip you up a gimlet or any other classic cocktail (around €10) your heart desires. Barcelona cocktail guru Javier Muelas is behind this and several other cocktail bars around the city, so you can be sure of excellent drinks, some with a creative twist.

EL XAMPANYET
WINE BAR

Map p300 (Carrer de Montcada 22; ☺lunch & dinner Tue-Sat, lunch Sun; ⓜJaume I) Nothing has changed for decades in this, one of the city's best-known *cava* bars. Plant yourself at the bar or seek out a table against the decoratively tiled walls for a glass or three of *cava* (Catalan version of champagne) and an assortment of tapas, such as the tangy *boquerons en vinagre* (white anchovies in vinegar).

MIRAMELINDO
BAR

Map p300 (☎93 319 53 76; Passeig del Born 15; ☺8pm-2.30am; ⓜJaume I) A spacious tavern in a Gothic building, this remains a classic on Passeig del Born for mixed drinks, while soft jazz and soul sounds float overhead. Try for a comfy seat at a table towards the back before it fills to bursting. Several similarly barnsized places line this side of the *passeig*.

LA FIANNA
BAR

Map p300 (www.lafianna.com; Carrer dels Banys Vells 15; ☺6pm-1.30am Sun-Wed, to 2.30am Thu-Sat; ⓜJaume I) There is something medieval about this bar, with its bare stone walls, forged iron candelabra and cushion-covered lounges. But don't think chill-out. This place heaves and as the night wears on it's elbow room only. Earlier in the evening you can indulge in a little snack food, too.

MAGIC
CLUB

Map p300 (☎93 310 72 67; Passeig de Picasso 40; ☺11pm-6am Wed-Sun; ⓜBarceloneta) Although it sometimes hosts live acts in its sweaty, smoky basement, it's basically a straightforward, subterranean nightclub offering rock, mainstream dance faves and Spanish pop.

UPIAYWASI
CLUB

Map p300 (☎93 268 01 54; Carrer d'Allada Vermell 11; ☺5pm-2am Mon-Thu, 5pm-3am Fri & Sat, 4pm-1am Sun; ⓜBarceloneta) Slide into this dimly lit cocktail bar, which crosses a chilled ambience with Latin American music. A mix of lounges and intimate table settings, chandeliers and muted decorative tones lends the place a pleasingly conspiratorial feel.

☆ ENTERTAINMENT

TOP CHOICE PALAU DE LA MÚSICA CATALANA
LIVE MUSIC

Map p300 (☎902 442882; www.palaumusica. org; Carrer de Sant Francesc de Paula 2; ☺box office 10am-9pm Mon-Sat; ⓜUrquinaona) A feast for the eyes, this Modernista confection is also the city's traditional venue for classical and choral music. Just being here for a performance is an experience. Sip a preconcert

tipple in the foyer, its tiled pillars all a-glitter. Head up the grand stairway to the main auditorium, a whirlpool of Modernista whimsy. The *palau* has a wide-ranging program.

FLOW
PERFORMING ARTS

Map p300 (✆93 310 06 67; Carrer de la Fusina 6; ⏰8pm-3am Tue-Sun; Ⓜ Jaume I) A touched-up old-time bar, with a mirror ball and a little-used pool table, this is a curious spot for a mixed drink, where you may witness anything from experimental classical music to amateur theatre.

TABLAO NERVIÓN
DANCE

Map p300 (✆93 315 21 03; www.restaurantenerv ion.com; Carrer de la Princesa 2; show & set dinner €35, show only with one drink €12; ⏰shows 10pm-1am Fri; Ⓜ Jaume I) For very tourist-oriented flamenco, this place has unbeatable offers. Come along to the second show at midnight and the only obligation is to have a drink for €6. If you come at 11pm, you pay €12 for the show and a drink (beer or sangria). Or you can do the whole dinner and show thing from 10pm.

🛍 SHOPPING

The former commercial heart of medieval Barcelona is today still home to a cornucopia of old-style specialist food and drink shops, a veritable feast of aroma and atmosphere. They have been joined, since the late 1990s, by a raft of hip little fashion stores.

TOP CHOICE CASA GISPERT
FOOD

Map p300 (✆93 319 75 35; www.casagispert. com; Carrer dels Sombrerers 23; Ⓜ Jaume I) The wonderful, atmospheric and wood-fronted Casa Gispert has been toasting nuts and selling all manner of dried fruit since 1851. Pots and jars piled high on the shelves contain an unending variety of crunchy titbits: some roasted, some honeyed, all of them moreish. Your order is shouted over to the till, along with the price, in a classic display of old-world accounting.

COQUETTE
FASHION

Map p300 (✆93 295 42 85; www.coquettebcn. com; Carrer del Rec 65; Ⓜ Barceloneta) With its spare, cut-back and designer look, this fashion store is automatically attractive in

its own right. Women will love to browse through casual, feminine wear by such designers as Tsunoda, Vanessa Bruno, Chloé Baño and Hoss Intropia.

VILA VINITECA
DRINK

Map p300 (✆902 327777; www.vilaviniteca.es; Carrer dels Agullers 7; ⏰8.30am-8.30pm Mon-Sat; Ⓜ Jaume I) One of the best wine stores in Barcelona (and Lord knows, there are a few), this place has been searching out the best in local and imported wines since 1932. On a couple of November evenings it organises what has by now become an almost riotous wine-tasting event in Carrer dels Agullers and surrounding lanes, at which cellars from around Spain present their young new wines. At No 9 it has another store devoted to gourmet food products.

GALERIA MAEGHT
ART

Map p300 (✆93 310 42 45; www.maeght.com; Carrer de Montcada 25; ⏰11am-2pm & 3-7pm Tue-Fri, 11am-2pm Sat; Ⓜ Jaume I) This high-end gallery, housed in one of the fine medieval mansions for which this street is known, specialises in 20th-century masters. It is as enticing for the building as the art.

EL MAGNÍFICO
COFFEE

Map p300 (✆93 319 60 81; www.cafeselmagnifico. com; Carrer de l'Argenteria 64; Ⓜ Jaume I) All sorts of coffee has been roasted here since the early 20th century. The variety of coffee (and tea) available is remarkable – and the aromas hit you as you walk in. Across the road, the same people run the exquisite and much newer tea shop **Sans i Sans** (Map p300; ✆93 319 60 81; Carrer de l'Argenteria 59).

HOFMANN PASTISSERIA
FOOD

Map p300 (✆93 268 82 21; www.hofmann-bcn. com; Carrer dels Flassaders 44; Ⓜ Jaume I) With old timber cabinets, this bite-sized gourmet patisserie has an air of timelessness, although it is quite new. Choose between jars of delicious chocolates, the day's croissants and more dangerous pastries, or an array of cakes and other sweets.

LA BOTIFARRERIA
FOOD

Map p300 (✆93 319 91 23; www.labotifarreria. com; Carrer de Santa Maria 4; Ⓜ Jaume I) Say it with a sausage! Although this delightful deli sells all sorts of goodies, the mainstay is an astounding variety of handcrafted sausages, the *botifarra*. Not just the pork variety either – these sausages stuffed with anything from green pepper and whiskey to apple curry!

OLISOLIVA FOOD

Map p300 (📞93 268 14 72; www.olisoliva.com; Avinguda de Francesc Cambó; ⓂJaume I) Inside the Mercat de Santa Caterina, this simple, glassed-in store is stacked with olive oils and vinegars from all over Spain. Taste some of the products before deciding. Some of the best olive oils come from southern Spain. The range of vinegars is astounding too.

EL REY DE LA MAGIA SPECIALTY

Map p300 (📞93 319 39 20; www.elreydelamagia. com; Carrer de la Princesa 11; ⓧ11am-2pm & 5-8pm Mon-Fri, 10am-2pm Sat; ⓂJaume I) For more than 100 years, the people behind this box of tricks have been keeping locals both astounded and amused. Should you decide to stay in Barcelona and make a living as a magician, this is the place to buy levitation brooms, glasses of disappearing milk and decks of magic cards.

NU SABATES SHOES, ACCESSORIES

Map p300 (📞93 268 03 83; www.nusabates.com; Carrer dels Cotoners 14; ⓂJaume I) A couple of modern-day Catalan cobblers have put together some original handmade leather shoes (and a handful of bags and other leather items) in their stylish locale.

CUSTO BARCELONA FASHION

Map p300 (📞93 268 78 93; www.custo-barcelona. com; Plaça de les Olles 7; ⓂJaume I) The psychedelic decor and casual atmosphere lend this avant-garde Barcelona fashion store a youthful edge. Custo presents daring new women's and men's collections each year on the New York catwalks. The dazzling colours and cut of anything from dinner jackets to hot pants are for the uninhibited. It has five other stores around town.

Catalan Culture

As the proud capital of Catalonia, Barcelona takes centre stage for many age-old Catalan traditions that are still alive and well in the 21st century.

On weekends year-round, devotees of the folk dance *sardana* gather in front of La Catedral, while a 10-piece band puts everyone in motion. Catalans of all ages come out for the dance, which takes place in a circle, with dancers holding hands. Together they move right, back and then left, hopping, raising their arms and generally building momentum as the tempo picks up. All are welcome to join in, though you'll have to watch a few rounds to get the hang of it.

The building of human *castells* (castles) is another Catalan tradition, one that dates back to the 18th century. Teams from across the region compete to build human towers up to 10 storeys tall. These usually involve levels of three to five people standing on each other's shoulders. A crowd of teammates forms a supporting scrum around the thickset lads at the base. To successfully complete the castle, a young (light!) child called the *anxaneta* must reach the top and signal with his or her hand.

Speaking of festivals, Catalonia's best celebrations tend to revolve around religious holidays. Fests dedicated to *Nostra Senyora de la Mercè* (Our Lady of Mercy) and Santa Eulàlia – Barcelona's two patron saints – are the city's biggest bashes. You'll see plenty of *sardana* and *castell*-building there. You'll also see *gegants* (huge papier-mâché giants: lords, princesses, sultans, fisherman and historic and contemporary figures) and *capgrossos* (oversized heads worn by costumed actors). Another feature of these Catalan fests is the *correfoc* (fire run): horned devils brandishing fireworks-spouting pitchforks wreak mayhem in the streets. They are sometimes accompanied by fireworks-spouting dragons, or even wooden carts that are set alight. Stand clear!

Clockwise from top left
1. *Sardana* dancers 2. Spanish and Catalan flags
3. Festive fireworks 4. A *castell* in progress

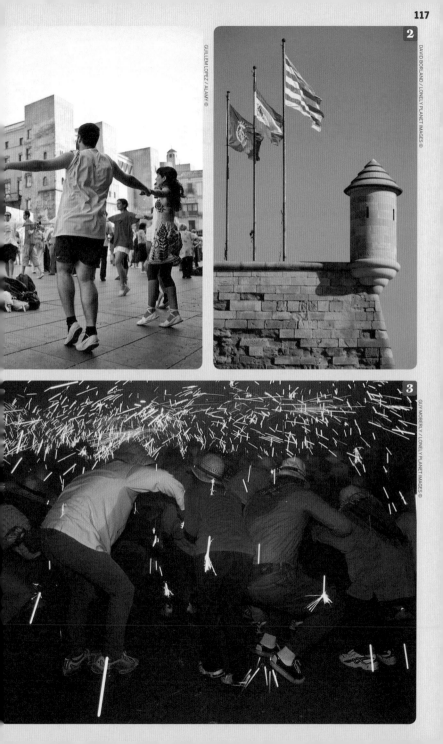

Barceloneta & the Waterfront

PORT VELL | PORT OLÍMPIC, EL POBLENOU & EL FÒRUM | BARCELONETA

Neighbourhood Top Five

1 Learning about the Romans, Muslims, feudal lords and civil war freedom fighters in the proud and interactive **Museu d'Història de Catalunya** (p121); afterwards, head to the rooftop for a meal with panoramic views.

2 Stepping back in time in the Gothic shipyards of the **Museu Marítim** (p120).

3 Walking through the eerie shark tunnel inside the massive **Aquarium** (p121).

4 Frolicking in the sea off the sands of **Platja de la Mar Bella** (p121).

5 Taking a **bike ride** (p125) along the beachside promenade from Barceloneta to Parc del Fòrum.

For more detail of this area, see Maps p302 and p304 ➡

Explore: Barceloneta & the Waterfront

Barcelona's long, sun-drenched waterfront provides a pleasant escape when you need a break from Gothic lanes and Modernisme. Heading northeast from the old city, you'll soon find yourself amid tempting seafood restaurants and waterfront bars, with a palm-lined promenade taking cyclists, joggers and strollers out to the beaches running some 4km up to Parc del Fòrum.

The transformed area of Port Vell, once an industrial wasteland, draws locals and tourists alike who come to stroll the peaceful pedestrian bridge of Rambla de Mar, which leads out to the shops and restaurants in Maremàgnum mall and the first-rate aquarium next door. Several small parks and plazas provide fine vantage points.

East of there lie upscale, open-air restaurants overlooking a marina and the Museu d'Historia de Catalunya. Nearby is Barceloneta, an old fishing quarter laid out in the mid-18th century. Head into its narrow (and tourist-free) lanes for lively tapas bars, old-fashioned seafood joints and bohemian drinking spots.

Where Barceloneta abuts the water, you'll find open-air restaurants with views of the promenade and the beaches beyond. On summer days the area fills with sun-seekers, making their way to and from the people-packed sands nearby. From here heading north to El Fòrum, it's beaches all the way; rustic shacks called *chiringuitos* dole out music and cocktails day and night on the sands.

Inland from these modern artificial beaches lies the high-tech zone of 22@bcn, not a big draw for many tourists, although Jean Nouvel's Torre Agbar draws a few architecture aficionados. The waterside district ends at El Fòrum, which has a worthwhile new science museum; it's also the setting for outdoor summer concerts and funfairs.

Local Life

➡ **Hangouts** *Cava* bars Vaso de Oro (p126) and Xampanyeria Can Paixano (p126) are long-time favourites.

➡ **Markets** Port Vell hosts Port Antic (p128), a small weekend antiques market; near the marina is the craft market of Feria de Artesanía del Palau de Mar (p128).

➡ **Beach Action** From June to September, head to the *chiringuitos* for cold drinks and festive ambience.

Getting There & Away

➡ **Foot** La Rambla and Via Laietana are the main pedestrian access points across busy Ronda del Litoral.

➡ **Metro** Drassanes (Línia 3) services Port Vell; Línia 4 stops at Barceloneta, Ciutadella Vila Olímpica (for Port Olímpic) and El Maresme Fòrum (for Parc del Fòrum).

Lonely Planet's Top Tip

If you'd like to explore the sea and the mountains in the same day, take advantage of the Transbordador Aeri (p122), which whisks passengers from Barceloneta up to Montjuïc in a rather vintage-looking cable car. The tower also has a top-end restaurant, a fine destination in its own right.

✖ Best Places to Eat

➡ Els Pescadors (p126)
➡ Can Majó (p124)
➡ Maians (p124)
➡ La Cova Fumada (p124)
➡ Torre d'Alta Mar (p124)

For reviews, see p124 ➡

☕ Best Places to Drink

➡ Xampanyeria Can Paixano (p126)
➡ Absenta (p127)
➡ Ké? (p127)
➡ Opium Mar (p127)

For reviews, see p126 ➡

◉ Best Sights

➡ Barceloneta's beaches (p121)
➡ Museu Marítim (p120)
➡ Museu d'Història de Catalunya (p121)
➡ L'Aquàrium (p121)
➡ Transbordador Aeri (p122)

For reviews, see p120 ➡

TOP SIGHTS
MUSEU MARÍTIM

Venice had its Arsenal and Barcelona the Reials Drassanes (Royal Shipyards), from which Don Juan of Austria's flagship galley was launched to lead a joint Spanish-Venetian fleet into the momentous Battle of Lepanto against the Turks in 1571.

These mighty Gothic shipyards are not as extensive as their Venetian counterparts but they're an extraordinary piece of civilian architecture nonetheless. Today the broad arches shelter the Museu Marítim, the city's seafaring-history museum and one of the most fascinating museums in town.

The shipyards were, in their heyday, among the greatest in Europe. Begun in the 13th century and completed by 1378, the long, arched bays (the highest arches reach 13m) once sloped off as slipways directly into the water, which lapped the seaward side of the Drassanes until at least the end of the 18th century.

Replica of Don Juan of Austria's Flagship

The centre of the shipyards is dominated by a full-sized replica (made in the 1970s) of Don Juan of Austria's flagship. A clever audiovisual display aboard the vessel brings to life the ghastly existence of the slaves, prisoners and volunteers (!) who, at full steam, could haul this vessel along at 9 knots. They remained chained to their seats, four to an oar, at all times. Here they worked, drank (fresh water was stored below decks, where the infirmary was also located), ate, slept and went to the loo. You could smell a galley like this from miles away.

Exhibitions

Fishing vessels, old navigation charts, models and dioramas of the Barcelona waterfront make up the rest of this engaging museum. Temporary exhibitions are also held (an intriguing show on the centennial of the Titanic was held here in 2012). The museum was being largely overhauled at the time of writing, and should continue through 2013. When it reopens, visitors will encounter a greatly expanded collection with multimedia exhibits evoking more of Spain's epic history on the high seas. While this work continues, only a limited selection of the museum's objects can be seen.

Ictíneo

The pleasant museum **cafe** offers courtyard seating and a small assortment of bites, as well as a decent *menú de mediodía* (set-price menu) at lunchtime. Also in the courtyard, you can have a look at a swollen replica of the Ictíneo, one of the world's first submarines. It was invented and built in 1858 by Catalan polymath Narcis Monturiol, and was operated by hand-cranked propellers turned by friends of Monturiol who accompanied him on dozens of successful short dives (two hours maximum) in the harbour. He later developed an even larger submarine powered by a combustion engine that allowed it to dive to 30m and remain submerged for seven hours. Despite impressive demonstrations to awestruck crowds he never attracted the interest of the navy, and remains largely forgotten today.

DON'T MISS...

➡ The replica of Don Juan of Austria's flagship

➡ Temporary exhibitions

➡ Ictíneo

➡ The courtyard cafe

PRACTICALITIES

➡ Map p296

➡ ☏93 342 99 20

➡ www.mmb.cat

➡ Avinguda de les Drassanes

➡ adult/child under 7yr/senior & student €2.50/free/1.25, 3-8pm Sun free

➡ ⊘10am-8pm

➡ MDrassanes

A series of pleasant beaches stretch northeast from Port Olímpic. They are largely artificial, but this doesn't stop an estimated seven million bathers from piling in every year!

The southernmost beach, **Platja de la Nova Icària**, is the busiest. Behind it, across the Avinguda del Litoral highway, is the Plaça dels Campions, site of the rusting three-tiered platform used to honour medallists in the sailing events of the 1992 games. Much of the athletes' housing-turned-apartments are in the blocks immediately behind Carrer de Salvador Espriu.

The next beach is **Platja de Bogatell**. Just in from the beach is the **Cementiri de L'Est**, circa 1773. Its central monument commemorates the victims of a yellow-fever epidemic that swept across Barcelona in 1821. The cemetery is full of bombastic family memorials, but a disquieting touch is the sculpture El Petó de la Mort (The Kiss of Death), in which a winged skeleton kisses a young lifeless body.

Platja de la Mar Bella (with its brief nudist strip and sailing school) and **Platja de la Nova Mar Bella** follow, leading into the new residential and commercial waterfront strip, the Front Marítim, part of the Diagonal Mar project in the Fòrum district. It is fronted by the last of these artificial beaches to be created, **Platja del Llevant**.

DON'T MISS...

➡ The vibrant bustle of Platja de la Nova Icària

➡ The poignant El Petó de la Mort sculpture in the Cementiri de L'Est

PRACTICALITIES

➡ Map p304

➡ 🚌36 or 41, Ⓜ Ciutadella Vila Olímpic, Bogatell, Llacuna or Selva de Mar

⊙ SIGHTS

⊙ Port Vell & Barceloneta

MUSEU MARÍTIM   MUSEUM
See p120.

L'AQUÀRIUM   AQUARIUM
Map p302 (📞93 221 74 74; www.aquariumbcn.com; Moll d'Espanya; adult/child €18/13, dive €300; ⊙9.30am-11pm Jul & Aug, to 9pm Sep-Jun, dive 9.30am-2pm Wed, Fri & Sat; Ⓜ Drassanes) It is hard not to shudder at the sight of a shark gliding above you, displaying its toothy, wide-mouthed grin. But this, the 80m shark tunnel, is the highlight of one of Europe's largest aquariums. It has the world's best Mediterranean collection and plenty of colourful fish from as far off as the Red Sea, the Caribbean and the Great Barrier Reef. All up, some 11,000 fish (including a dozen sharks) of 450 species reside here.

Back in the shark tunnel, which you reach after passing a series of themed fish tanks with everything from bream to sea horses, various species of shark (white tip, sand tiger, bonnethead, black tip, nurse and sand-bar) flit around you, along with a host of other critters, from flapping rays to bloated sunfish. An interactive zone, Planeta Agua, is host to a family of Antarctic penguins and a tank of rays that you watch close up.

Divers with a valid dive certificate may dive in the main tank with the sharks.

MUSEU D'HISTÒRIA DE CATALUNYA   MUSEUM
Map p302 (Museum of Catalonian History; 📞93 225 47 00; www.mhcat.net; Plaça de Pau Vila 3; adult/child permanent exhibition only €4/3, permanent & temporary exhibitions €5/4, 1st Sun of month free ; ⊙10am-7pm Tue & Thu-Sat, to 8pm Wed, to 2.30pm Sun; Ⓜ Barceloneta) The **Palau de Mar** (Map p302) building facing the harbour once served as warehouses, but was transformed in the 1990s. Inside is the Museu d'Història de Catalunya, something of a local patriotic statement, but interesting nonetheless.

The permanent display covers the 2nd and 3rd floors, taking you from the Stone Age through to the early 1980s. It is a busy hotchpotch of dioramas, artefacts, videos, models, documents and interactive bits: all up, an entertaining exploration of 2000 years of Catalan history.

WORTH A DETOUR

EXPLORING CATALAN IMMIGRATION

The **Museu d'Història de la Immigració de Catalunya** (☑93 381 26 06; www.mhic.net; Carretera de Mataró 124; ⏰10am-2pm & 5-8pm Tue & Thu, 10am-2pm Wed, Fri & Sat ; Ⓜ Verneda) is dedicated to the history of immigration in Catalonia. The star piece of this museum is a wagon of the train known as El Sevillano, which trundled between Andalucía and Catalonia in the 1950s, jammed with migrants on an all-stops trip that often lasted more than 30 hours! The one-room exhibition in the former country house Can Serra (now surrounded by light industry, ring roads and warehouses) contains a display of photos, text (in Catalan) and various documents and objects that recall the history of immigration to Catalonia from the 19th century on. There's also an engaging video with images of migrant life decades ago and today.

See how the Romans lived, listen to Arab poetry from the time of the Muslim occupation of the city, peer into the dwelling of a Dark Ages family in the Pyrenees, try to mount a knight's horse or lift a suit of armour.

When you have had enough of all this, descend into a civil-war air-raid shelter, watch a video in Catalan on post-Franco Catalonia or head upstairs to the first-rate rooftop restaurant and cafe, **1881**.

The temporary exhibitions are often as interesting as the permanent display. Outside the museum, you'll find a string of elegant open-air restaurants serving up classic seafood dishes.

TRANSBORDADOR AERI   CABLE CAR
Map p302 (www.telefericodebarcelona.com; Passeig Escullera; 1 way/return €10/15; ⏰11am-7pm, closed Jan–mid-Feb; Ⓜ Barceloneta, 🚌17, 39 or 64) This cable car strung across the harbour to Montjuïc provides a eagle-eye view of the city. The cabins float between the Torre de Sant Sebastià (in La Barceloneta) and Miramar (Montjuïc), with a midway stop at the Torre de Jaume I in front of the World Trade Center. At the top of the Torre de Sant Sebastià is a spectacularly located restaurant, Torre d'Alta Mar.

PAILEBOT DE SANTA EULÀLIA   SHIP
(Moll de la Fusta; adult/child incl Museu Marítim €4/free; ⏰noon-7.30pm Tue-Fri, 10am-7pm Sat & Sun; Ⓜ Drassanes) This 1918 three-mast schooner, restored by the Museu Marítim, is moored along the palm-lined promenade Moll de la Fusta. You can see it perfectly well without going aboard, and there's not an awful lot to behold below decks. On occasion it sets sail for demonstration trips up and down the coast.

ESGLÉSIA DE SANT
MIQUEL DEL PORT   CHURCH
Map p302 (☑93 221 65 50; Plaça de la Barceloneta; ⏰7am-1.30pm Mon-Fri, 8am-1.30pm Sat; Ⓜ Barceloneta) Finished in 1755, this sober baroque church was the first building completed in La Barceloneta. Built low so that the cannon in the then Ciutadella fort could fire over it if necessary, it bears images of St Michael (Miquel) and two other saints considered protectors of the Catalan fishing fleet: Sant Elm and Santa Maria de Cervelló.

Just behind the church is the bustling marketplace, worth an early-morning browse. Ferdinand Lesseps, the French engineer who designed the Suez Canal, did a stint as France's consul-general in Barcelona and lived in the house to the right of the church.

⊙ Port Olímpic, El Poblenou & El Fòrum

TORRE AGBAR   ARCHITECTURE
Map p304 (☑93 342 21 29; www.torreagbar.com; Avinguda Diagonal 225; Ⓜ Glòries) Barcelona's very own cucumber-shaped tower, Jean

LOCAL KNOWLEDGE

BURYING THE PAST

Buried beneath the concrete expanses, bathing zone and marina created in El Fòrum lies the memory of more than 2000 people executed in the fields of Camp de la Bota between 1936 and 1952, most of them under Franco from 1939 onward. To their memory, *Fraternitat* (Brotherhood), a sculpture by Miquel Navarro, stands on Rambla de Prim.

Nouvel's luminous Torre Agbar (which houses the city water company's headquarters), is the most daring addition to Barcelona's skyline since the first towers of La Sagrada Família went up. Completed in 2005, it shimmers at night in shades of midnight blue and lipstick red. Unfortunately, you can only enter the foyer on the ground floor, frequently used to host temporary exhibitions on water-related topics.

PARC DEL CENTRE DEL POBLENOU   PARK

Map p304 (Avinguda Diagonal; ⊙10am-sunset; MPoblenou) Barcelona is sprinkled with parks whose principal element is cement, and Jean Nouvel's Parc del Centre del Poblenou, with its stylised metal seats and items of statuary, is no exception. However, the park's Gaudí-inspired cement walls are increasingly covered by sprawling bougainvillea and, inside, some 1000 trees of mostly Mediterranean species are complemented by thousands of smaller bushes and plants. Nouvel's idea is that the trees, sustained by local ground water, will eventually form a natural canopy over the park.

EL FÒRUM   NEIGHBOURHOOD

Map p304 (☑93 356 10 50; ⊙Zona de Banys 11am-8pm summer, amusement park 11am-2.30pm & 5-9pm Sat & Sun Jun-Sep; MEl Maresme Fòrum) Where before there was wasteland, half-abandoned factories and a huge sewage-treatment plant in the city's northeast corner, there are now high-rise apartment blocks, luxury hotels, a marina (Port Fòrum), a shopping mall and a conference centre.

The most striking element is the eerily blue, triangular *2001: A Space Odyssey*-style **Edifici Fòrum** building by Swiss architects Herzog & de Meuron. The navy blue raised facades look like sheer cliff faces, with angular crags cut into them as if by divine laser. Grand strips of mirror create fragmented reflections of the sky.

Next door, Josep Lluís Mateo's **Centre de Convencions Internacional de Barcelona** (CCIB) has capacity for 15,000 delegates. The huge space around the two buildings is used for major outdoor events, such as concerts (eg during the Festes de la Mercè) and the Feria de Abril.

A 300m stroll east from the Edifici Fòrum is the **Zona de Banys**, with kayaks and bikes available for rent, the option to learn diving, and other activities. This tranquil seawater swimming area was won

READING & PLAYING ON THE BEACH

From July to September, the city sets up several small lending libraries on the beach. These are free for use, and even tourists can take part. You'll find magazines, newspapers and a small foreign-language selection among the Spanish titles. It happens in two places: at **El Centre de la Platja** (Passeig Marítim de la Barceloneta 25; ⊙10am-7pm Mon-Sat, 11am-2pm Sun Jul-Sep; MCiutadella or Vila Olímpica), located underneath the boardwalk, just up from the Parc de la Barceloneta, and at **l'Espigó de Bac de Roda jetty** (⊙11am-2pm & 3-7pm Mon-Fri Jul-Sep; MPoblenou) near Platja de la Mar Bella.

At the same locations, you can also hire out frisbees, volleyballs and nets, beach rackets and balls and *petanque* games; for the kiddies, you'll find buckets, spades and watering cans. All you need to hire out the books or gear is your ID.

from the sea by the creation of massive cement-block dykes. At its northern end, like a great rectangular sunflower, an enormous photovoltaic panel turns its face up to the sun to power the area with solar energy. Along with another set of solar panels in the form of porticoes, it generates enough electricity for 1000 households. Just behind it spreads **Port Fòrum**, Barcelona's third marina. The area is unified by an undulating esplanade and walkways (with wheelchair access) that are perfect for walking, bikes and skateboards. In summer, a weekend **amusement park** sets up with all the usual suspects: rides, shooting galleries, snack stands, inflatable castles and dodgem cars.

The **Parc de Diagonal Mar**, designed by Enric Miralles, contains pools, fountains, a didactic botanical walk (with more than 30 species of trees and other plants) and modern sculptures.

MUSEU BLAU   MUSEUM

Map p304 (Blue Museum; ☑93 256 60 02; Parc del Fòrum; adult/child €6/2.70; ⊙10am-7pm Tue-Fri, to 8pm Sat & Sun; MEl Maresme Fòrum) Set inside the vaguely futuristic Edifici Fòrum, the Museu Blau, which opened in 2011, takes visitors on a journey all across the natural world. Multimedia and interactive exhibits explore topics like the history of evolution, earth's formation and the great scientists who have helped shaped human knowledge. There are also specimens from the animal, plant and mineral kingdoms – plus dinosaur skeletons – all rather dramatically set amid the sprawling 9000 sq metres of exhibition space. There's also a 'science nest' (open weekends only), where kids can take part in hands-on activities. Science geeks of all ages will enjoy spending a few hours here.

EATING

✖ Port Vell & Barceloneta

In the Maremàgnum complex on the Moll d'Espanya you can eat close to the water's edge at a handful of fun, if fairly slapdash, joints. For good food and atmosphere, head around to La Barceloneta, the lanes of which bristle with everything from good-natured, noisy tapas bars to upmarket seafood restaurants. Almost everything shuts on Sunday and Monday evenings.

CAN MAJÓ   SEAFOOD €€
Map p302 (☑93 221 54 55; Carrer del Almirall Aixada 23; mains €18-24; ☺lunch & dinner Tue-Sat, lunch Sun; ☐45, 57, 59, 64 or 157, MBarceloneta) Virtually on the beach (with tables outside in summer), Can Majó has a long and steady reputation for fine seafood, particularly its rice dishes and bountiful *suquets* (fish stews). The *bollabessa de peix i marisc* (fish and seafood bouillabaisse) is succulent. Or try a big *graellada* (mixed seafood grill). Sit outside and admire the beach goers.

MAIANS   TAPAS €
Map p302 (Carrer de Sant Carles 28; tapas €4-6; ☺Wed-Sun; MBarceloneta) This tiny jovial bar and eatery in Maians serves excellent tapas to a hip, largely neighbourhood crowd. Highlights include the not-to-be-missed *cazón en adobo* (marinated fried dogfish) and *mejillones a la marinera* (mussels in a rich tomato broth) followed by hearty *arroz negra* (paella with cuttlefish).

LA COVA FUMADA   TAPAS €
Map p302 (☑93 221 40 61; Carrer de Baluard 56; tapas €3-6; ☺9am-3.20pm Mon-Wed, 9am-3.20pm & 6-8.20pm Thu & Fri, 9am-1.20pm Sat ; MBarceloneta) There's no sign and few tourists in sight, but this tiny, buzzing family-run tapas spot always packs in a crowd. The secret? Mouth-watering *pulpo* (octopus), *calamar*, *sardinias* and 15 or so other small plates cooked up to perfection in the small open kitchen near the door. The *bombas* (potato and ham croquettes served with *ali-oli*, a mixture of crushed garlic and olive oil) and grilled *carxofes* (artichokes) are good, but everything is amazingly fresh. The restaurant doesn't even have a fridge – seafood comes straight from market to table.

TORRE D'ALTA MAR   MEDITERRANEAN €€€
Map p302 (☑93 221 00 07; www.torredealtamar. com; Torre de Sant Sebastià; mains around €30; ☺lunch & dinner Tue-Sat, dinner Sun & Mon; ☐17, 39, 57 or 64, MBarceloneta) Head 75m skyward to the top of the Torre de Sant Sebastià and take a ringside seat for magnificent city and waterfront views while dining on first-rate seafood. Menu hits include creamy rice with grilled prawns; scallops with artichoke, asparagus and ham; and roasted monkfish. Prices are steep (a multicourse lunch runs €48) and would seem poor value apart from the fine vistas.

CAN ROS   SEAFOOD €€
Map p302 (☑93 221 45 79; Carrer del Almirall Aixada 7; mains €16-28; ☺Tue-Sun; ☐45, 57, 59, 64 or 157, MBarceloneta) The fifth generation is now at the controls of this immutable seafood favourite, which first opened in 1911. In a restaurant where the decor is a reminder of simpler times, there's a straightforward guiding principle: serve juicy fresh fish cooked with a light touch. Can Ros also does a rich *arròs a la marinera* (seafood rice), *fideuà* (similar to paella, but using vermicelli noodles as the base) with shrimp and clams and a mixed seafood platter for two.

RESTAURANT 7 PORTES   SEAFOOD €€
Map p302 (☑93 319 30 33; www.7portes.com; Passeig d'Isabel II 14; mains €14-28; ☺1pm-1am; MBarceloneta) Founded in 1836 as a cafe and converted into a restaurant in 1929, this is a classic. It exudes an old-world atmosphere with its wood panelling, tiles, mirrors and plaques naming some of the famous – such as Orson Welles – who have passed through. Paella is the specialty, or go for the surfeit of seafood in the *gran plat de marisc* (literally 'big plate of seafood'), big enough for two.

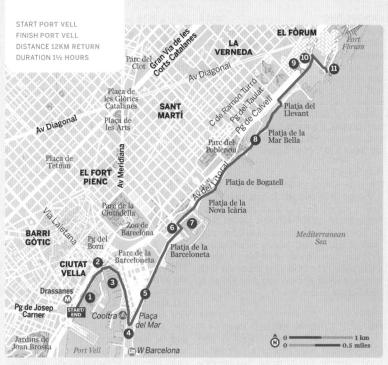

START PORT VELL
FINISH PORT VELL
DISTANCE 12KM RETURN
DURATION 1½ HOURS

Neighbourhood Bike-Ride
The New Barcelona

This bike tour takes in boardwalks, beaches, sculpture and architecture along Barcelona's ever-changing waterfront. It's a flat and safe ride along a dedicated bike path separate from traffic – though watch out for pedestrians. There are several convenient bike and scooter hires nearby, including BarcelonaBiking.com (p263) and Cooltra (p263).

With Columbus at your back make your way northeast along the waterfront. Keep an eye out for the three-mast schooner, **1 Pailebot de Sant Eulàlia**, built in 1918.

Another 400m up the road, you'll pass the colourful **2 Barcelona Head** sculpture by US pop artist Roy Lichtenstein.

As you make your way along the **3 Marina**, you may have to dismount amid the throng of strollers and open-air restaurants.

Hop back on and pedal to the Plaça del Mar, which sports an elegant sculpture entitled **4 Homenatge als Nedadors** (Homage to the Swimmers).

Follow the crowds north, past another well-known sculpture, the **5 Homenatge a la Barceloneta**, which commemorates the old-fashioned shacks that once lined the beach.

Cycle another kilometre and you'll pass beneath the copper-hued **6 Peix** (Fish) sculpture designed by Frank Gehry.

Next up is the marina of **7 Port Olímpic**, which is lined on both sides by popular back-to-back restaurants and bars. From here you'll pass the city's **8 beaches**, which in summer teem with snack-bars-cum-cocktail-bars.

It's another 2.5km or so to the end, where you'll find the **9 Parc del Fòrum**. Dominating this empty plaza is the rather harsh-looking sculpture **10 Fraternitat**, dedicated to hundreds executed here during the Franco years.

The protected bathing area **11 Zona de Banys** is a popular summer attraction for families. Just behind it looms the giant solar panel that powers the area.

VASO DE ORO
TAPAS €

Map p302 (Carrer de Balboa 6; tapas €5-9; ☺10am-midnight; Ⓜ Barceloneta) Always packed, this narrow bar gathers a festive, beer-swilling crowd who come for fantastic tapas. Fast-talking, white-jacketed waiters will serve up a few quick quips with your plates of grilled *gambes* (prawns), *foie a la plancha* (grilled liver pâté) or *solomillo* (sirloin) chunks. Want something a little different to drink? Ask for a *flauta cincuenta* – half lager and half dark beer.

CAN MAÑO
SPANISH €

Map p302 (Carrer del Baluard 12; mains €8-12; ☺Mon-Sat; Ⓜ Barceloneta) It may look like a dive, but you'll need to be prepared to wait before being squeezed in at a packed table for a raucous night of *raciones* (larger portions of tapa dishes; posted on a board at the back) over a bottle of *turbio* – a cloudy white plonk. The seafood is abundant with first-rate squid, shrimp and fish served at rock-bottom prices.

BITÁCORA
TAPAS €

Map p302 (Carrer de Balboa 1; tapas €4-8; ☺10am-11pm Mon-Fri, to 5pm Sat; Ⓜ Barceloneta) This youthful little gem is a neighbourhood favourite for its simple but congenial ambience and well-priced tapas plates, which come in ample portions. There's also a small hidden terrace in back. Top picks: *calamares, boquerones* (anchovies), *gambas* (shrimp) and *vedella amb rulo de cabra* (veal with goat cheese).

🍴 Port Olímpic, El Poblenou & El Fòrum

The Port Olímpic marina is lined on two sides by dozens of restaurants and tapas bars, popular in spring and summer but mostly underwhelming. A more upmarket series of places huddles at the northeast end of Platja de la Barceloneta – it's hard to beat the sand, sea and palm tree backdrop. Otherwise, the search for culinary curios will take you behind the scenes in El Poblenou, where a few nuggets glitter.

TOP CHOICE ELS PESCADORS
SEAFOOD €€

Map p304 (☎93 225 20 18; www.elspescadors. com; Plaça de Prim 1; mains €16-28; ☺daily; Ⓜ Poblenou) Set on a picturesque square lined with low houses and *bella ombre* trees

long ago imported from South America, this bustling family restaurant continues to serve some of the city's great seafood-and-rice dishes. There are three dining areas inside: two quite modern, while the main one preserves its old tavern flavour. Sitting outside is better. All the products – fish, meat and vegetables – are trucked in fresh from various parts of Catalonia.

EL CANGREJO LOCO
SEAFOOD €€

Map p304 (☎93 221 05 33; www.elcangrejoloco. com; Moll de Gregal 29-30; mains €13-25, menú del día €25; ☺daily; Ⓜ Ciutadella Vila Olímpica) Of the hive of eating activity along the docks of Port Olímpic, the 'Mad Crab' is among the best. Fish standards, such as *bacallà* (cod) and *rap* (monkfish), are served in various guises and melt in the mouth. The rich *paella de llamàntol* (lobster paella) is superb.

XIRINGUITO D'ESCRIBÀ
SEAFOOD €€

Map p304 (☎93 221 07 29; www.escriba.es; Ronda Litoral 42; mains €18-22; ☺lunch daily year-round, 8-11.30pm Thu-Sat Apr-Sep; Ⓜ Llacuna) The clan that brought you Escribà sweets and pastries also operates one of Barcelona's most popular waterfront seafood eateries. This is one of the few places where one person can order from a selection of paella and *fideuà* (normally reserved for a minimum of two people). You can also choose from a selection of Escribà pastries for dessert – worth the trip alone.

🍷 DRINKING & NIGHTLIFE

🍷 Port Vell & Barceloneta

The northeastern end of the beach on the Barceloneta waterfront near Port Olímpic is a pleasant corner of evening chic that takes on a balmy, almost Caribbean air in the warmer months. A selection of restaurant-lounges and trendy bar-clubs vies for your attention. Several other attractive options are scattered about away from this core of night-time entertainment.

XAMPANYERIA CAN PAIXANO
WINE BAR

Map p302 (☎93 310 08 39; Carrer de la Reina Cristina 7; tapas €3-6; ☺9am-10.30pm Mon-Sat, to 1pm Sun; Ⓜ Barceloneta) This lofty old champagne bar has long been on a winning formula. The standard poison is bubbly rosé in elegant little glasses, combined with bite-sized *bocadillos* (filled rolls). This place is jammed to the rafters, and elbowing your way to the bar to ask harried staff for menu items can be a titanic struggle.

ABSENTA
BAR

Map p302 (Carrer de Sant Carles 36; MBarceloneta) Decorated with old paintings, vintage lamps and curious sculpture (including a dangling butterfly woman and face-painted TVs), this whimsical and creative drinking den takes its liquor seriously. Stop in for the house-made vermouth or for more bite try one of many absinthes on hand. Absenta gathers a hipsterish but easygoing crowd.

KÉ?
BAR

Map p302 (Carrer del Baluard 54; ⊙11am-2am; MBarceloneta) An eclectic and happy crowd hangs about this hippie-ish little bar near Barceloneta's market. Pull up a padded 'keg chair' or grab a seat on one of the worn lounges in back and join in the animated conversation wafting out over the street.

OPIUM MAR
CLUB

Map p302 (☑902 267486; www.opiummar.com; Passeig Marítim de la Barceloneta 34; ⊙8pm-6am; MCiutadella Vila Olímpica) This seaside dance place has a spacious dance floor that attracts a mostly foreign crowd. It only begins to fill from about 3am and is best in summer, when you can spill onto a terrace overlooking the beach. The beachside outdoor section also works as a chilled restaurant-cafe.

CDLC
LOUNGE

Map p302 (www.cdlcbarcelona.com; Passeig Marítim de la Barceloneta 32; ⊙noon-3am; MCiutadella Vila Olímpica) Seize the night by the scruff at the Carpe Diem Lounge Club, where you can lounge in Asian-inspired surrounds. Ideal for a slow warm-up before heading to the nearby clubs. You can come for the food or wait until about midnight, when they roll up the tables and the DJs and dancers take full control.

BAR LEO
BAR

Map p302 (Carrer de Sant Carles 34; ⊙noon-9.30pm; MBarceloneta) Bar Leo is a hole-in-the-wall drinking spot plastered with images of late Andalucian singer and heartthrob Bambino, and a jukebox mostly dedicated to flamenco. For a youthful, almost entirely *barcelonin* crowd, Bar Leo is it! It's liveliest on weekends.

SANTA MARTA
BAR

Map p302 (Carrer de Guitert 60; ⊙10.30am-7pm Sun, Mon, Wed & Thu, to 10pm Fri & Sat; ☐45, 57, 59 & 157, MBarceloneta) This chilled bar just back from the beach attracts a garrulous mix of locals and expats, who come for light meals, beers and prime people-watching at one of the outdoor tables near the boardwalk. It has some tempting food too: a mix of local and Italian items, with a range of *bocatas* (filled rolls).

SHÔKO
LOUNGE

Map p302 (www.shoko.biz; Passeig Marítim de la Barceloneta 36; ⊙noon-3am Tue-Sun; MCiutadella Vila Olímpica) This stylish restaurant, club and beachfront bar brings in a touch of the Far East via potted bamboo, Japanese electro and Asian-Med fusion cuisine. As the food is cleared away, Shôko transforms into a deep-grooving nightspot with international DJs like Groove Armada and Felix da Housecat spinning for the beautiful crowd. The open-sided beachfront lounge is a popular spot for a sundowner.

CATWALK
CLUB

Map p302 (☑93 224 07 40; www.clubcatwalk.net; Carrer de Ramon Trias Fargas 2-4; admission €15-18; ⊙midnight-6am Thu-Sun; MCiutadella Vila Olímpica) A well-dressed crowd piles in here for good house music, occasionally mellowed down with more body-hugging electro, R&B, hip hop and funk. Alternatively, you can sink into a fat lounge for a quiet tipple and whisper. Popular local DJ Jekey leads the way most nights.

⬤ Port Olímpic, El Poblenou & El Fòrum

Several options present themselves along the coast. The line-up of raucous bars along the marina at Port Olímpic is one. More chilled are the beach bars. In deepest Poblenou you'll find some clubs, among them one of Barcelona's classics, Razzmatazz.

RAZZMATAZZ
CLUB

Map p304 (☑93 320 82 00; www.salarazzmatazz.com; Carrer de Pamplona 88; admission €15-30; ⊙midnight-3.30am Thu, to 5.30am Fri & Sat; MMarina or Bogatell) Bands from far and wide occasionally create scenes of near hysteria in this, one of the city's classic live-music and clubbing venues. Bands can appear throughout the week (check the website), with different start times. On weekends the live music then gives way to club sounds.

Five different clubs in this huge post-industrial space attract people of all dance persuasions and ages. The main space, the Razz Club, is a haven for the latest international rock and indie acts. The Loft does house and electro, while the Pop Bar offers anything from garage to soul. The Lolita room is the land of techno pop and deep house, and upstairs in the Rex Room guys and girls sweat it out to high-rhythm electro-rock.

⭐ ENTERTAINMENT

MONASTERIO   LIVE MUSIC
Map p302 (☎616 287197; Passeig d'Isabel II, 4; ◷9pm-2.30am; ⓜBarceloneta) Wander downstairs to the brick vaults of this jamming basement music den. There's a little of everything, from jazz on Sunday night to blues jams on Thursdays, rock and roll on Tuesdays and up-and-coming singer/songwriters on Mondays. Monasterio has Murphy's on tap, along with several other imported beers.

YELMO CINES ICÀRIA   CINEMA
Map p304 (☎93 221 75 85; www.yelmocines.es; Carrer de Salvador Espriu 61; ⓜCiutadella Vila Olímpica) This vast cinema complex screens movies in the original language on 15 screens, making for plenty of choice. Aside from the screens, you'll find several cheerful eateries, bars and the like to keep you occupied before and after the movies.

 SHOPPING

Aside from several weekend markets and the mall mayhem of Maremàgnum, there aren't many shopping options along the waterfront.

MAREMÀGNUM   MALL
Map p302 (www.maremagnum.es; Moll d'Espanya 5; ◷10am-10pm; ⓜDrassanes) Created out of largely abandoned docks, this buzzing shopping centre, with its bars, restaurants and cinemas, is pleasant enough for a stroll virtually in the middle of the old harbour. The usual labels are on hand, including the youthful Spanish chain Mango, mega-retailer H&M and eye-catching fashions from Barcelona-based Desigual. Football fans will be drawn to the paraphernalia at FC Barcelona. The big news is that shops here open on Sundays, pretty much unheard of anywhere else in the city.

WATERFRONT MARKETS

On weekends, Port Vell springs to life with a handful of markets selling a mix of antiques, contemporary art and crafts at key points along the waterfront.

At the base of La Rambla, the small **Port Antic** (Map p302; Plaça del Portal de la Pau; ◷10am-8pm Sat & Sun; ⓜDrassanes) market is a requisite stop for strollers and antique hunters. Here you'll find old photographs, frames, oil paintings, records, shawls, cameras, vintage toys and other odds and ends. Go early to beat the crowds.

Near the Palau de Mar, you'll find **Feria de Artesanía del Palau de Mar** (Map p302; Moll del Dipòsit; ◷10am-8pm Sat & Sun; ⓜBarceloneta), with artisans selling a range of crafty items, including jewellery, graphic T-shirts, handwoven hats, fragrant candles and soaps, scarves and decorative items. In July and August the market runs daily.

Take a stroll along the pedestrian-only Rambla de Mar to reach the weekend art fair **Mercado de Pintores** (Map p302; Passeig d'Ítaca; ◷10am-8pm Sat & Sun; ⓜDrassanes), with a broad selection of paintings both collectable and rather forgettable.

🏃 SPORTS & ACTIVITIES

If gazing at the deep blue Mediterranean leaves you yearning for something a bit more immersive, there are plenty of ways to experience the life aquatic: joining a harbour cruise, taking a sailing course, or swimming laps in one of several athletic clubs on the waterfront.

CLUB NATACIÓ
ATLÈTIC-BARCELONA   SWIMMING

Map p302 (www.cnab.cat; Plaça del Mar; adult/child €11.20/6.50; ☉7am-11pm Mon-Sat, 8am-8pm Sun; ☐17, 39, 57, 64, Ⓜ Barceloneta) This athletic club has one indoor and two outdoor pools. Of the latter, one is heated for lap swimming in winter. Admission includes use of the gym and private beach access. Membership costs €38 a month, plus €75 joining fee.

POLIESPORTIU MARÍTIM   SWIMMING

Map p302 (www.claror.cat; Passeig Marítim de la Barceloneta 33-35; general admission Mon-Fri €16, Sat, Sun & holidays €19; ☉7am-midnight Mon-Fri, 8am-9pm Sat, 8am-4pm Sun; Ⓜ Ciutadella Vila Olímpica) Water babies will squeal with delight in this *thalassotherapeutic* (seawater therapy) sports centre. In addition to the small pool for lap swimming, there is a labyrinth of hot, warm and freezing-cold spa pools, along with thundering waterfalls for massage relief.

BASE NAUTICA
MUNICIPAL   SAILING, WINDSURFING

Map p304 (☎93 221 04 32; www.basenautica.org; Avinguda de Litoral; Ⓜ Poblenou) Have you come to Barcelona to become a sea dog? If so, head to this place, just back from Platja de la Mar Bella, and enrol in a course in pleasure-boat handling, kayaking (€132 for 10 hours' tuition), windsurfing (€196 for 10 hours' tuition) or catamaran sailing (€229 for 12 hours' tuition).

ORSOM   CRUISE

Map p302 (☎93 441 05 37; www.barcelona-orsom.com; Moll de les Drassanes; adult/child €14/11; ☉Apr-Oct; Ⓜ Drassanes) Aboard a large sailing catamaran, Orsom makes the 90-minute journey past Port Olímpic, the beaches and out to the Fòrum and back. There are three departures per day (four on weekends in July and August), and the last is a jazz cruise, scheduled around sunset. The same company also runs five daily, 50-minute speedboat tours (adult/child €12/8).

LAS GOLONDRINAS   CRUISE

Map p302 (☎93 442 31 06; www.lasgolondrinas.com; Moll de las Drassanes; 35min tour adult/child €6.80/2.60; Ⓜ Drassanes) Golondrinas offers several popular cruises from its dock in front of Mirador de Colom. The 90-minute catamaran tour takes you out past Barceloneta and the beaches to the Forum and back. If you just want a peak at the area around the port, you can opt for the 35-minute excursion to the breakwater and back. Both run frequently throughout the day.

On the Waterfront

Once an industrial eyesore, Barcelona's waterfront was dramatically transformed in the run-up to the 1992 Olympics, when city planners laid down artificial beaches, parks, a long seaside promenade and a host of other development. Marinas, hotels, shopping malls and waterfront bars and restaurants are all part of the scenic new landscape.

Cycling

1 Stretching for over 4km from Barceloneta to Parc del Fòrum, the beachside bike path makes a breezy setting for a spin. Open-air cafes and restaurants are ideal pitstops along the way. Finish up with a swim.

Seafood

2 Scores of outdoor restaurants dot the waterfront, offering a winning combination of market-fresh seafood and unbeatable views. For a classic Catalan dish, try a *suquet* (seafood stew).

Beach Bars

3 From April to October, *chiringuitos* (open-air shacks) arrive on the beach, bringing a tropical air to the city with music, cocktails and a laid-back vibe. Other beachside bars and clubs run year-round and always draw a weekend crowd.

Beaches

4 Barcelona's beaches are a major draw on warm days, when sun-seekers hit the sand for volleyball, football, picnics and refreshing dips in the sea.

Mediterranean Meander

5 You can get a good view of the everchanging waterfront from the deck of a cruise boat or catamaran. Excursion boats regularly take leisurely sails along the coast.

....

Clockwise from top left
1. Homenatge a la Barceloneta (p125) by Rebecca Horns, at Platja de la Barceloneta **2.** Paella at Xiringuito d'Escribà (p126) **3.** Beach bar on Platja de la Barceloneta

La Sagrada Família & L'Eixample

L'ESQUERRA DE L'EIXAMPLE | LA DRETA DE L'EIXAMPLE

Neighbourhood Top Five

1 Seeing history being made at **La Sagrada Família** (p134).

2 Witnessing groundbreaking architecture at **La Pedrera** (p139).

3 Marvelling at the almost-alive, swirling interior of **Casa Batlló** (p140).

4 Deciphering contemporary art at the fascinating **Fundació Antoni Tàpies** (p141).

5 Tracing the timeline of Catalan Modernism at the **Museu del Modernisme Català** (p141).

For more detail of this area, see Maps p306 and p310 ➡

Explore: L'Eixample

In the 1820s, ranks of trees were planted on either side of the road linking Barcelona and the town of Gràcia. Thus was born the Passeig de Gràcia, a strollers' boulevard. L'Eixample's grid streets radiate from the Passeig de Gràcia and are home to the majority of the city's most expensive shops and hotels, a range of eateries and several nightspots. This is the area to head to for Modernista architecture, the best of which – apart from La Sagrada Família – are clustered on or near Passeig de Gràcia. Eating is at the high end (though set-lunch options are available for lower budgets), and the emphasis is on design-led outfits that cater to designer-shopping locals and tourists alike, though there are some notable exceptions.

La Dreta de L'Eixample (The Right Side of L'Eixample), stretching from Passeig de Gràcia to Passeig de Sant Joan and beyond, contains much-desired real estate, although it has a dowdy feel closer to La Sagrada Família. L'Esquerra de L'Eixample (The Left Side of L'Eixample), running southwest from Passeig de Gràcia, changes character several times. The area between Carrer d'Aribau, Passeig de Sant Joan, Avinguda Diagonal and Ronda de Sant Pere has been known since the early 20th century as the Quadrat d'Or (Golden Square) thanks to its high-end shops purveying everything from teak furniture to designer clothes, gourmet nibbles and shoes.

At night L'Esquerra de L'Eixample has its own flavour. From Thursday to Saturday, Carrer d'Aribau becomes a busy nightlife axis. Closer to the Universitat is the heart of the 'Gaixample', a cluster of gay and gay-friendly bars and clubs in an area bounded by Carrer de Balmes and Carrer de Muntaner.

Local Life

➡ **Markets** L'Eixample is all about wealth, but you can find some quirky bargains at the buzzing flea market of Els Encants Vells (p154).

➡ **Garden Concerts** Get a ticket for a local favourite – a summertime garden concert at the beautiful Palau Robert (p154).

➡ *Cava* **Supply** Try some of Barcelona's best *cava*, sold at Xampany (p155) to a loyal local clientele.

Getting There & Away

➡ **Metro** Four Metro lines criss-cross L'Eixample, three stopping at Passeig de Gràcia for La Manzana de la Discordia. Línia 3 stops at Diagonal for La Pedrera, while Línies 2 and 5 stop at Sagrada Família.

➡ **Train** FGC lines from Plaça de Catalunya take you one stop to Provença, in the heart of L'Eixample.

Lonely Planet's Top Tip

L'Eixample's restaurants can be quite pricey, but you can still sample their food at budget prices if you head over for the lunchtime *menú del día* (set menu), which, although simpler in choice, is always good value.

✕ Best Places to Eat

➡ Tapaç 24 (p145)
➡ Can Kenji (p145)
➡ Alkímia (p145)
➡ Cata 1.81 (p147)
➡ Taktika Berri (p148)

For reviews, see p145 ➡

Best Places to Drink

➡ Monvínic (p150)
➡ La Fira (p151)
➡ Les Gens Que J'Aime (p153)
➡ Dry Martini (p151)

For reviews, see p150 ➡

Best Places to Shop

➡ Vinçon (p154)
➡ Els Encants Vells (p154)
➡ El Bulevard dels Antiquaris (p154)
➡ Xampany (p155)

For reviews, see p154 ➡

LA SAGRADA FAMÍLIA & L'EIXAMPLE

TOP SIGHTS
LA SAGRADA FAMÍLIA

If you have time for only one sightseeing outing, this should be it. La Sagrada Família inspires awe by its sheer verticality, and, in the manner of the medieval cathedrals it emulates, it's still under construction after more than 100 years. When completed, the highest tower will be more than half as high again as those that stand today.

A Holy Mission

The Temple Expiatori de la Sagrada Família (Expiatory Temple of the Holy Family) was Antoni Gaudí's all-consuming obsession. Given the commission by a conservative society that wished to build a temple as atonement for the city's sins of modernity, Gaudí saw its completion as his holy mission. As funds dried up, he contributed his own, and in the last years of his life he was never shy of pleading with anyone he thought a likely donor.

Gaudí devised a temple 95m long and 60m wide, able to seat 13,000 people, with a central tower 170m high above the transept (representing Christ) and another 17 of 100m or more. The 12 along the three facades represent the Apostles, while the remaining five represent the Virgin Mary and the four evangelists. With his characteristic dislike for straight lines (there were none in nature, he said), Gaudí gave his towers swelling outlines inspired by the weird peaks of the holy mountain Montserrat outside Barcelona, and encrusted them with a tangle of sculpture that seems an outgrowth of the stone.

At Gaudí's death, only the crypt, the apse walls, one portal and one tower had been finished. Three more towers were added by 1930, completing the northeast (Nativity) facade. In 1936, anarchists burned and smashed the interior, including workshops, plans

DON'T MISS...

➡ The apse, the extraordinary pillars and the stained glass

➡ Nativity Facade

➡ Passion Facade

➡ Museu Gaudí

PRACTICALITIES

➡ Map p306

➡ ☎93 207 30 31

➡ www.sagrada familia.org

➡ Carrer de Mallorca 401

➡ adult/child under 10yr/senior & student €13/free/11

➡ ◷9am-8pm Apr-Sep, to 6pm Oct-Mar

➡ Ⓜ Sagrada Família

and models. Work began again in 1952, but controversy has always clouded progress. Opponents of the continuation of the project claim that the computer models based on what little of Gaudí's plans survived the anarchists' ire have led to the creation of a monster that has little to do with Gaudí's plans and style. It is a debate that appears to have little hope of resolution. Like or hate what is being done, the fascination it awakens is undeniable.

Guesses on when construction might be complete range from the 2020s to the 2040s. Even before reaching that point, some of the oldest parts of the church, especially the apse, have required restoration work.

The Interior & the Apse

Inside, work on roofing over the church was completed in 2010. The roof is held up by a forest of extraordinary angled pillars. As the pillars soar towards the ceiling, they sprout a web of supporting branches, creating the effect of a forest canopy. The tree image is in no way fortuitous – Gaudí envisaged such an effect. Everything was thought through, including the shape and placement of windows to create the mottled effect one would see with sunlight pouring through the branches of a thick forest. The pillars are of four different types of stone. They vary in colour and load-bearing strength, from the soft Montjuïc stone pillars along the lateral aisles through to granite, dark grey basalt and finally burgundy-tinged Iranian porphyry for the key columns at the intersection of the nave and transept. The stained glass, divided in shades of red, blue, green and ochre, creates a hypnotic, magical atmosphere when the sun hits the windows. Tribunes built high above the aisles can host two choirs: the main tribune up to 1300 people and the children's tribune up to 300.

Nativity Facade

The Nativity Facade is the artistic pinnacle of the building, mostly created under Gaudí's personal supervision. You can climb high up inside some of the four towers by a combination of lifts and narrow spiral staircases – a vertiginous experience. Do not climb the stairs if you have cardiac or respiratory problems. The towers are destined to hold tubular bells capable of playing complex music at great volume. Their upper parts are decorated with mosaics spelling out *'Sanctus, Sanctus, Sanctus, Hosanna in Excelsis, Amen, Alleluia'*. Asked why he lavished so much care on the tops of the spires, which no one would see from close up, Gaudí answered: 'The angels will see them.'

Unfinished it may be, but La Sagrada Família attracts around 2.8 million visitors a year and is the most visited monument in Spain. The most significant tourist in recent times was Pope Benedict XVI, who consecrated the church in a huge ceremony in November 2010.

A HIDDEN PORTRAIT

Careful observation of the Passion Facade will reveal a special tribute from sculptor Josep Subirachs to Gaudí. The central sculptural group (below Christ crucified) shows, from right to left, Christ bearing his cross, Veronica displaying the cloth with Christ's bloody image, a pair of soldiers and, watching it all, a man called the evangelist. Subirachs used a rare photo of Gaudí, taken a couple of years before his death, as the model for the evangelist's face.

A TIMELINE

1882 Francesc del Villar is commissioned to construct a neo-Gothic church.

1883 Antoni Gaudí takes over as chief architect, and plans a far more ambitious church to hold 13,000 faithful.

1926 Death of Gaudí; work continues under Domènec Sugrañes. Much of the **apse 1** and **Nativity Facade 2** is complete.

1930 Bell towers 3 of the Nativity Facade completed.

1936 Construction is interrupted by Spanish Civil War; anarchists destroy Gaudí's plans.

1939-40 Architect Francesc de Paula Quintana i Vidal restores the crypt and meticulously reassembles many of Gaudí's lost models, some of which can be seen in the **museum 4**.

1976 Completion of **Passion Facade 5**.

1986-2006 Sculptor Josep Subirachs adds sculptural details to the Passion Facade including the panels telling the story of Christ's last days, amid much criticism for employing a style far removed from what was thought typical of Gaudí.

2000 Central nave vault 6 completed.

2010 Church completely roofed over; Pope Benedict XVI consecrates the church; work begins on a high-speed rail tunnel that will pass beneath the church's **Glory Facade 7**.

2026-2028 Projected completion date.

TOP TIPS

➡ **Light** The best light through the stained-glass windows of the Passion Facade bursts through into the heart of the church in late afternoon.

➡ **Time** Visit at opening time on weekdays and purchase tickets online to avoid the worst of the crowds.

➡ **Views** Head up the Nativity Facade bell towers for the views, as long queues generally await at the Passion Facade towers.

KRZYSZTOF DYDYNSKI/LPI ©

Nativity Facade
Gaudí used plaster casts of local people and even of the occasional corpse from the local morgue as models for the portraits in the Nativity scene.

Spiral staircase

Central nave vault

Apse
Built just after the crypt in mostly neo-Gothic style, it is capped by pinnacles that show a hint of the genius that Gaudí would later deploy in the rest of the church.

MICHELLE CHAPLOW/ALAMY ©

Bell towers
The towers (eight completed) of the three facades represent the 12 Apostles. Lifts whisk visitors up one tower of the Nativity and Passion Facades (the latter gets longer queues) for fine views.

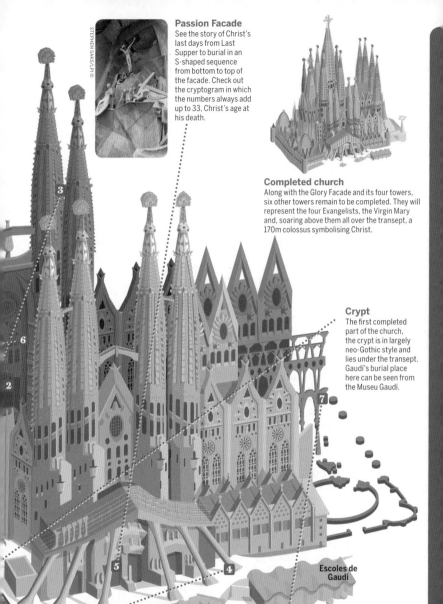

Passion Facade
See the story of Christ's last days from Last Supper to burial in an S-shaped sequence from bottom to top of the facade. Check out the cryptogram in which the numbers always add up to 33, Christ's age at his death.

Completed church
Along with the Glory Facade and its four towers, six other towers remain to be completed. They will represent the four Evangelists, the Virgin Mary and, soaring above them all over the transept, a 170m colossus symbolising Christ.

Crypt
The first completed part of the church, the crypt is in largely neo-Gothic style and lies under the transept. Gaudí's burial place here can be seen from the Museu Gaudí.

Escoles de Gaudí

Museu Gaudí
Jammed with old photos, drawings and restored plaster models that bring Gaudí's ambitions to life, the museum also houses an extraordinarily complex plumb-line device he used to calculate his constructions.

Glory Facade
This will be the most fanciful facade of all, with a narthex boasting 16 hyperboloid lanterns topped by cones that will look something like an organ made of melting ice cream.

Three sections of the portal represent, from left to right, Hope, Charity and Faith. Among the forest of sculpture on the Charity portal you can see, low down, the manger surrounded by an ox, an ass, the shepherds and kings, and angel musicians. Some 30 different species of plant from around Catalonia are reproduced here, and the faces of the many figures are taken from plaster casts done of local people and the occasional one made from corpses in the local morgue!

Directly above the blue stained-glass window is the Archangel Gabriel's Annunciation to Mary. At the top is a green cypress tree, a refuge in a storm for the white doves of peace dotted over it. The mosaic work at the pinnacle of the towers is made from Murano glass, from Venice.

To the right of the facade is the curious Claustre del Roser, a Gothic style mini-cloister tacked on to the outside of the church (rather than the classic square enclosure of the great Gothic church monasteries). Once inside, look back to the intricately decorated entrance. On the lower right-hand side you'll notice the sculpture of a reptilian devil handing a terrorist a bomb. Barcelona was regularly rocked by political violence, and bombings were frequent in the decades prior to the civil war. The sculpture is one of several on the 'temptations of men and women'.

Passion Facade

The southwest Passion Facade, on the theme of Christ's last days and death, was built between 1954 and 1978 based on surviving drawings by Gaudí, with four towers and a large, sculpture-bedecked portal. The sculptor, Josep Subirachs, worked on its decoration from 1986 to 2006. He did not attempt to imitate Gaudí, instead producing angular, controversial images of his own. The main series of sculptures, on three levels, are in an S-shaped sequence, starting with the Last Supper at the bottom left and ending with Christ's burial at the top right. Decorative work on the Passion facade continues even today, as construction of the Glory facade moves ahead.

To the right, in front of the Passion Facade, the Escoles de Gaudí is one of his simpler gems. Gaudí built this as a children's school, creating an original, undulating roof of brick that continues to charm architects to this day. Inside is a re-creation of Gaudí's modest office as it was when he died, and explanations of the geometric patterns and plans at the heart of his building techniques.

Glory Facade

The Glory Facade is under construction and will, like the others, be crowned by four towers – the total of 12 representing the Twelve Apostles. Gaudí wanted it to be the most magnificent facade of the church. Inside will be the narthex, a kind of foyer made up of 16 'lanterns', a series of hyperboloid forms topped by cones. Further decoration will make the whole building a microcosmic symbol of the Christian church, with Christ represented by a massive 170m central tower above the transept, and the five remaining planned towers symbolising the Virgin Mary and the four evangelists.

Museu Gaudí

Open the same times as the church, Museu Gaudí, below ground level, includes interesting material on Gaudí's life and other works, as well as models and photos of La Sagrada Família. You can see a good example of his plumb-line models that showed him the stresses and strains he could get away with in construction. A side hall towards the eastern end of the museum leads to a viewing point above the simple crypt in which the genius is buried. The crypt, where Masses are now held, can also be visited from the Carrer de Mallorca side of the church.

TOP SIGHTS
LA PEDRERA

This undulating beast is another madcap Gaudí masterpiece, built from 1905 to 1910 as a combined apartment and office block. Formally called Casa Milà after the businessman who commissioned it, it is better known as La Pedrera (the Quarry) because of its uneven grey stone facade, which ripples around the corner of Carrer de Provença.

When commissioned by Pere Milà to design this apartment building, Gaudí wanted to top anything else done in L'Eixample. Milà had married the older – and far richer – Roser Guardiola, the widow of Josep Guardiola, and clearly knew how to spend his new wife's money. As Milà was one of the city's first car owners, Gaudí built parking space into this building, this itself a first.

The Fundació Caixa Catalunya has opened the top-floor apartment, attic and roof, together called the Espai Gaudí (Gaudí Space), to visitors. The roof is the most extraordinary element, with its giant chimney pots looking like multicoloured medieval knights. Gaudí wanted to put a tall statue of the Virgin up here, too: when the Milà family said no, fearing it might make the building a target for anarchists, Gaudí resigned from the project in disgust.

One floor below the roof, where you can appreciate Gaudí's taste for parabolic arches, is a modest museum dedicated to his work.

The next floor down is the apartment (El Pis de la Pedrera). It is fascinating to wander around this elegantly furnished home, done up in the style a well-to-do family might have enjoyed in the early 20th century. There are sensuous curves and unexpected touches in everything from light fittings to bedsteads, from door handles to balconies.

DON'T MISS...

➡ The marvellous roof
➡ The apartment
➡ The stone facade

PRACTICALITIES

➡ Casa Milà
➡ Map p310
➡ ☎902 400973
➡ www.fundacio caixacatalunya.es, in Spanish
➡ Carrer de Provença 261-265
➡ adult/child/student €15/7.50/13.50
➡ ⏰9am-8pm Mar-Oct, to 6.30pm Nov-Feb
➡ Ⓜ Diagonal

TOP SIGHTS
CASA BATLLÓ

this is Gaudí at his hallucinatory best: Casa Batlló is one of the strangest residential buildings in Europe. The facade, sprinkled with bits of blue, mauve and green tiles and studded with wave-shaped window frames and balconies, rises to an uneven blue-tiled roof with a solitary tower. Casa Barlló and neighbouring Casa Amatller (p141) and Casa Lleó Morera (p142) comprise La Manzana de la Discordia (the Block of Discord), and together represent Modernisme's eclecticism.

When Gaudí was commissioned to refashion this building, he went to town inside and out. The internal light wells shimmer with tiles of deep sea blue. Gaudí eschewed the straight line, and so the staircase wafts you up to the 1st (main) floor, where the salon looks on to Passeig de Grà-cia. Everything swirls: the ceiling is twisted into a vortex around its sunlike lamp; the doors, window and skylights are dreamy waves of wood and coloured glass. The attic features Gaudí's trademark hyperboloid arches. Twisting tiled chimney pots add a surreal touch to the roof.

Locals know Casa Batlló variously as the *casa dels ossos* (house of bones) or *casa del drac* (house of the dragon). It's easy enough to see why. The balconies look like the bony jaws of some strange beast and the roof represents Sant Jordi (St George) and the dragon – each shiny scale changes colour as you walk around. Each paving piece outside carries stylised images of an octopus and a starfish, designs Gaudí originally cooked up for Casa Batlló.

La Manzana de la Discordia is still known by its Spanish, rather than Catalan, name to preserve a pun on *manzana,* which means 'block' and 'apple'. In Greek mythology, the Apple of Discord was tossed onto Mt Olympus by Eros (Discord), with orders that it be given to the most beautiful goddess, sparking jealousies that were the catalyst for the Trojan War.

DON'T MISS...

➡ The facade and balconies

➡ The swirling interior

➡ The dragon-back roof

PRACTICALITIES

➡ Map p310

➡ 93 216 03 06

➡ www.casabatllo.es

➡ Passeig de Gràcia 43

➡ adult/child under 7yr/student, child 7-18yr & senior €18.15/free/14.55

➡ 9am-8pm

➡ Passeig de Gràcia

SIGHTS

L'Esquerra de L'Eixample

CASA BATLLÓ ARCHITECTURE

See p140.

FUNDACIÓ ANTONI TÀPIES GALLERY

Map p310 (✆93 487 03 15; www.fundaciotapies. org; Carrer d'Aragó 255; adult/child under 16yr €7/5.60; ⊙10am-8pm Tue-Sun; ⓂPasseig de Gràcia) The Fundació Antoni Tàpies is both a pioneering Modernista building (completed in 1885) and the major collection of leading 20th-century Catalan artist Antoni Tàpies. A man known for his esoteric work, Tàpies died in February 2012, aged 88; he leaves behind a powerful range of paintings and a foundation intended to promote contemporary artists.

The building, designed by Domènech i Montaner for the publishing house Editorial Montaner i Simón (run by a cousin of the architect), combines a brick-covered iron frame with Islamic-inspired decoration. Tàpies crowned it with the meanderings of his own mind, a work called *Núvol i Cadira* (Cloud and Chair) that spirals above the building like a storm.

Although it's difficult to understand the art of Antoni Tàpies, it's worth seeing the one-hour documentary on his life, on the top floor, to understand his influences, method and the course of his interesting life. In his work, Tàpies expressed a number of themes, such as left-wing politics and humanitarianism; the practices of Zen meditation and its relationship between nature and insight; incarnation as seen in Christian faith; and art as an alchemy or magic.

He launched the Fundació in 1984 to promote contemporary art, donating a large part of his own work. The collection spans the arc of Tàpies' creations (with more than 800 works) and contributions from other contemporary artists. In the main exhibition area (level 1, upstairs) you can see an ever-changing selection of around 20 of Tàpies' works, from early self-portraits of the 1940s to grand items like *Jersei Negre* (Black Jumper; 2008). Level 2 hosts a small space for temporary exhibitions. Rotating exhibitions take place in the basement levels.

MUSEU DEL MODERNISME CATALÀ MUSEUM

Map p310 (✆93 272 28 96; www.mmcat.cat; Carrer de Balmes 48; adult/child under 5yr/child 5-16yr/student €10/free/5/7; ⊙10am-8pm Mon-Sat, to 3pm Sun; ⓂPasseig de Gràcia) Housed in a Modernista building, the ground floor seems a like a big Modernista furniture showroom. Several items by Antoni Gaudí, including chairs from Casa Batlló and a mirror from Casa Calvet, are supplemented by a host of items by his lesser-known contemporaries, including some typically whimsical, mock medieval pieces by Puig i Cadafalch.

The basement, showing off Modernista traits like mosaic-coated pillars, bare brick vaults and metal columns, is lined with Modernista art, including paintings by Ramon Casas and Santiago Rusiñol, and statues by Josep Llimona and Eusebi Arnau.

FREE **CASA AMATLLER** ARCHITECTURE

Map p310 (✆93 487 72 17; www.amatller.org; Passeig de Gràcia 41; ⊙10am-8pm Mon-Sat, to 3pm Sun, guided tour in English noon Fri, in Catalan & Spanish noon Wed; ⓂPasseig de Gràcia) One of Puig i Cadafalch's most striking bits of Modernista fantasy, Casa Amatller combines Gothic window frames with a stepped gable borrowed from Dutch urban architecture. But the busts and reliefs of dragons, knights and other characters dripping off the main facade are pure caprice.

The pillared foyer and staircase lit by stained glass are like the inside of some romantic castle.

The building was renovated in 1900 for the chocolate baron and philanthropist Antoni Amatller (1851–1910) and it will one day open partly to the public. Renovation due for completion in 2012 – though still continuing at the time of research – will see the 1st (main) floor converted into a museum with period pieces, while the 2nd floor will house the Institut Amatller d'Art Hispanic (Amatller Institute of Hispanic Art).

For now, you can wander into the foyer, admire the staircase and lift, and head through the shop to see the latest temporary exhibition out the back. Depending on the state of renovation, it is also possible to join a 1½-hour guided tour of the 1st floor, with its early-20th-century furniture and decor intact, and Amatller's photo studio.

Amatller was a keen traveller and photographer (his absorbing shots of turn-of-the-20th-century Morocco are occasionally

LA SAGRADA FAMÍLIA & L'EIXAMPLE SIGHTS

show). The tour also includes a tasting of Amatller chocolates in the original kitchen.

CASA LLEÓ MORERA ARCHITECTURE

Map p310 (Passeig de Gràcia 35; MPasseig de Gràcia) Domènech i Montaner's 1905 contribution to La Manzana de la Discordia, with Modernista carving outside and a bright, tiled lobby in which floral motifs predominate, is perhaps the least odd-looking of the three main buildings on the block. If only you could get inside – they are private apartments. The 1st floor is giddy with swirling sculptures, rich mosaics and whimsical decor.

FUNDACIÓN FRANCISCO GODIA GALLERY

Map p310 (☑93 272 31 80; www.fundacionfgodia. org; Carrer de la Diputació 250; adult/child under 5yr/student €6.50/free/3.50; ⊙10am-8pm Mon & Wed-Sun; MPasseig de Gràcia) Francisco Godia (1921–90), head of one of Barcelona's great establishment families, liked fast cars (he came sixth in the 1956 Grand Prix season driving Maseratis) and fine art. An intriguing mix of ceramics and medieval and modern art make up this varied collection.

The gallery is housed in Casa Garriga Nogués, a stunning, carefully restored Modernista residence originally built for a rich banking family by Enric Sagnier in 1902–05.

The ground floor is given over to a display of Godia's driving trophies (and goggles) and a video on his feats behind the wheel, as well as occasional temporary exhibitions.

The art is up the languidly curvaceous marble stairway on the 1st floor and organised along roughly chronological lines across 17 rooms. The first five are given over mostly to Romanesque and Gothic wooden sculptures. Some of these are especially arresting because of their well-preserved colouring. The early-14th-century wood cut of Joseph of Armithea (room 1), with its bright-red pyjamalike outfit, is a case in point. Jaume Huguet is represented in room 5 by *Santa Maria Magdalena,* a bright, Gothic representation of Mary Magdalene dressed in red ermine.

Room 6 is a long and overwhelming rococo room with aqua-green walls and a selection of Godia's extensive ceramics collection, with pieces from all the historic porcelain production centres in Spain (including Manises in Valencia and Talavera de la Reina in Castilla-La Mancha). Admire the fine Modernista stained-glass windows in room 8.

Godia's interests ranged from the Neapolitan baroque painter Luca Giordano to Catalan Modernisme and Valencia's Joaquim Sorolla. Room 17, a gallery around the central staircase, contains several works by Modernista and Noucentista painters, like Ramon Casas, Santiago Rusiñol and Isidre Nonell. There's even a modest Miró.

MUSEU DEL PERFUM MUSEUM

Map p310 (☑93 216 01 21; www.museudelperfum. com; Passeig de Gràcia 39; adult/student & senior €5/3; ⊙10.30am-1.30pm & 4.30-8pm Mon-Fri, 11am-2pm Sat; MPasseig de Gràcia) Housed in the back of the Regia perfume store (p157), this museum contains everything from ancient Egyptian and Roman (the latter mostly from the 1st to 3rd centuries AD) scent receptacles to classic eau-de-cologne bottles – all in all, some 5000 bottles of infinite shapes, sizes and histories.

You can admire anything from ancient bronze Etruscan tweezers to little early-19th-century potpourris made of fine Sèvres porcelain. Also on show are old catalogues and advertising posters.

UNIVERSITAT DE BARCELONA ARCHITECTURE

Map p310 (☑93 402 11 00; www.ub.edu; Gran Via de les Corts Catalanes 585; ⊙9am-9pm Mon-Fri; MUniversitat) Although a university was first set up in the 16th century on what is now La Rambla, the present, glorious mix of (neo) Romanesque, Gothic, Islamic and Mudéjar architecture is a caprice of the 19th century (built 1863–82). Wander into the main hall, up the grand staircase and around the various leafy cloisters or take a stroll in the rear gardens.

On the 1st floor, the main hall for big occasions is the Mudéjar-style Paranimfo.

FREE MUSEU I CENTRE D'ESTUDIS DE L'ESPORT DR MELCIOR COLET MUSEUM

Map p306 (☑93 419 22 32; Carrer de Buenos Aires 56-58; ⊙9am-2pm & 3-5.30pm Mon-Fri; ☐27, 32, 59, 66, 67 or 68) Puig i Cadafalch's Casa Company (1911) looks like an odd Tyrolean country house and is marvellously out of place. A collection of photos, documents and other sports memorabilia stretches over two floors – from an incongruous 1930s pair of skis and boots to the skull-decorated swimming costume of a champion Catalan water-polo player.

A curio on the ground floor is the replica of a stone commemoration in Latin of Lucius Minicius Natal, a Barcelona boy who won a quadriga (four-horse chariot) race at the 227th Olympic Games...in AD 129.

XALET GOLFERICHS   ARCHITECTURE

Map p306 (☑93 323 77 90; www.golferichs. org; Gran Via de les Corts Catalanes 491; ⓢ5.30-9.30pm Mon-Sat; ⓜRocafort) This quirky mansion is an oddity of another era on one of the city's busiest boulevards. Its owner, businessman Macari Golferichs, wanted a Modernista villa and he got one. Brick, ceramics and timber are the main building elements of the house, which displays a distinctly Gothic flavour. It came close to demolition in the 1970s but was saved by the town hall and converted into a cultural centre. Opening times can vary depending on temporary exhibitions and other cultural activities.

◉ La Dreta de L'Eixample

LA SAGRADA FAMÍLIA   CHURCH
See p134.

LA PEDRERA   ARCHITECTURE
See p139.

HOSPITAL DE LA SANTA
CREU I DE SANT PAU   ARCHITECTURE

(☑93 317 76 52; www.rutadelmodernisme.com; Carrer de Cartagena 167; guided tour adult/senior & student €10/5; ⓢtours 10am, 11am, noon & 1pm in English, others in Catalan, French & Spanish; ⓜHospital de Sant Pau) Domènech i Montaner outdid himself as architect and philanthropist with this Modernista masterpiece, long considered one of the city's most important hospitals. The complex, including 16 pavilions – together with the Palau de la Música Catalana, a joint World Heritage Site – is lavishly decorated and each pavilion is unique.

Domènech i Montaner wanted to create a unique environment that would also cheer up patients. Among artists who contributed statuary, ceramics and artwork was the prolific Eusebi Arnau. The hospital facilities have been transferred to a new complex on the premises, freeing up the century-old structures, which are being restored to their former glory in a plan to convert the complex into an international centre on the Mediterranean.

MODERNISME UNPACKED

Travellers interested in running the gamut of L'Eixample's Modernista gems should consider the Ruta del Modernisme pack (p33). It includes a guide (in various languages) and discounted entry prices to the city's major Modernista sights.

Guided tours are the only way the curious get inside this unique site – but the building might one day open up for more regular visits.

MUSEU DE LA MÚSICA   MUSEUM

Map p306 (☑93 256 36 50; www.museumusica. bcn.cat; Carrer de Lepant 150; adult/senior & student €5/4, 3-8pm Sun free ; ⓢ10am-6pm Mon & Wed-Sat, to 8pm Sun; ⓜMonumental) Some 500 instruments (less than a third of those held) are on show in this museum, housed on the 2nd floor of the administration building in L'Auditori, the city's main classical-music concert hall.

Instruments range from a 17th-century baroque guitar through to lutes (look out for the 1641 archilute from Venice), violins, Japanese kotos, sitars from India, eight organs (some dating from the 18th century), pianos, a varied collection of drums and other percussion instruments from across Spain and beyond, along with all sorts of phonographs and gramophones. There are some odd pieces indeed, like the *buccèn*, a snake-head-adorned brass instrument.

Much of the documentary and sound material can be enjoyed through audiovisual displays as you proceed. An audio device allows you to listen to how some of the instruments sound, although it is sometimes a trifle hard to hear the recording above the continually changing ambient music.

The museum organises occasional concerts in which well-known musicians perform on rare instruments held in the collection.

FUNDACIÓ SUÑOL   GALLERY

Map p310 (☑93 496 10 32; www.fundaciosunol. org; Passeig de Gràcia 98; adult/concession €5/3; ⓢ4-8pm Mon-Sat; ⓜDiagonal) Rotating exhibitions of portions of this private collection of mostly 20th-century art (some 1200 works in total) offer anything from Man Ray's photography to sculptures by Alberto

Giacometti. Over two floors, you are most likely to run into Spanish artists, anyone from Picasso to Jaume Plensa, along with a sprinkling of others from abroad.

It makes a refreshing pause between the crush of crowded Modernista monuments on this boulevard. Indeed, you get an interesting side view of one of them, La Pedrera, from out the back.

FREE PALAU DEL BARÓ QUADRAS ARCHITECTURE

Map p310 (Casa Asia; ☑93 368 08 36; www.casaasia.es; Avinguda Diagonal 373; ☺10am-8pm Tue-Sat, to 2pm Sun; ⓜDiagonal) Puig i Cadafalch designed Palau del Baró Quadras (built 1902–06) in an exuberant Gothic-inspired style. The main facade is its most intriguing, with a soaring, glassed-in gallery. Take a closer look at the gargoyles and reliefs – the pair of toothy fish and the sword-wielding knight clearly have the same artistic signature architect brought to Casa Amatller.

Decor inside is eclectic, but dominated by Middle Eastern and East Asian themes. The setting is appropriate for its occupant: Casa Asia is a cultural centre celebrating the relationship between Spain and the Asia-Pacific region. Visiting the varied temporary exhibitions (mostly on the 2nd floor) allows you to get a good look inside this intriguing building. Take in the views from the roof terrace.

CASA DE LES PUNXES ARCHITECTURE

Map p310 (Casa Terrades; Avinguda Diagonal 420; ⓜDiagonal) Puig i Cadafalch's Casa Terrades is better known as the Casa de les Punxes (House of Spikes) because of its pointed turrets. This apartment block, completed in 1905, looks like a fairy-tale castle and has the singular attribute of being the only fully detached building in L'Eixample.

FREE FUNDACIÓ JOAN BROSSA GALLERY

Map p310 (☑93 467 69 52; www.fundaciojoanbrossa.cat; Carrer de Provença 318; ☺10am-2pm & 3-7pm Mon-Fri; ⓜDiagonal) Pop into this basement gallery to get an insight into the mind of one of the city's cultural icons, Joan Brossa, a difficult-to-classify mix of poet, artist, theatre man, Catalan nationalist and all-round visionary. You'll see a panoply of objects of art (like *Porró amb Daus*, a typical Spanish wine decanter with dice), followed by samples of his visual poems.

MUSEU EGIPCI MUSEUM

Map p310 (☑93 488 01 88; www.museuegipci.com; Carrer de València 284; adult/senior & student €11/8; ☺10am-8pm Mon-Sat, to 2pm Sun; ⓜPasseig de Gràcia) Hotel magnate Jordi Clos has spent much of his life collecting ancient Egyptian artefacts, brought together in this private museum. It's divided into different thematic areas (the Pharaoh, religion, funerary practices, mummification, crafts etc) and boasts an interesting variety of exhibits.

There are statuary, funereal implements and containers, jewellery (including a fabulous golden ring from around the 7th century BC), ceramics and even a bed made of wood and leather. In the basement is an exhibition area and library, displaying volumes including original editions of works by Carter, the Egyptologist who led the Tutankhamen excavations. On the rooftop terrace is a pleasant cafe.

ESGLÉSIA DE LA PURÍSSIMA CONCEPCIÓ I ASSUMPCIÓ DE NOSTRA SENYORA CHURCH

Map p310 (Carrer de Roger de Llúria 70; ☺8am-1pm & 5-9pm; ⓜPasseig de Gràcia) One hardly expects to run into a medieval church on the grid-pattern streets of the late-19th-century city extension, yet that is just what this is. This 14th-century church was transferred stone by stone from the old centre in 1871–88. It features a pretty 16th-century cloister with a peaceful garden.

Behind is a Romanesque-Gothic bell tower (11th to 16th century), moved from another old town church that didn't survive, Església de Sant Miquel. This is one of a handful of such old churches shifted willy-nilly from their original locations to L'Eixample.

PALAU MONTANER ARCHITECTURE

Map p310 (☑93 317 76 52; www.rutadelmodernisme.com; Carrer de Mallorca 278; adult/child & senior €6/3; ☺guided visit in English 10.30am & in Spanish 12.30pm Sat, in Catalan 10.30am, in Spanish 11.30am & in Catalan 12.30pm Sun; ⓜPasseig de Gràcia) It's interesting on the outside – and made all the more enticing by its gardens – but this 1896 creation by Domènech i Montaner is spectacular on the inside. Its central feature is a grand staircase beneath a broad, ornamental skylight. The interior is laden with sculptures (some by Eusebi Arnau), mosaics and fine woodwork. It is advisable to call ahead if you want to visit, as the building is sometimes closed to the public on weekends.

MUSEU DE
CARROSSES FÚNEBRES   MUSEUM

Map p306 (☑902 076902; Carrer de Sancho d'Àvila 2; ⊙10am-1pm & 4-6pm Mon-Fri, 10am-1pm Sat, Sun & holidays; ⓂMarina) If late-18th-century to mid-20th-century hearses (complete with period-dressed dummies) are your thing, then this museum, probably the city's weirdest sight, is where to contemplate the pomp and circumstance of people's last earthly ride. The funeral company claims it is the biggest museum of its kind in the world.

From the reception desk you are taken into the rather gloomy basement by a security guard. Alongside a metallic Buick hearse and a couple of earlier motorised hearses are lined up 11 horse-drawn carriage-hearses in use in the 19th and early 20th centuries – four of them with horses and accompanying walkers in powdered wigs and tricorn hats. It's a strange little display, easily done in half an hour.

ESGLÉSIA DE LES SALESES   CHURCH

Map p310 (☑93 265 39 12; Passeig de Sant Joan; ⊙10am-2pm & 5-9pm Mon-Sat; ⓂTetuan) A singular neo-Gothic effort, this church is interesting because it was designed by Joan Martorell i Montells (1833–1906), Gaudí's architecture professor. Raised in 1878–85 with an adjacent convent (badly damaged in the civil war and now a school), it offers hints of what was to come with Modernisme, with his use of brick, mosaics and sober stained glass.

EATING

Most of this huge area's many varied and enticing restaurants are concentrated in the Quadrat d'Or between Carrer de Pau Claris and Carrer de Muntaner, Avinguda Diagonal and Gran Via de les Corts Catalanes. There is no shortage of perfectly acceptable bar-restaurants (often with street-side tables) that offer reasonable *menús del día* (set menus) and stock-standard dishes *a la carta*. In among these places are sprinkled real finds, offering both local and international cuisine.

✖ La Dreta de L'Eixample

TOP CHOICE TAPAÇ 24   TAPAS €€

Map p310 (www.carlesabellan.com; Carrer de la Diputació 269; mains €10-20; ⊙9am-midnight Mon-Sat; ⓂPasseig de Gràcia) Carles Abellán, master of Comerç 24 in La Ribera, runs this basement tapas haven known for its gourmet versions of old faves. Specials include the *bikini* (toasted ham and cheese sandwich – here the ham is cured and the truffle makes all the difference) and a thick black *arròs negre de sípia* (squid-ink black rice).

The inventive McFoie-Burguer is fantastic and, for dessert, choose *xocolata amb pa, sal i oli* (delicious balls of chocolate in olive oil with a touch of salt and wafer). You can't book but it's worth the wait.

TOP CHOICE ALKÍMIA   CATALAN €€€

(☑93 207 61 15; www.alkimia.cat; Carrer de l'Indústria 79; set menu €38-84; ⊙lunch & dinner Mon-Fri Sep-Jul; ⓂVerdaguer) Jordi Vila, a culinary alchemist, serves up refined Catalan dishes with a twist in this elegant, white-walled locale well off the tourist trail. Dishes such as his *arròs de nyore i safrà amb escamarlans de la costa* (saffron and sweet-chilli rice with crayfish) earned Vila his first Michelin star. He presents a series of set menus from €38 to €84.

CAN KENJI   JAPANESE €

Map p306 (☑93 476 18 23; www.cankenji.com; Carrer del Rosselló 325; mains €6-12; ⊙1-3.30pm & 8.30-11.30pm Mon-Sat; ⓂVerdaguer) If you want to go Japanese in Barcelona, this is the place. The chef of this understated little *izakaya* (the Japanese version of a pub/eatery) gets his ingredients fresh from the city's markets, with traditional Japanese recipes receiving a Mediterranean touch, so you'll get things like sardine tempura with an aubergine, miso and anchovy puree, or *tataki* (lightly grilled meat) of bonito (tuna) with *salmorejo* (a Córdoban cold tomato and bread soup). This is fusion at its very best.

NOTI   MEDITERRANEAN €€

Map p310 (☑93 342 66 73; http://noti-universal. com; Carrer de Roger de Llúria 35; mains €10-15; ⊙lunch & dinner Mon-Fri, dinner Sat; ⓂPasseig de Gràcia) Once home to the *Noticiero Universal* newspaper, Noti has an ample dining room plastered with mirrors that seem to multiply the steely designer tables. Try the

START CASA CALVET
FINISH CASA MACAYA
DISTANCE 4KM
DURATION 1HOUR

Neighbourhood Walk
More Modernisme in L'Eixample

Gaudí's most conventional contribution to L'Eixample is **1** **Casa Calvet**, built in 1900. Inspired by baroque, the noble ashlar facade is broken up by protruding wrought-iron balconies. Inside, the main attraction is the staircase, which you can admire if you eat in the swanky restaurant.

2 **Casa Enric Batlló** was completed in 1896 by Josep Vilaseca (1848–1910), part of the Comtes de Barcelona hotel. The brickwork facade is especially graceful when lit up at night.

Puig i Cadafalch let his imagination loose on **3** **Casa Serra** (1903–08), a neo-Gothic whimsy that is home to government offices. With its central tower topped by a witch's hat, grandly decorated upper-floor windows and tiled roof, it must have been a strange house to live in!

4 **Casa Comalatis**, built in 1911 by Salvador Valeri (1873–1954), is similarly striking. Note Gaudí's obvious influence on the main facade, with its wavy roof and bulging balconies. Head around the back to Carrer de Còrsega to see a more playful facade, with its windows stacked like cards.

Completed in 1912, **5** **Casa Thomas** was one of Domènech i Montaner's earlier efforts – the ceramic details are a trademark and the massive ground-level wrought-iron decoration (and protection?) is magnificent. Wander inside to the Cubiñá design store to admire his interior work.

6 **Casa Llopis i Bofill** is an interesting block of flats designed by Antoni Gallissà (1861–1903) in 1902. The graffiti-covered facade is particularly striking to the visitor's eye. The use of elaborate parabolic arches on the ground floor is a clear Modernista touch, as are the wrought-iron balconies.

Puig i Cadafalch's **7** **Casa Macaya** (1901) has a wonderful courtyard and features the typical playful, pseudo-Gothic decoration that characterises many of the architect's projects. It belongs to La Caixa bank and is occasionally used for temporary exhibitions, when visitors are permitted to enter.

fresh fish from the Boqueria market with ratatouille of courgette and lemon butter or perhaps a meat dish – anything from steak tartare to chicken curry. Start the evening with the cocktail of the day at the bar.

It has lunch menus from €14 to €24, and an evening set menu at €36.

PATAGONIA   SOUTH AMERICAN €€€

Map p310 (⚐93 304 37 35; Gran Via de les Corts Catalanes 660; meals €40-45; ⊘lunch & dinner; ⓂPasseig de Gràcia) An elegant Argentinean beef-fest awaits in this stylish restaurant. Start with empanadas (tiny meat-crammed pies). You might want to skip the *achuras* (offal) and head for a hearty meat main, such as a juicy beef *medallón con salsa de colmenillas* (a medallion in a morel sauce) or such classics as *bife de chorizo* (sirloin with spicy sausage) or Brazilian *picanha* (rump). You can choose from one of five side dishes to accompany your pound of flesh.

CASA CALVET   CATALAN €€

Map p310 (⚐93 412 40 12; www.casacalvet.es; Carrer de Casp 48; mains €15-30; ⊘lunch & dinner Mon-Sat; ⓂUrquinaona) An early Gaudí masterpiece loaded with his trademark curvy features now houses a swish restaurant (just to the right of the building's main entrance). Dress up and ask for an intimate *taula cabina* (wooden booth). You could opt for sole and lobster on mashed leeks, with balsamic vinegar and Pedro Ximénez reduction, and artichoke chips. It has various tasting menus for up to €70.

DE TAPA MADRE   CATALAN €€

Map p310 (⚐93 459 31 34; www.detapamadre.cat; Carrer de Mallorca 301; mains €8-15; ⊘8am-1am Mon-Sat; ⓂVerdaguer) A chatty atmosphere greets you from the bar from the moment you swing open the door. A few tiny tables line the window, but head upstairs for more space in the gallery, which hovers above the array of tapas on the bar below, or go deeper inside past the bench with the ham legs. The *arròs caldós amb llagostins* (a hearty rice dish with king prawns) is delicious.

EMBAT   MEDITERRANEAN €€

Map p310 (⚐93 458 08 55; www.restaurantembat.es; Carrer de Mallorca 304; mains €10-20; ⊘lunch Tue & Wed, lunch & dinner Thu-Sat; ⓂGirona) Enthusiastic young chefs turn out beautifully presented dishes in this basement eatery, the brown and cream decor of which might not enchant all comers. You can eat three fish or meat courses for around €20 to €25 at lunch.

Indulge perhaps in *raviolis de pollo amb bacon i calabassó* (chicken ravioli bathed in a sauce of finely chopped bacon, zucchini and other vegetables) followed by melt in the mouth *lluç amb pa amb tomàquet, carxofes i maionesa de peres* (a thick cut of hake on a tomato-drenched clump of bread dressed with artichoke slices and a pear mayonnaise).

CASA AMALIA   CATALAN €

Map p310 (⚐93 458 94 58; Passatge del Mercat 4-6; mains €8-16; ⊘lunch & dinner Tue-Sat, lunch Sun Sep-Jul; ⓂGirona) This formal restaurant is popular for its hearty Catalan cooking that uses fresh produce, mainly sourced from the busy market next door. On Thursdays during winter it offers the Catalan mountain classic, *escudella*. Otherwise, you might try light variations on local cuisine, such as the *bacallà al allioli de poma* (cod in an apple-based aioli sauce). The four-course *menú del día* is exceptional lunchtime value at €12.

The orange and white decorated joint has split-level dining that makes the most of its space.

CASA ALFONSO   SPANISH €

Map p310 (⚐93 301 97 83; www.casaalfonso.com; Carrer de Roger de Llúria 6; mains €8; ⊘9am-1am Mon-Sat; ⓂUrquinaona) In business since 1934, Casa Alfonso is perfect for a morning coffee or a tapas stop at the long marble bar. Timber panelled and festooned with old photos and swinging hams, it attracts a faithful local clientele at all hours for its *flautas* (thin custom-made baguettes with your choice of filling), hams, cheeses, hot dishes and homemade desserts. Consider rounding off with an *alfonsito* (a tiny Irish coffee).

✖ L'Esquerra de L'Eixample

CATA 1.81   TAPAS €€

Map p310 (⚐93 323 68 18; www.cata181.com; Carrer de València 181; tapas €7-12; ⊘dinner Mon-Sat; ⓂPasseig de Gràcia) This beautifully designed venue (with many small lights, some trapped in birdcages) is the place to come for fine wines and dainty gourmet dishes like *raviolis amb bacallà* (salt-cod dumplings) or *truita de patates i tòfona negre* (thick potato tortilla with a delicate trace of black truffle).

The best option is to choose from one of several tasting-menu options (€28 to €45).

The cheapest option is the fixed lunchtime menu at €16. Since wines feature so highly here, let rip with the list of fine Spanish tipples.

TAKTIKA BERRI
BASQUE, TAPAS €€

Map p310 (Carrer de València 169; mains €15; ⓢlunch & dinner Mon-Fri, lunch Sat; ⓜHospital Clínic) Get in early because the bar teems with punters from far and wide, anxious to wrap their mouths around some of the best Basque tapas in town. The hot morsels are snapped up as soon as they arrive from the kitchen, so keep your eyes peeled. The seated dining area out the back is also good. In the evening, it's all over by about 10.30pm.

SPEAKEASY
INTERNATIONAL €€

Map p310 (☎93 217 50 80; www.drymartinibcn.com; Carrer d'Aribau 162-166; mains €10-15; ⓢlunch & dinner Mon-Fri, dinner Sat Sep-Jul; ⓜDiagonal) This clandestine restaurant lurks behind the Dry Martini (p151) bar. You will be shown a door through the open kitchen area to the 'storeroom', lined with hundreds of bottles of backlit, quality tipples. Dark decorative tones, a few works of art, low lighting, light jazz music and smooth service complete the setting. The menu has tempting options like the huge hunk of burrata cheese with white asparagus and strips of ravishing *jamón* (cured ham).

FASTVÍNIC
CAFE €

Map p310 (☎93 487 32 41; www.fastvinic.com; Carrer de la Diputació 251; sandwiches €6-10; ⓢnoon-midnight Mon-Sat; ⓜPasseig de Gràcia) A project in sustainability all round, this is slow food done fast, with ingredients, wine and building materials all sourced from Catalonia. Designed by Alfons Tost, there are air-purifying plants, energy-efficient LED lighting, and a water and food recycling system.

It's all sandwiches on the menu, with some wonderful choices of roast beef, mustard and honey, or more adventurous crunchy suckling pig, banana chutney and coriander; there is also a self-service wine machine with quality Spanish choices. The interior is sleek and calm, with classical music accompanying your food. There are large tables for groups and smaller niches for quieter affairs – a word of warning: don't sit at the table right between the sliding door and the food recycling machine or

you'll be subjected to hot/cold draughts and food blitzing.

CINC SENTITS
INTERNATIONAL €€

Map p310 (☎93 323 94 90; www.cincsentits.com; Carrer d'Aribau 58; mains €10-20; ⓢlunch & dinner Tue-Sat; ⓜPasseig de Gràcia) Enter this somewhat overlit realm of the 'Five Senses' to indulge in a tasting menu (from €49 to €69), consisting of a series of small, experimental dishes. A key is the use of fresh local produce, such as fish landed on the Costa Brava and top-quality suckling pig from Extremadura. Less ambitious, but cheaper, is the set lunch at €30.

MELTON
ITALIAN €€

Map p306 (☎93 363 27 76; Carrer de Muntaner 189; mains €12-20; ⓢTue-Sat; ⓜHospital Clínic) You know you're onto something when Italians recommend an Italian restaurant. This slick place offers well-prepared pasta and risotto dishes (the latter, for example, with foie gras) and a tempting array of meat and fish mains. For an unusual pasta option, try the *lasagnetta de tòfona negra i múrgules* (little lasagne with black truffle and morel mushrooms). There is a tasting menu at €55.

ALBA GRANADOS
SPANISH, MEDITERRANEAN €€

Map p310 (☎93 454 61 16; Carrer d'Enric Granados 34; mains €12; ⓢlunch & dinner Mon-Sat, lunch Sun; ⓡFGC Provença) In summer ask for one of the romantic tables for two on the 1st-floor balcony. Overlooking the trees, it is a unique spot, with little traffic. Inside, the ground- and 1st-floor dining areas are huge, featuring exposed brick and dark parquet. The menu offers a little of everything but the best dishes revolve around meat, such as *solomillo a la mantequilla de trufa con tarrina de patata y beicon* (sirloin in truffle butter, potato and bacon terrine).

TERRABACUS
TAPAS €€

Map p306 (☎93 410 86 33; www.terrabacus.com; Carrer de Muntaner 185; mains €12-15; menú del día €18; ⓢlunch & dinner Tue-Fri, dinner Mon & Sat; ⓜHospital Clínic) Food exists to accompany wine, or so one could be led to believe here. In this 'Land of Bacchus', one of the joys is sampling from the extensive wine list and choosing bites to go down with the nectar. You might try the various cheese platters or select a dish of high-grade Joselito cured ham. More substantial dishes range from risotto to steak tartare.

CERVESERIA BRASSERIA GALLEGA
TAPAS €€

Map p306 (☎93 439 41 28; Carrer de Casanova 238; mains €10-20; ☺lunch & dinner Mon-Sat; MHospital Clínic) You could walk right by this modest establishment without giving it a second glance. If you did, you'd notice it was chock-full of locals immersed in animated banter and surrounded by plates of abundant Galician classics. The fresh *pulpo a la gallega* (spicy octopus chunks with potatoes) as starter confirms this place is a cut above the competition.

Waiters have little time for loitering, but always a quick quip. The setting is simple, the meat dishes are succulent and the *fideuà* (similar to paella but with vermicelli noodles as the base) is full of seafood flavour.

LA BODEGUETA PROVENÇA
TAPAS €

Map p310 (☎93 215 17 25; Carrer de Provença 233; mains €7-10; ☺lunch & dinner; MDiagonal) The 'Little Wine Cellar' offers classic tapas presented with a touch of class, from *calamares a la andaluza* (lightly battered calamari rings) to *cecina* (dried cured veal meat). The house specialty is *ous estrellats* (literally 'smashed eggs') – a mix of scrambled egg white, egg yolk, potato and then ingredients ranging from foie gras to *morcilla* (black pudding). Wash it all down with a good Ribera del Duero or *caña* (little glass) of beer.

KOYUKI
JAPANESE €€

Map p310 (Carrer de Còrsega 242; mains €14; ☺lunch & dinner Tue-Sat, dinner Sun; MDiagonal) This unassuming basement Japanese diner is one of those rough-edged diamonds that it pays to revisit. Sit at a long table and order from the cheesy menu complete with pictures courtesy of the Japanese owner – you won't be disappointed. The variety of *sashimi moriawase* is generous and constantly fresh. The *tempura udon* is a particularly hearty noodle option. Splash it all down with Sapporo beer.

BODEGA SEPÚLVEDA
CATALAN €

Map p306 (☎93 323 59 44; www.bodega sepulveda.net; Carrer de Sepúlveda 173bis; tapas €4-12; ☺lunch & dinner Mon-Fri, dinner Sat; MUniversitat) This tavern has been showering tapas on its happy diners since 1952. The range of dishes is a little overwhelming

and mixes traditional (Catalan faves like *cap i pota* – chunks of fatty beef in gravy) with more surprising options like *carpaccio de calabacín con bacalao y parmesán* (thin zucchini slices draped in cod and parmesan cheese). You can hang out until 1am.

The main dining area is out the back and downstairs, with a small, low-ceilinged area upstairs.

CERVESERIA CATALANA
TAPAS €

Map p310 (☎93 216 03 68; Carrer de Mallorca 236; mains €8; ☺lunch & dinner; MPasseig de Gràcia) The 'Catalan Brewery' is good for breakfast, lunch and dinner. Come in for your morning coffee and croissant, or wait until lunch to enjoy choosing from the abundance of tapas and *montaditos* (canapés). You can sit at the bar, on the pavement terrace or in the restaurant at the back. The variety of hot tapas, salads and other snacks draws a well-dressed crowd of locals and outsiders.

EL RINCÓN MAYA
MEXICAN €

Map p310 (☎93 451 39 46; Carrer de València 183; mains €5-10; ☺lunch & dinner Tue-Sat, dinner Mon; MPasseig de Gràcia) Getting a seat in this Mexican eatery can be a trial. The setting is warm, modest and simple. The pocket-sized serves of nachos, guacamole and fajitas all burst with flavour. You'll also discover lesser-known items like *tacos de pibil* (pork tacos) and *tinga* (little pasta pockets of chicken). There are also more substantial dishes for €9.50. The owner-chef spent much of his life in the restaurant business in Mexico City.

RESTAURANTE JARDÍN ROSA
CHINESE €

Map p306 (☎93 325 71 95; Avinguda Mistral 54; mains €8; ☺lunch & dinner; MEspanya) As in any other city, there's no shortage of cheap and cheerful Chinese joints, but this is the real McCoy. Go for the first part of the menu, where you'll find pig's-blood soup, and black chicken in ginger, frogs' legs, and strips of eel with leek. The chintzy decor one normally associates with Chinese eateries is considerably more sober here.

AMALTEA
VEGETARIAN €

Map p306 (www.amalteaygovinda.com; Carrer de la Diputació 164; mains €5; ☺lunch & dinner Mon-Sat; ☑; MUrgell) The ceiling fresco of blue sky sets the scene in this popular vegetarian eatery. The weekday set lunch (€10.50) offers a series of dishes that change frequently with the seasons. At night, the set two-course dinner (€15) offers good value. The homemade desserts are tempting. The place is something of an alternative lifestyle centre, with yoga, t'ai chi and belly-dancing classes.

CRUSTO
CAFE €

Map p310 (☑93 487 05 51; www.crusto.es; Carrer de València 246; bread & pastry from €2; ⊗lunch & dinner Mon-Sat; MPasseig de Gràcia) A French-inspired bakery and pastry shop, its wonderful perfume of freshly baked bread, baguettes, croissants and countless pastries will be enough to convince you that it's worth pulling up a stool here for a long and tasty breakfast.

MAURI
PASTELERÍA €

Map p310 (☑93 215 10 20; Rambla de Catalunya 102; pastries from €1.50; ⊗8am-9pm Mon-Sat, to 3pm Sun; MDiagonal) Ever since it opened in 1929, this grand old pastry shop has had its regular customers salivating over the endless range of sweets, chocolate croissants and gourmet delicatessen items.

CREMERIA TOSCANA
GELATERIA €

Map p306 (☑93 539 38 25; Carrer de Muntaner 161; gelati from €1.50; ⊗1-9pm Tue-Sun Oct-Easter, 1pm-midnight Tue-Sun Easter-Sep; MHospital Clínic) Yes, you can stumble across quite reasonable ice cream in Barcelona, but close your eyes and imagine yourself across the Mediterranean with the real ice-cream wizards. Creamy *stracciatella* and wavy *nocciola*...and myriad other flavours await at the most authentic gelato outlet in town. Buy a cone or a tub!

ESCRIBÀ
DESSERTS €

Map p310 (☑93 454 75 35; www.escriba.es; Gran Via de les Corts Catalanes 546; pastries from €2; ⊗8am-3pm & 5-9pm Mon-Fri, 8am-9pm Sat, Sun & holidays; MUrgell) Antoni Escribà carries forward a family tradition (since 1906) of melting *barcelonins'* hearts with remarkable pastries and criminal chocolate creations. Try the Easter *bunyols de xocolata* (little round pastry balls filled with chocolate cream). Escribà has another branch in a Modernista setting at La Rambla de Sant Josep 83 (Map p292).

ORXATERIA SIRVENT
ICE CREAM €

Map p306 (☑93 441 76 16; Ronda de Sant Pau 3; horchata from €3, ice cream from €1.50; ⊗11am-2pm & 4-9pm Oct-Apr, 11am-9pm Jun-Sep; MSant Antoni or Paral.lel) *Barcelonins'* favourite source of *orxata/horchata* (tiger-nut drink) since 1926, this busy locale serves up the best you'll try without having to catch the train down to this drink's spiritual home, Valencia. This place also purveys ice cream, *granissat* (iced fruit crush) and *turrón* (nougat).

🍷 DRINKING & NIGHTLIFE

Much of middle-class L'Eixample is dead at night, but several streets are exceptions. Noisy Carrer de Balmes is lined with a rowdy adolescent set. Much more interesting is the cluster of locales lining Carrer d'Aribau between Avinguda Diagonal and Carrer de Mallorca. They range from quiet cocktail bars to '60s retro joints. Few get going much before midnight and are generally closed or dead Sunday to Wednesday. Lower down, on and around Carrer del Consell de Cent and Carrer de la Diputació, is the heart of Gaixample, with several gay bars and clubs.

🍷 L'Esquerra de L'Eixample

TOP CHOICE MONVÍNIC
WINE BAR

Map p310 (☑932 72 61 87; www.monvinic.com; Carrer de la Diputació 249 ; ⊗wine bar 1.30-11.30pm, restaurant 1.30-3.30pm & 8.30-10.30pm; MPasseig de Gracia) Proclaimed as 'possibly the best wine bar in the world' by the *Wall Street Journal*, and apparently considered unmissable by El Bulli's sommelier, Mondvínic is an ode – a rhapsody, even – to wine loving. The interactive wine list sits on the bar for you to browse on a digital tablet similar to an iPad and boasts more than 3000 varieties.

But that's not to say that it's for connoisseurs only; enthusiasts can also come here to taste wine by the glass – there are 60 selections. You can search by origin, year or grape, from a vast international range. Prices start at €3.50 for a glass of Albariño, and go up – and you can, of course, order by the bottle, too. There is an emphasis on affordability, but if you want to splash out, there are fantastic vintage wines. Feel free to talk to one of the six sommeliers who work on the list. At the back is the restaurant that specialises in Mediterranean cuisine, with ingredients that are sourced locally from Catalan farmers.

LA FIRA   BAR
Map p310 (www.lafiraclub.com; Carrer de Provença 171; admission €8-12; ⊙10.30pm-3am Wed-Sat; ⌴FGC Provença) A designer bar with a difference. Wander in past distorting mirrors and ancient fairground attractions from Germany. Put in coins and listen to hens squawk. Speaking of squawking, the music swings wildly from whiffs of house through '90s hits to Spanish pop classics. You can spend the earlier part of the night trying some of the bar's shots – it claims to have 500 varieties (but we haven't counted them up).

DRY MARTINI   BAR
Map p310 (☑93 217 50 72; www.drymartinibcn. com; Carrer d'Aribau 162-166; ⊙5pm-3am; ⌴Diagonal) Waiters with a discreetly knowing smile will attend to your cocktail needs here. The house drink, taken at the bar or in one of the plush green leather lounges, is a safe bet. The gin and tonic comes in an enormous mug-sized glass – a couple of these and you're well on the way! Out the back is a restaurant, Speakeasy (p148).

COSMO   CAFE
Map p310 (www.galeriacosmo.com; Carrer d'Enric Granados 3; ⊙10am-10pm Mon-Thu, noon-2am Fri & Sat, noon-10pm Sun; ☏; ⌴Universitat) This groovy space – with psychedelic colouring in the tables and bar stools, high white walls out back for exhibitions and events, a nice selection of teas, pastries and snacks, all set on a pleasant pedestrian strip just behind the university – is perfect for a morning session on your laptop or a civilised evening tipple while admiring the art.

ÁTAME   GAY BAR
Map p310 (☑93 454 92 73; Carrer del Consell de Cent 257; ⊙7pm-3am; ⌴Universitat) Cool for a coffee in the early evening, Átame (Tie Me Up) heats up later in the night when the gay crowd comes out to play. There is usually a raunchy show on Friday nights and a happy hour on Thursdays.

BACON BEAR   GAY BAR
Map p310 (Carrer de Casanova 64; ⊙6pm-2.30am; ⌴Urgell) Every bear needs a cave to go to, and this is a rather friendly one. It's really just a big bar for burly gay folk. On weekends the music cranks up enough for a bit of bear-hugging twirl.

CAFÉ SAN TELMO   BAR
Map p306 (☑934 39 17 09; www.cafesantelmo. com; Carrer de Buenos Aires 60; ⊙9am-2.30pm Mon-Fri, 9am-3.30pm Sat & Sun; ⌴Diagonal) This narrow bar has an appealingly busy feel, with big windows along Carrer de Casanova revealing the crowds and traffic of nearby Avinguda Diagonal. Perch at the bar for a couple of low-key afternoon drinks while you ponder the evening ahead (some of the area's key bars and clubs are just over the other side of Avinguda Diagonal).

DACKSY   GAY BAR
Map p310 (☑93 217 50 72; Carrer del Consell de Cent 247; ⊙1pm-2am Sun-Thu, to 3am Fri & Sat; ⌴Universitat) Eye-candy bartenders know their stuff when it comes to mixing, shaking and/or stirring their way to your heart with a fine selection of cocktails in this chilled lounge in the heart of the Gaixample action. It makes a perfect start to the evening, or a nice way to finish off if clubbing is not on the night's agenda.

LA CHAPELLE   GAY BAR
Map p310 (☑93 453 30 76; Carrer de Muntaner 67; ⊙6pm-2am Mon-Thu, to 3am Fri & Sat; ⌴Universitat) A typical, long, narrow L'Eixample bar with white-tiled walls like a 1930s hospital, it houses a plethora of crucifixes and niches that far outdo what you'd find in any other 'chapel'. This is a relaxed gay meeting place that welcomes all comers. No need for six-pack bellies here.

MEDITERRÁNEO   BAR
Map p310 (☑678 211253; Carrer de Balmes 129; ⊙11pm-3am; ⌴Diagonal) This smoky, studenty jam joint is a great hang-out that attracts a mostly casual student set. Order a beer, enjoy the free nuts and chat at one of the tiny tables while waiting for the next act to tune up at the back. Sometimes the young performers are surprisingly good.

MILANO   COCKTAIL BAR
Map p310 (www.camparimilano.com; Ronda de la Universitat 35; ⊙noon-2.30am; ⌴Catalunya) You may not know what to expect when heading down to this cocktail den. Then you're confronted by its vastness and the happily imbibing crowds ensconced at tables or perched at the broad, curving bar to the right.

MUSEUM
GAY BAR

Map p306 (Carrer de Sepúlveda 178; ⊗6.30pm-3am; MUniversitat) 'Kitsch gone mad' is the artistic theme here, where chandeliers meet mock Renaissance sculpture and light pop. Drinks are served behind a stage-lit bar and can be hard to come by from 1.30am on. Twinks and muscle builders mix happily in this gay starter bar perfectly located for a hop over to Metro later on.

PLATA BAR
BAR

Map p310 (☎93 452 46 36; Carrer del Consell de Cent 235; ⊗8pm-3am; MUniversitat) A summer seat on the corner terrace of this wide-open bar attracts a lot of lads hopping the area's gay bars in the course of an evening. Inside, metallic horse-saddle stools are lined up at the bar and high tables, the music drifts through modes of dance and trance and waiters whip up drinks from behind a couple of candelabra on the bar.

PREMIER
BAR

Map p310 (Carrer de Provença 236; ⊗6pm-2.30am Mon-Thu, to 3am Fri & Sat; ℝFGC Provença) A little cross-pollination has happened in this funky little French-run wine bar. The rather short wine list is mostly French – or you can opt for a Moritz beer or a *mojito*. Hug the bar, sink into a lounge or hide up on the mezzanine. Later in the evening, a DJ adds to the ambience.

PUNTO BCN
GAY BAR

Map p310 (☎93 453 61 23; www.arenadisco.com; Carrer de Muntaner 63-65; ⊗6pm-3am; MUniversitat) It's an oldie but a goody. A big bar over two levels with a crowd ranging from their 20s to their 40s and beyond, this place fills to bursting on Friday and Saturday nights. It's a friendly early stop on a gay night out, and you can shoot a round of pool if you feel so inclined.

QUILOMBO
BAR

Map p310 (☎93 439 54 06; Carrer d'Aribau 149; ⊗7pm-2.30am daily Jun-Sep, Wed-Sun Oct-May; ℝFGC Provença) Some formulas just work, and this place has been working since the 1970s. Set up a few guitars in the back room, which you pack with tables and chairs, add some cheapish pre-prepared mojitos and plastic tubs of nuts, and let the punters do the rest. They pour in, creating plenty of *quilombo* (fuss).

AIRE
LESBIAN CLUB

Map p310 (☎93 487 83 42; www.arenadisco.com; Carrer de València 236; ⊗11pm-3am Thu-Sat; MPasseig de Gràcia) A popular locale for lesbians, the dance floor is spacious and there is usually a DJ in command of the tunes, which range from hits of the '80s and '90s to techno. As a rule, only male friends of the girls are allowed entry, although in practice the crowd tends to be fairly mixed. Things can heat up on Thursday nights with live music.

ARENA CLASSIC
CLUB

Map p310 (☎93 487 83 42; www.arenadisco.com; Carrer de la Diputació 233; admission €6-12; ⊗12.30am-6.30am Fri & Sat; MPasseig de Gràcia) This place is a little more sedate than its wilder – and almost exclusively gay – partner around the corner, Arena Madre, and tends to get more of a mixed crowd. The dominant sound is commercial house music.

ARENA MADRE
GAY CLUB

Map p310 (☎93 487 83 42; www.arenadisco.com; Carrer de Balmes 32; admission €6-12; ⊗12.30am-5.30am; MPasseig de Gràcia) Popular with a hot young crowd, Arena Madre is one of the top clubs in town for boys seeking boys. Keep an eye out for the striptease shows on Mondays and drag queens on Wednesdays, along with the usual combination of disco and Latin music to get those butts moving. Heteros are welcome but a minority.

CITY HALL
CLUB

Map p310 (☎93 238 07 22; www.grupo-ottozutz.com; Rambla de Catalunya 2-4; admission €12; ⊗midnight-5am Mon-Thu, to 6am Fri & Sat; MCatalunya) A corridor leads to the dance floor of this place, located in a former theatre. House and other electric sounds dominate, including a rather forward-sounding session of cutting-edge funk called Get Funkd! on Tuesdays. Wednesday night is electro-house, while different guest DJs pop up on Thursdays. Out back from the dance floor is a soothing terrace.

LA BASE
GAY CLUB

Map p306 (Carrer de Casanova 201; ⊗10pm-3am Mon-Fri, midnight-5am Sat & Sun; MHospital Clínic) This heavy, heated gay bar and club has something for just about everyone: nude nights, rude nights, leather cruising evenings and dark rooms. There's even music!

METRO
GAY CLUB

Map p306 (📞93 323 52 27; www.metrodiscobcn.
com; Carrer de Sepúlveda 185; ⏰1am-5am Mon,
midnight-5am Sun & Tue-Thu, midnight-6am Fri &
Sat; Ⓜ️Universitat) Metro attracts a casual gay
crowd with its two dance floors, three bars
and very dark room. Keep an eye out for
shows and parties, which can range from parades of models to bingo nights (on Thursday
nights, with sometimes-interesting prizes).
On Wednesday nights there's a live sex show.

OPIUM CINEMA
CLUB

Map p310 (📞93 414 63 62; www.opiumcinema.
com; Carrer de París 193-197; ⏰9pm-2.30am Tue-
Thu, to 3am Fri & Sat; Ⓜ️Diagonal) Reds, roses
and yellows dominate the colour scheme in
this wonderful former cinema. Barcelona's
beautiful people, from a broad range of ages,
gather to drink around the central rectangular bar, dance a little and eye one another
up. Some come earlier for a bite. Wednesday
nights are for R&B and Brazilian music.

ROXY BLUE
CLUB

Map p310 (📞93 272 66 97; www.roxyblue.es; Carrer del Consell de Cent 294; ⏰midnight-5am Wed
& Thu, to 6am Fri & Sat; Ⓜ️Passeig de Gràcia) Blue
is indeed the predominant colour in this
split-level miniclub. Tastes in music swing
from New York beats to Brazil night on
Sunday. On weekends you are likely to find
queues of 20-somethings waiting to pile in.
Sit out the music on long leather lounges or
investigate the couple of different bars.

🍷 La Dreta de L'Eixample

LES GENS QUE J'AIME
BAR

Map p310 (Carrer de València 286; ⏰6pm-2.30am
Sun-Thu, to 3am Fri & Sat; Ⓜ️Passeig de Gràcia)
This intimate basement relic of the 1960s
follows a deceptively simple formula:
chilled jazz music in the background,
minimal lighting from an assortment of
flea-market lamps and a cosy, cramped
scattering of red velvet-backed lounges
around tiny dark tables.

CAFÈ DEL CENTRE
CAFE

Map p310 (📞93 488 11 01; Carrer de Girona 69;
⏰8.30am-midnight Mon-Fri; Ⓜ️Girona) Step
back a century in this cafe, in business since
1873. The timber-top bar extends down the
right side as you enter, fronted by a slew
of marble-topped tables and dark timber

chairs. It exudes an almost melancholy air
by day but gets busy at night.

GARAJE HERMÉTICO
BAR

Map p310 (Avinguda Diagonal 440; ⏰11pm-4am;
Ⓜ️Diagonal) It's a pool-playing, rock and
roll kinda world in this popular late-night
haunt, where those without disco desire but
in search of one (or two) more drinkies con-
verge when most of the other bars in Barcelona have closed. It's a no-nonsense place
and full of beans after 3am.

NEW CHAPS
GAY BAR

Map p310 (📞93 215 53 65; www.newchaps.com;
Avinguda Diagonal 365; ⏰9pm-3am Sun-Thu, to
3.30am Fri & Sat; Ⓜ️Diagonal) Leather lovers
get in some close-quarters inspection on the
dance floor and more, especially in the dark
room, downstairs past the fairly dark loos in
the vaulted cellars. It's a classic handlebar-
moustache gay-porn kinda place.

DBOY
GAY CLUB

Map p310 (📞93 453 05 10; Ronda de Sant Pere
19-21; ⏰midnight-6am Sat; Ⓜ️Urquinaona) With
pink laser lights and dense crowds of fit
young lads, this is one of the big dance-club
locations on a Saturday night. Electronic
music dominates the dance nights here
and, in spite of the 6am finish, for many
this is only the start of the 'evening'. You
need to look your gorgeous best to get in
past the selective doormen.

⭐ ENTERTAINMENT

BEL-LUNA JAZZ CLUB
JAZZ

Map p310 (📞93 302 22 21; www.bel-luna.
com; Rambla de Catalunya 5; admission €5-15;
⏰9pm-2am Sun-Thu, to 3am Fri & Sat; Ⓜ️Cat-
alunya) This basement restaurant-cum-bar-
cum-club is not the prettiest location but
attracts a full jazz program, seven nights a
week, with local and visiting acts. You can
join in for dinner, but frankly you're better
off dining elsewhere. When the last act fin-
ishes, the place turns into a kind of preclub
club with tunes from the 1980s and '90s.

DIETRICH GAY TEATRO CAFÉ
CABARET

Map p310 (📞93 451 77 07; Carrer del Consell de
Cent 255; ⏰10.30pm-3am; Ⓜ️Universitat) It's
show time at 1am, with at least one drag-
queen gala a night in this cabaret-style locale
dedicated to Marlene Dietrich. Soft house is

the main musical motif and the place has an interior garden. In between performances, gogo boys heat up the ambience.

L'AUDITORI
CLASSICAL MUSIC

Map p306 (☑93 247 93 00; www.auditori. org; Carrer de Lepant 150; admission €10-60; ⊙box office 3-9pm Mon-Sat; MMonumental) Barcelona's modern home for serious music lovers, L'Auditori (designed by Rafael Moneo) puts on plenty of orchestral, chamber, religious and other music. L'Auditori is perhaps ugly on the outside (to the less kindhearted it looks like a pile of rusting scrap metal) but beautifully tuned on the inside. It is home to the Orquestra Simfònica de Barcelona i Nacional de Catalunya.

PALAU ROBERT
CLASSICAL MUSIC

Map p310 (☑93 238 40 00; www.gencat.cat/palaurobert; Passeig de Gràcia 107; admission €4; MDiagonal) Once a month concerts are held in the peaceful gardens at the back of this fine building or its main hall. Concerts are usually held around 8pm on a Wednesday. You need to pick up a pass the afternoon before (between 5pm and 7pm) or on the morning of the performance (from 10am to noon), as places are limited.

TEATRE NACIONAL DE CATALUNYA
PERFORMING ARTS

Map p306 (☑93 306 57 00; www.tnc.cat; Plaça de les Arts 1; admission €12-32; ⊙box office 3-7pm Wed-Fri, 3-8.30pm Sat, 3-5pm Sun & 1hr before show; MGlòries or Monumental) Ricard Bofill's ultra neoclassical theatre, with its bright, airy foyer, hosts a wide range of performances, principally drama (anything from King Lear in Catalan to La Fura dels Baus) but occasionally dance and other performances.

TEATRE TÍVOLI
THEATRE

Map p310 (☑902 332211; www.grupbalana.com; Carrer de Casp 8-12; admission €20-50; ⊙box office 5pm to start of show; MCatalunya) A grand old theatre with three storeys of boxes and a generous stage, the Tívoli has a fairly rapid turnover of drama and musicals, with pieces often not staying on for more than a couple of weeks.

MÉLIÈS CINEMES
CINEMA

Map p310 (☑93 451 00 51; www.cinesmelies.net; Carrer de Villarroel 102; admission €3-5; MUrgell) A cosy cinema with two screens, the Méliès specialises in old classics from Hollywood and European cinema.

RENOIR FLORIDABLANCA
CINEMA

Map p306 (☑93 426 33 37; www.cinesrenoir.com; Carrer de Floridablanca 135; MSant Antoni) With seven screens, this is one of a small chain of art-house cinemas in Spain showing quality flicks. It is handily located just beyond El Raval, so you can be sure that there is no shortage of postfilm entertainment options nearby.

🛍 SHOPPING

Most of the city's classy shopping spreads across the heart of L'Eixample, in particular along Passeig de Gràcia, Rambla de Catalunya and adjacent streets. A surprisingly diverse array of specialty stores are also interspersed.

VINÇON
HOMEWARES

Map p310 (☑93 215 60 50; www.vincon.com; Passeig de Gràcia 96; ⊙10am-8.30pm Mon-Sat; MDiagonal) An icon of the Barcelona design scene, Vinçon has the slickest furniture and household goods (particularly lighting), both local and imported. Not surprising, really, since the building, raised in 1899, belonged to the Modernista artist Ramon Casas. Head upstairs to the furniture area – from the windows and terrace you get close side views of La Pedrera.

ELS ENCANTS VELLS
MARKET

Map p306 (Fira de Bellcaire; ☑93 246 30 30; www. encantsbcn.com; Plaça de les Glòries Catalanes; ⊙7am-6pm Mon, Wed, Fri & Sat; MGlòries) Also known as the Fira de Bellcaire, the 'Old Charms' flea market is the biggest of its kind in Barcelona. The markets moved here in 1928 from Avinguda de Mistral, near Plaça d'Espanya. It's all here, from antique furniture through to secondhand clothes. A lot of it is junk, but occasionally you'll stumble across a *ganga* (bargain).

The most interesting time to be here is from 7am to 9am on Monday, Wednesday and Friday, when the public auctions take place. Debate on a future location for the market has ebbed and flowed for years but at the time of writing it was still firmly anchored to its spot on the north flank of the Plaça de les Glòries Catalanes.

EL BULEVARD DELS ANTIQUARIS
ANTIQUES

Map p310 (☑93 215 44 99; www.bulevarddelsanti quaris.com; Passeig de Gràcia 55-57; ⊙10.30am-

8.30pm Mon-Sat; **M**Passeig de Gràcia) More than 70 stores (most are open from 11am to 2pm and from 5pm to 8.30pm) are gathered under one roof (on the floor above the more general Bulevard Rosa arcade) to offer the most varied selection of collector's pieces, ranging from old porcelain dolls through to fine crystal, from Asian antique furniture to old French goods, and from African and other ethnic art to jewellery.

XAMPANY   DRINK

Map p310 (☑610 845011; Carrer de València 200; ⊘4.30-10pm Mon-Fri, 10am-2pm Sat; **M**Passeig de Gràcia) This 'Cathedral of Cava' has been distributing bubbly since 1981. It's a veritable Aladdin's cave of *cava* (Catalan sparkling wine), with bottles of the stuff crammed high and into every possible chaotic corner of this dimly lit locale.

CASA DEL LLIBRE   BOOKS

Map p310 (☑902 026407; www.casadellibro.com; Passeig de Gràcia 62; ⊘9.30am-9.30pm Mon-Sat; **M**Passeig de Gràcia) With branches elsewhere in Spain, the 'Home of the Book' is a well-stocked general bookshop with reasonable sections devoted to literature in English, French and other languages. The website is a good place to look for Spanish literature if the shop is a walk too far.

COME IN   BOOKS

Map p310 (☑93 453 12 04; www.libreriainglesa. com; Carrer de Balmes 129bis; **M**Diagonal) English teachers, Shakespeare enthusiasts and those thirsting for the latest thrillers in English will all find something to awaken their curiosity in this, one of the city's main English-language bookshops. There are even a few odds and ends in other languages.

LAIE   BOOKS

Map p310 (☑93 318 17 39; www.laie.es; Carrer de Pau Claris 85; ⊘10am-9pm Mon-Fri, 10.30am-9pm Sat; **M**Catalunya or Urquinaona) Laie has novels and books on architecture, art and film in English, French, Spanish and Catalan. Better still, it has a great upstairs cafe where you can examine your latest purchases or browse through the newspapers provided for customers in true Central European style.

CACAO SAMPAKA   FOOD

Map p310 (☑93 272 08 33; www.cacaosampaka. com; Carrer del Consell de Cent 292; ⊘9am-9pm Mon-Sat; **M**Passeig de Gràcia) Chocoholics will be convinced they have died and passed

---

ℹ

SHOPPING OUT OF HOURS

Got the munchies at 4am? Forgot to buy the paper from your local kiosk? Need something on a Sunday? **Open 25** (Map p310; www.open25.es; Carrer de Còrsega 241; **M**Diagonal) is Barcelona's only 24-hour store, selling useful items like snacks, chocolate bars, magazines and newspapers.

---

on to a better place. Load up in the shop or head for the bar out the back where you can have a classic *xocolata calenta* (hot chocolate) and munch on exquisite chocolate cakes, tarts, ice cream, sweets and sandwiches.

NORMA COMICS   BOOKS

Map p306 (☑93 244 84 23; www.normacomics. com; Passeig de Sant Joan 7-9; **M**Arc de Triomf) With a huge range of comics, both Spanish and international, this is Spain's biggest dealer – everything from Tintin to some of the weirdest sci-fi and sex comics can be found here. Also on show are armies of model superheroes and other characters produced by fevered imaginations. Kids from nine to 99 can be seen snapping up items to add to their collections.

EL CORTE INGLÉS   DEPARTMENT STORE

Map p310 (☑902 400222; www.elcorteingles.es; Plaça de Catalunya 14; **M**Catalunya) 'The English Cut' is Spain's flagship department store, with everything you'd expect, from computers to cushions, and high fashion to homewares. The top floor is occupied by a so-so restaurant with fabulous city views. El Corte Inglés has other branches, including at **Portal de l'Àngel 19-21** (Map p292), **Avinguda Diagonal 617** (Map p314) and **Avinguda Diagonal 471-473** (Map p306), near Plaça de Francesc Macià.

CUBIÑA   HOMEWARES

Map p310 (☑93 476 57 21; www.cubinya.es; Carrer de Mallorca 291; **M**Verdaguer) Even if interior design doesn't ring your bell, it's worth a visit to this extensive temple to furniture, lamps and just about any home accessory your heart might desire just to see this Domènech i Montaner building. Admire the enormous and whimsical wrought-iron decoration at street level before heading inside to marvel at the ceiling, timber work, brick columns and windows. Oh, and don't forget the furniture.

LA SAGRADA FAMÍLIA & L'EIXAMPLE SHOPPING

WORTH A DETOUR

AN OUTLET OUTING

For the ultimate discount fashion overdose, head out of town for some outlet shopping at **La Roca Village** (☑93 842 39 39; www.larocavillage.com; ☺11am-8.30pm Mon-Thu, 11am-9pm Fri, 10am-10pm Sat). Here, a village has been given over to consumer madness. At a long line of Spanish and international fashion boutiques you'll find clothes, shoes, accessories and designer homewares at (they claim) up to 60% off normal retail prices.

To get here, follow the AP-7 tollway north from Barcelona, take exit 12 (marked Cardedeu) and follow the signs for La Roca. The **Sagalés bus company** (☑902 130014; www.sagales.com) organises shuttles from Plaça de Catalunya (€12 return, 40 minutes, 10am, 4pm and 6pm Monday to Saturday from May to September, Monday, Friday and Saturday from October to April). Alternatively, take a slower bus of the same company from Fabra i Puig metro station (€2.90 each way, up to four departures Monday to Friday, does not run in August) or a *rodalies* train to Granollers and pick up the shuttle (Monday to Friday only) or a taxi there.

ADOLFO DOMÍNGUEZ
FASHION

Map p310 (☑93 487 41 70; www.adolfodominguez shop.com; Passeig de Gràcia 32; ⓜPasseig de Gràcia) One of the stars of Spanish prêt-à-porter, this label produces classic men's and women's garments from quality materials. Encompassing anything from regal party gowns to kids' outfits (that might have you thinking of British aristocracy), the broad range generally oozes a conservative air, with elegant cuts that make no concessions to rebellious urban ideals.

ANTONIO MIRÓ
FASHION

Map p310 (☑93 487 06 70; www.antoniomiro. es; Carrer del Consell de Cent 349; ⓒ10am-8pm Mon-Sat; ⓜPasseig de Gràcia) Antonio Miró is one of Barcelona's haute couture kings. The entrance to the airy store, with dark hardwood floor, seems more like a hip hotel reception. Miró concentrates on light, natural fibres to produce smart, unpretentious men's and women's fashion. High-end evening dresses and shimmering, smart suits lead the way. Or you could just settle for an Antonio Miró T-shirt.

ARMAND BASI
FASHION

Map p310 (☑93 215 14 21; www.armandbasi. com; Passeig de Gràcia 49; ⓒ10am-8pm Mon-Sat; ⓜPasseig de Gràcia) Local design star Basi appeals to a 30s and 40s crowd with a slick line in casual elegance. Suits that are perfect without ties and made to impress at dinner or in the town's top clubs match with stylish evening dresses. More casual shirts, trousers, tops and frocks broaden the range. Leather jackets and footwear complete the picture.

GI JOE
FASHION

Map p306 (☑93 329 96 52; Ronda de Sant Antoni 49; ⓜLiceu) Recently moved to this new address, this is the best central army-surplus warehouse. Get your khakis here, along with urban army fashion T-shirts. Throw in a holster, gas mask or sky-blue UN helmet for a kinkier effect.

LOEWE
FASHION

Map p310 (☑93 216 04 00; www.loewe.com; Passeig de Gràcia 35; ⓒ10am-8.30pm Mon-Sat; ⓜPasseig de Gràcia) Loewe is one of Spain's leading and oldest fashion stores, founded in 1846. It specialises in luxury leather (shoes, accessories and travel bags), and also has lines in perfume, sunglasses, cuff links, silk scarves and jewellery. This branch opened in 1943 in the Modernista Casa Lleó Morera.

PURIFICACIÓN GARCÍA
FASHION

Map p310 (☑93 487 72 92; www.purificacion garcia.es; Passeig de Gràcia 21; ⓒ10am-8.30pm Mon-Sat; ⓜPasseig de Gràcia) Ms García has an enormous spread of offerings over two floors in this generous corner store. Not only is the building extraordinary but so too are her collections, if only because of their breadth. You'll find women's cardigans and men's ties, as well as light summer dresses and jeans.

FLORISTERÍA NAVARRO
FLOWERS

Map p310 (☑934574099; www.floristeriasnavarro. com; Carrer de València 320; ⓒ24hr; ⓜDiagonal) You never know when you might need flowers. What better way to follow up the first night of a new romance than with a bunch of roses? No problem, because this florist never closes!

JOAN MURRIÀ   FOOD

Map p310 (☎93 215 57 89; www.murria.cat; Carrer de Roger de Llúria 85; ⓂPasseig de Gràcia) Ramon Casas designed the century-old Modernista shop-front advertisements featured at this culinary temple. For a century the gluttonous have trembled at this altar of specialty food goods from Catalonia and beyond.

NOSOTRAOS   GAY & LESBIAN

Map p310 (☎93 451 51 34; http://nosotras.cat; Carrer de Casanova 56; ⓂUrgell) Everything from gay girl calendars to bear T-shirts and books appear in this multifaceted gay and lesbian store in the heart of the 'Gaixample'.

BAGUÉS   JEWELLERY

Map p310 (☎93 216 01 74; www.bagues.com; Passeig de Gràcia 41; ⓂPasseig de Gràcia) This jewellery store, in business since the 19th century, is in thematic harmony with its location in the Modernista Casa Amatller. Some of the classic pieces of jewellery to come out of the Bagués clan's workshops have an equally playful, Modernista bent.

SERGIO ARANDA   JEWELLERY

Map p310 (☎93 451 44 04; www.sergioaranda.com; Carrer de València 201; ⓂDiagonal) Trained in Switzerland in the art of jewellery creation, Aranda produces an original line of goods, including jewellery made using ancient coins. He also specializes in pearls, making all sorts of original and even daring necklaces and other items for ladies looking for something combining the extroverted and unique with the classic.

REGIA   PERFUME

Map p310 (☎93 216 01 21; www.regia.es; Passeig de Gràcia 39; ◷9.30am-8.30pm Mon-Fri, 10.30am-8.30pm Sat; ⓂPasseig de Gràcia) Regia has been in business since 1928, and is reputed to be one of the best perfume stores in the city. It stocks all the name brands and also has a private perfume museum (p142) out the back. It also sells all sorts of creams, lotions and colognes and has its own line of bath products.

CAMPER   SHOES

Map p310 (☎93 215 63 90; www.camper.com; Carrer de València 249; ⓂPasseig de Gràcia) What started as a modest Mallorcan family business (the island has a long shoemaking tradition) has, over the decades, become the Clarks of Spain. Camper shoes, from the eminently sensible to the stylishly fashionable,

are known for reliability and are sold all over the world, with eight shops in Barcelona.

FARRUTX   SHOES

Map p310 (☎93 215 06 85; www.farrutx.es; Carrer de Rosselló 218; ⓂDiagonal) Mallorcan shoemaker Farrutx specializes in exclusive upmarket footwear for uptown gals. You might fall for high-heeled summer sandals or elegant winter boots. There are matching bags and leather jackets, and even a limited line in men's footwear.

🏃 SPORTS & ACTIVITIES

ANTILLA BCN ESCUELA DE BAILE   CLASSES

Map p310 (☎610 900558, 93 451 45 64; www.antillasalsa.com; Carrer d'Aragó 141; 10 1hr classes €120; ⓂUrgell) The *salsateca* in town, this is the place to come for Cuban *son*, merengue, salsa and a whole lot more. If you don't know how to dance to any of this, you may feel a little silly (as a guy) but women will probably get free lessons. The guys can come back at another time and pay for classes.

BABYLON IDIOMAS   LANGUAGE COURSE

Map p310 (☎93 467 36 36; www.babylon-idiomas.com; Carrer del Bruc 65; ⓂGirona) This small school offers a high degree of flexibility – you can study for a week or enlist for a half-year intensive course in Spanish. The big selling point is class size, with a maximum of eight students per class. A week of tuition (30 hours plus five hours of culture) costs €260.

BARCELONA WALKING TOURS   WALKING TOUR

Map p310 (☎93 285 38 34; www.barcelonaturisme.com; Plaça de Catalunya 17-S; ⓂCatalunya) The Oficina d'Informació de Turisme de Barcelona organises guided walking tours. One explores the **Barri Gòtic** (adult/child €14/5; ◷in English 9.30am daily); another follows in the footsteps of **Picasso** (adult/child €20/7; ◷in English 3pm Tue, Thu & Sun) and winds up at the Museu Picasso (entry is included in the price); and a third takes in the main jewels of **Modernisme** (adult/child €14/5; ◷in English 4pm Fri & Sat Oct-May, 6pm Fri & Sat Jun-Sep). Also offered is a **gourmet tour** (adult/child €20/7; ◷in English 10am Fri & Sat, in Spanish & Catalan 10.30am Sat) of traditional purveyors of fine foodstuffs across the old city (tastings included).

Gràcia & Park Güell

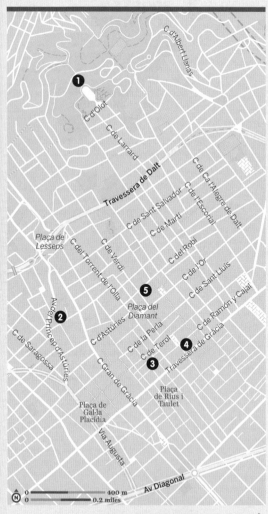

Neighbourhood Top Five

1 Getting lost along the winding paths of **Park Güell** (p160) and exploring its more-natural-than-nature sculptures, mosaics and columns, then resurfacing on one of the park's sunny plazas.

2 Checking out the swirling patterns of the facade of **Casa Vicens** (p162), Gaudí's first commission.

3 Wandering around and taking in the sun on one of **Gràcia's many squares** (p163).

4 Getting high on chocolate with the locals at **La Nena** (p164).

5 Stocking up on Portuguese delicacies and wine in **A Casa Portuguesa** (p168).

For more detail of this area, see Map p312 ➡

Explore: Gràcia & Park Güell

Once a separate village north of L'Eixample, and an industrial district famous for its Republican and liberal ideas, Gràcia was incorporated into the city of Barcelona in 1897, much to the disgust of the locals. The neighbourhood retains its distinct character today, with a boho feel that varies between chic and downtrodden. It's home to artists, local luminaries, young families and a fair number of tramps.

You know you are in Gràcia when you hit its maze of narrow streets and lanes. The heart of the neighbourhood is bounded by Carrer de Còrsega and Avinguda Diagonal in the south, Via Augusta and Avinguda del Príncep d'Astúries to the west, Carrer de Sardenya to the east and Travessera de Dalt to the north. The official district of Gràcia extends beyond, taking in the residential valley of Vallcarca, which nuzzles up alongside Park Güell.

Start the day by exploring Park Güell, moving down to the centre of Gràcia. Plunge into the atmosphere of its narrow streets and small plazas, and the bars and restaurants on and around them. The liveliest are Carrer de Verdi, where you will find wonderful cafes, bars and shops; Plaça del Sol, a raucous square populated by cool bars and (often loud) drunks; Plaça de la Vila de Gràcia (formerly de Rius i Taulet), dotted with cafes and restaurants; Plaça de la Revolucio de Setembre de 1868, a family-friendly square with a playground and ice-cream parlour; and the tree-lined Plaça de la Virreina, a particularly lovely square with cafes, shops and a chilled-out feel.

Gràcia is great during the day or at night – the squares are sunny and relaxed for breakfast or lunch, and lively at night with youngsters enjoying a drink alfresco.

Local Life

➡ **Markets** Locals get their fresh produce from Mercat de la Llibertat (p162), the neighbourhood's emblematic larder – queue up and sample some wonderful food.

➡ **Independent Stores** Wander up Carrer de Verdi for an insight into what Gràcia does best. Local boutiques and food shops abound on this tree-lined street.

➡ **Gourmet Tapas** Gràcia churns out great food in unremarkable local bars – Sureny (p164) is especially fine.

Getting There & Away

➡ **Underground Rail** Metro Línia 3 (Fontana stop) leaves you halfway up Carrer Gran de Gràcia and close to a network of busy squares.

➡ **On Foot** Strolling up Passeig de Gràcia from Plaça de Catalunya is a wonderful way to reach the neighbourhood, but it does take around 45 minutes.

Lonely Planet's Top Tip

A wonderful way to take in Gràcia's atmosphere is from a cafe or restaurant on one of its many squares. Arrive after dusk and watch as the place comes to life in the post-work hours.

✖ Best Places to Eat

➡ Botafumeiro (p162)
➡ Sureny (p164)
➡ O'Gràcia! (p164)
➡ La Nena (p164)

For reviews, see p162 ➡

🍷 Best Places to Drink

➡ La Cigale (p166)
➡ Raïm (p166)
➡ Le Journal (p166)

For reviews, see p166 ➡

☆ Best Entertainment

➡ Heliogàbal (p167)
➡ Elèctric Bar (p167)
➡ Sala Beckett (p167)

For reviews, see p167 ➡

Park Güell – north of Gràcia and about 4km from Plaça de Catalunya – is where Gaudí turned his hand to landscape gardening. It's a strange, enchanting place where this iconic Modernista's passion for natural forms really took flight, to the point where the artificial almost seems more natural than the natural.

A City Park

Park Güell originated in 1900, when Count Eusebi Güell bought the tree-covered hillside of El Carmel (then outside Barcelona) and hired Gaudí to create a miniature city of houses for the wealthy, surrounded by landscaped grounds. The project was a commercial flop and was abandoned in 1914 – but not before Gaudí had created, in his inimitable manner, steps, a plaza, two gatehouses and 3km of roads and walks. In 1922 the city bought the estate for use as a public park. The park became a Unesco World Heritage site in 2004.

Just inside the main entrance on Carrer d'Olot, immediately recognisable by the two Hansel-and-Gretel gatehouses, is the park's newly refurbished Centre d'Interpretació, in the Pavelló de Consergeria, which is a typically curvaceous former porter's home that hosts a display on Gaudí's building methods and the history of the park. There are nice views from the top floor.

Sala Hipóstila (The Doric Temple)

The steps up from the entrance, guarded by a mosaic salamander (a copy of which you can buy in many downtown souvenir shops), lead to the Sala Hipóstila (aka the Doric Temple). This forest of 88 stone columns – some leaning like mighty trees bent by

DON'T MISS...

➡ Learning about Gaudí's building methods at the Centre d'Interpretació

➡ The Sala Hipóstila's stone forest

➡ The life of the artist at Casa-Museu Gaudí

PRACTICALITIES

➡ ☎93 413 24 00

➡ Carrer d'Olot 7

➡ admission free

➡ ⊙10am-9pm Jun-Sep, 10am-8pm Apr, May & Oct, 10am-7pm Mar & Nov, 10am-6pm Dec-Feb

➡ ▯24, Ⓜ Lesseps or Vallcarca

the weight of time – was originally intended as a market. To the left curves a gallery, with twisted stonework columns and roof that give the effect of a cloister beneath tree roots – a motif repeated in several places in the park.

On top of the Sala Hipóstila is a broad open space. Its centrepiece is the Banc de Trencadís, a tiled bench curving sinuously around its perimeter, which was designed by one of Gaudí's closest colleagues, architect Josep Maria Jujol (1879–1949). With Gaudí, however, there is always more than meets the eye. This giant platform was designed as a kind of catchment area for rainwater washing down the hillside. The water is filtered through a layer of stone and sand, and it drains down through the columns to an underground cistern.

Casa-Museu Gaudí

The spired house to the right of the entrance is the Casa-Museu Gaudí, where Gaudí lived for almost the last 20 years of his life (1906–26). It contains furniture he designed (including items that were once at home in La Pedrera, Casa Batlló and Casa Calvet) along with other memorabilia. The house was built in 1904 by Francesc Berenguer i Mestres as a prototype for the 60 or so houses that were originally planned here.

Much of the park is still wooded, but it's laced with pathways. The best views are from the cross-topped Turó del Calvari in the southwest corner.

GETTING HERE

The walk from Metro stop Lesseps is signposted. From the Vallcarca stop, the walk is marginally shorter and the uphill trek eased by escalators. Bus 24 drops you at an entrance near the top of the park.

The park is extremely popular (it gets an estimated 4 million visitors a year, about 86% of them tourists) and there is talk of limiting access to keep a lid on damage done by the overkill. Its quaint nooks and crannies are irresistible to photographers, who on busy days have trouble keeping out of each other's pictures.

GRÀCIA & PARK GÜELL PARK GÜELL

TOP SIGHTS
PARK GÜELL

GAUDÍ OFF THE BEATEN TRACK

Gaudí, like any freelancer, was busy all over town. While his main patron was Eusebi Güell and his big projects were bankrolled by the wealthy bourgeoisie, he also took on smaller jobs. One example is the Casa Vicens (p162) in Gràcia. Another is the **Col. legi de les Teresianes** (Map p314; ☑93 212 33 54; Carrer de Ganduxer 85-105; ⓕFGC Tres Torres), to which he added some personal touches in 1889. Although you can see parts of the wing he designed (to the right through the entrance gate) from the outside, the most unique features are those hardest to see – the distinctive parabolic arches inside. Unfortunately, it is no longer possible to view the school's interior.

Gaudí fanatics might also want to reach **Bellesguard** (Map p314; Carrer de Bellesguard; ⓕFGC Avinguda Tibidabo, ☐60), a private house he built in 1909 on the site of the ancient palace of the Catalan count-king Martí I. You can get a reasonable idea of the house peering in from the roadside. The castlelike appearance is reinforced by the heavy stonework, generous wrought iron and a tall spire. Gaudí also worked in some characteristically playful mosaic and colourful tiles.

◉ SIGHTS

PARK GÜELL
PARK

See p160.

FREE MERCAT DE LA LLIBERTAT
MARKET

Map p312 (☑93 217 09 95; Plaça de la Llibertat; ◷8am-8.30pm Mon-Fri, 8am-3pm Sat; ⓕFGC Gràcia) Built in the 1870s, the 'Liberty Market' was covered over in 1893 in typically fizzy Modernista style, employing generous whirls of wrought iron. It got a considerable facelift in 2009 and has lost some of its aged charm, but the market remains emblematic of the Gràcia district: full of life and all kinds of fresh produce. The man behind the 1893 remake was Francesc Berenguer i Mestres (1866–1914), Gaudí's longtime assistant.

FUNDACIÓ FOTO COLECTANIA
GALLERY

Map p312 (☑93 217 16 26; www.colectania.es; Carrer de Julián Romea 6; admission €3; ◷11am-2pm & 5-8.30pm Mon-Sat, closed Aug; ⓕFGC Gràcia) Photography lovers should swing by here to see the latest exhibition; they change over about three times a year. When you reach what seems like offices, head through to the back on the ground floor, where two floors of exhibition space await. The exhibits may come from the foundation's own collection of Spanish and Portuguese snappers from the 1950s onwards, but more likely will be temporary exhibitions.

CASA VICENS
ARCHITECTURE

(www.casavicens.es; Carrer de les Carolines 22; ⓕFGC Plaça Molina) The angular, turreted 1888 Casa Vicens was one of Gaudí's first commissions. Tucked away west of Gràcia's main drag, this private house (which was up for sale at the time of writing, and couldn't be viewed inside) is awash with ceramic colour and shape.

As was frequently the case, Gaudí sought inspiration from the past, in this case the rich heritage of building in the Mudéjar-style brick, typical in those parts of Spain reconquered from the Muslims. Mudéjar architecture was created by those Arabs and Berbers allowed to remain in Spain after the Christian conquests.

✖ EATING

All sorts of enticing options are spread along this busy quarter, from simple tapas bars to top-class seafood. Gràcia is loaded with Middle Eastern and, to a lesser extent, Greek restaurants, which are chirpy and good value. Several classic Catalan taverns tick along nicely with a strong local following. There's little of interest, however, around Park Güell.

BOTAFUMEIRO
SEAFOOD €€

Map p312 (☑93 218 42 30; www.botafumeiro.es; Carrer Gran de Gràcia 81; meals €15-25; ◷1pm-1am; ⓜFontana) It is hard not to mention this classic temple of Galician shellfish and other briny delights, long a magnet for VIPs visiting Barcelona. You can bring the price down by sharing a few *medias raciones* (medium tapas plates) to taste a range of marine offerings or a *safata especial del Mar Cantàbric* (seafood platter) between two. Try the

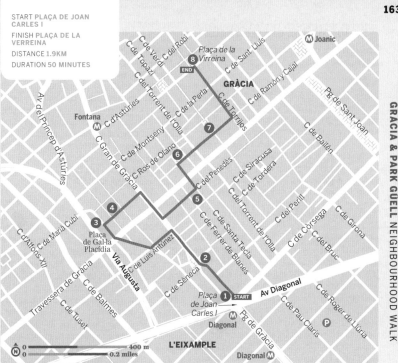

GRÀCIA & PARK GÜELL NEIGHBOURHOOD WALK

Neighbourhood Walk
The Squares of Gràcia

The obelisk at **1 Plaça de Joan Carles I** honours Spain's present king for stifling an attempted coup d'état in February 1981, six years after Franco's death. Under the dictatorship, the avenue that passes through the square was known as Avenida de Francisco Franco. To locals it was simply 'La Diagonal'. That name stuck.

Where Carrer Gran de Gràcia leads you into Gràcia proper, a grand Modernista edifice now turned hotel, **2 Casa Fuster** (p221), rises in all its glory.

3 Plaça de Gal.la Placidia recalls the brief sojourn of the Roman empress-to-be Galla Placidia, captive and wife of the Visigothic chief Athaulf in the 5th century AD. She had been hauled across from Italy, where she hastily returned upon her captor-husband's death.

4 Plaça de la Llibertat (Liberty Square) is home to the bustling Modernista produce market of the same name. It was designed by one of Gaudí's colleagues, Francesc Berenguer.

Popular **5 Plaça de la Vila de Gràcia** was until recently named after the mayor under whom Gràcia was absorbed by Barcelona, Francesc Rius i Taulet. It is fronted by the local town hall (designed by Berenguer). At its heart stands the Torre del Rellotge (Clock Tower), long a symbol of Republican agitation.

Possibly the rowdiest of Gràcia's squares, **6 Plaça del Sol** (Sun Square) is lined with bars and eateries and comes to life on long summer nights.

7 Plaça de la Revolució de Setembre de 1868 commemorates the toppling of Queen Isabel II, a cause of much celebration in this working-class stronghold.

Pleasant terraces adorn pedestrianised **8 Plaça de la Virreina**, notable for its shady trees and presided over by the 17th-century Església de Sant Joan. It was largely destroyed by anarchists during the unrest of the Setmana Tràgica (Tragic Week) of 1909. Rebuilt by Berenguer, it was damaged again during the civil war.

percebes, the strangely twisted goose barnacles harvested along Galicia's north Atlantic coast, which many Spaniards consider the ultimate seafood delicacy.

SURENY
CATALAN €

Map p312 (☎93 213 75 56; Plaça de la Revolució de Setembre de 1868; meals €8-10; ☉Tue-Sun; MFontana) Appearances can be deceiving: the cooks in this unremarkable-looking corner restaurant dedicate themselves to producing gourmet tapas ranging from exquisite *vieiras* (scallops) to a serving of *secreto ibérico*, a particular tasty cut of pork meat (near the porcine equivalent of the armpit – perhaps that's the 'secret'). The *menú del día* (set menu) is decent value at €9.90.

O'GRÀCIA!
MEDITERRANEAN €€

Map p312 (Plaça de la Revolució de Setembre de 1868, 15; meals €10-12; ☉Tue-Sat; MFontana) This is an especially popular lunch option, with the *menú del día* outstanding value at €10.50. The *arròs negre de sepia* (black rice with cuttlefish) makes a good first course, followed by a limited set of meat and fish options with vegetable sides. Serves are decent, presentation is careful and service is attentive. There's a more elaborate tasting menu at €24.50.

LA NENA
CAFE €

Map p312 (☎93 285 14 76; Carrer de Ramon i Cajal 36; ☉9am-2pm & 4-10pm Mon-Sat, 10am-10pm Sun & holidays; MFontana) A French team has created this delightfully chaotic space for indulging in cups *suïssos* (rich hot chocolate), served with a plate of heavy homemade whipped cream and *melindros* (spongy sweet biscuits), fine desserts and even a few savoury dishes (including crêpes). The place is strewn with books and the area out the back is designed to keep kids busy, with toys, books and a blackboard with chalk, making it an ideal family rest stop.

RESTAURANT ROIG ROBÍ
CATALAN €€

Map p312 (☎93 218 92 22; www.roigrobi.com; Carrer de Sèneca 20; meals €15-20; ☉lunch & dinner Mon-Fri, dinner Sat; MDiagonal) This is an altar to refined traditional cooking. Try the *textures de carxofes amb vieires a la plantxa* (artichokes with grilled scallops) for the delicate scent of artichoke wafting over the prized shellfish. The restaurant also does several seafood-and-rice dishes and offers half portions for those with less of an appetite.

CON GRACIA
FUSION €€€

Map p312 (☎93 238 02 01; www.congracia.es; Carrer de Martínez de la Rosa 8; set menus €59; ☉lunch & dinner Tue-Fri, dinner Sat; MDiagonal) This teeny hideaway (seating about 20 in total) is a hive of originality, producing delicately balanced Mediterranean cuisine with Asian touches. On offer is a regularly changing surprise tasting menu or the set 'traditional' one, which includes such items as *sopa de foie y miso con aceite de trufa blanca* (miso and foie gras soup with white truffle oil) and a nice Chilean sea bass. At lunch, only groups are accepted. Book ahead.

IPAR-TXOKO
BASQUE €€€

Map p312 (☎93 218 19 54; Carrer de Mozart 22; meals €40-50; ☉Tue-Sat Sep-Jul; MDiagonal) Inside this Basque eatery the atmosphere is warm and traditional. Hefty timber beams hold up the Catalan vaulted ceiling, and the bar (with tapas available) has a garish green columned front. Getxo-born Mikel turns out traditional cooking from northern Spain, including a sumptuous *chuletón* (T-bone steak for two – look at the size of that thing!) or a less gargantuan *tortilla de bacalao* (a thick salted-cod omelette).

There are also curiosities like *kokotxas de merluza*, heart-shaped cuts from the hake's throat. The wine list is daunting but Mikel is on hand to explain everything – in English, too.

BILBAO
SPANISH €€

Map p312 (☎93 458 96 24; Carrer del Perill 33; meals €10-15; ☉Mon-Sat; MDiagonal) It doesn't look much from the outside, but Bilbao is a timeless classic, where reservations for dinner are imperative. The back dining room, with bottle-lined walls, stout timber tables and a yellow light evocative of a country tavern, will appeal to carnivores especially, although some fish dishes are also on offer. Consider opting for a *chuletón* (T-bone steak), accompanied with a good Spanish red wine.

TIBET
CATALAN €€€

(☎93 284 50 45; Carrer de Ramiro de Maetzu 34; meals €35; ☉lunch & dinner Mon & Wed-Sat, lunch Sun; ☐24 or 39, MAlfons X) This Catalan restaurant, nestled in a semi-rustic setting not far from Park Güell, has as much to do with Tibet as this author does with Outer Mongolia. For 50 years it has been sizzling meat on the grill and dishing up snails, one of the house specialities.

CAL BOTER
CATALAN €

Map p312 (☎93 458 84 62; Carrer de Tordera 62; meals €10; ☺Tue-Sun; MJoanic) Families and noisy groups are drawn to this classic eatery for *cargols a la llauna* (snails sautéed in a tin dish), *filet de bou a la crema de foie* (a thick clump of tender beef drowned in an orange and foie gras sauce), and other Catalan specialities, including curious *mar i muntanya* (sea and mountain) combinations like *bolets i gambes* (mushrooms and prawns). The *menú del día* (lunch Tuesday to Friday) comes in at a good-humoured €9.80.

ENVALIRA
CATALAN €

Map p312 (Plaça del Sol 13; meals €8; ☺lunch & dinner Tue-Sat, lunch Sun; MFontana) You might not notice the modest entrance to this delicious relic, surrounded as it is by cool hang-outs, Lebanese eateries and grunge bars. Head for the 1950s time-warp dining room out the back. Serious waiters deliver all sorts of seafood and rice dishes to your table; try *arròs a la milanesa* (savoury rice with chicken, pork and a light cheese gratin) or a *bullit de lluç* (slice of white hake boiled with herb-laced rice and a handful of clams).

LAC MAJÙR
ITALIAN €€€

Map p312 (☎93 285 15 03; Carrer de Tordera 33; meals €25; ☺Mon-Sat; MVerdaguer) Inside this cosy slice of northwest Italy all sorts of home-cooking delights await, including the house pasta specials, gnocchi and trofie. The latter are twists of pasta, usually served with pesto sauce, from Liguria. Try the mascarpone and ham variant followed by, say, a *saltimbocca alla romana* (a veal slice cooked with ham, sage and sweet Marsala wine).

LA PANXA DEL BISBE
TAPAS €€€

Map p312 (☎93 213 70 49; www.lapanxadelbisbe. com; Carrer de Rabassa 37; meals €25; ☺Tue-Sat; MJoanic) With low lighting and a hip, young feel, the 'Bishop's Gut' is a great place to indulge in some gourmet tapas, washed down with a fine wine, like the Albariño white from Galicia, for a surprisingly modest outlay.

EL GLOP
CATALAN €€€

Map p312 (☎93 213 70 58; www.tavernaelglop. com; Carrer de Sant Lluís 24; meals €25; MJoanic) This raucous eatery is decked out in country Catalan fashion, with gingham tablecloths and no-nonsense, slap-up meals. The secret is hearty serves of simple dishes, such as *bistec a la brasa* (grilled steak), perhaps preceded by *alberginies farcides* (stuffed aubergines) or *calçots* (spring onions) in winter. To finish try the *tocinillo*, a caramel dessert. Open until 1am, El Glop is a useful place to have up your sleeve for a late bite.

LA LLAR DE FOC
CATALAN €€

Map p312 (☎93 284 10 25; Carrer de Ramón i Cajal 13; meals €20; MFontana) For a hearty sit-down meal at rock-bottom prices, the 'Hearth' is hard to beat. At lunch, it has a €9 *menú del día*. You could start with a mixed salad or *empanadita* (big slice of tuna pie), followed by chicken in a mild curry sauce or *costellas* (ribs). Go for flan for dessert, as the ice creams are on a stick.

HIMALI
NEPALESE €€

Map p312 (☎93 285 15 68; Carrer de Milà i Fontanals 60; meals €15-20; ☺Tue-Sun; ☑; MJoanic) Spacious and simple, with gruff service and paper placemats, this is a great spot for Nepalese chow and vegetarian dishes. A vegetarian set dinner menu costs €14.95; the meatier version is €16.95. Carnivores can also opt for mixed grills with rice and naan, or *kukhurako fila* (roast chicken in walnut sauce). Mains come in at €8 to €10.

NOU CANDANCHÚ
TAPAS €

Map p312 (☎93 237 73 62; Plaça de la Vila de Gràcia 9; meals €5-7; ☺Wed-Mon; MFontana) The liveliest locale on the square, Nou Candanchú is a long-time favourite for various reasons. Many flock to its sunny terrace just for a few drinks. Accompany the liquid refreshment with one of the giant *entrepans* (filled rolls) for which this place is famous. Otherwise, it offers a limited range of tapas and reasonable grilled-meat dishes.

EL ROURE
TAPAS €

Map p312 (☎93 218 73 87; Carrer de la Riera de Sant Miquel 51; meals €7-9; ☺Mon-Sat; MFontana) This old-time locals' bar is what Hemingway meant by a 'clean, well-lighted place'. Sidle up to the bar or pull up a little wooden chair and tuck into good-value tapas from the bar, washed down by a few cold Estrellas. The *bunyols de bacallà* are delightful battered balls of cod that demand to be gobbled up. The place is full to bursting most of the time.

VRENELI
CAFE €

Map p312 (☎93 217 61 01; Plaça de la Vila de Gràcia 8; ☺8am-9pm Tue-Fri, 9am-9pm Sat & Sun; cakes from €3; MFontana) For banana or carrot cake and a cup of coffee on a grey winter's day, this long, narrow bar with soft mood music is a good place to come in out of the cold.

CANTINA MACHITO
MEXICAN €

Map p312 (☏932 17 34 14; www.cantinamachito.com; Carrer Torrijos 47; meals €8-11; ☉1-4pm, 7pm-1.30am; ⓜFontana or Joanic) On the leafy Torrijos street, the colourful Machito – which seems devoted to the image of Frida Kahlo – gets busy with locals, and the outside tables are a great place to eat and drink until late. You'll find all the standard Mexican delights like quesadillas, tacos, enchiladas and so on, and some wonderfully refreshing iced water flavoured with honey and lime, mint and fruit.

MONTY CAFÉ
CAFE, ITALIAN €€

Map p312 (☏93 368 28 82; www.montycafe.com; Carrer de la Riera de Sant Miquel 29; meals €6-19; ☉8am-10pm Mon & Tue, 8am-midnight Wed & Thu, 8am-2am Fri & Sat; ☂; ⓜDiagonal) This laid-back Italian-run cafe has a terracotta floor, art on the walls, classic marble-top tables and a series of varied, secondhand lounges down one side and a bar at the back. Great for coffee, a long list of teas and cocktails, it also offers food from pasta to bruschetta. It's a great place to lounge around over your laptop.

🍷 DRINKING & NIGHTLIFE

Gràcia is a quirky place. In many ways it's its own world, with rowdy young beer swillers, trendy music bars and a couple of the city's big clubs.

LA CIGALE
BAR

Map p312 (☏93 457 58 23; http://poesialacigale.blogspot.co.uk; Carrer de Tordera 50; ☉6pm-2.30am Sun-Thu, 6pm-3am Fri & Sat; ⓜJoanic) A very civilised place for a cocktail (or two for €8 before 10pm) and hearing some poetry readings. Prop up the zinc bar, sink into a secondhand lounge chair around a teeny table or head upstairs. Music is chilled, conversation is lively and you're likely to see Charlie Chaplin in action on the silent flat-screen TV. You can also snack on wok-fried dishes.

The same brothers run the equally pleasant **La Fourmi** (Map p312; ☏93 213 30 52; Carrer de Milà i Fontanals 58; ⓜJoanic) around the corner, which is open for breakfast.

RAÏM
BAR

Map p312 (www.raimbcn.com; Carrer del Progrés 48; ☉8pm-2.30am; ⓜDiagonal) The walls in Raïm are alive with black-and-white photos of Cubans and Cuba. Tired old wooden chairs of another epoch huddle around marble tables, while grand old timber-lined mirrors hang from the walls. They just don't make old Spanish taverns like this anymore.

LE JOURNAL
BAR

Map p312 (☏93 218 04 13; Carrer de Francisco Giner 36; ☉6pm-2.30am Sun-Thu, 6pm-3am Fri & Sat; ⓜFontana) Students love the conspiratorial basement air of this narrow bar, whose walls and ceiling are plastered with newspapers (hence the name). Read the headlines of yesteryear while reclining in an old lounge. For a slightly more intimate feel, head upstairs to the rear gallery. It's a smokers' paradise.

ALFA
BAR

Map p312 (☏93 415 18 24; Carrer Gran de Gràcia 36; ☉11pm-3.30am Thu-Sat; ⓜDiagonal) Aficionados of good old-fashioned rock love this unchanging bar-cum-minidisco, a Gràcia classic. Records hang from the ceiling as if to remind you that most of the music comes from the pre-CD era, '60s to '80s and the occasional later intruder. Take up a stool for a drink and chat or head for the no-frills dance area just beyond. There's another bar right up the back.

BAR CANIGÓ
BAR

Map p312 (☏93 213 30 49; Carrer de Verdi 2; ☉5pm-2am Mon-Thu, 5pm-3am Fri & Sat; ⓜFontana) Especially welcoming in winter, this corner bar overlooking Plaça de la Revolució de Setembre de 1868 is an animated spot to simply sip on an Estrella beer around rickety old marble-top tables, as people have done here for decades. There's also a pool table.

LA BAIGNOIRE
WINE BAR

Map p312 (Carrer de Verdi 6; ☉7pm-2.30am Sun-Thu, 7pm-3am Fri & Sat; ⓜFontana) This inviting, tiny wine bar is always packed. Grab a stool and high table and order fine wines by the glass (beer and cocktails available, too). It's perfect before and after a movie at the nearby Verdi cinema.

MUSICAL MARIA — BAR

Map p312 (Carrer de Maria 5; ⏰9pm-3am; ⓜDiagonal) Even the music hasn't changed since this place got going in the late 1970s. Those longing for rock 'n' roll crowd into this animated bar, listen to old hits and knock back beers. Out back there's a pool table and the bar serves pretty much all the variants of the local Estrella Damm brew.

NOISE I ART — BAR

Map p312 (✆93 217 50 01; Carrer de Topazi 26; ⏰6pm-2.30am Tue & Wed, 7pm-3am Thu-Sat, 6pm-1.30am Sun; ⓜFontana) Step back into the 1980s in this retro den. Red, green and other bold colours dominate the decor in a place where you might encounter Boney M on the video music play. Drape yourself on the circular red lounge, have a light meal (served up on old LPs) at red-lit tables alongside floor-to-ceiling glass windows, or perch yourself at the bar. The daiquiris may not be the best you've ever had, but are probably the biggest!

SABOR A CUBA — BAR

Map p312 (Carrer de Francisco Giner 32; ⏰10pm-2.30am Mon-Thu, 10pm-3am Fri & Sat; ⓜDiagonal) Ruled since 1992 by the charismatic Havana-born Angelito is this home of *ron y son* (rum and sound). A mixed crowd of Cubans and fans of the Caribbean island come to drink *mojitos* and shake their stuff in this diminutive, good-humoured hang-out.

SOL SOLER — BAR

Map p312 (✆93 217 44 40; Plaça del Sol 21-22; ⏰noon-1am; ⓜFontana) A pleasant place with old tile floors, wood panelling and little marble tables perfect for an early beer or glass of red and a chat. Drop by earlier in the day for wi-fi (available to 6.30pm) and, if hunger strikes, order in some bar snacks (the chicken wings are delicious).

⭐ ENTERTAINMENT

HELIOGÀBAL — LIVE MUSIC

Map p312 (www.heliogabal.com; Carrer de Ramón i Cajal 80; ⏰9pm-2am Sun-Thu, 9pm-3am Fri & Sat; ⓜJoanic) This compact bar is a veritable hive of cultural activity where you never quite know what to expect. The eclectic live-music program is a pleasant surprise:. jazz groups are often followed by open jam sessions, and experimental music of all persuasions gets a run. While many performers are local, international acts also get a look-in.

ELÈCTRIC BAR — LIVE MUSIC

Map p312 (www.electricbarcelona.com; Travessera de Gràcia 233; ⏰7pm-2am Sun-Thu, 7pm-3am Fri & Sat; ⓜJoanic) Concerts get under way between 10pm and 11pm in this long and somewhat dingy bar. Generally, we're looking at home-grown bands revelling in the chance to bring jazz, blues, funk, bossa nova and much more to a small stage and appreciative crowd. It can get pretty crowded in here but often the bands are fresh and fun.

SALA BECKETT — THEATRE

Map p312 (✆93 284 53 12; www.salabeckett.com; Carrer de Ca l'Alegre de Dalt 55; ⏰box office 10am-2pm & 4-8pm Mon-Fri & 1hr before start of show; ⓜJoanic) One of the city's principal alternative theatres, the Sala Beckett is a smallish space that does not shy away from challenging theatre, contemporary or otherwise, and usually has a heterodox mix of local productions and foreign drama.

TEATRENEU — THEATRE

Map p312 (✆93 285 37 12; www.teatreneu.com; Carrer de Terol 26; ⏰box office 1hr before show; ⓜFontana or Joanic) This lively theatre (with a bustling, rambling downstairs bar facing the street) dares to fool around with all sorts of material, from monologues to social comedy. Aside from the main theatre, two cafe-style spaces serve as more intimate stage settings for small-scale productions. Films are also shown.

CASABLANCA KAPLAN — CINEMA

Map p312 (✆93 218 43 45; Passeig de Gràcia 115; ⓜDiagonal) A smallish, popular local cinema (with three screens) that always shows movies in the original language.

VERDI — CINEMA

Map p312 (✆93 238 79 90; www.cines-verdi.com; Carrer de Verdi 32; ⓜFontana) This popular original-language movie house in the heart of Gràcia is handy to lots of local eateries and bars for pre- and post-film enjoyment.

VERDI PARK — CINEMA

Map p312 (✆93 238 79 90; www.cines-verdi. com; Carrer de Torrijos 49; ⓜFontana) The Verdi Park is a block away from its sister cimena, Verdi, and follows the same art-house philosophy.

🛍 SHOPPING

A wander along the narrow lanes of Gràcia turns up all sorts of surprises, mostly tiny enterprises producing a variety of pretty garments and trinkets. These places tend to come and go, so you never quite know what you might turn up. Carrer de Verdi has plenty of interesting threads shops.

A CASA PORTUGUESA
FOOD

Map p312 (☎933 68 35 28; www.acasaportuguesa.com, in Spanish; Carrer de Verdi 58; ⏱5-10pm Tue-Fri, 11am-3pm & 5-10pm Sat & Sun; ⓂFontana) Come here to try Barcelona's best Portuguese custard tarts, *pastéis de Belém*. Unfortunately, and because of Gràcia's draconian restaurant laws, A Casa Portuguesa had to be turned into a non-seating-and-eating kind of place; although you can taste wine and stand here for a while, you can no longer sit down for food and drink.

No matter – at the time of writing, the owners were in the process of opening a bistro on 111 Carrer d'Aragò, where you'll be able to sample the vast variety of Portuguese food and wine, and a *menú del día* offering typical Portuguese delicacies. The new place should be open by the time you're reading this. In this Gràcia outlet, however, you can get your shopping bag full of cheeses, little pies and pastries, and have a picnic on a local square.

NOSTÀLGIC
PHOTOGRAPHY

Map p312 (☎933 68 57 57; www.nostalgic.es; Carrer de Goya 18; ⏱11am-2pm & 5-9pm daily; closed Mon mornings; ⓂFontana) A beautiful space with exposed brick walls and wooden furniture specialising in all kinds of modern and vintage photography equipment – you'll find camera bags and tripods for the digital snappers, and the inevitable collection of Lomo cameras, with their quirky variations. There is also a decent collection of photography books to buy or browse.

HIBERNIAN
BOOKS

Map p312 (☎93 217 47 96; Carrer de Montseny 17; ⏱4-8.30pm Mon, 10.30am-8.30pm Tue-Sat; ⓂFontana) The biggest secondhand English bookshop in Barcelona stocks thousands of titles covering all sorts of subjects, from cookery to children's classics.

ÉRASE UNA VEZ
FASHION

Map p312 (☎93 217 29 77; Carrer de Goya 7; ⓂFontana) 'Once Upon a Time' is the name of this fanciful boutique, which brings out the princess in you (if you have one in there, that is). It offers women's clothes, almost exclusively evening wear to suit most tastes and occasions, as well as wedding dresses. Local designers such as Llamazares y de Delgado and Zazo & Brull are behind these sometimes-sumptuous creations.

🏃 SPORTS & ACTIVITIES

AQUA URBAN SPA
DAY SPA

Map p312 (☎93 238 41 60; www.aqua-urbanspa.com; Carrer Gran de Gràcia 7; 75min session €65-99; ⏱9am-9.30pm Mon-Fri, 9am-8.30pm Sat; ⓂDiagonal) With sessions for anything from stress to tired legs (helpful for diehard sightseers!), this spa offers smallish pool and shower areas, along with steam baths, Roman-style baths and a series of beauty treatment options.

FLOTARIUM
FLOTARIUM

Map p312 (☎93 217 36 37; www.flotarium.com; Plaça de Narcís Oller 3; 1hr session €35; ⏱10am-10pm daily; ⓂDiagonal) Be suspended in zero gravity and feel the stress ebb away. Each flotarium, like a little space capsule with water, is in a private room, with shower, towels and shampoo, and Epsom salts that allow you to float as if in the Dead Sea.

Camp Nou, Pedralbes & La Zona Alta

SANT GERVASI | TIBIDABO | SARRIÀ | PEDRALBES | ZONA UNIVERSITÀRIA

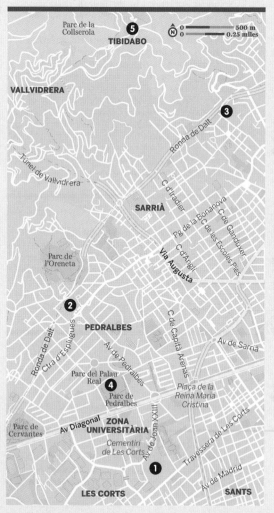

Neighbourhood Top Five

1 Reliving the great moments of one the world's legendary football teams at the multimedia museum of **Camp Nou** (p171). Or, better yet, seeing a game live.

2 Walking the 14th-century cloister and gazing at exquisite murals at peaceful **Museu-Monestir de Pedralbes** (p172).

3 Getting a taste of the Amazon, and travelling through earth's evolution at warp speed at **CosmoCaixa** (p176).

4 Discovering 1000 years of ceramic treasures inside the fascinating **Palau Reial de Pedralbes** (p173).

5 Travelling by tram and funicular railway up to **Tibidabo** (p174) for its lovely views and old-fashioned amusement park.

For more detail of this area, see Maps p314 and p316 ➡

Lonely Planet's Top Tip

To make the most of the neighbourhood, try to visit on a weekend. Saturday and Sunday are the only days when you can peek inside the Pavellons Güell (with guided visits in English offered twice daily) at Palau Reial de Pedralbes. The weekend is also the best time to catch the tram up to Tibidabo.

✖ Best Places to Eat

➡ Via Veneto (p175)
➡ La Molina (p175)
➡ Hofman (p176)
➡ La Balsa (p176)
➡ El Asador de Aranda (p177)

For reviews, see p175 ➡

☐ Best Places to Drink

➡ Mirablau (p177)
➡ Elephant (p177)
➡ Marcel (p178)

For reviews, see p177 ➡

◉ Best Parks & Gardens

➡ Parc de Collserola (p174)
➡ Jardins del Laberint d'Horta (p175)
➡ Parc de la Creueta del Coll (p173)

For reviews, see p173 ➡

Explore: Camp Nou, Pedralbes & La Zona Alta

This vast area, which runs north of L'Eixample and west of Gràcia, includes some intriguing sites, yet few tourists make the journey here. The Collserola hills, a major draw for outdoor enthusiasts, frame the north end of 'the High Zone'. The rugged Parc de Collserola attracts cyclists and walkers, and has a sprinkling of historic sites for those wanting to explore Barcelona off the tourist path.

Nearby Tibidabo (512m), topped by the towering Temple del Sagrat Cor, marks the city's highest point. Getting here – via tram and funicular – is half the fun.

Standout attractions in the upscale neighbourhood of Pedralbes include an atmospheric monastery and the artwork-filled Palau Reial de Pedralbes.

To the south is Camp Nou, the enshrined playing field of FC Barça, one of the world's best football teams.

To the northeast lies Sarrià, a small, quaint neighbourhood of brick streets, tiny plazas and medieval buildings, with a lively collection of shops, restaurants and bars. For an authentic and charming side of Barcelona, relatively untouristed, this is the place to come.

The drawbacks to this area are its remoteness from town, and the distances between sights. Aside from Sarrià, the other area that's worth exploring on foot is Sant Gervasi, with its handful of upscale restaurants and bars. It is geographically (and thematically) close to Gràcia.

Local Life

➡ **Outdoors** Go for a run or a mountain-bike ride in the vast hillside reserve of Parc de Collserola (p174).
➡ **Nightlife** Start with drinks in the bars near Carrer de Muntaner, followed by dancing at Otto Zutz (p178).
➡ **Village Days** Wander through the picturesque narrow lanes of Sarrià, stopping for cakes at Foix de Sarrià (p177) and tapas at Bar Tomàs (p177).

Getting There & Away

➡ **Metro** Línia 3 passes Jardins del Laberint d'Horta (Mundet) and Camp Nou and Palau Reial de Pedralbes (Palau Reial).
➡ **Train** FGC trains are handy for getting close to sights in and around Tibidabo and the Parc del Collserola.
➡ **Tram** The *tramvia blau* runs from Avinguda de Tibidabo station to Plaça del Doctor Andreu.
➡ **Funicular** The funicular del Tibidabo runs between Plaça del Doctor Andreu and Plaça del Doctor Tibidabo; the funicular de Vallvidrera runs between Peu del Funicular and Vallvidrera Superior.

KRZYSZTOF DYDYNSKI / LONELY PLANET IMAGES ©

◉ TOP SIGHTS
CAMP NOU

Among Barcelona's most-visited sites is the massive stadium of Camp Nou (which means New Field in Catalan), home to the legendary Futbol Club Barça. Football fans who aren't able to attend a game can get a taste of all the excitement at the museum, with its multimedia exhibits, and a guided tour of the stadium.

Museu del Futbol Club Barcelona

The **museum** (☑93 496 36 00; www.fcbarcelona.es; Carrer d'Aristides Maillol; adult/child €8.50/6.80; ◷10am-8pm Mon-Sat, 10am-2.30pm Sun & holidays mid-Apr–mid-Oct, 10am-6.30pm Mon-Sat, 10am-2.30pm Sun & holidays mid-Oct–mid-Apr; ⓜCollblanc), renovated in 2010, provides a high-tech view into the club, with massive touch-screens allowing visitors to explore arcane aspects of the legendary team.

The best bits of the museum itself are the photo section, the goal videos and the views out over the stadium. You can admire the (in at least one case literally) golden boots of great goalscorers of the past and learn about the greats who have played for Barça over the years, including Maradona, Ronaldinho, Kubala and many others.

The Stadium

Gazing out across Camp Nou is an experience in itself. The stadium, built in 1957 and enlarged for the 1982 World Cup, is one of the world's biggest, holding 99,000 people. The club has a world-record membership of 173,000. The guided tour of the stadium takes in the team's dressing rooms, heads out through the tunnel, onto the pitch and winds up in the presidential box. You'll also get to visit the television studio, the press room and the commentary boxes. Set aside about 2½ hours for the whole visit.

DON'T MISS...

➡ Hearing the rousing Barça anthem sung before the team takes the field

➡ The museum's footage of the team's best goals

➡ A guided tour of the stadium

PRACTICALITIES

➡ Map p314

➡ ☑93 496 36 00

➡ www.fcbarcelona. com

➡ Carrer d'Aristides Maillol

➡ adult/child €22/17

➡ ◷10am-8pm Mon-Sat, to 2.30pm Sun

➡ ⓜPalau Reial

 TOP SIGHTS
MUSEU-MONESTIR DE PEDRALBES

This peaceful old convent was first opened to the public in 1983 and is now a museum of monastic life (the few remaining nuns have moved into more modern neighbouring buildings). It's full of architectural treasures and provides a fascinating glimpse into centuries past. Perched at the top of busy Avinguda de Pedralbes in what was once unpeopled countryside, the monastery remains a divinely quiet corner of Barcelona.

The Cloister & Chapel

The architectural highlight is the large, elegant, three-storey cloister, a jewel of Catalan Gothic, built in the early 14th century. Following its course to the right, stop at the first chapel, the Capella de Sant Miquel, the **murals** of which were done in 1346 by Ferrer Bassá, one of Catalonia's earliest documented painters.

The Refectory & Dormidor

As you head around the ground floor of the cloister, you can peer into the restored refectory, kitchen, stables, stores and a reconstruction of the infirmary – all giving a good idea of convent life. Eating in the refectory must not have been a whole lot of fun, judging by the **enscriptions** around the walls exhorting Silentium (Silence) and Audi Tacens (Listen and Keep Quiet).

Upstairs is a grand hall that was once the *dormidor* (sleeping quarters). It was lined by tiny night cells but they were long ago removed. Today a modest collection of the monastery's art, especially Gothic devotional works, and furniture grace this space.

DON'T MISS...

➡ Ferrer Bassá's murals
➡ The three-storey Gothic cloister
➡ The refectory's admonishing enscriptions

PRACTICALITIES

➡ Map p314
➡ ☎93 256 34 34
➡ www.museuhistoria.bcn.cat
➡ Baixada del Monestir 9
➡ adult/child €7/5
➡ ⊙10am-5pm Tue-Sat, to 8pm Sun
➡ ⓡFGC Reina Elisenda, ⎙22, 63, 64 or 75

⦿ SIGHTS

CAMP NOU STADIUM
See p171.

**MUSEU-MONESTIR
DE PEDRALBES** MONASTERY
See p172.

PALAU REIAL DE PEDRALBES PALACE
Map p314 (☑93 256 34 65; Avinguda Diagonal 686; all collections adult/student & senior €5/3, 1st Sun of month & 3-6pm Sun free; ⊘museums 10am-6pm Tue-Sun, 10am-3pm holidays, park 10am-6pm daily; ⓜPalau Reial) Across Avinguda Diagonal from the main campus of the Universitat de Barcelona is the entrance to **Parc del Palau Reial**. In the park is the Palau Reial de Pedralbes, an early-20th-century building that belonged to the family of Eusebi Güell (Gaudí's patron) until they handed it over to the city in 1926 to serve as a royal residence. Among its guests have been King Alfonso XIII, the president of Catalonia and General Franco.

The palace houses three museums, two of them temporarily housed here.

The **Museu de Ceràmica** (Map p314; www.museuceramica.bcn.es) has a good collection of Spanish ceramics from the 10th to 19th centuries, including work by Picasso and Miró. Spain inherited from the Muslims, and then further refined, a strong tradition in ceramics – here you can compare some exquisite work (tiles, porcelain tableware and the like) from some of the greatest centres of pottery production across Spain, including Talavera de la Reina in Castilla-La Mancha, Manises and Paterna in Valencia, and Teruel in Aragón.

The **Museu de les Arts Decoratives**, across the hall from the Museu de Ceràmica on the 1st floor, brings together an eclectic assortment of furnishings, ornaments and knick-knacks dating as far back as the Romanesque period. The **Museu Tèxtil i d'Indumentària** (www.museutextil.bcn.es), on the 2nd floor, contains some 4000 items that range from 4th-century Coptic textiles to 20th-century local embroidery. The heart of the collection is the assortment of clothing from the 16th century to the 1930s. These two collections will form the bedrock of the new **Disseny Hub** (Design Hub; www.dhub-bcn.cat) museum being built at Plaça de les Glòries Catalanes and due to open in 2013.

Over by Avinguda de Pedralbes are the stables and porter's lodge designed by Gaudí for the Finca Güell, as the Güell estate here was called. Known also as the **Pavellons Güell** (☑93 317 76 52; www.rutadelmodernisme.com; guided tour adult/senior & child under 18yr €6/3; ⊘in English 10.15am & 12.15pm, in Catalan 11.15am, in Spanish 1.15pm Fri-Mon), they were built in the mid-1880s, when Gaudí was strongly impressed by Islamic architecture. Outside visiting hours, there is nothing to stop you admiring Gaudí's wrought-iron dragon gate from the exterior.

PARC DE LA CREUETA DEL COLL PARK
(☑93 413 24 00; www.bcn.cat/parcsijardins; Passeig de la Mare de Déu del Coll 77; ⊘10am-sunset; ⓜPenitents) This refreshing public park, not far from Park Güell, has a pleasantly meandering, splashing pool. The pool, along with swings, showers and snack bar, makes for a relaxing family stop on hot summer days and is strictly a local affair. The park area is open all year; only the lake-pool closes outside summer.

The park is set inside a deep crater left by long years of stone quarrying. On one side of it, an enormous cement sculpture,

---

LOCAL KNOWLEDGE

A WANDER THROUGH OLD SARRIÀ

Although it hugs the left flank of thundering Via Augusta, the old centre of Sarrià is a largely pedestrianised haven. Sarrià, most likely founded in the 13th century, was only incorporated into Barcelona in 1921. It was shaped by the sinuous **Carrer Major de Sarrià**, today a mix of old and new, with a sprinkling of shops and restaurants. At its top end is the **Plaça de Sarrià** (from where Passeig de la Reina Elisenda de Montcada leads west to the Museu-Monestir de Pedralbes). Here you'll want to check out Foix De Sarrià (p177), an exclusive pastry shop. As you wander downhill, duck into **Plaça del Consell de la Vila**, **Plaça de Sant Vicenç de Sarrià** and Carrer de Rocaberti, at the end of which is the neo-Gothic cloister of the **Monestir de Santa Isabel**. The monestery was built in 1886 to house Clarissan nuns, whose order had first set up in El Raval in the 16th century. It was abandoned during the civil war and used as an air-raid shelter.

TIBIDABO: GARDENS OF EARTHLY DELIGHTS

Framing the north end of the city, the forest-covered mountain of Tibidabo, which tops out at 512m, is the highest peak in Serra de Collserola. Aside from the superb views from the top, the highlights of Tibidabo include an 8000-hectare park, an old-fashioned amusement park, a telecommunications tower with viewing platform and a looming church that's visible from many parts of the city. Tibidabo gets its name from the devil, who, trying to tempt Christ, took him to a high place and said, in Latin: *'Haec omnia tibi dabo si cadens adoraberis me'* ('All this I will give you if you fall down and worship me').

To reach the church and amusement park, take an FGC train to Avinguda de Tibidabo station. From there, hop on the *tramvia blau,* which runs past fancy Modernista mansions to Plaça del Doctor Andreu (one way/return €3/4.70, 30 minutes). From Plaça del Doctor Andreu the Tibidabo funicular railway climbs to the top of the hill (return €7.50, five minutes). Departures start around 10am and continue until shortly after the Parc d'Atraccions' closing time.

An alternative is bus T2, the 'Tibibús', from Plaça de Catalunya to Plaça de Tibidabo (€2.80, 30 minutes).

For Parc de Collserola, take an FGC train to Baixador de Vallvidrera. Alternatively, you can stop one station earlier at Peu del Funicular and ride to the top via funicular railway.

Bus 111 runs between Tibidabo and Vallvidrera (passing in front of the Torre de Collserola).

Parc de Collserola

Barcelonins (people of Barcelona) needing an escape from the city without heading too far into the countryside seek out the vast **Parc de Collserola** (☑93 280 35 52; www.parcnaturalcollserola.cat; Carretera de l'Església 92; ☺Centre d'Informació 9.30am-3pm, Can Coll 9.30am-3pm Sun & holidays, closed Jul & Aug; ☑FGC Peu del Funicular, Baixador de Vallvidrera) in the hills. It is a great place to hike and bike and bristles with eateries and snack bars. Pick up a map from the Centre d'Informació.

Aside from nature, the principal point of interest is the sprawling Museu-Casa Verdaguer, 100m from the information centre and a short walk from the train station. Catalonia's revered writer Jacint Verdaguer lived in this late-18th-century country house before his death on 10 July 1902, and it remains remarkably well preserved.

Temple del Sagrat Cor

The **Temple del Sagrat Cor** (Church of the Sacred Heart; ☑93 417 56 86; Plaça de Tibidabo; admission free, lift €2; ☺8am-7pm, lift 10am-7pm), looming above the top funicular station, is meant to be Barcelona's answer to Paris' Sacré-Cœur. The church, built from 1902 to 1961 in a mix of styles with some Modernista influence, is certainly as visible as its Parisian namesake, and even more vilified by aesthetes. It's actually two churches, one on top of the other. The top one is surmounted by a giant statue of Christ and has a lift to take you to the roof for the panoramic views.

Parc d'Atraccions

The reason most *barcelonins* come up to Tibidabo is for some thrills in this **funfair** (☑93 211 79 42; www.tibidabo.cat; Plaça de Tibidabo 3-4; adult/child €25.20/9; ☺closed Jan-Feb), close to the top funicular station. Here you'll find whirling high-speed rides and high-tech 4D cinema, as well as old-fashioned amusement, including an old steam train and the Museu d'Autòmats, with its collection of automated puppets going as far back as 1880. Check the website for opening times.

Torre de Collserola

Sir Norman Foster designed the 288m-high **Torre de Collserola** (Map p314; ☑93 406 93 54; www.torredecollserola.com; Carretera de Vallvidrera al Tibidabo; adult/child €5/3; ☺noon-2pm & 3.15-8pm Wed-Sun Jul & Aug, noon-2pm & 3.15-6pm Sat, Sun & holidays Sep-Jun, closed Jan & Feb; Funicular de Vallvidrera, ☑111) telecommunications tower, which was completed in 1992. The visitors' observation area, 115m up, offers magnificent views – up to 70km on a clear day.

JARDINS DEL LABERINT D'HORTA

Laid out in the twilight years of the 18th century by Antoni Desvalls, Marquès d'Alfarras i de Llupià, this carefully manicured **park** (📞93 413 24 00; Passeig del Castanyers 1; adult/ student €2.20/1.40, Wed & Sun free; ⏰10am-sunset; Ⓜ️Mundet) remained a private family idyll until the 1970s, when it was opened to the public. Many a fine party and theatrical performance was held here over the years, but it now serves as a kind of museum-park.

The gardens take their name from a maze in their centre, but other paths take you past a pleasant artificial lake (estany), waterfalls, a neoclassical pavilion and a false cemetery. The last is inspired by 19th-century romanticism, characterised by an obsession with a swooning, anaemic (some might say silly) vision of death.

The labyrinth, in the middle of these cool gardens (somehow odd in this environment, with modern apartments and ring roads nearby), can be surprisingly frustrating! Aim to reach the centre from the bottom end, and then exit towards the ponds and neoclassical pavilion. This is a good one for kids.

Scenes of the film adaptation of Patrick Süsskind's novel *Perfume* were shot in the gardens.

To reach the gardens, take the right exit upstairs at Mundet Metro station; on emerging, turn right and then left along the main road (with football fields on your left) and then the first left uphill to the gardens (about five minutes).

Elogio del Agua (Eulogy to Water) by Eduardo Chillida, is suspended. You can wander the trails around the high part of this hill-park and enjoy views of the city and Tibidabo. From the Penitents Metro station it's a 15-minute walk. Enter from Carrer Mare de Déu del Coll.

OBSERVATORI FABRA   OBSERVATORY

Map p314 (📞93 431 21 39; www.fabra.cat; Carretera del Observatori; admission €10; 🚇FGC Avinguda Tibidabo then 🚋Tramvia Blau) Inaugurated in 1904, this Modernista observatory is still a functioning scientific foundation. It can be visited on certain evenings to allow people to observe the stars through its grand old telescope. Visits, generally in Catalan or Spanish (Castilian) have to be booked. From mid-June to mid-September an option is to join in for the nightly Sopars amb Estrelles (Dinner under the Stars). You dine outside, tour the building, peer into the telescope and get a lecture (in Catalan) on the heavens. The evening starts at 8.30pm and costs €67 per person. The easiest way here is by taxi.

✖ EATING

Some of the grandest kitchens in the city are scattered across La Zona Alta, from Tibidabo across Sant Gervasi (as far down as Avinguda Diagonal, west of Gràcia) to Pedralbes. Plenty of places of all cuisines and qualities abound, often tucked away in quiet, unassuming residential streets far from anything of interest to tourists. Eating in La Zona Alta can be both a culinary and, with a couple of notable exceptions, a genuinely local experience.

✖ Sant Gervasi

VIA VENETO   CATALAN €€

Map p316 (📞93 200 72 44; www.viavenetorestaurant.com; Carrer de Ganduxer 10; mains €30-46; ⏰lunch & dinner Mon-Fri, dinner Sat, closed Aug; 🚇FGC La Bonanova) Dalí used to regularly waltz into this high-society eatery after it opened in 1967. The vaguely art-deco setting (note the oval mirrors), orange-rose tablecloths, leather chairs and fine cutlery may cater to more conservative souls, but the painter was here for the kitchen exploits. Catalan dishes dominate, with delicacies such as roast suckling pig or salt-baked sea bass with black rice and razor clams.

LA MOLINA   CATALAN €€

Map p314 (📞93 417 11 24; Passeig de Sant Gervasi 65; mains €9-16; ⏰1pm-12.30am Mon-Fri, 11am-5pm Sat & Sun; 🚇FGC Avinguda Tibidabo) La Molina looks like a typical tapas bar at first glance – pavement tables, nondescript bar in front – but head to the back room, and you'll discover one of the great unsung Catalan restaurants in the neighbourhood.

TOP SIGHTS
COSMOCAIXA

Kids (and kids at heart) are fascinated by displays here and the museum has become one of the city's most popular attractions. The single greatest highlight is the re-creation over 1 sq km of a chunk of flooded **Amazon** rainforest (Bosc Inundat). More than 100 species of Amazon flora and fauna (including anacondas, colourful poisonous frogs and caymans) prosper in this unique, living diorama in which you can even experience a tropical downpour. In another original section, the Mur Geològic, seven great chunks of rock (90 tonnes in all) have been assembled to create a **Geological Wall**.

These and other displays on the lower 5th floor (the bulk of the museum is underground) cover many fascinating areas of science, from fossils to physics, and from the alphabet to outer space. To gain access to other special sections, such as the **Planetari** (planetarium), check for guided visits. Most of these activities are interactive and directed at children, and cost €2/1.50 per adult/child. The Planetari has been adapted so that the vision or hearing impaired may also enjoy it.

Outside, there's a nice stroll through the extensive Plaça de la Ciència, with the modest garden of flourishing Mediterranean flora.

DON'T MISS...

➡ A tropical storm in the Amazon
➡ The Geological Wall
➡ The Planetari

PRACTICALITIES

➡ Museu de la Ciència
➡ Map p314
➡ ☎93 212 60 50
➡ www.fundacio.lacaixa.es
➡ Carrer de Isaac Newton 26
➡ adult/child €3/2
➡ ☺10am-8pm Tue-Sun
➡ ☒60, ☒FGC Avinguda Tibidabo

Dishes are made with great care and beautifully presented in delicious combinations like foie gras with duck egg and parmentier, rice with sea urchin and squid, and tuna tataki with mango and avocado.

HOFMANN
MEDITERRANEAN €€€

Map p316 (☎93 218 71 65; www.hofmann-bcn.com; Carrer de Granada del Penedès 14-16; mains around €45, 3-course lunch €47; ☺lunch & dinner Mon-Fri; ☒FGC Gràcia) What's cooking here are the trainee chefs, helped along by their instructors. Dishes are generally elegant renditions of classic Mediterranean food, followed by such delicious desserts that some people prefer a starter and two sweets, skipping the main course altogether.

FLASH FLASH
SPANISH €

Map p316 (☎93 237 09 90; Carrer de la Granada del Penedès 25; mains €8-12; ☺1pm-1.30am; ☒Gracia) Decorated with black-and-white murals and all-white interior, Flash Flash has a fun and kitschy pop-art aesthetic that harks back to its opening in 1969. Fluffy tortillas (omelettes) are the specialty, with more than 50 varieties, as well as massive bunless hamburgers.

LIADÍSIMO
CAFE €

(Carrer de Guillem Tell 23-25; mains €5-7; ☺7.30am-9pm Mon-Fri, 8.30am-9pm Sat; ☒St Gervasi or Molina) This bright and enticing cafe has an art-loving soul with changing artwork adorning the walls, whimsical light fixtures and a backdrop of films playing silently against a textured back wall. There's also a lush garden, which is a relaxing retreat to enjoy the fresh juices and smoothies, sweet or savoury crêpes, pastas, grilled sandwiches and decent coffees.

✖ Tibidabo

LA BALSA
MEDITERRANEAN €€€

Map p314 (☎93 211 50 48; www.labalsarestaurant.com; Carrer de la Infanta Isabel 4; mains €18-24; ☺lunch Tue-Sun, dinner Mon-Sat, in Aug dinner only 9pm-midnight; ☒FGC Avinguda Tibidabo) With its grand ceiling and the scented gardens that surround the main terrace dining area, La Balsa is one of the city's top dining experiences. The menu changes frequently and is a mix of traditional Catalan and off-centre inventiveness. Lounge over a cocktail at the bar before being ushered to your table.

EL ASADOR DE ARANDA
SPANISH €€€

Map p314 (📞93 417 01 15; www.asadordearanda. com; Av del Tibidabo 31; mains €20-22; ⊙closed Sun dinner; 🚇FGC Avinguda Tibidabo) A great place for a meal after visiting Tibidabo, El Asador de Aranda is set in a striking art nouveau building, complete with stained-glass windows, Moorish-style brick arches and elaborate ceilings. You'll find a fine assortment of tapas plates for sharing, though the specialty is the meat (roast lamb, spare ribs, beef), beautifully prepared in a wood oven.

✗ Sarrià

BAR TOMÀS
TAPAS €

Map p314 (📞93 203 10 77; Carrer Major de Sarrià 49; tapas €3-5; ⊙noon-10pm Thu-Tue; 🚇FGC Sarrià) Many barcelonins have long claimed that Bar Tomàs is by far the best place in the city for patatas bravas (potato chunks in a slightly spicy tomato sauce), prepared here with a special variation on the traditional sauce. It's a rough-edged bar, but that doesn't stop the well-off citizens of Sarrià piling in, particularly for lunch on weekends.

FOIX DE SARRIÀ
PASTELERÍA €

Map p314 (📞93 203 04 73; www.foixdesarria.com; Plaça de Sarrià 12-13; desserts €2-5; ⊙8am-8pm; 🚇FGC Reina Elisenda) Since 1886 this exclusive pastry shop has been selling the most exquisite desserts. You can take them away or head out back to sip tea, coffee or hot chocolate while sampling the little cakes and other wizardry.

WORTH A DETOUR

CAN TRAVI NOU
CATALAN €€€

(📞93 428 03 01; www.gruptravi.com; Carrer de Jorge Manrique 8; mains €20-28; ⊙lunch & dinner Mon-Sat, lunch Sun; 🅿; 🚇Montbau) This expansive 18th-century mansion has several dining areas that stretch out across two floors. The warm colours, grandfather clock and wholesome, rustic air make for a magical setting for a Catalan splurge.

🍷 DRINKING & NIGHTLIFE

North of Avinguda Diagonal, the *pijos* (cashed-up mama's boys and papa's girls) are in charge. Whether you sample the bars around Carrer de Marià Cubí (and surrounding streets) or try the clubs around Carrer d'Aribau or Tibidabo, expect to be confronted by perma-tanned Audi- and 4WD-driving folks in designer threads. What do you care? The eye candy more than compensates for the snobbery.

🍷 Sarrià & Tibidabo

MIRABLAU
BAR

Map p314 (Plaça del Doctor Andreu; ⊙11am-4.30am Sun-Thu, to 5am Fri & Sat; 🚇FGC Avinguda Tibidabo then 🚋Tramvia Blau) Gaze out over the entire city from this privileged balcony restaurant on the way up to Tibidabo. Wander downstairs to join the folk in the tiny dance space. In summer you can step out onto the even smaller terrace for a breather.

CAFFÈ SAN MARCO
CAFE

Map p314 (📞93 280 29 73; Carrer de Pedro de la Creu 15; ⊙9am-9.30pm; 🚇FGC Reina Elisenda) For one of the best coffees you're likely to have, it is hard to beat this place. It boasts a charming atmosphere where you can settle in to read the paper or simply watch passers-by.

🍷 Pedralbes & Zona Universitària

ELEPHANT
CLUB

Map p314 (📞93 334 02 58; www.elephantbcn. com; Passeig dels Til.lers 1; ⊙11.30pm-4am Thu, to 5am Fri & Sat ; 🚇Palau Reial) Getting in here is like being invited to a private fantasy party in Beverly Hills. Models and wannabes mix with immaculately groomed lads who most certainly didn't come by taxi. A big tent-like dance space is the main game here, but smooth customers slink their way around a series of garden bars in summer, too.

UP AND DOWN CLUB
CLUB

Map p314 (📞93 448 61 15; http://upanddown barcelona.com; Avinguda del Doctor Marañón 17; admission €15; ⊙11.30pm-5.30am Thu-Sat; 🚇Palau Reial) This concept club has moved

WORTH A DETOUR

MAKING A SPLASH

Guys and gals board their metal steeds on hot summer nights to bear down on one of the top outdoor club scenes in town (or rather out of town, since it's in neighbouring L'Hospitalet de Llobregat). **Liquid** (☏670 221209; www.liquidbcn.com; Carrer de Manuel Azaña 21-23, Complex Esportiu Hospitalet Nord; ⊗Jun-Sep; ⋒Zona Universitaria) says what it is. A palm-studded islet is surrounded by a bottom-lit azure moat that tempts surprisingly few folks to plunge in while dancing the night away in this megaclub. Local and foreign DJs keep the punters, a mixed crowd from all over town, in the groove in a series of different internal spaces, as well as poolside.

in to replace what for years was the Ibiza-inspired Pachá, becoming one of the city's top nightspots. The main, ground floor is enormous, with a stage and several separate VIP sections. Upstairs, the lounge room is a more intimate space, bathed in shimmering light and with a strange bloblike seating arrangement in the middle.

🍸 Sant Gervasi

MARCEL
BAR

Map p316 (☏93 209 89 48; Carrer de Santaló 42; ⊗10am-2am Mon-Thu, to 3am Fri & Sat; ⋒FGC Muntaner) A classic meeting place, Marcel has a homey but classy old-world feel, with a timber bar, black-and-white floor tiles and high windows. It offers a few snacks and tapas as well. Space is somewhat limited and customers inevitably spill out onto the footpath.

BERLIN
BAR

Map p316 (Carrer de Muntaner 240; ⊗10am-2am Mon-Thu, to 3am Fri & Sat; ⋒Diagonal or Hospital Clínic) This elegant corner bar offers views over Avinguda Diagonal. There is a cluster of tables outside on the ground floor and designer lounges downstairs. Service can be harried but the location is excellent for starting an uptown night. All ages and creeds snuggle in and many kick on to Luz de Gas, virtually next door, afterwards.

BOCAYMA
BAR

Map p316 (☏93 430 28 38; Carrer de l'Avenir 50; ⊗11pm-2am Tue & Wed, to 3am Thu-Sat; ⋒FGC Muntaner) Bocayma starts in quiet fashion with patrons gathered around its low tables lined up on one side of the rear bar area. Two backlit bars also keep the drinks coming to this spot of good-looking 20- and 30-somethings. After 1am the music takes off and punters rev up for an outing to

nearby clubs. It often opens beyond its official hours.

BUBBLIC BAR
BAR

Map p316 (☏93 414 54 01; www.bubblicbar.com; Carrer de Marià Cubí 183; ⊗11pm-2am Tue & Wed, to 3am Thu-Sat; ⋒FGC Muntaner) In the heart of Zona Alta's nightlife centre, Bubblic is a multilevel space with a tight upstairs lounge – and inviting terrace in the summer – and a subterranean level with bars running alongside dance areas where DJs spin a mixed medley of anything from rock and pop to house and trance.

OTTO ZUTZ
CLUB

Map p316 (www.ottozutz.com; Carrer de Lincoln 15; admission €15; ⊗midnight-6am Tue-Sat; ⋒FGC Gràcia) Beautiful people need only apply for entry to this three-floor dance den. Shake it all up to house on the ground floor, or head upstairs for funk and soul. DJs come from the Ibiza rave mould and the top floor is for VIPs (although at some ill-defined point in the evening the barriers all seem to come down). Friday and Saturday it's hip hop, R&B and funk on the ground floor and house on the 1st floor.

SALA BECOOL
CLUB

Map p316 (☏93 362 04 13; www.salabecool.com; Plaça de Joan Llongueras 5; admission €10-15; ⊗midnight-6am Thu-Sun; ☐27, 32, 59, 66, 67 or 68) Electro is the leitmotif in this middle-sized dance place dominated by a single giant mirror ball at the stage end, where earlier in the night you might catch a concert (from 9pm). The secondary Redrum space runs at a slower pace, with indie music to the fore.

SUTTON THE CLUB
CLUB

Map p316 (www.thesuttonclub.com; Carrer de Tuset 13; admission €15; ⊗midnight-5am Wed-Thu, midnight-6am Fri & Sat, 10.30pm-4am Sun; ⋒Diagonal) A classic disco with mainstream sounds on the dance floor, some hopping house in a side bar and a fair spread of eye candy, this place inevitably attracts just about everyone pouring in and out of the nearby bars at some stage of the evening. The main dance floor is akin to a writhing bear pit. The people are mostly beautiful and the bouncers can be tough.

LUZ DE GAS
CLUB

Map p316 (☎93 209 77 11; www.luzdegas.com; Carrer de Muntaner 246; admission up to €20; ⏰11.30pm-6am; MDiagonal then ☐6, 7, 15, 27, 32, 33, 34, 58 or 64) Several nights a week this club, set in a grand former theatre, stages concerts ranging through soul, country, salsa, rock, jazz and pop. You can hang back in the relative obscurity of the bars or plunge down into the pit and boogie away before the grand stage. It's like being at a rock concert of old. From about 2am, the place turns into a club that attracts a well-dressed crowd with varying musical tastes, depending on the night. It gets a little sweaty in the dedicated club room Sala B, which opens on Friday and Saturday nights only.

 **ENTERTAINMENT**

BIKINI
LIVE MUSIC

Map p316 (☎93 322 08 00; www.bikinibcn.com; Av Diagonal 547; admission €10-20; ⏰midnight-6am Wed-Sat; ☐6, 7, 33, 34, 63, 67 or 68, MEntença) This grand old star of the Barcelona night-life scene has been keeping the beat since the darkest days of Franco. Every possible kind of music gets a run, from Latin and Brazilian beats to 1980s disco, depending on the night and the space you choose. It frequently stages quality local and foreign acts in a wide range of genres. Performances generally start between 8pm and 10pm (the club doesn't happen until midnight).

RENOIR-LES CORTS
CINEMA

Map p314 (☎93 490 55 10; www.cinesrenoir.com; Carrer de Eugeni d'Ors 12; MMaria Cristina or Les Corts) With six cinemas, this is a somewhat distant alternative from central Barcelona for original versions.

SHOPPING

Although many of Barcelona's better-off folks descend from the 'High Zone' to L'Eixample to shop, there are still plenty of trendy little boutiques scattered around La Zona Alta. Passeig de la Bonanova, for example, has quite a liberal spread. It's perhaps a little far off to be of much interest to tourists but can nevertheless make for an interesting shopping experience.

BEA BEA
FASHION

Map p316 (☎93 414 29 55; Carrer de Calvet 39; ☒FGC Muntaner) On a street dotted with small boutiques, this women's clothing shop has something to suit most generations

---

DEATH BY CHOCOLATE

Spain has been importing cocoa from its South American colonies since the 16th century and, ever since, the pastry makers of Barcelona have been doing it greatest justice. The city's love affair with chocolate is exemplified in the existence of a museum dedicated to the stuff. Traditional purveyors of fine chocolates have long operated alongside *granjas* (milk bars) and other similar outlets for sipping cups of the thick hot stuff. Since the 1980s they have been joined by a slew of chocolatiers whose creativity seems to know no bounds. Chocoholics should seek out the following:

➡ **Enric Rovira** (Map p316; ☎93 419 25 47; www.enricrovira.com; Avinguda de Josep Tarradellas 113; ⏰Mon-Sat, closed Aug; MEntença)

➡ **Oriol Balaguer** (Map p316; ☎93 201 18 46; www.oriolbalaguer.com; Plaça de Sant Gregori Taumaturg 2; ☒FGC La Bonanova)

➡ **Pastisseria Natcha** (Map p316; ☎93 430 10 70; www.natcha.cat; Avinguda de Sarrià 45; MHospital Clínic)

➡ **Richart** (Map p316; ☎93 202 02 40; www.richart.com; Carrer de Muntaner 463; ⏰Mon-Sat; ☒FGC La Bonanova)

and tastes. Younger, carefree styles sit side by side with more classical skirts, jackets and accoutrements for uptown dames.

SIETE BESOS
FASHION

Map p316 (☎93 200 67 34; Carrer d'Amigó 55; ⓡFGC Muntaner) A bijou store surrounded by bigger and shriller competition, the 'Seven Kisses' is an attractive treasure treat for women's fashion. Styles can be cheeky and nonconformist but not at all vintage or jeansy. Pretty, light-hearted dresses vie for your attention with pants and tops, all at pretty reasonable prices considering the neighbourhood.

FC BOTIGA
SOUVENIRS

(☎93 492 31 11; http://shop.fcbarcelona.com; Carrer de Arístides Maillol; ⓧ10am-9pm Mon-Sat; ⓜCollblanc) For some, football is the meaning of life. If you fall into that category, your idea of shopping heaven may well be this store at the football museum next to Camp Nou stadium. Here you will find footballs, shirts, scarves, socks, wallets, bags, sneakers, iPhone covers – pretty much anything you can think of, all featuring Barça's famous red-and-blue insignia. It has branches all over town, including at Maremàgnum and Carrer de Jaume I, 18 (p86).

✦ SPORTS & ACTIVITIES

CAMP NOU
SPECTATOR SPORT

Map p314 (☎902 189 900; www.fcbarcelona.com; Carrer d'Aristides Maillol; tickets €19-265; ⓧbox office 10am-7.45pm Mon-Sat, to 2.15pm Sun, 11am to kick-off on match days; ⓜPalau Reial or Collblanc) Seeing an FC Barça football match inside the massive Camp Nou stadium is an experience not to be missed. You can purchase tickets at the stadium box office, from FNAC and Carrerfour stores and from Servicaixa ATMs.

RITUELS D'ORIENT
SPA

Map p316 (☎93 419 14 72; www.rituelsdorient.com; Carrer de Loreto 50; baths only €28; ⓧwomen only 1-9pm Tue, 10.30am-8pm Wed, 1-4pm Fri, mixed 1-10pm Thu, 4-10pm Fri, 10.30am-8pm Sat; ⓜHospital Clínic) True to name, Rituels d'Orient offers a setting that resembles a Moroccan fantasy with its dark woods, window grills, candle lighting and ancient-looking stone walls. It's a fine setting for luxuriating in hammams and indulging in massages, body scrubs and other treatments.

Montjuïc

MONJUÏC | SANTS | EL POBLE SEC

Neighbourhood Top Five

❶ Dedicating a day to the world's most important collection of early-medieval art in the Romanesque art section of the **Museu Nacional d'Art de Catalunya (MNAC)** (p183), and exploring the stunning Gothic art, plus two fascinating private collections.

❷ Admiring the beauty of Josep Lluís Sert's **Fundació Joan Miró** (p188), which houses the work of Barcelona's best-known 20th-century artist.

❸ Taking in the **Caixa-Forum** (p189), the premier art space that showcases the Barcelona bank's extensive global collection.

❹ Watching the colours and water come alive in the evening display of **Font Màgica** (p190).

❺ Getting inside a **cable car** (p190) and watching Montjuïc from the air.

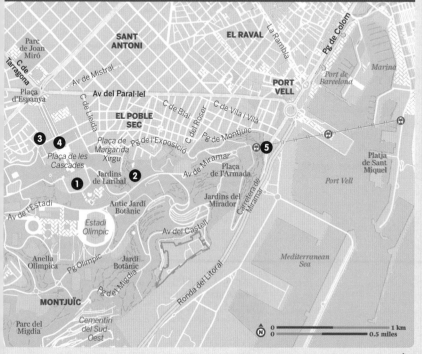

For more detail of this area, see Map p318 ➡

Lonely Planet's Top Tip

Take advantage of the cable-car services that transport you to and across Montjuïc – the short trip is beautifully silent and affords views not just of the verdant hill, but of wider Barcelona.

✕ Best Places to Eat

➡ Tickets (p193)

➡ Quimet i Quimet (p193)

➡ Xemei (p194)

➡ Restaurant Evo (p194)

➡ Barramòn (p194)

For reviews, see p193 ➡

🍷 Best Places to Drink

➡ La Caseta del Migdia (p196)

➡ Terrrazza (p196)

➡ Tinta Roja (p196)

➡ Barcelona Rouge (p196)

For reviews, see p196 ➡

👁 Best for Art

➡ Museu Nacional d'Art de Catalunya (MNAC) (p183)

➡ Fundació Joan Miró (p188)

➡ CaixaForum (p189)

For reviews, see p183 ➡

Explore: Montjuïc

Montjuïc is home to some of the city's finest art collections – the CaixaForum, MNAC and Fundació Joan Miró, and it hosts several lesser museums, curious sights like the Poble Espanyol, the sinister Castell de Montjuïc and the beautiful remake of Mies van der Rohe's 1929 German pavilion. The bulk of the Olympic installations of the 1992 games are also here. Come at night and witness the spectacle of Font Màgica, several busy theatres and a couple of nightclubs. Throw in various parks and gardens and you have the makings of an extremely full couple of days.

You can approach the hill from Plaça d'Espanya on foot and take advantage of a series of escalators from the west side of the Palau Nacional up to Avinguda de l'Estadi; alternatively, and spectacularly, you can get onto a cable car from La Barceloneta and take in the beautiful aerial views of the verdant hill.

The swirling traffic roundabout of Plaça d'Espanya marks the boundary between Montjuïc and the *barri* (neighbourhood) of Sants, an area worth seeing if you are keen on witnessing everyday life of residential, tourist-free Barcelona.

Sloping down the north face of Montjuïc is the tight warren of working-class El Poble Sec. Though short on sights, it hides various interesting bars and eateries best visited on warm evenings to take advantage of the pavement seating. Avinguda del Paral.lel was, until the 1960s, the centre of Barcelona nightlife, and a handful of theatres and cinemas survive.

Local Life

➡ **Hangouts** To eat like the locals, head for Carrer de Blai. Sample tapas from the Canaries at Barramòn (p194), or go on a tapas crawl down the lively street.

➡ **Nightlife** Catch a burlesque show at the Sala Apolo club and experience Paral.lel's lively nightlife.

➡ **Greenery** Join the locals on a stroll through the gardens of Montjuic and catch all that art on the way.

Getting There & Around

➡ **Metro** Metro Línia 3 runs through El Poble Sec, stopping at Espanya, Poble Sec and Paral.lel.

➡ **Bus** Bus 55 runs across town via Plaça de Catalunya, terminating at the Estació Parc Montjuïc funicular station. The 193 (Parc de Montjuïc) line does a circle trip from Plaça d'Espanya to the Castell de Montjuïc.

➡ **Funicular** Take the Metro (Línia 2 or 3) to the Paral.lel stop and pick up the funicular railway, part of the Metro fare system, to Estació Parc Montjuïc.

From across the city, the flamboyant neobaroque silhouette of the Palau Nacional can be seen on the slopes of Montjuïc. Built for the 1929 World Exhibition and restored in 2005, it houses a vast collection of mostly Catalan art spanning the early Middle Ages to the early 20th century. The high point is the collection of extraordinary Romanesque frescoes.

The Romanesque Masterpieces

The real highlight here is the Romanesque art section, considered the most important concentration of early medieval art in the world. Rescued from neglected country churches across northern Catalonia in the early 20th century, the collection consists of 21 frescoes, woodcarvings and painted altar frontals (low-relief wooden panels that were the forerunners of the elaborate altarpieces that adorned later churches). The insides of several churches have been re-created and the frescoes – in some cases fragmentary, in others extraordinarily complete and alive with colour – have been placed as they were when in situ.

The two most striking fresco sets follow one after the other. The first, in Àmbit 5, is a magnificent image of Christ in Majesty done around 1123. Based on the text of the Apocalypse, we see Christ enthroned on a rainbow with the world at his feet. He holds a book open with the words *Ego Sum Lux Mundi* (I am the Light of the World) and is surrounded by the four Evangelists. The images were taken from the apse of the Església de Sant Climent de Taüll in northwest Catalonia. In Àmbit 7 are frescoes done around the same time in the nearby Església de Santa Maria de Taüll. This

DON'T MISS

→ The Romanesque pieces
→ Gothic artworks
→ The paintings of the Cambo Bequest and Thyssen-Bornemisza collections
→ Modernista furniture and decoration

PRACTICALITIES

→ Map p318
→ ☑93 622 03 76
→ www.mnac.es
→ Mirador del Palau Nacional
→ adult/senior & child under 15yr/student €10/free/7, 1st Sun of month free
→ ⊙10am-7pm Tue-Sat, 10am-2.30pm Sun & holidays, library 10am-6pm Mon-Fri, to 2.30pm Sat
→ Ⓜ Espanya

THE FRESCO STRIPPERS

The Stefanoni brothers, Italian art restorers, brought the secrets of *strappo* (stripping of frescoes from walls) to Catalonia in the early 1900s. The Stefanoni would cover frescoes with a sheet of fabric, stuck on with a glue made of cartilage. When dry, this allowed the image to be stripped off the wall and rolled up. For three years the Stefanoni roamed the Pyrenean countryside, stripping churches and chapels and sending the rolls back to Barcelona, where they were eventually put back up on walls and inside purpose-built church apses to reflect how they had appeared in situ.

The Museu Nacional d'Art de Catalunya's displays account for little more than 20% of its holdings. The rest is kept in storerooms that, since 2010, can be visited on a guided tour (€5). Since the displays themselves already represent an enormous chunk to absorb in a day, a separate day should be set aside for visiting the reserves.

time the central image taken from the apse is of the Virgin Mary and Christ Child. These images were not mere decoration but tools of instruction in the basics of Christian faith for the local population – try to set yourself in the mind of the average medieval citizen: illiterate, ignorant, fearful and in most cases eking out a subsistence living. These images transmitted the basic personalities and tenets of the faith and were accepted at face value by most.

The Gothic Collection

Opposite the Romanesque collection on the ground floor is the museum's Gothic art section. In these halls you can see Catalan Gothic painting and works from other Spanish and Mediterranean regions. Look out especially for the work of Bernat Martorell in Àmbit 32 and Jaume Huguet in Àmbit 34. Among Martorell's works figure images of the martyrdom of St Vincent and St Llúcia. Huguet's *Consagració de Sant Agustí,* in which St Augustine is depicted as a bishop, is dazzling in its detail.

The Cambò Bequest & the Thyssen-Bornemisza Collection

The Cambò Bequest by Francesc Cambò spans the history of European painting between the 14th century and the beginning of the 19th century, and the Thyssen-Bornemisza collection presents a selection of European painting and sculpture produced between the 13th and the 18th centuries on loan to the MNAC by the Museo Thyssen-Bornemisza in Madrid. The Thyssen-Bornemisza collection's highlight is Fra Angelico's *Madonna of Humility,* whereas the Cambò Bequest holds wonderful works by the Venetian Renaissance masters Veronese, Titian and Canaletto, along with those of Rubens and even England's Gainsborough, its grand finale being examples of work by Francisco de Goya.

Modern Catalan Art

Up on the next floor, the collection turns to modern Catalan art belonging to Carmen Thyssen-Bornemisza. It is an uneven affair, but it is worth looking out for Modernista painters Ramon Casas (Àmbit 71) and Santiago Rusiñol (Àmbit 72), as well as the recently deceased Antoni Tàpies.Also on show are items of Modernista furniture and decoration, which include a mural by Ramon Casas (depicting the artist and Pere Romeu on a tandem bicycle) that once adorned the legendary bar and restaurant Els Quatre Gats.

After all this, you can relax in the museum restaurant, which offers great views north towards Plaça d'Espanya.

MUSEU NACIONAL D'ART DE CATALUNYA

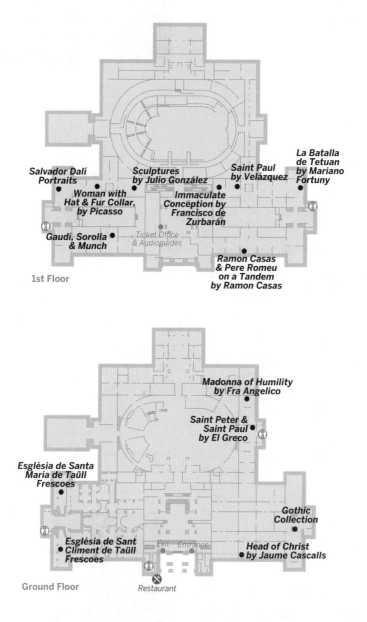

1st Floor

Salvador Dalí Portraits

Woman with Hat & Fur Collar, by Picasso

Sculptures by Julio González

Immaculate Conception by Francisco de Zurbarán

Saint Paul by Velázquez

La Batalla de Tetuan by Mariano Fortuny

Gaudí, Sorolla & Munch

Ticket Office & Audioguides

Ramon Casas & Pere Romeu on a Tandem by Ramon Casas

Ground Floor

Madonna of Humility by Fra Angelico

Saint Peter & Saint Paul by El Greco

Església de Santa Maria de Taüll Frescoes

Església de Sant Climent de Taüll Frescoes

Gothic Collection

Head of Christ by Jaume Cascalls

Exit   Entrance

Restaurant

TOP SIGHTS
MUSEU NACIONAL D'ART DE CATALUNYA

A ONE-DAY ITINERARY

Montjuïc, perhaps once the site of pre-Roman settlements, is today a hilltop green lung looking over city and sea. Interspersed across varied gardens are major art collections, a fortress, an Olympic stadium and more. A solid one-day itinerary can take in the key spots.

Alight at Espanya metro stop and make for **CaixaForum 1**, always host to three or four free top-class exhibitions. The nearby **Pavelló Mies van der Rohe 2** is an intriguing study in 1920s futurist housing by one of the 20th century's greatest architects. Uphill, the Romanesque art collection in the **Museu Nacional d'Art de Catalunya 3** is a must, and its restaurant is a pleasant lunch stop. Escalators lead further up the hill towards the **Estadi Olímpic 4**, scene of the 1992 Olympic Games. The road leads east to the **Fundació Joan Miró 5**, a shrine to the master surrealist's creativity. Contemplate ancient relics in the **Museu d'Arqueologia de Catalunya 6**, then have a break in the peaceful **Jardins de Mossèn Cinto Verdaguer 7**, the prettiest on the hill, before taking the cable car to the **Castell de Montjuïc 8**. If you pick the right day, you can round off with the gorgeously kitsch **La Font Màgica 9** sound and light show, followed by drinks and dancing in an open-air nightspot in **Poble Espanyol 10**.

TOP TIPS

➡ **Moving views** Ride the Transbordador Aeri from Barceloneta for a bird's eye approach to Montjuïc. Or take the Teleféric de Montjuïc cable car to the Castell for more aerial views.

➡ **Summer fun** The Castell de Montjuïc features outdoor summer cinema and concerts (see http://sala montjuic.org).

➡ **Beautiful bloomers** Bursting with colour and serenity, the Jardins de Mossèn Cinto Verdaguer are exquisitely laid out with bulbs, especially tulips, and aquatic flowers.

JEAN-PIERRE LESCOURRET

CaixaForum
This former factory and barracks designed by Josep Puig i Cadafalch is an outstanding work of Modernista architecture; like a Lego fantasy in brick.

Piscines Bernat Picornell

Olympic Needle

Poble Espanyol
Amid the rich variety of traditional Spanish architecture created in replica for the 1929 Barcelona World Exhibition, browse the art on show in the Fundació Fran Daurel.

NEIL SETCHFIELD

Pavelló Mies van der Rohe
Admire the inventiveness of the great German architect Ludwig Mies van der Rohe in this recreation of his avant garde German pavillion for the 1929 World Exhibition.

La Font Màgica
Take a summer evening to behold the Magic Fountain come to life in a unique 15-minute sound and light performance, when the water glows like a cauldron of colour.

9

3

Museu Etnològic

6

Teatre Grec

5

Museu Nacional d'Art de Catalunya
Make a beeline for the Romanesque art selection and the 12th-century polychrome image of Christ in majesty, which was recovered from the apse of a country chapel in northwest Catalonia.

7

Museu Olímpic i de l'Esport

4

Estadi Olímpic

Jardí Botànic

8

Jardins de Mossèn Cinto Verdaguer

Castell de Montjuïc
Enjoy the sweeping views of the sea and city from atop this 17th-century fortress, once a political prison and long a symbol of oppression.

Fundació Joan Miró
Take in some of Joan Miró's giant canvases, and discover little-known works from his early years in the Sala Joan Prats and Sala Pilar Juncosa.

Museu d'Arqueologia de Catalunya
Seek out the Roman mosaic depicting the Three Graces, one of the most beautiful items in this museum, which was dedicated to the ancient past of Catalonia and neighbouring parts of Spain.

TOP SIGHTS
FUNDACIÓ JOAN MIRÓ

Joan Miró, the city's best-known 20th-century artistic progeny, bequeathed this art foundation to his home town in 1971. Its light-filled buildings, designed by close friend and architect Josep Lluís Sert (who also built Miró's Mallorca studios), are crammed with seminal works, from Miró's earliest timid sketches to paintings from his last years.

Sert's Temple to Miró's Art

Sert's shimmering white temple to one of Spain's artistic luminaries is considered one of the world's most outstanding museum buildings. The architect designed it after spending many of Franco's dictatorship years in the USA as the head of the School of Design at Harvard University. The foundation rests amid the greenery of the mountains and holds the greatest single collection of the artist's work, containing around 220 of his paintings, 180 sculptures, some textiles and more than 8000 drawings spanning his entire life. Only a small portion is ever on display.

The Collection

The exhibits give a broad impression of Miró's artistic development. The first couple of rooms (11 and 12) hold various works, including a giant tapestry in his trademark primary colours. Room 13, a basement space called Espai 13, leads you downstairs to a small room for temporary exhibitions.

Next (oddly enough) comes room 16, the Sala Joan Prats, with works spanning the early years until 1931, entitled The Early Years and Paris and Surrealism. Here, you can see how the young Miró moved away, under surrealist influence, from his relative realism (for instance his 1917 painting *Ermita de Sant Joan d'Horta*) towards his own unique style that uses primary colours and morphed shapes symbolising the moon, the female form and birds.

This theme is continued upstairs in room 17, the Sala Pilar Juncosa (named after his wife), which covers the years 1932–55, his surrealist years. Rooms 18–19 contain masterworks of the years 1956–83, and room 20 a series of paintings done on paper. Room 21 hosts a selection of the private Katsuka collection of Miró works from 1914 to the 1970s. Room 22 rounds off the permanent exhibition with some major paintings and bronzes from the 1960s and 1970s. On the way here, you will see *Mercury Fountain* by Alexander Calder, a rebuilt work that was originally created for the 1937 Paris Fair and represented Spain at the Spanish Republic's Pavilion.

The basement rooms 14 and 15, together labelled Homenatge a Joan Miró (Homage to Joan Miró), are dedicated to photos of the artist, with a 15-minute video on his life and a series of works from some of his contemporaries, like Henry Moore, Antoni Tàpies, Eduardo Chillida, Yves Tanguy, Fernand Léger and others.

The museum library contains Miró's personal book collection.

The Garden

Outside on the eastern flank of the museum is the Jardí de les Escultures, a small garden with various pieces of modern sculpture. The green areas surrounding the museum, together with the garden, are perfect for a picnic in the shade after a hard day's sightseeing.

DON'T MISS

- ➡ Sert's architectural design
- ➡ Masterworks in rooms 18 & 19
- ➡ Miro's move to Surrealism, room 16
- ➡ The beautiful garden

PRACTICALITIES

- ➡ Map p318
- ➡ www.bcn.fjmiro.es
- ➡ Plaça de Neptu
- ➡ adult/senior & child €10/7
- ➡ ⊙10am-8pm Tue, Wed, Fri & Sat, to 9.30pm Thu, to 2.30pm Sun & holidays
- ➡ 🚌50, 55, 193, Ⓜ Paral.lel

⊙ SIGHTS

**MUSEU NACIONAL D'ART
DE CATALUNYA (MNAC)**   MUSEUM
See p183.

FUNDACIÓ JOAN MIRÓ   MUSEUM
See p188.

CAIXAFORUM   GALLERY
Map p318 (www.fundacio.lacaixa.es; Avinguda
de Francesc Ferrer i Guàrdia 6-8; adult/student
& child €3/2, first Sunday of the month free;
☺10am-8pm Tue-Fri & Sun, to 10pm Sat; Ⓜ Espanya) The Caixa building society prides itself
on its involvement in (and ownership of)
art, in particular all that is contemporary.
Its premier art expo space in Barcelona
hosts part of the bank's extensive collection
from around the globe.

The setting is a completely renovated
former factory, the Fàbrica Casaramona,
an outstanding Modernista brick structure
designed by Puig i Cadafalch. From 1940 to
1993 it housed the First Squadron of the police cavalry unit – 120 horses in all.

Now it is home to major exhibition space.
On occasion portions of La Caixa's own collection of 800 works of modern and contemporary art go on display, but more often
than not major international exhibitions
are the key draw.

In the courtyard where the police horses
used to drink is a steel tree designed by the
Japanese architect Arata Isozaki. Musical
recitals are sometimes held in the museum,
especially in the warmer months.

FREE **CASTELL DE
MONTJUÏC**   FORTRESS, GARDENS
Map p318 (☺9am-9pm Tue-Sun Apr-Sep, to 7pm
Tue-Sun Oct-Mar; Ⓜ Telefèric) The forbidding
Castell (castle or fort) de Montjuïc dominates
the southeastern heights of Montjuïc and
enjoys commanding views over the Mediterranean. It dates, in its present form, from the
late 17th and 18th centuries. For most of its
dark history, it has been used to watch over
the city and as a political prison and killing
ground.

Anarchists were executed here around
the end of the 19th century, fascists during
the civil war and Republicans after it – most
notoriously Lluís Companys in 1940. The
castle is surrounded by a network of ditches
and walls (from which its strategic position
over the city and port become clear).

Until 2009 the castle was home to a somewhat fusty old military museum, closed since
the Ministry of Defence handed the fortress
over to the city after protracted negotiations.
The artillery that once stood in the central
courtyard has been removed, but some of
the seaward big guns remain in place.

In the coming years, it is planned to establish an international peace centre in the
castle, as well as a display on its history.
There will also be an interpretation centre
dedicated to Montjuïc. While waiting for
this to happen, a modest temporary exhibition has been established in one of the
castle's bastions, on the right as soon as you
enter. Called **Barcelona Té Castell** (Barcelona Has a Castle), it explains something of the
history of the place as well as detailing plans
for its future. Perhaps when all this is done,
the tombstones (some dating to the 11th century) from the one-time Jewish cemetery on
Montjuïc will get a more imaginative exhibition space than the drab room once set aside
for them in the military museum.

The views from the castle and the surrounding area looking over the sea, port
and city below are the best part of making
the trip up.

Catalan and Spanish speakers can join
free guided tours of the castle on Saturdays
and Sundays (11.30am in Catalan, 1pm in
Spanish). Group tours (€65 to €80) can also
be booked (also in English and French).

Around the seaward foot of the castle is an
airy walking track, the **Camí del Mar**, which
offers breezy views of city and sea. Towards
the foot of this part of Montjuïc, above the
thundering traffic of the main road to Tarragona, the **Jardins de Mossèn Costa i Llobera**
(Map p318; admission free; ☺10am-sunset) have a
good collection of tropical and desert plants –
including a veritable forest of cacti. Near the
Estació Parc Montjuïc funicular/Telefèric station are the ornamental **Jardins de Mossèn
Cinto de Verdaguer**. These sloping, verdant
gardens are home to various kinds of bulbs
and aquatic plants. Many of the former (some
80,000) have to be replanted each year. They
include tulips, narcissus, crocus, varieties of
dahlia and more. The aquatic plants include
lotus and water lilies.

From the **Jardins del Mirador**, opposite
the Mirador Transbordador Aeri (Telefèric)
station, you have fine views over the port
of Barcelona. A little further downhill, the
Jardins de Joan Brossa (Map p318; admission
free; ☺10am-sunset) are charming, landscaped

MONTJUÏC SIGHTS

ℹ️ MAR I MUNTANYA: SEA AND MOUNTAIN

The quickest way from the beach to the mountain is via the **Transbordador Aeri** (Map p318; www.telefericodebarcelona.com; Av de Miramar, Jardins de Miramar; 1 way/return €10/15; ⊙11am-7pm; 🚌50 & 153), the cable car that runs between Torre de Sant Sebastiá in La Barceloneta and the Miramar stop on Montjuïc (from mid-June to mid-September only). From Estació Parc Montjuïc, the Teleféric de Montjuïc cable car carries you to the Castell de Montjuïc via the Mirador (a lookout point).

gardens on the site of a former amusement park near **Plaça de la Sardana** (Map p318). These gardens contain many Mediterranean species, from cypresses to pines and a few palms. There are swings and things, thematic walking trails and some good city views.

ESTADI OLÍMPIC — STADIUM

Map p318 (Avinguda de l'Estadi; ⊙10am-8pm; 🚌50, 61 or 193) The Estadi Olímpic was the main stadium of Barcelona's Olympic Games. If you saw the Olympics on TV, the 65,000-capacity stadium may seem surprisingly small. So might the Olympic flame holder into which an archer spectacularly fired a flaming arrow during the opening ceremony. The stadium was opened in 1929 and restored for 1992.

MUSEU OLÍMPIC I DE L'ESPORT — MUSEUM

Map p318 (www.museuolimpicbcn.com; Avinguda de l'Estadi 60; adult/student €4/2.50; ⊙10am-8pm; 🚌50, 61 or 193) The Museu Olímpic i de L'Esport is an information-packed interactive museum dedicated to the history of sport and the Olympic Games. After picking up tickets, you wander down a ramp that snakes below ground level and is lined with displays on the history of sport, starting with the ancients.

FONT MÀGICA — FOUNTAIN

Map p318 (Avinguda de la Reina Maria Cristina; ⊙every 30min 7-9pm Fri & Sat Oct-late Jun, 9-11.30pm Thu-Sun late Jun-Sep; MEspanya) The main fountain of a series that sweeps up the hill from Avinguda de la Reina Maria Cristina to the grand facade of the Palau Nacional, Font Màgica is a unique performance in which the water can look like seething fireworks or a mystical cauldron of colour.

It is wonderful that an idea that was cooked up for the 1929 World Exposition has, since the 1992 Olympics, again become a magnet. With a flourish, the 'Magic Fountain' erupts into a feast of musical, backlit aquatic life. On hot summer evenings especially, this 15-minute spectacle (repeated several times throughout the evening) mesmerises onlookers. On the last evening of the Festes de la Mercè in September, a particularly spectacular display includes fireworks.

POBLE ESPANYOL — TOURISM CENTRE, ARTS & CRAFTS

Map p318 (www.poble-espanyol.com; Avinguda de Francesc Ferrer i Guàrdia; adult/child €9.50/5.60; ⊙9am-8pm Mon, to 2am Tue-Thu, to 4am Fri, to 5am Sat, to midnight Sun; 🚌50, 61 or 193, MEspanya) Welcome to Spain! All of it! This 'Spanish Village' is both a cheesy souvenir hunters' haunt and an intriguing scrapbook of Spanish architecture built for the Spanish crafts section of the 1929 World Exhibition. You can meander from Andalucía to the Balearic Islands in the space of a couple of hours, visiting surprisingly good copies of Spain's characteristic buildings.

You enter from beneath a towered medieval gate from Ávila. Inside, to the right, is an information office with free maps. Straight ahead from the gate is the Plaza Mayor (Town Square), surrounded with mainly Castilian and Aragonese buildings. It is sometimes the scene of summer concerts. Elsewhere you'll find an Andalucian barrio, a Basque street, Galician and Catalan quarters and even a Dominican monastery (at the eastern end). The buildings house dozens of restaurants, cafes, bars, craft shops and workshops (for glass-artists and other artisans), and some souvenir stores.

Spare some time for the **Fundació Fran Daurel** (Map p318; www.fundaciofrandaurel.com; admission free; ⊙10am-7pm), an eclectic collection of 300 works of art including sculptures, prints, ceramics and tapestries by modern artists ranging from Picasso and Miró to more contemporary figures, including Miquel Barceló. The foundation also has a sculpture garden, boasting 27 pieces, nearby within the grounds of Poble Espanyol (look for the Montblanc gate). Frequent temporary exhibitions broaden the offerings further.

At night the restaurants, bars and especially the discos become a lively corner of Barcelona's nightlife.

Children's groups can participate in the Joc del Sarró. Accompanied by adults, the kids go around the *poble* seeking the answers to various mysteries outlined in a kit distributed to each group. Languages catered for include English.

PAVELLÓ MIES VAN DER ROHE ARCHITECTURE

Map p318 (☏93 423 40 16; www.miesbcn.com; Avinguda de Francesc Ferrer i Guàrdia; adult/child under 18yr/student €4.75/free/2.60; ⊙10am-8pm 10am Sat free guided tour; Ⓜ Espanya) The Pavelló Mies van der Rohe is not only a work of breathtaking beauty and simplicity, it is a highly influential building emblematic of the modern movement. The structure has been the subject of many studies and interpretations, and it has inspired several generations of architects.

Designed in 1929 by Ludwig Mies van der Rohe (1886–1969) as the Pavelló Alemany (German Pavilion) for the World Exhibition, it was removed after the show and reconstructed only in 1980, after the building had been consistently referred to as one of the key works of modern architecture. The Pavelló was built using glass, steel and marble, reflecting Mies van der Rohe's originality in the use of materials – he admired their visual rigour and precision, and their embodiment of modernity.

Mies van der Rohe also designed the Barcelona Chair for the pavilion, an iconic piece of furniture that can be seen in design-conscious spaces across the world today. Watch out for the graceful copy of a statue of *Alba* (Dawn) by Berlin sculptor Georg Kolbe (1877–1947) in one of the exterior areas.

MUSEU D'ARQUEOLOGIA DE CATALUNYA (MAC) MUSEUM

Map p318 (Archaeology Museum; www.mac.cat; Passeig de Santa Madrona 39-41; adult/student €3/2.10; ⊙9.30am-7pm Tue-Sat, 10am-2.30pm Sun; ☐55 or 193) This archaeology museum, housed in what was the Graphic Arts palace during the 1929 World Exposition, covers Catalonia and cultures from elsewhere in Spain. Items include copies of pre-Neanderthal skulls, Carthaginian necklaces and jewel-studded Visigothic crosses.

There's good material on the Balearic Islands (rooms X to XIII) and Empúries (Emporion, the Greek and Roman city on the Costa Brava; rooms XIV and XVII). The

Roman finds upstairs were mostly dug up in and around Barcelona. The most beautiful piece is a mosaic depicting Les Tres Gràcies (The Three Graces), unearthed near Plaça de Sant Jaume in the 18th century. In the final room, dedicated to the dying centuries of the Roman world, a beautiful golden disk depicting Medusa stands out. The museum has been renovated slowly over recent years, and the displays are now updated with a more modern design and interactive displays.

MUSEU ETNOLÒGIC MUSEUM

Map p318 (www.museuetnologic.bcn.cat; Passeig de Santa Madrona 16-22; adult/senior & student €3.50/1.75; ⊙noon-8pm Tue-Sat, 11am-3pm Sun; ☐55) Barcelona's ethnology museum presents a curious permanent collection that explores how various societies have worked down the centuries, as seen through collections of all sorts of objects. The entire museum was closed at the time of writing for major refurbishments. Check the website for reopening date.

Prior to the refurbishment, the museum started with a general look at ethnology in an introductory section, Orígens (Origins). Thereafter, collections covered the Pyrenees region in Catalonia (including traditional instruments and archive images of traditional dances) and Salamanca in central Spain, looking at a now largely extinct rural society. Further collections explored Japan, Nuristan (an area straddling Pakistan and Afghanistan), Morocco, Ethiopia, Australia, Papua New Guinea and the Americas (in particular Ecuador's Amazon region). The museum typically displays only a fraction of its collections at a time, showcasing a number of countries at different intervals, including for temporary exhibitions.

JARDÍ BOTÀNIC GARDENS

Map p318 (www.jardibotanic.bcn.es; Carrer del Doctor Font i Quer 2; adult/student €3.50/1.70; ⊙10am-8pm; ☐50, 61 or 193) This botanical garden is dedicated to Mediterranean flora

---

WHAT'S HAPPENING ON THE HILL?

To find out what temporary art exhibitions are on at Montjuïc's main art centres (the Museu Nacional d'Art de Catalunya, CaixaForum and the Fundació Joan Miró), take a look at **ArtMontjuïc** (www.artmontjuic.cat).

MONTJUÏC SIGHTS

WORTH A DETOUR

COLÒNIA GÜELL

Apart from La Sagrada Família, Gaudí's last big project was the creation of a utopian textile workers' complex for his magnate patron Eusebi Güell outside Barcelona at Santa Coloma de Cervelló. Gaudí's main role was to erect the colony's church, **Colònia Güell** (☎93 630 58 07; www.coloniaguellbarcelona.com; Carrer de Claudi Güell 6; adult/student €8/6.60; ⊙10am-7pm Mon-Fri, to 3pm Sat & Sun; ®FGC lines S4, S7, S8 or S33). Work began in 1908 but the idea fizzled eight years later and Gaudí only finished the crypt, which still serves as a working church.

This structure is a key to understanding what the master had in mind for his magnum opus, La Sagrada Família. The mostly brick-clad columns that support the ribbed vaults in the ceiling are inclined at all angles in much the way you might expect trees in a forest to lean. That effect was deliberate, but also grounded in physics. Gaudí worked out the angles so that their load would be transmitted from the ceiling to the earth without the help of extra buttressing. Similar thinking lay behind his plans for La Sagrada Família, whose Gothic-inspired structure would tower above any medieval building, without requiring a single buttress. Gaudí's hand is visible down to the wavy design of the pews. The primary colours in the curvaceous plant-shaped stained-glass windows are another reminder of the era in which the crypt was built.

Near the church spread the cute brick houses designed for the factory workers and still inhabited today. A short stroll away, the 23 factory buildings of a Modernista industrial complex, idle since the 1970s, were brought back to life in the early 2000s, with shops and businesses moving into the renovated complex.

In a five-room display with audiovisual and interactive material, the history and life of the industrial colony and the story of Gaudí's church are told in colourful fashion.

and has a collection of some 40,000 plants and 1500 species that thrive in areas with a climate similar to that of the Mediterranean, such as the Eastern Mediterranean, Spain (including the Balearic and Canary Islands), North Africa, Australia, California, Chile and South Africa.

The garden is a work in progress and the plan is to reach 4000 species.

PLAÇA D'ESPANYA
& AROUND   SQUARE, NEIGHBOURHOOD

(Ⓜ Espanya) The whirling roundabout of Plaça d'Espanya, distinguished by its so-called Venetian towers (because they are vaguely reminiscent of the belltower in Venice's St Mark's Square), was built for the 1929 World Exhibition and is the junction of several major thoroughfares.

It is flanked on its northern side by the facade of the former Plaça de Braus Las Arenas bullring. Built in 1900 and once one of three bullrings in the city, it was recently converted into a shopping and leisure centre by Lord Richard Rogers. There are good views of the city from its 4th-floor rooftop terrace.

Behind the bullring is the **Parc de Joan Miró** (Map p318), created in the 1980s – worth a quick detour for Miró's phallic sculpture

Dona i Ocell (Map p318) (Woman and Bird) in the western corner. Locals know the park (which apart from Miró is a dispiriting affair) as the Parc de l'Escorxador (Abattoir Park), as that's what once stood here – not surprising given the proximity to the bullring.

A couple of blocks west and just south of Estació Sants is **Parc d'Espanya Industrial** (Map p318; Carrer de Sant Antoni, Sants; ⊙10am-sunset; Sants Estació). With its ponds, little waterfalls, green spaces, trees, children's swings, bar, and the odd towers that look for all the world like sci-fi prison-camp searchlight towers, it is a strange park indeed.

CEMENTIRI DEL SUD-OEST   CEMETERY

(⊙8am-6pm; 🚍193) On the hill to the south of the Anella Olímpica stretches this huge cemetery, the Cementiri del Sud-Oest or Cementiri Nou, which extends down the southern side of the hill. Opened in 1883, it's an odd combination of elaborate architect-designed tombs for rich families and small niches for the rest. It includes the graves of numerous Catalan artists and politicians.

Among the big names are Joan Miró, Carmen Amaya (the flamenco dance star from La Barceloneta), Jacint Verdaguer (the 19th-century priest and poet to whom the rebirth of Catalan literature is attributed),

Francesc Macià and Lluís Companys (nationalist presidents of Catalonia; Companys was executed by Franco's henchmen in the Castell de Montjuïc in 1940), Ildefons Cerdà (who designed L'Eixample) and Joan Gamper (the founder of the FC Barcelona football team, aka Hans Gamper). Many victims of Franco's postwar revenge were buried in unmarked graves here – the last of them in 1974. From the 193 bus stop, it's about an 800m walk southwest. Otherwise, bus 38 from Plaça de Catalunya stops close to the cemetery entrance.

MUHBA REFUGI 307 — HISTORIC SITE

Map p318 (☎93 256 21 22; www.museuhistoria. bcn.cat; Carrer Nou de la Rambla 169; admission incl tour €3; ☺tours 11am-2pm Sat & Sun; MParal.lel) Part of the Museu d'Història de Barcelona (MUHBA), this is a shelter that dates back to the days of the Spanish Civil War. Barcelona was the city most heavily bombed from the air during the Spanish Civil War and had more than 1300 air-raid shelters. Local citizens started digging this one under a fold of Montjuïc in March 1937.

In the course of the next two years, the web of tunnels was slowly extended to 200m, with a theoretical capacity for 2000 people. People were not allowed to sleep overnight in the shelter – when raids were not being carried out work continued on its extension. Vaulted to displace the weight above the shelter to the clay brick walls (clay is porous, which allowed the bricks to absorb the shock waves of falling bombs without cracking), the tunnels were narrow and winding. Coated in lime to seal out humidity and whitewashed to relieve the sense of claustrophobia, they became a second home for many El Poble Sec folks.

When the civil war ended, Franco had some extensions made because he considered the option of entering WWII on Hitler's side. When he decided not to join the war, this and other shelters were largely abandoned. In the tough years of famine and rationing during the 1940s and 1950s, families from Granada took up residence here rather than in the shacks springing up all over the area, as poor migrants arrived from southern Spain. Later on, an enterprising fellow grew mushrooms here for sale on the black market.

The half-hour tours (in Catalan or Spanish; book ahead for English or French) explain all this and more.

✘ EATING

Montjuïc is largely bereft of notable eating options, for the obvious reason that it is mostly parks and gardens. In gruff old El Poble Sec, however, you'll turn up all sorts of priceless nuggets, from historic taverns offering Catalan classics to a handful of smart, new-wave eateries. The pickings in Sants are slimmer, but there are still some worthy exceptions.

✘ El Poble Sec

TOP CHOICE TICKETS — CATALAN €€

Map p306 (www.ticketsbar.es; Avinguda del Paral.lel 164; tapas from €4-12; ☺lunch & dinner daily; MParal.lel) This is, literally, one of the sizzling tickets in the restaurant world. It's the new tapas bar opened by Ferran Adrià, of the legendary El Bulli, and his brother Albert. And unlike El Bulli, it's an affordable venture – if you can book a table, that is (you can only book online, and two months in advance).

It's a fairly flamboyant and modern affair in terms of decor, playing with circus images and theatre lights, while the food has kept some of the El Bulli greats such as the 'air baguette' – a crust larded with Iberico ham, or the slightly bonkers 'cotton candy tree', with fruit-studded candyfloss clouds served up on a small bush. The seafood bar serves a slightly more serious option of oysters, tuna belly, and delicate fish skin in a paper cone. At the back is the bar, 41° – go through the curtain for cocktail classics with an Adrià twist: the ice has had the oxygen sucked out so it sparkles like a diamond.

QUIMET I QUIMET — TAPAS €€

Map p318 (Carrer del Poeta Cabanyes 25; tapas €3-11; ☺lunch & dinner Mon-Fri, noon-6pm Sat; MParal.lel) Quimet i Quimet is a family-run business that has been passed down from generation to generation. There's barely space to swing a calamari in this bottle-lined, standing-room-only place, but it is a treat for the palate. Look at all those gourmet tapas waiting for you! Let the folk behind the bar advise you, and order a drop of fine wine to accompany the food.

XEMEI — ITALIAN €€

Map p318 (☎93 553 51 40; Passeig de l'Exposició 85; mains €10-20; ☺Wed-Mon; MParal.lel) Xemei ('twins' in Venetian, because it is run

WORTH A DETOUR

HIGH IN THE SKY

For a five-star dining experience 105m above ground, grab a cab to **Restaurant Evo** (📞93 413 50 30; www.evores taurante.com; Avinguda Gran Via, 144, L'Hospitalet de Llobregat, ; fixed lunch menus Mon-Fri €38 & €70, mains €31-54, tasting menu €146; ⊘10am-midnight Mon-Sat; Ⓜ Hospital de Bellvitge, 🚌46, 94 & 95, 🚆FGC Bellvitge), located in Hotel Hesperia Tower in L'Hospitalet de Llobregat. This is gourmet dining literally under the stars (of which one comes from Michelin). The high point is the presentation of Mediterranean market cooking – try the *consomé de faisà amb els seus raviolis de foie i tòfona negra* (a pheasant consommé with foie-gras ravioli and black truffle).

by a pair of twins from Italy's lagoon city) is a wonderful slice of Venice in Barcelona. To the accompaniment of gentle jazz, you might try an entrée of mixed *cicheti* (Venetian seafood tapas), followed with *bigoi in salsa veneziana* (thick spaghetti in an anchovy and onion sauce).

BARRAMÒN   CANARIAN €
Map p318 (📞934 42 30 80; www.barramon.es; Carrer de Blai 28; mains €6-14; Ⓜ Paral.lel) On the lively Carrer de Blai, Barramòn is a great little bar that serves Canarian food and is a bit rock and roll at the same time. Try the Ropa Vieja (an infinitely more flavoursome version of its eponymous Cuban cousin), a wonderful stew of chickpeas and shredded pork; *papas arrugadas* (baked new potatoes with a spicy sauce); and *almogrote* (cured cheese topped with olive oil, garlic and red pepper).

LA TOMAQUERA   CATALAN €
Map p318 (📞93 441 85 18; Carrer de Margarit 5; mains €7; ⊘lunch & dinner Tue-Sat; Ⓜ Poble Sec) The waiters shout and rush about this classic place, while carafes of wine are sloshed about the long wooden tables. You can't book, so it's first in, first seated (queues are the norm). Try the house specialty of snails or go for hearty meat dishes. The occasional seafood option, such as *cassola de cigales* (crayfish hotpot) might also tempt. And cash is king.

ROSAL 34   TAPAS €€
Map p318 (📞93 324 90 46; www.rosal34.com; Carrer del Roser 34; mains €15-20; ⊘lunch & din

ner Tue-Sat; Ⓜ Poble Sec) Exposed brick and stone walls and a sinuous bar, accompanied by wafting lounge sounds, set the scene for a gourmet experience. You can opt for one of two tasting menus (€48/60) or search the menu for such numbers as *saltejat de xipironets de platja amb trompeta de la mort i ou escalfat* (sautéed small beach cuttlefish with mushrooms and egg).

TAVERNA CAN MARGARIT   CATALAN €€
Map p318 (Carrer de la Concòrdia 21; mains €8-10; ⊘dinner Mon-Sat; Ⓜ Poble Sec) For decades this former wine store has been dishing out dinner to often raucous groups. Traditional Catalan cooking is the name of the game. Surrounded by aged wine barrels, take your place at old tables and benches and perhaps order the *conejo a la jumillana* (fried rabbit served with garlic, onion, bay leaves, rosemary, mint, thyme and oregano).

LA BELLA NAPOLI   PIZZA €
Map p318 (📞93 442 50 56; www.bellanapoli.net; Carrer de Margarit 14; pizzas €7-21; ⊘lunch & dinner daily; Ⓜ Paral.lel) There are pizza joints all over Barcelona. And then there's the real thing: the way they make it in Naples. This place even *feels* like Naples. The waiters are mostly from across the Med and have that cheeky southern Italian approach to food, customers and everything else. The pizzas are good, ranging from the simple *margherita* to a heavenly black-truffle number.

RESTAURANT ELCHE   SPANISH €€
Map p318 (📞93 441 30 89; Carrer de Vila i Vilà 71; mains €10-12; ⊘lunch & dinner; Ⓜ Paral.lel) With tables spreading over two floors, and old-world style in service and settings, this spot has been doing some of Barcelona's best paella (of various types) and *fideuá* (vaguely similar to paella, but made with vermicelli noodles) since the 1960s.

✕ Monjuïc

MIRAMAR   MEDITERRANEAN, ASIAN €€
Map p318 (📞93 443 66 27; www.club-miramar.es; Carretera de Miramar 40; mains €10-15, lunchtime 3-course fixed menu €19.50; ⊘lunch & dinner Tue-Sat, lunch Sun; 🚌50 & 193) With several terraces and a cool designer main dining area, this restaurant's key draw is the views it offers over Barcelona's waterfront. Hovering just above the Transbordador Aeri cable-car station, you can linger over a coffee or

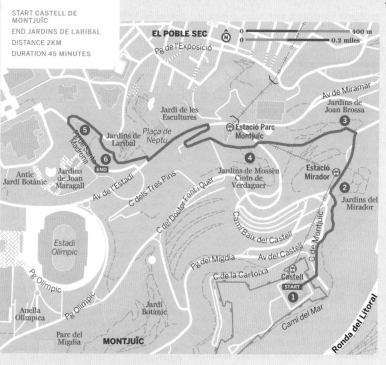

START CASTELL DE MONTJUÏC
END JARDINS DE LARIBAL
DISTANCE 2KM
DURATION 45 MINUTES

Neighbourhood Walk
Views & Gardens on Montjuïc

Although the ❶ **Castell de Montjuïc** itself is long synonymous with oppression, the building's dark history is today overshadowed by the fine views it commands over the city and sea. The ride up on the Telefèric is the perfect way to get there.

A short stroll down the road or the parallel Camí del Mar pedestrian trail leads to another fine viewpoint over the city and sea, the ❷ **Jardins del Mirador**. Take a weight off on the park benches or partake in a picnic lunch.

Further downhill is the multi-tiered ❸ **Jardins de Joan Brossa**. The entrance is on the left just beyond Plaça de la Sardana, with the sculpture of people engaged in the classic Catalan folk dance. More fine city views can be had from among the many Mediterranean trees and plants.

Exiting the Jardins de Joan Brossa at the other (west) side, you cross Camí Baix del Castell to the painstakingly laid-out ❹ **Jardins de Mossèn Cinto de Verdaguer**. This is a beautiful setting for a slow meander among tulip beds and water lilies.

Dropping away behind the Fundació Joan Miró, the ❺ **Jardins de Laribal** are a combination of terraced gardens linked by paths and stairways. The pretty sculpted watercourses along some of the stairways were inspired by Granada's Muslim-era palace of El Alhambra.

Finally, revivie with yourself with a snack at the cafe in the ❻ **Centre Gestor del Parc de Montjuïc**.

tuck into an elegant meal with a creative Catalan and Mediterranean slant, or opt for an extensive Asian menu.

✗ Sants

ZARAUTZ
BASQUE €

Map p318 (☎93 325 28 13; Carrer de l'Elisi 13; mains €10; ☺8am-11.30pm Mon-Sat Sep-Jul; ☒Tarragona) A short hop away from the train station, you can take in some quality Basque tapas at the bar any time of the day, or retire to the restaurant for a full meal, such as *carpaccio de carn amb formatge Idiazábal* (beef carpaccio with a tangy Basque cheese). The owner is a dessert specialist, so save some room. It's a rough-and-tumble-looking joint, but don't let that put you off.

🍷 DRINKING & ⚱ NIGHTLIFE

A couple of curious bars in El Poble Sec (literally 'Dry Town'!) make a good prelude to the clubs that hold sway up in the wonderfully weird fantasy world of the Poble Espanyol. A couple of clubs on the lower end of Avinguda del Paral.lel are worth seeking out too.

🍷 El Poble Sec

┌─────┐
┌─TOP─┐
│CHOICE│ LA CASETA DEL MIGDIA
BAR

Map p318 (☎617 956572, 93 301 91 77; www.laca seta.org; Mirador del Migdia; ☺6pm-2.30am Thu-Sat, noon-1am Sun Jun-Sep, noon-7pm Sat & Sun Oct-May; ☒Paral.lel) The effort of getting to what is, for all intents and purposes, a simple *chiringuito* (makeshift cafe-bar) is well worth it. Stare out to sea over a beer or coffee by day. As sunset approaches the atmosphere changes, as lounge music (from samba to funk) wafts out over the hammocks.

Walk below the walls of the Montjuïc castle along the dirt track or follow Passeig del Migdia – watch out for signs for the **Mirador del Migdia** (Map p318).

TINTA ROJA
BAR

Map p318 (Carrer de la Creu dels Molers 17; ☺8.30pm-2am Thu, to 3am Fri & Sat; ☒Poble Sec) A succession of nooks and crannies, dotted with what could be a flea market's collec-

tion of furnishings and dimly lit in violets, reds and yellows, makes the 'Red Ink' an intimate spot for a drink and the occasional show in the back – with anything from actors to acrobats. You never quite know what to expect in this one-time *vaqueria* (small dairy farm), where they kept cows out the back and sold fresh milk at the front!

BARCELONA ROUGE
BAR

Map p318 (☎93 442 49 85; Carrer del Poeta Cabanyes 21; ☺11pm-2am Tue-Thu, to 3am Fri & Sat; ☎; ☒Poble Sec) Decadence is the word that springs to mind in this bordello-red lounge–cocktail bar, with acid jazz, drum and bass and other soothing sounds drifting along in the background. The walls are laden with heavy-framed paintings, dim lamps and mirrors, and no two chairs are alike. Stick to simple drinks, as the €10 glamour cocktails are on the watery side.

GRAN BODEGA SALTÓ
BAR

Map p318 (http://bodegasalto.net; Carrer de Blesa 36; ☺7pm-3am Wed-Sat, noon-2am Sun; ☒Paral.lel) You can tell by the ranks of barrels that this was once an old-fashioned wine store. Now, after a little homemade psychedelic redecoration, with odd lamps, figurines and old Chinese beer ads, this is a magnet for an eclectic barfly crowd. Mohicans and tats abound, but the crowd is mixed and friendly.

⚱ Monjuïc

TERRAZZA
CLUB

Map p318 (www.laterrrazza.com; Avinguda de Francesc Ferrer i Guàrdia; admission €10-20; ☺midnight-5am Thu, to 6am Fri & Sat; ☒Espanya) One of the city's top summertime dance locations, Terrazza attracts squadrons of the beautiful people, locals and foreigners alike, for a full-on night of music and cocktails partly under the stars inside the Poble Espanyol complex.

ONE
CLUB

Map p318 (www.theonebarcelona.com; Avinguda de Francesc Ferrer i Guàrdia; admission €18; ☺midnight-6am Fri & Sat; ☒Espanya) A classic dance place inside the fantasy land of Poble Espanyol. The main dance floor has the latest in lighting effects and video screens. Shuttle buses ferry revellers from Plaça de Catalunya and Plaça d'Espanya from midnight to 3.30am and back down into town from 5am to 6.30am.

⭐ ENTERTAINMENT

SALA APOLO
LIVE MUSIC

Map p318 (☎93 441 40 01; www.sala-apolo.com; Carrer Nou de la Rambla 113; admission €6-12; ⏱12.30-6am Fri & Sat, midnight-5am Sun-Thu; MParal.lel) This is a fine old theatre, where red velvet dominates and you feel as though you're in a movie-set dancehall scene featuring Eliot Ness. 'Nasty Mondays' and 'Crappy Tuesdays' are aimed at a diehard, we-never-stop-dancing crowd. Earlier in the evening, concerts generally take place. Tastes are as eclectic as possible, from local bands to name international acts. Wednesday night is Rumba night in Sala 2, the smaller of the two spaces.

SANT JORDI CLUB
LIVE MUSIC

Map p318 (Passeig Olimpic 5-7; ⬚50, 55, 193) With capacity for more than 4500 people, this concert hall, annexed to the **Palau Sant Jordi** (Map p318), is used for big gigs that do not reach the epic proportions of headlining international acts. For concert information, keep your eyes out for listings sections in newspapers, flyers and magazines like the *Guía del Ocio*. Admission prices and opening times vary with the concerts.

TEATRE LLIURE
THEATRE

Map p318 (☎93 289 27 70; www.teatrelliure.com; Plaça de Margarida Xirgu 1; admission €13-26; ⏱box office 5-8pm; MEspanya) Housed in the magnificent former Palau de l'Agricultura building on Montjuïc (opposite the Museu d'Arqueologia) and consisting of two modern theatre spaces (Espai Lliure and Sala Fabià Puigserver), the 'Free Theatre' puts on a variety of quality drama (mostly in Catalan), contemporary dance and music.

TEATRE VICTÒRIA
THEATRE

Map p318 (☎93 329 91 89; www.teatrevictoria. com; Avinguda del Paral.lel 67-69; admission €15-45; ⏱box office 5pm to start of show; MParal.lel) This modern (and, on the street, rather nondescript-looking) theatre is on what used to be considered Barcelona's version of Broadway. It often stages ballet (including the Bolshoi in 2010), contemporary dance and even flamenco.

Day Trips from Barcelona

Girona p199
A splendid cathedral, a maze of narrow cobbled streets and Catalonia's finest medieval Jewish quarter are part of this riverside town's charms.

Figueres p202
The Teatre-Museu Dalí is a place of pilgrimage for any fan of Salvador Dalí, as well as the artist's final resting place.

Montserrat p205
Catalonia's most important shrine is in this mountain monastery, complete with Europe's oldest choir and superb scenic walks.

Sitges p207
A superb string of beaches, great nightlife and a hedonistic carnival await visitors at Costa Daurada's premier seaside town.

Tarragona p208
Sunny port city with a beautiful medieval core, boasting some of Spain's most extensive Roman ruins and studded with tempting eating options.

Girona

Explore

Girona's big draw is its Old Town, a tight huddle of ancient arcaded houses, grand churches and climbing cobbled streets, so head first for the star attraction – the Catedral – either by strolling along the lazy Río Onyar or by taking the high road along the medieval walls. Followed this with a visit to El Call (the medieval Jewish quarter) and the excellent Museu d'Història dels Jueus de Girona before taking your pick of the restaurants in the nearby streets.

After lunch, continue your exploration of other Old Town sights, such as the wonderfully intact Banys Àrabs or the attractive cloisters and verdant grounds of the Monestir de Sant Pere de Galligant, before finding a bar around the Plaça Independencia to while away the evening.

The Best...

➡ **Sight** La Catedral (p199)

➡ **Place to Eat** El Celler de Can Roca (p201)

➡ **Place to Drink** Lola Cafe (p202)

Top Tip

For the best views of the city, take a walk along Girona's medieval walls, accessed either from across the street from the Banys Àrabs or from near Plaça Catalunya.

Getting There & Away

➡ **Car** Take the AP-7 freeway via Granollers.

➡ **Train** At least 20 trains per day run from Barcelona Sants station (from €9.70, up to 1½ hours).

Need to Know

➡ **Area Code** 972

➡ **Location** 85km northeast of Barcelona

➡ **Tourist Office** (☑972 22 65 75; www.girona. cat/turisme; Rambla de la Llibertat 1; ☑9am-8pm Mon-Fri, 9am-2pm & 4-8pm Sat, 9am-2pm Sun)

---

❶ FIVE IN ONE

The **GironaMuseus card** (www. gironamuseus.cat) covers the five main Girona museums. You pay the full entrance fee at the first museum you visit and then get a 50% discount at the remainder. It's valid for six months.

◉ SIGHTS

TOP CHOICE LA CATEDRAL   CHURCH
(www.catedraldegirona.org; Plaça de la Catedral; museum adult/child €5/1.20, Sun free; ☑10am-8pm Apr-Oct, 10am-7pm Nov-Mar) The billowing baroque facade of the cathedral seems all the grander, standing at the head of a majestic flight of 86 steps rising from Plaça de la Catedral. Though the beautiful Romanesque **cloister** dates back to the 12th century, most of the building has been repeatedly altered over the centuries, giving it the second-widest Gothic nave (23m) in Christendom. The cathedral's **museum** contains numerous ecclesiastic treasures, including the masterly Romanesque *Tapís de la Creació* (Tapestry of the Creation) and a Mozarabic illuminated *Beatus* manuscript, dating from 975.

TOP CHOICE MUSEU D'HISTÒRIA
DELS JUEUS DE GIRONA   MUSEUM
(Carrer de la Força 8; adult/child €2/free; ☑Museu d'Història dels Jueus de Girona 10am-8pm Mon-Sat, 10am-2pm Sun Jul & Aug, shorter hours rest of year) The restored Centre Bonstruc ça Porta, named after Jewish Girona's most illustrious figure – a 13th-century cabbalist philosopher and mystic – houses the excellent Museu d'Història dels Jueus de Girona, which shows genuine pride in Girona's Jewish heritage without shying away from the less salubrious aspects, such as persecution by the Inquisition and forced conversions. Other well-presented displays deal with Girona's Jewish contribution to medieval astronomy and medicine, the synagogue, everyday life and rituals in the Jewish community and the Jewish diaspora; standout objects include funerary slabs and the original documents ordering the expulsion of Jews from Spain.

Girona

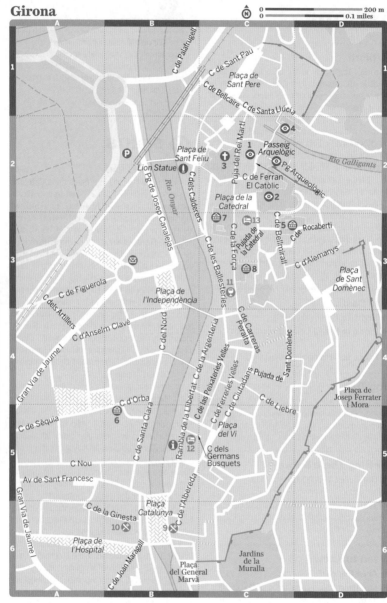

BANYS ÀRABS BATHHOUSE

(www.banysarabs.org; Carrer de Ferran Catòlic; adult/child €2/1; ⊗10am-7pm Mon-Sat Apr-Sep, shorter hours rest of year, 10am-2pm Sun & holidays) This is the only public bathhouse discovered from 12th-century Christian Spain. Possibly in reaction to Muslim enthusiasm for water and cleanliness (and a widely held view that water carried disease), washing almost came to be regarded as ungodly. The baths contain an *apodyterium* (changing room), followed by a *frigidarium* and *tepidarium* (with cold and warm water respectively) and a *caldarium* (a kind of sauna).

Girona

MONESTIR DE SANT PERE DE GALLIGANTS
MONASTERY

(www.mac.cat/cat/Seus/Girona; Carrer de Santa Llúcia; adult/senior & child/16-18 year old €2.30/free/1.61; ⊙10.30am-1.30pm & 4-7pm Tue-Sat Jun-Sep, 10am-2pm & 4-6pm Tue-Sat Oct-May, 10am-2pm Sun & holidays) This 11th- and 12th-century Romanesque Benedictine monastery has a lovely cloister, featuring otherworldly animals and mythical creatures on its pillars. It is home to the **Museu Arqueològic** (adult/senior & child €2.30/free), with exhibits that range from prehistoric to medieval times.

MUSEU D'HISTÒRIA DE LA CIUTAT
MUSEUM

(www.girona.cat; Carrer de la Força 27; adult/student/child €4/2/free; ⊙10am-2pm & 5-7pm Tue-Sat, 10am-2pm Sun & holidays) The engaging and well-presented museum does Girona's long and impressive history justice, its displays covering everything from the city's Roman origins, through the siege of the city by Napoleonic troops to the *sardana* (Catalonia's national folk dance) tradition and edgy temporary art.

FREE ESGLÉSIA DE SANT FELIU
CHURCH

(Plaça de Sant Feliu; ⊙9.30am-2pm & 4-7pm Mon-Sat, 10am-noon Sun) The 17th-century main facade of Girona's second great church, with its landmark single tower, is on Plaça de Sant Feliu. The nave has 13th-century Romanesque arches but 14th- to 16th-century Gothic upper levels and a baroque tower. The northernmost of the chapels is graced by a masterly Catalan Gothic sculpture,

DAY TRIPS FROM BARCELONA GIRONA

WORTH A DETOUR

COOKING UP A THREE-STAR STORM

➡ Once a simple bar and grill clutching onto a rocky perch high above the bare Mediterranean beach of Cala Montjoi and accessible only by dirt track from Roses, 6km to the west, **El Bulli** (www.elbulli.com) held three Michelin stars and the title of 'Best Restaurant in the World' a record five times, thanks to star chef Ferran Adrià, the 'Dalí of gastronomy', dedicated to presenting traditional flavours in very nontraditional forms. Though he closed El Bulli's doors in 2011, to open the El Bulli Foundation instead (an academy for advanced cuisine, expected in 2014), fear not, gourmands! Catalonia still has three three-star Michelin establishments, including the much-beloved El Celler de Can Roca, which was quick to slip into El Bulli's place.

➡ **El Celler de Can Roca** (☑972 22 21 57; www.cellercanroca.com; Carrer Can Sunyer 48; 5/9 course menus €130/160; ⊙lunch & dinner Tue-Sat), set 2km west of central Girona in a refurbished country house, is run by three brothers – Joan, Josep and Jordi – who focus on 'emotional cuisine': bringing back happy memories of your childhood and such through their ever-changing takes on Mediterranean cuisine. The style is playful – how about a 'dry gambini' (with a prawn serving the olive role in a dry martini)? – and the five- and nine-course tasting menus are reasonably priced (€130 to €160, plus wine).

> ### SLEEPING IN GIRONA
>
> ⇒ **Casa Cúndaro** (☏972 22 35 83; www.casacundaro.com; Pujada de la Catedral 9; d €60-80; ☎) Medieval Jewish house featuring five sumptuous rooms and four self-catering apartments – all combining original exposed stone walls with modern luxuries such as satellite TV. The location is practically on top of the cathedral.
>
> ⇒ **Bed & Breakfast Bells Oficis** (☏972 22 81 70; www.bellsoficis.com; Carrer dels Germans Busquets 2; r incl breakfast €40-85; ❋☎) Six very desirable rooms in a 19th-century building. Some have unusual pebble art in the bathrooms; others share bathrooms and some have views over the street.

Aloi de Montbrai's alabaster **Crist Jacent** (Recumbent Christ).

MUSEU D'ART GALLERY

(www.museuart.com; Plaça de la Catedral 12; admission €2; ◷10am-7pm Tue-Sat Mar-Sep, to 6pm Oct-Feb, 10am-2pm Sun & holidays) The Museu d'Art's collection includes around 8500 artworks from the Girona region, ranging from Romanesque woodcarvings and stained-glass tables to Modernista sculptures by Olot-born Miquel Blay and early-20th-century paintings by Francesc Vayreda.

MUSEU DEL CINEMA MUSEUM

(www.museudelcinema.org; Carrer de Sèquia 1; adult/child €5/free; ◷10am-8pm Jul-Aug, shorter hours & closed Mon rest of year) The Casa de les Aigües houses Spain's only cinema museum. The Tomás Mallol (Girona film director) collection includes not only displays tracing the history of cinema from the late 19th century debut of the Lumiére brothers, but also a parade of hands-on items for indulging in shadow games, optical illusions and the like – it's great for kids.

 EATING & DRINKING

L'ALQUERIA CATALAN €€

(☏972 22 18 82; www.restaurantalqueria.com; Carrer de la Ginesta 8; mains €18-22; ◷lunch & dinner Wed-Sat, lunch only Tues & Sun) This smart minimalist *arrocería* (a restaurant specialising in rice dishes) serves the finest *arrós negre* (rice cooked in cuttlefish ink) and *arrós a la Catalan* (Catalan paella, cooked in an earthenware pot, without saffron) in the city, as well as around 20 other superbly executed rice dishes. Book ahead for dinner.

+CUB TAPAS €

(Plaça Catalunya; 3 tapas €10.40; ◷lunch daily, dinner Mon-Sat; ✐) Ubercentral cafe-bar distinguished by the friendly service, innovative tapas – from black pudding with pistachio to salad with black fig sorbet – fresh fruit juice combos, shakes and Girona's own La Moska microbrew.

LOLA CAFE BAR

(Carrer de la Força 7; ◷6pm-3am) Re-creating a sultry Latin night in the midst of medieval Girona with occasional live salsa and rumba, this bar really hits the spot if you happen to have a weakness for *caipirinhas*, *mojitos* and more.

Figueres

Explore

An early start is essential for visiting the incomparable Teatre-Museu Dalí – it's Spain's second-most popular museum and from mid-morning, coachloads of tourists from the Costa Brava can make its narrow corridors quite claustrophobic. You'll want to spend the whole morning here, admiring everything from the exterior to the bizarre decorative touches and Dalí's distinctive works before partaking of some of the finest cuisine in the region, just out of town, or just grabbing a quick bite nearby.

There's more to Figueres than just Dalí, and there are several other attractions worth your time if you have the stamina in the afternoon: the vast Castell de Sant Ferran, perfect for a stroll around, or else the two entertaining museums in the centre.

The Best...

⇒ **Sight** Teatre-Museu Dalí (p204)

⇒ **Place to Eat** El Motel (p204)

⇒ **Place to Drink** Sidrería Txot's (p204)

Top Tip

Visit the Teatre-Museu Dalí outside the weekends and public holidays; in spring or early summer, get here for opening time or stay in Figueres the night before.

Getting There & Away

➡ **Car** Take the AP-7 freeway via Granollers and Girona.

➡ **Train** At least 18 trains daily from Barcelona Sants station via Girona (€9.40 to €12.80, 1½ to 2¼ hours).

Need to Know

➡ **Area Code** 972

➡ **Location** 139km northeast of Barcelona

➡ **Tourist Office** (☑972 50 31 55; www.figueresciutat.com; Plaça del Sol; ◷9am-8pm Mon-Sat, 10am-2pm Sun Jul-Sep, shorter hours rest of year)

◉ SIGHTS

CASTELL DE SANT FERRAN　　　　　　CASTLE

(www.lesfortalesescatalanes.info; admission €6; ◷10.30am-8pm Easter & Jul–mid-Sep, 10.30am-6pm mid-Sep–Oct & April-Jun, until 3pm rest of year) The impregnable-looking 18th-century fortress – the largest in Europe – has commanding views of the surrounding plain from a low hill 1km northwest of the centre. Built in 1750 to repel any French invaders and large enough to house 16,000 men, it nevertheless fell to their Gallic neighbours – both in 1794 and 1808. During the civil war, after abandoning Barcelona, Spain's Republican government held its final meeting (8 February 1939) in the dungeons. Peek inside the vast stables to get some idea of the size of the cavalry the castle held during its heyday. A stroll around the outside of the castle takes around forty-five minutes.

MUSEU DEL JOGUET　　　　　　MUSEUM

(www.mjc.cat; Carrer de Sant Pere 1; adult/child €5.80/free; ◷10am-7pm Mon-Sat, 11am-6pm Sun

DAY TRIPS FROM BARCELONA FIGUERES

WORTH A DETOUR

DALLYING WITH DALÍ DELIRIUM

Dalí was born in Figueres in 1904, but his career took him to Madrid, Barcelona, Paris and the USA. He remained true to his roots and has left his mark in several locations around Catalonia, particularly at his seaside residence in Portlligat and his inland 'castle', Castell de Púbol.

Portlligat, a 1.25km walk north of Cadaqués, is a tiny fishing settlement on a quiet, enchanting bay. Between 1930 and 1982, Dalí spent more than half his adult life here, in what was originally a fisherman's hut but has since grown into the **Casa-Museu Salvador Dalí** (☑972 25 10 15; www.salvador-dali.org; adult/child €11/free; ◷by advance reservation only), a whitewashed complex of quirky rooms, narrow corridors and terraces, the bizarre furnishings reflecting Dalí's personality. Dalí had not here come by choice. His father had forbidden him to return to the family house in Cadaqués after Dalí presented an image of the Sacred Heart in Paris, with *Parfois je crache par plaisir sur le portrait de ma mère* (Sometimes I spit for pleasure on my mother's picture) written across it. His father never forgave him this.

The **Castell de Púbol** (www.salvador-dali.org; Plaça de Gala Dalí; adult/student & senior €8/5; ◷10am-8pm daily mid-Jun–mid-Sep, shorter hours rest of year), in the village of La Pera, just south of the C-66 road between Girona and Palafrugell, is a Gothic and Renaissance mansion, purchased by Dalí in 1969 as a retreat for his wife, Gala, who lived here until her death at 88 in 1982. An inconsolable Dalí then moved in himself, but was removed by friends after starting a fire in 1984. Though much of the castle was decorated according to Gala's taste, Dalí touches do creep in in the form of spindly-legged elephant statues in the mazelike garden, a see-through table with a horse visible below and a stuffed giraffe staring at Gala's tomb in the crypt.

The Castell de Púbol can easily be reached by Palafrugell-bound buses from Girona (€ 2.50; 40 minutes). Alight at the second La Pera stop along the C66 and walk the 2km to the castle. For Portlligat, take a Sarfa bus to Cadaqués from Figueres (€5.30, one hour, 3-7 daily) or Girona (€3.50, 1 3/4 hours, 2-3 daily).

Jun-Sep, shorter hours rest of year) Spain's only toy museum has more than 3500 toys from the ages, from the earliest board games involving coloured stones and ball-in-a-cup – that timeless classic! – through to intricate dolls' houses, 1920s dolls with the creepiest expressions, Dinky Toys, and Catalonia- and Valencia-made religious processions with tiny figures. Absolutely mesmerising, and not just for the kids!

MUSEU DE L'EMPORDÀ MUSEUM
(www.museuemporda.org; La Rambla 2; adult/child €2/free; ⊙11am-8pm Tue-Sat May-Oct, 11am-7pm Tue-Sat Nov-Apr, 11am-2pm Sun & holidays) This local museum combines Greek, Roman and medieval archaeological finds with a size-able collection of art, mainly by Catalan artists, but there are also some works on loan from the Prado in Madrid. Admission is free with a Teatre-Museu Dalí ticket.

✕ EATING & DRINKING

TOP CHOICE **EL MOTEL** CATALAN €€€
(☑972 50 05 62; www.elmotel.cat; Avinguda Salvador Dalí I Doménech 170, Hotel Empordá; tasting menus €35-55, s/d from €93/109; ⊙lunch & dinner) Jaume Subirós, the chef and owner of this restaurant, located inside the Hotel Empordá on a busy road 1km north of the centre, is widely hailed for making the transition from traditional Catalan home cooking to the polished, innovative creature it is today. Gourmands have been making pilgrimages here for decades for dishes such as sea urchins from Cadaqués, cod with truffle and calf's cheek in red wine.

SIDRERÍA TXOT'S BASQUE €€
(www.sidreriatxots.com; Avinguda Salvadór Dalí 114; mains €12-20; ⊙lunch & dinner) Perch on a wooden seat and watch your Basque cider being poured from on high from the barrel before tucking into cured meats, cheeses and salads, as well as dishes such as chorizo in cider and L'Escala anchovies on toast.

◎ TOP SIGHTS
TEATRE-MUSEU DALÍ

This red castlelike building, topped with Dalí's trademark giant eggs and stylised Oscar-like statues and studded with plaster-covered croissants, is an entirely appropriate final resting place for the master of surrealism, its entrance watched over by medieval suits of armour balancing baguettes on their heads.

Inside, the ground floor (1st level) includes a semi-circular garden area; in its centre is **Taxi Plujós** (Rainy Taxi), composed of an early Cadillac – put a coin in the slot and water washes all over the occupant of the car. The **Sala de Peixateries** (Fish Shop Room) holds a collection of Dalí oils, including the famous **Autoretrat Tou amb Tall de Bacon Fregit** (Soft Self-Portrait with Fried Bacon). Beneath the former stage of the theatre is the crypt, with Dalí's plain tomb, located at 'the spiritual centre of Europe', as Dalí modestly described it.

The presence of Gala, Dalí's wife and lifelong muse, is seen throughout, from **Gala Mirando el Mar Mediterráneo** (Gala Looking at the Mediterranean Sea) on the 2nd level, which also appears to be a portrait of Abraham Lincoln from afar, to the classic the **Leda Atómica** (Atomic Leda).

Don't Miss
➡ The museum's whimsical exterior
➡ Taxi Plujós
➡ Gala Mirando el Mar Mediterráneo

Practicalities
➡ www.salvador-dali.org
➡ Plaça de Gala i Salvador Dalí 5
➡ adult/child €12/free
➡ ⊙9am-8pm Jul-Sep, 9.30am-6pm Mar-Jun & Oct, shorter hours for the rest of the year

SLEEPING IN FIGUERES

➡ **Hotel Durán** (☎972 50 12 50; www.
hotelduran.com; Carrer de Lasauca 5;
s/d from €74/89; [P][❄][🛜]) Staying at
this mid-19th century hotel is very
much in keeping with the Dalí theme
as he and his wife used to frequent
the place themselves. The rooms
are modern with forgettable soft
beige, brown and white decor but the
restaurant is like a royal banquet hall,
with smooth service and a fantastic
€20 lunch menu which features such
expertly-prepared delights as seared
tuna steak and rabbit loin.

➡ **Mas Pau** (☎972 54 61 54; www.mas
pau.com; Avinyonet de Puigventós; s/d
from €80/100; [P][❄][🛜]) This enchanting 16th-century *masia* (farmhouse)
features rustic chic rooms and a
Michelin-starred restaurant offering
a seasonal menu with an emphasis
on fresh local ingredients.

Montserrat

Explore

Though the monastery complex itself is
compact, allow a whole day for the visit if
you want to take advantage of the many
splendid mountain walks. Take the earliest
cremallera (rack-and-pinion train) or cable
car up the mountain to beat the crowds and
begin with the exploration of the monastery
complex, paying a visit to the Virgin and
then the worthwhile Museu de Montserrat
before grabbing an early lunch at the cafeteria. Season permitting, you might be able
to catch a performance by Europe's oldest
boys' choir (p206) inside the basilica.

Afterwards, ride the funiculars, or else
take a walk down to the Santa Cova –
the spot where the Virgin was originally
found – or up to the Sant Jeroni peak for a
splendid view of the valley below.

The Best...

➡ **Sight** Monestir de Montserrat (p206)
➡ **Place to Eat** Hotel Abat Cisneros (p207)
➡ **Walk** Sant Jeroni (p205)

Top Tip

To commune with La Moreneta in solitude
and enjoy the stillness and the silence of the
mountain, stay overnight to make it to the
chapel by the 7am opening time.

Getting There & Away

➡ **Train, rack railway & cable car** TheR5
line trains operated by **FGC** (www.fgc.net)
run hourly from Plaça d'Espanya station,
starting at 8.36am (52 to 56 minutes). They
connect with the **cable car** (☎93 835 00 05;
www.aeridemontserrat.com) at the Montserrat
Aeri stop (one way/return €5/7.90, 17
minutes, 9.40am to 7pm March to October,
10.10am to 5.45pm Monday to Saturday,
10.10am to 6.45pm Sunday & holidays
November to February) and the **cremallera**
(☎90 231 20 20; www.cremalleradmontserrat.
com) at Monistrol de Montserrat (one way/
return €6/9, five minutes).

Need to Know

➡ **Area Code** 938
➡ **Location** 50km northwest of Barcelona
➡ **Tourist Office** (☎938 77 77 01; www.
montserratvisita.com; ⊙9am-5.45pm Mon-Fri, to
6.45pm Sat & Sun)

⊙ SIGHTS

SANT JERONI   MOUNTAIN
You can explore the mountain above the
monastery on a web of paths leading to
some of the peaks and to 13 empty and
picturesquely dilapidated hermitages.
The **Sant Joan funicular** (one way/return
€5.05/8; ⊙every 20min 10am-6.50pm, closed

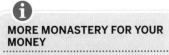

❶ MORE MONASTERY FOR YOUR MONEY

The all-inclusive **Tot Montserrat
ticket** from Plaça d'Espanya comprises train, *cremallera*, museum, funiculars, three-course cafeteria lunch
and the audiovisual show and costs
€39.95, which saves you a few euros
overall if you're interested in getting
as much as you can out of your visit.

Jan & Feb) will carry you up the first 250m from the monastery. If you prefer to walk, the road past the funicular's bottom station leads to its top station in about one hour (3km).

From the top station, it's a 20-minute stroll (signposted) to the **Sant Joan chapel**, with fine westward views. More exciting is the one-hour walk northwest to Montserrat's highest peak, Sant Jeroni, from where there's an awesome sheer drop on the north face.

SANTA COVA

(one way/return €2/3.20; ☺every 20min 10am-5.30pm) To see the chapel on the spot where the holy image of the Virgin was discovered (currently housing a replica La Moreneta), take the **Santa Cova funicular** (one way/return €2/3.20; ☺every 20min 10am-5.30pm) or else just stroll down, then follow the precipitous mountain path with fabulous views of the valley below.

SLEEPING IN MONTSERRAT

➡ **Hotel Abat Cisneros** (☎93 877 77 01; s/d €60/104; P ❄) The only hotel in the monastery complex has modern, comfortable rooms, some of which look over Plaça de Santa Maria. It has a good restaurant serving imaginative Catalonian dishes (meals €36).

 EATING

CAFETERIA FAST FOOD €

(meals €15-20; ☺lunch noon-4pm) At this central self-service spot you can grab a sandwich or more substantial mains: *calamares a la romana* (deep-fried calamari rings), meatballs, burgers – the usual suspects.

⭐ **ENTERTAINMENT**

MONTSERRAT BOYS CHOIR

(www.escolania.cat; ☺performances 1pm & Mon-Thu, 1pm Fri, noon Sun late Aug-late Jun)

TOP SIGHTS
MONESTIR DE MONTSERRAT

The monastery, the second most important pilgrimage centre in Spain after Santiago de Compostela, was founded in 1025 to commemorate a vision of the Virgin on the mountain, seen by – you guessed it – shepherds. The Black Virgin icon, allegedly carved by St Luke and hidden in the mountains by St Peter to protect it from the Moors, was subsequently discovered. Pilgrims come from far and wide to venerate the Virgen de Montserrat, affectionately known as **La Moreneta** ('the little brown one' or 'the Black Madonna'). She has been Catalonia's patron since 1881 and her blessing is particularly sought by newly married couples; Barcelona FC dedicate their victories to her and during the civil war she was courted by Franco.

The two-part **Museu de Montserrat** (Plaça de Santa Maria; adult/student €6.50/5.50; ☺10am-6pm) has an excellent collection ranging from an Egyptian mummy and Gothic altarpieces to art by El Greco, Monet, Degas and Picasso, as well as modern art and some fantastically gruesome 14th-century Russian icons. From Plaça de Santa Maria you enter the courtyard of the 16th-century **Basilica** (admission €5; ☺7.30am-8pm). From here, stairs lead to the narrow **Cambril de la Mare de Déu** (☺7-10.30am & noon-6.30pm), which houses La Moreneta.

Don't Miss

➡ La Moreneta shrine
➡ Montserrat Boys Choir performing at the basilica
➡ A walk up Montserrat's Sant Jeroni peak

Practicalities

➡ www.abadia montserrat.net
➡ ☺9am-6pm

Escolania, Europe's oldest music school, has a boys' choir, the Montserrat Boys' Choir, which sings in the basilica daily. It is a rare (if brief) treat; they tend to sing *Virolai*, written by Catalonia's national poet Jacint Verdaguer. The 40 to 50 *escolanets,* aged between 10 and 14, go to boarding school at Montserrat and must endure a two-year selection process to join the choir. Performance times are subject to change, so we recommend checking the website for the latest schedule.

hooks up with the C-32 after Castelldefels, but it is often busy and slow.

➡ **Train** Four R2 *rodalies* trains an hour, from about 6am to 10pm, run from Barcelona's Passeig de Gràcia and Estació Sants to Sitges (€3.60, 27 to 46 minutes depending on stops).

Need to Know

➡ **Area Code** 938

➡ **Location** 32km southwest of Barcelona

➡ **Tourist Office** (☑938 11 06 11; Passeig de la Ribera; ☺10am-2pm & 4-8pm)

Sitges

Explore

Sitges is perfect for seafront promenading and sun worshipping, so in warmer weather you'll find the most central beaches quite crowded. Luckily, there are quite a few to choose from, so pick your spot for a morning of sunbathing (or skinny dipping off the nudist beach) before choosing a seafood restaurant nearby.

If you have an interest in contemporary art and in the Modernisme movement, the Museu Cau Ferrat (p207) is well worth an hour of your time in the afternoon, as is the Fundació Stämpfli Museu d'Art Contemporani (p207) (Friday to Sunday only), followed by a central tapas bar for an afternoon drink. If you're particularly hard core, stay on and party until daybreak at one of the many clubs on the outskirts of town.

The Best...

➡ **Sight** Beaches (p207)

➡ **Place to Eat** eF & Gi (p208)

➡ **Place to Drink** Sweet Pachá (p208)

Top Tip

To find out the latest gay nightlife hotspots, head to the Parrots Hotel (p208); if you're coming to Sitges for the bacchanalian weeklong Carnaval in February/March, book well ahead.

Getting There & Away

➡ **Car** The best road from Barcelona is the C-32 tollway. More scenic is the C-31, which

⊙ SIGHTS

TOP CHOICE FUNDACIÓ STÁMPFLI MUSEU D'ART CONTEMPORANI   GALLERY

(www.fundacio-stampfli.org; Plaća Ajuntament; adult €3.50; ☺9.30am-2pm & 4-7pm Fri & Sat, 10am-3pm Sun) This excellent new art gallery opened in late 2010, with a focus on 20th-century art from the 1960s onwards. The striking paintings and sculptures by artists from all over the world, spread throughout the two renovated historical buildings, include works by Richard 'Buddy' di Rosa, Oliver Mosset and Takis.

PLATJAS   BEACHES

There are 12 beaches altogether in Sitges: the main beach, flanked by the attractive seafront **Passeig Maritim**, dotted with *chiringuitos* (beach bars) and divided into nine sections with different names by a series of breakwaters, as well as Sant Sebastiá, Balmins and D'aiguadolç beaches running east of the headland that's crowded with museums and graced by the striking **Església de Sant Bartomeu i Santa Tecla**. Though Bassa Rodona used to be the unofficial 'gay beach', gay sunbathers are now spread out pretty evenly, while Balmins is the sheltered bay favoured by nudists.

MUSEU CAU FERRAT   MUSEUM

(Carrer de Fonollar) Built in the 1890s as a house-cum-studio by artist Santiago Rusiñol (a pioneer of the art nouveau movement, whose statue graces the main beach), this whitewashed mansion is full of his own art and that of his contemporaries, including his friend Picasso, as well as a couple of El Grecos. The interior, with its exquisitely

SLEEPING IN SITGES

➡ **Parrots Hotel** (☏93 894 13 50; www.parrots-group.com; Calle Joán Torrida 16; s/d from €96/106 in high season; ❀🛉) It's hard to miss this bright blue gay hotel; the thoroughly modern rooms come with cable TV and air-con (a godsend in summer), there are balconies for people-watching and a sauna to get steamy in.

➡ **Hotel Romàntic** (☏93 894 83 75; www.hotelromantic.com; Carrer de Sant Isidre 33; s/d from €70/100 in high season; ❀) These three adjoining 19th-century villas are presented in sensuous Modernista style, with a leafy dining courtyard and friendly service, though the rooms are smallish and could do with sprucing up. Just around the corner is its charming sister hotel, **Hotel de la Renaixença** (☏93 894 06 43; www.hotelromantic.com; Carrer d'Illa de Cuba 45; s/d from €70/100 in high season), which is actually better value.

➡ **Pensió Maricel** (☏93 894 36 27; www.milisa.com; Carrer d'En Tacó 13; d €60-70 in high season) This spot, just back from the beach in a tight lane, is one of the cheapest deals in town. The 10 simple rooms are clean and spartan. Interior rooms are cheaper but have no view to speak of, while the exterior ones yield glimpses of the sea if you lean out the window.

tiled walls and lofty arches, is enchanting. Under renovation at the time of writing, the museum should have reopened by the time you read this.

✖ EATING & DRINKING

TOP CHOICE **EF & GI** INTERNATIONAL €€
(www.efgirestaurant.com; Carrer Major 33; meals €35-50; ⊘dinner Tue-Sat mid-Jan–mid-Dec) Fabio and Greg (eF & Gi) are not afraid to experiment and the results are startlingly good: the mostly Mediterranean menu with touches of Asian inspiration throws out such delights as chargrilled beef infused with lemongrass and kaffir lime, and tuna loin encrusted with peanuts and calamata olives with mango chutney. Don't skip the dessert, either.

EL POU TAPAS €€
(www.elpoudesitges.com; Carrer de Sant Pau 5; meals €30; ⊘lunch & dinner Wed-Mon) The tiny Wagyu beef burgers at this friendly gourmet tapas place are an absolute delight, and the rest of their offerings don't lag far behind; the traditional tapas fare sits alongside the likes of *mojama* (salted dried tuna) with almonds and fried aubergine with cane molasses. The sumptuous meatballs with squid are guaranteed to leave anyone in raptures.

SWEET PACHÁ CLUB CLUB
(www.sweetpacha.com; Avinguda Port d'Aiguadolç 9) The white leather seats are perfect for a pause in between cocktail-fuelled sessions on the dance floor and there's a decent seafood restaurant for those wanting a quieter night. It's located just back from the Aiguadolç Marina, 1.2km east along the coast from the Museu Maricel del Mar.

L'ATLÀNTIDA CLUB CLUB
(www.clubatlantida.com; Platja de Les Coves; ⊘Fri & Sat plus two more nights per week Jun-Sep) An Ibiza-esque big mama of a beachside nightclub with a large open air dance floor, about 3.5km west of the centre.

Tarragona

Explore

Since the Museu d'Història de Tarragona tends to be busiest from mid-morning onwards, it's best to start with its Amfiteatre Romà and the Pretori i Circ Romans first, or the excellent Museu Nacional Arqueològic de Tarragona. Later, head for the Catedral, followed by lunch in one of the many gourmet establishments nearby.

The Roman sights are spread out, so in the afternoon you may want to take a taxi to the Necròpolis Paleocristians, followed by the impressive Pont del Diable aqueduct. Alternatively (and especially if you have the Tarrago!na Card), leave the rest of the Roman remains until the following morning and instead have a peaceful wander along the Passeig Arqueológic Muralles – a walk between the medieval walls, followed by a seafood meal at the fishermen's quarter of Serallo.

The Best...

➡ **Sight** Museu d'Història de Tarragona (p210)

➡ **Place to Eat** Arcs Restaurant (p210)

➡ **Place to Drink** El Candil (p211)

Top Tip

The 48-hour Tarrago!na Card, available from the tourist office for €15, gives you free access to all of the city's museums, as well as discounts in select restaurants and shops.

Getting There & Away

➡ **Car** Take the C-32 toll road along the coast via Castelldefels or the AP-7 (if following Avinguda Diagonal west out of town).

➡ **Train** More than 40 regional and long-distance trains per day run to/from Barcelona's Estació Sants (from €5.70 to €6.40 for regional and from €19.80 for long-distance, high-speed trains; 55 minutes to 1¾ hours).

Need to Know

➡ **Area Code** 977

➡ **Location** 96km southwest of Barcelona

➡ **Tourist Office** (✆977 25 07 95; www. tarragonaturisme.es; Carrer Major 39; ☺10am-9pm Mon-Sat, 10am-2pm Sun Jul-Sep, 10am-2pm & 4-7pm Mon-Sat, 10am-2pm Sun & holidays Oct-Jun)

◉ SIGHTS

MUSEU NACIONAL ARQUEOLÒGIC DE TARRAGONA
MUSEUM

(www.mnat.es; Plaça del Rei 5; adult/child €3.50/ free; ☺10am-8pm Tue-Sat, 10am-2pm Sun & holidays Jun-Sep, shorter hours rest of year) This excellent museum does justice to the cultural and material wealth of Roman Tarraco. The mosaic collection traces the changing trends, from the simple black-and-white designs to complex full-colour creations; a highlight is the large, almost complete *Mosaic de Peixos de la Pineda,* showing fish and sea creatures. In the section on everyday arts, you can admire ancient fertility aids, including an oversized stone penis, symbol of the god Priapus.

Admission entitles you to enter the museum at the **Necròpolis Paleocristians** (www. mnat.cat; Avinguda de Ramón i Cajal 80; ☺9am-8.30pm Tue-Sat, 10am-2pm Sun Jun-Sep, shorter hours rest of year), a vast Roman-Christian city of the dead consisting of over 2000 elaborate tombs. While you can only look at the tombs through the fence, the museum features curious funereal objects and sarcophagi.

LA CATEDRAL
CHURCH

(Pla de la Seu; adult/child €4/1.40; ☺10am-7pm Mon-Sat Jun–mid-Oct, shorter hours rest of year) Tarragona's cathedral has been undergoing a major facelift for some time and much of it was closed, albeit scheduled to reopen soon, at the time of writing. The length of its construction (between 1171 and 1331) has endowed it with both Romanesque and Gothic features, as typified by the main facade on Pla de la Seu. Its fortresslike exterior suggests fears of a Moorish invasion.

The cloister has Gothic vaulting and Romanesque carved capitals, one of which shows rats conducting what they imagine to be a cat's funeral...until the cat comes back to life! It's a lesson about passions seemingly lying dormant until they reveal themselves. The rooms off the cloister house the **Museu Diocesà**, with an extensive collection extending from Roman hairpins to some lovely 12th- to 14th-century polychrome woodcarvings of a breastfeeding Virgin.

The interior houses the arm of St Thecla, Tarragona's patron saint; the marble main **altar**, carved in the 13th century, depicts scenes from the life of St Thecla.

PASSEIG ARQUEOLÒGIC MURALLES
HISTORIC SITE

(€3; ☺9am-9pm Tue-Sat, 9am-3pm Sun Easter-Oct, shorter hours rest of year) The Passeig Arqueològic is a peaceful walk around part of the perimeter of the old town between two lines of city walls; the inner ones are

TOP SIGHTS
MUSEU D'HISTÒRIA DE TARRAGONA

The 'museum' title is somewhat misleading, as this is in fact four separate Roman sites (which together have constituted a Unesco World Heritage site since 2000).

Start by exploring the **Pretori i Circ Romans** (Plaça del Rei), which includes part of the vaults of the Roman circus, where chariot races were once held, ending at the Pretori tower on Plaça de Rei.

Near the beach is the crown jewel of Tarragona's Roman sites, the **Amfiteatre Romá** (Plaça d'Arce Ochotorena; ⊙9am-9pm Tue-Sat, 9am-3pm Sun Easter-Sep, 9am-5pm Tue-Sat, 10am-3pm Sun & holidays Oct-Easter). Much of the amphitheatre was picked to bits, the stone used to build the port, so what you see now is a partial reconstruction.

The northwest half of **Fórum Roma** (Carrer del Cardenal Cervantes) was occupied by a judicial basilica (where legal disputes were settled), from where the rest of the forum stretched downhill to the southwest. Linked to the site by a footbridge is another excavated area which includes a stretch of Roman street.

The so-called **Pont del Diable** (Devil's Bridge) is actually the Aqüeducte de les Ferreres, a Roman relic and an irrigation engineer's wet dream. In its glory days, it delivered water from the Ríu Gayo to over 200,000 people .

Don't Miss
➡ Pretori i Circ Romans
➡ Amfiteatre Roma
➡ Pont del Diable, the Devil's Bridge

Practicalities
➡ www.museutgn.com
➡ adult/child per site €3/free, all MHT sites €10/free
➡ ⊙9am-9pm daily Easter-Sep, shorter hours for the rest of the year

mainly Roman and date back to the 3rd century BC, while the outer ones were put up by the British in 1709 during the War of the Spanish Succession. Prepare to be awed by the vast gateways built by the Iberians, and clamber up onto the battlements from the doorway to the right of the entrance for all-encompassing views of the city. The walk starts from the Portal del Roser on Avenida Catalunya.

pumpkin soup with *morcilla* (black pudding) and goat's cheese to the most intense *salmorejo* (a thicker, more savoury gazpacho) outside Andalucía.

AQ CATALAN €€
(☎977 21 59 54; www.aq-restaurant.com; Carrer de les Coques 7; menus from €18; ⊙lunch & dinner Tue-Sat) This is a bubbly designer haunt with stark colour contrasts (black, lemon and cream linen), slick lines and intriguing plays on traditional cooking, such as *ven-*

🍴 EATING & DRINKING

TOP CHOICE ARCS RESTAURANT MEDITERRANEAN €€
(☎977 21 80 40; www.restaurantarcs.com; Carrer Misser Sitges 13; menu €23; ⊙lunch & dinner Tue-Sat) Inside a medieval cavern with bright splashes of colour in the form of contemporary art, you are served some wonderful takes on Mediterranean dishes, from *tartar de atún* (tuna carpaccio) and the inspired

SLEEPING IN TARRAGONA
➡ **Hotel Plaça de la Font** (☎977 24 61 34; www.hotelpdelafont.com; Plaça de la Font 26; s/d €55/70; ❄) Simple, spick-and-span rooms overlooking a bustling terrace in a you-can't-get-more-central-than-this location, right on the popular Plaça de la Font.

tresca de tonyina amb ceba caramelitzada, tomàquet, formatge de cabra i olives (tuna belly meat with caramelised onion, tomato, goat's cheese and olives).

EL VARADERO   SEAFOOD €

(Carrer de Trafalgar 13; raciones €7-9; ☺lunch & dinner) El Varadero is an informal, locally popular spot serving simple, mouth-wateringly delicious seafood dishes, which might include *tigres* (stuffed, breaded and fried mussels), *ostrón* (fat oyster) and *cigalas a la plancha* (grilled crayfish).

EL CANDIL   CAFE €

(Plaça de la Font 13; hot chocolate €3; ☺11am-3pm & 5pm-midnight) There are over 30 different hot-chocolate combinations on the menu at this cavelike cafe-bar, as well as a good selection of beers and *cava*.

🛏 Sleeping

Barcelona has an excellent range of accommodation, with luxury hotels, small-scale boutique lodgings, and varied midrange and budget selections. The settings offer some fine choices in historic or seaside districts, or in the thick of charming neighbourhoods packed with restaurants and nightlife. The economic crisis has slowed price increases, yielding reasonable value overall.

Hotels

Hotels in Barcelona cover a broad range. At the bottom end there is often little to distinguish them from the better *pensiones* and *hostales*, and from there they run up the scale to five-star luxury. Some of the better features to look out for: rooftop pools and lounges, views (either of the sea or a cityscape – La Sagrada Família, Montjuïc, Barri Gòtic) and proximity to the important sights. For around €100 to €140 there are extensive options for good doubles across a broad range of areas. The top-end category starts at €250 for a double, but can easily rise to €500 (and beyond for suites).

Pensiones & Hostales

Depending on the season, you can pay as little as €15 to €25 for a dorm bed in a youth hostel. If dorm living is not your thing but you are still looking for a budget deal, check around the many *pensiones* (small private hotels) and *hostales* (budget hotels). These are family-run, small-scale hotels, often housed in sprawling apartments. Some are fleapits, others immaculately maintained gems. You're looking at a minimum of around €35/55 for basic individual/doble (single/double) rooms, mostly without a private bathroom. (It is occasionally possible to find cheaper rooms, but they can be unappetising.)

Some places, especially at the lower end, offer triples and quads, which can be good value for groups. If you want a double bed (as opposed to two singles), ask for a *llit/cama matrimonial* (Catalan/Spanish). If your budget is especially tight, look at the economical options on Barcelona 30.com.

Apartment & Room Rentals

A cosier (and sometimes more cost-effective) alternative to hotels can be short-term apartment rental. Typical prices are around €80 to €100 for two people per night. For four people it's an average of €160 a night.

One of the best options is Air BnB (www.airbnb.com). It also lists single rooms – a good way to meet locals and/or other travellers if you don't mind sharing common areas. Average prices for a room range from €30 to €60.

Other apartment-rental services include:
➡ Oh-Barcelona (www.oh-barcelona.com)
➡ Aparteasy (www.aparteasy.com)
➡ Feel at Home Barcelona.com (www.feelathomebarcelona.com)
➡ Barcelona On Line (www.barcelona-on-line.es)
➡ Friendly Rentals (www.friendlyrentals.com)
➡ Lodging Barcelona (www.lodgingbarcelona.com)
➡ Rent a Flat in Barcelona (www.rentaflatinbarcelona.com)
➡ MH Apartments (www.mhapartments.com)

If you're after a short-term house swap, check out www.loquo.com. Want to sleep on a local's couch? Try www.couchsurfing.com. To browse a large selection of accommodation at all price levels, check out hotels.lonelyplanet.com.

Travellers with Disabilities

Often hotels falsely claim to be equipped for guests with disabilities – check out www.accessiblebarcelona.com for help finding genuinely accessible accommodation. The same people also run www.accessible.travel.

Lonely Planet's Top Choices

Hotel Neri (p215) Beautiful, historic option on a tranquil spot in Barri Gòtic.

Casa Camper (p216) Stylish option in El Raval with Vinçon furniture and hammocks.

Hotel Arts Barcelona (p218) Utramodern waterfront high-rise with all the trappings of luxury.

W Barcelona (p217) Seafront luxury hotel with magical views and lovely palm-fringed pool.

Hotel Casa Fuster (p221) Plush rooms in a Modernista mansion in Gràcia.

Hotel Omm (p219) Fantastical Dalí-esque hotel with a 'peeling' facade.

Best Budget Options

€

Hostal Campi (p215)
Alberg Hostel Itaca (p215)
Hostel Mambo Tango (p223)
Pensió 2000 (p217)
Hotel Marina Folch (p218)

€€

El Jardí (p215)
Barceló Raval (p216)
Hotel San Agustín (p216)
Hotel Banys Orientals (p217)

Hotel Constanza (p220)
Hotel Praktik (p219)

€€€

Hotel 1898 (p215)
Hotel Majèstic (p219)
Hotel Rey Juan Carlos I (p222)

Best Rooms with a View

Hotel Arts Barcelona (p218)
W Barcelona (p217)
Hotel Rey Juan Carlos I (p222)
Eurostars Grand Marina Hotel (p218)
Hotel 54 (p218)
Hotel Colón (p215)

Best Hotel Pools

Comtes De Barcelona (p219)
Hotel Arts Barcelona (p218)
Hotel Majèstic (p219)
Hotel Rey Juan Carlos (p222)
Eurostars Grand Marina Hotel (p218)

Best Style Hotels

Barceló Raval (p216)
Hotel Banys Orientals (p217)
Hotel Sixtytwo (p219)
Hotel Axel (p221)
Chic & Basic (p217)

Where to Stay

Neighbourhood	For	Against
La Rambla & Barri Gòtic	Great location, close to major sights; perfect area for exploring on foot; good nightlife and dining options	Very touristy; noisy; some rooms are small, lack windows
El Raval	Central option, with good local nightlife and access to sights; bohemian vibe with few tourists	Can be noisy; seedy and run-down in parts; many fleapits best avoided; feels unsafe to walk late at night.
La Ribera	Great restaurant scene and neighbourhood exploring; central; top sights including the Museu Picasso and the Palau de la Música Catalana	Can be noisy; overly crowded; touristy
Barceloneta & the Waterfront	Excellent seafood restaurants; local easygoing vibe; handy access to the promenade and beaches	Very few sleeping options; outside of Barceloneta can be far from the action and better suited to business travellers
L'Eixample	Wide range of options for all budgets; close to Modernista sights; good restaurants and nightlife; prime gay scene (in the 'Gaixample')	Can be very noisy with lots of traffic; not a great area for walking; a little far from the old city.
Gràcia	Youthful, local scene with lively restaurants and bars	Far from the old city; few formal options (but lots of rooms for rent)
La Zona Alta	Good nightlife and restaurants in parts	Very far from the action; spread-out area, requires frequent metro travel; geared more towards business travellers
Montjuïc, Sants and El Poble Sec	Near the museums, gardens and views of Montjuïc; great local exploring in El Poble Sec; locations in El Poble Sec are also convenient to El Raval	Somewhat out of the way; can be a bit gritty up by El Sants train station

🛏 La Rambla & Barri Gòtic

La Rambla is lined with hotels, *pensiones* and fleapits, and countless others are scattered in the Barri Gòtic labyrinth. Carrer de Ferran is lined with popular but mostly cramped, noisy options – a little too close to ranks of pseudo-Irish pubs for comfort. Many of the smaller joints are nothing special, catering to an at times rowdy party crowd. But there are some real gems too.

HOTEL NERI   DESIGN HOTEL €€€
Map p292 (☑93 304 06 55; www.hotelneri.com; Carrer de Sant Sever 5; d from €270; ❄@🛜; MLiceu) This tranquil hotel occupies a beautifully adapted, centuries-old building backing onto Plaça de Sant Felip Neri. The sandstone walls and timber furnishings lend a sense of history, while the rooms feature cutting-edge technology, including plasma-screen TVs and infra-red lights in the stone-clad designer bathrooms. Choose from a menu of sheets and pillows, and sun yourself on the roof deck.

HOTEL 1898   HOTEL €€€
Map p292 (☑93 552 95 52; www.hotel1898.com; La Rambla 109; d €230-350; ❄@🛜🏊; MLiceu) The former Compañía de Tabacos Filipinas (Philippines Tobacco Company) has been resurrected as a luxury hotel, replete with idylic rooftop bar La Isabala. Some rooms are smallish but deluxe rooms and suites have their own terraces. All combine modern comfort and elegance, with hardwood floors and tasteful furniture. Some of the suites have access to a private indoor pool, while all guests can use the outdoor one.

HOTEL COLÓN   HOTEL €€
Map p292 (☑93 301 14 04; www.hotelcolon.es; Avinguda de la Catedral 7; s/d from €110/170; ❄@; MJaume I) The privileged position opposite the cathedral lends this hotel special grace. A range of rooms, from modest singles to light-filled doubles and suites, offers elegant accommodation. Decoration varies considerably (from hardwood floors to carpet) and the top-floor superior rooms with terrace are marvellous (and go for about €300).

HOTEL CONTINENTAL   HOTEL €€
Map p292 (☑93 301 25 70; www.hotelcontinental.com; La Rambla 138; s/d from €92/102; ❄🛜; MCatalunya) You can imagine being here in 1937, when George Orwell returned from the front during the Spanish Civil War, and Barcelona was tense with factional strife. The Continental's rooms are worn and rather spartan, but have romantic touches like ceiling fans, brass bedsteads and frilly bedclothes. An extra €20 yields a room with a small balcony overlooking La Rambla.

EL JARDÍ   HOTEL €€
Map p292 (☑93 301 59 00; www.eljardi-barcelona.com; Plaça de Sant Josep Oriol 1; d €65-120; ❄🛜; MLiceu) The 'Garden Hotel' has no garden but several boxy doubles with balcony overlooking one of the prettiest squares in the city. If you can snare one of them, it is well worth climbing up the stairs. If you can't get a room with a view, you are better off looking elsewhere.

HOTEL RACÓ DEL PI   BOUTIQUE HOTEL €€
Map p292 (☑93 342 61 90; www.hotelh10racodelpi.com; Carrer del Pi 7; d €100-198; ❄@🛜; MLiceu) This hotel was stylishly carved out of a historic Barri Gòtic building, and features 37 rooms with dark wood beams, parquet floors, colourful mosaic-tiled bathrooms and full soundproofing. The aesthetic in the rooms is modern: light colours blended with navy blue blankets and the occasional art print. The location is terrific.

HOSTAL CAMPI   HOSTAL €
Map p292 (☑93 301 35 45; www.hostalcampi.com; Carrer de la Canuda 4; s/d without bathroom €35/60, d with bathroom €70; @🛜; MCatalunya) This is an excellent budget deal appealing mostly to younger backpackers. The best rooms at this friendly, central *hostal* are the doubles with private bathrooms: these are spotlessly kept and extremely roomy and bright, with attractive tile floors. The building is located off La Rambla, protecting it from much of the street noise, and dates from the late 18th century.

ALBERG HOSTEL ITACA   HOSTEL €
Map p292 (☑93 301 97 51; www.itacahostel.com; Carrer de Ripoll 21; dm €11-26, d €60; @🛜; MJaume I) A bright, quiet hostel near the Catedral, Itaca has spacious dorms (sleeping six, eight or 12 people) with parquet floors and spring colours, and two doubles. It also features two nearby apartments for six people (€120 per night). There's a lively vibe, but not much in the way of common areas, apart from the tiny cafe-lounge at the entrance.

SLEEPING LA RAMBLA & BARRI GÒTIC

REGENCIA COLÓN
HOTEL

Map p292 (☎93 318 98 58; www.hotelregencia colon.com; Carrer de Sagristans 13; d €80-135; ☎; MJaume I) Although not as flashy as its sister property around the corner (the Hotel Colón), this efficient, modern 6-story hotel has clean, sizeable rooms done up in an easy-going colour scheme (pastels in most). Showers are strong and wi-fi is reliable. As elsewhere in Barri Gòtic, street noise can be a problem, but the location – just steps from La Catedral – is superb.

BONIC
B&B €€

Map p292 (☎62 605 34 34; www.bonic-barcelona. com; Carrer de Josep Anselm Clavé 9; s €55, d €90-95; ✱@☎; MDrassanes) Bonic is a small, cosy B&B that has eight rooms in varied styles, with wood or decorative tile floors, tall ceilings and attractive furnishings. Several are bright and cheerfully painted, and some lack exterior windows. Owing to the lack of private facilities – all guest rooms share three bathrooms – maximum occupancy is six or seven guests a night, although groups of friends can book the whole place to themselves.

🛏 El Raval

You're right in the thick of things when staying in this mildly wild side of the old town. Accommodation options are broad, from fleapits on dodgy lanes through to the latest in designer comfort. Hostels and cheap hotels abound.

CASA CAMPER
DESIGN HOTEL €€€

Map p296 (☎93 342 62 80; www.casacamper. com; Carrer d'Elisabets 11; s/d €240/270; ✱@; MLiceu) The massive foyer looks like a contemporary-art museum, but the rooms are the real surprise. Decorated in red, black and white, each room has a sleeping and bathroom area, where you can put on your Camper slippers, enjoy the Vinçon furniture and contemplate the hanging gardens outside your window. Across the corridor is a separate, private sitting room with balcony, TV and hammock. Get to the rooftop for sweeping cityscapes.

WHOTELLS
HOSTAL €€

Map p296 (☎93 443 08 34; www.whotells.com; Carrer de Joaquín Costa 28; apt from €180; ✱@☎; MUniversitat) These comfortable home-away-from-home apartments, decked out with Muji furniture, can sleep four to six people. Cook up a storm in the kitchen with products bought in the nearby La Boqueria market, or flop in front of the LCD TV. The owners also have apartments in L'Eixample and La Barceloneta. Prices fluctuate enormously in response to demand.

BARCELÓ RAVAL
DESIGN HOTEL €€

Map p296 (☎93 320 14 90; www.barceloraval. com; Rambla del Raval 17-21; d €160-230; ✱@; MLiceu) Part of the city's plans to pull the El Raval district up by the bootstraps, this oval-shaped designer hotel tower makes a 21st-century splash. The rooftop terrace offers fabulous views and the B-Lounge bar-restaurant is the toast of the town for meals and cocktails. Rooms have slick aesthetics (white with lime green or ruby-red splashes of colour), Nespresso machines and iPod docks.

HOTEL SAN AGUSTÍN
HOTEL €€

Map p296 (☎93 318 16 58; www.hotelsa.com; Plaça de Sant Agustí 3; r from €80-180; ✱@☎; MLiceu) This former 18th-century monastery opened as a hotel in 1840, making it the city's oldest. The location is perfect – a quick stroll off La Rambla on a curious square. Rooms sparkle, and are mostly spacious and light-filled. Consider an attic double with sloping ceiling and bird's-eye views.

HOTEL ESPAÑA
HOTEL €€

Map p296 (☎93 318 17 58; www.hotelespanya. com; Carrer de Sant Pau 9-11; s €100, d €125-155; ✱; MLiceu) Best known for its eccentric Modernista restaurants, in which architect Domènech i Montaner, sculptor Eusebi Arnau and painter Ramon Casas had a hand, this hotel offers clean, straightforward rooms in a building that still manages to ooze a little history. In the 1920s it was a favourite with bullfighters.

HOSTAL CHIC & BASIC
HOSTEL €€

Map p296 (☎93 302 51 83; www.chicandbasic. com; Carrer de Tallers 82; s €80, d €103-124; ✱@; MUniversitat) The colour scheme here is predominantly white, with exceptions like the screaming orange fridge in the communal kitchen and chill-out area. Rooms are also themed lily white, from the floors to the sheets. Finishing touches include the plasma-screen TVs and the option of plugging your iPod into your room's sound system. The street can get noisy.

HOSTAL GAT RAVAL   HOSTEL €

Map p296 (📞93 481 66 70; www.gataccommoda
tion.com; Carrer de Joaquín Costa 44; s/d without
bathroom €63/82; ❄ @ 🛜; Ⓜ Universitat) There's
pea-green and lemon-lime decor in this hip
2nd-floor *hostal* located on a bar-lined lane
dominated by resident migrants and wandering bands of uni students. The individual
rooms are pleasant and secure, but only some
have private bathrooms. The staff also run
the more upmarket **Hostal Gat Xino** (Map
p296; 📞93 324 88 33; www.gataccommodation.
com; Carrer de l'Hospital 149-155; s/d €80/115, ste
with terrace €140; ❄ @ 🛜; Liceu) nearby.

HOTEL PENINSULAR   HOTEL €

Map p296 (📞93 302 31 38; www.hpeninsular.
com; Carrer de Sant Pau 34; s/d €55/78; ❄ @ 🛜;
Ⓜ Liceu) An oasis on the edge of the slightly
dicey Barri Xinès, this former convent
(which was connected by tunnel to the Església de Sant Agustí) has a plant-draped
atrium extending its height and most of its
length. The 60 rooms are simple, with tiled
floors and whitewash, but mostly spacious
and well kept.

🛏 La Ribera

Several fine hotels are located on the fring-
es of the busy El Born area and a growing
number of the sometimes bombastic buildings on thundering Via Laietana are top-
end hotels.

CHIC & BASIC   DESIGN HOTEL €€

Map p300 (📞93 295 46 52; www.chicandbasic.
com; Carrer de la Princesa 50; s €96, d €132-192;
❄ @; Ⓜ Jaume I) This is a very cool hotel indeed, with its 31 spotlessly white rooms and
fairy-lights curtains that change colour,
adding an entirely new atmosphere to the
space. The ceilings are high and the beds
enormous. Many beautiful old features of
the original building have been retained,
such as the marble staircase. Chic & Basic
also runs a *hostal* in El Raval (p216).

HOTEL BANYS ORIENTALS   BOUTIQUE HOTEL €€

Map p300 (📞93 268 84 60; www.hotelbanysorien
tals.com; Carrer de l'Argenteria 37; s/d €88/105,
ste €130; ❄ @; Ⓜ Jaume I) Book well ahead
to get into this magnetically popular designer haunt. Cool blues and aquamarines
combine with dark-hued floors to lend this
clean-lined, boutique hotel a quiet charm.
All rooms, on the small side, look onto the

street or back lanes. There are more spacious suites in two other nearby buildings.

GRAND HOTEL CENTRAL   DESIGN HOTEL €€

Map p300 (📞93 295 79 00; www.grandhotel
central.com; Via Laietana 30; d €235; ❄ @ 🛏;
Ⓜ Jaume I) With super-soundproofed rooms
no smaller than 21 sq metres, this design
hotel, complete with rooftop pool, is one
of the standout hotel offerings along Via
Laietana. Rooms are decorated in style,
with high ceilings, muted colours (beiges,
browns and creams), dark timber floors
and subtle lighting.

PENSIÓN FRANCIA   HOSTEL €

Map p300 (📞93 319 03 76; www.pensionfrancia
-barcelona.com; Carrer de Rere Palau 4; s/d
€32/48; 🛜; Ⓜ Barceloneta) The homely smell of
laundry pervades this quaint little hostel in
a great location close to the shore, the Ciutadella park and the nightlife of El Born. The 11
simple rooms are kept spick and span, with
nothing much in the way of frills. Rooms
with balconies benefit from plenty of natural
light but little noise, as the lane is set away
from the busy nearby thoroughfares.

PENSIÓ 2000   PENSIÓN €

Map p300 (📞93 310 74 66; www.pensio2000.com;
Carrer de Sant Pere més Alt 6; s/d with bathroom
€60/80; @; Ⓜ Urquinaona) This 1st-floor, family-run place is opposite the anything-but-
simple Palau de la Música Catalana. Seven
reasonably spacious doubles (which can
be taken as singles) all have mosaic-tiled
floors; two have ensuite bathrooms. You can
eat your breakfast in the little courtyard.

🛏 Barceloneta & the Waterfront

The handful of seaside options around Port
Vell and La Barceloneta ranges from a rowdy youth hostel to a couple of grand five-
stars, one of which is destined to become an
iconic, waterfront landmark.

For years the breathtakingly located Hotel Arts Barcelona has been *the* place to stay
in Barcelona. It gets some tower-hotel competition in the Fòrum area, mostly aimed
at a business crowd and generally considerably cheaper.

W BARCELONA   LUXURY HOTEL €€€

Map p302 (📞93 295 28 00; www.w-barcelona.
com; Plaça de la Rosa del Vents 1; r from €310;

SLEEPING LA RIBERA

[P][✱][@][📶][🏊]; [🚇]17, 39, 57 or 64, [M]Barceloneta) This spinnaker-shaped beach-adjacent tower of glass contains 473 rooms and suites that are the last word in contemporary hotel chic. Self-indulgence is a byword and guests can flit between gym, infinity pool (with bar) and spa. There's avant-garde dining on the 2nd floor in Carles Abellán's Bravo restaurant, and hip cocktail sipping in the top-floor Eclipse bar.

HOTEL ARTS BARCELONA   LUXURY HOTEL €€€

Map p304 ([✆]93 221 10 00; www.hotelartsbarce lona.com; Carrer de la Marina 19-21; r from €480; [P][✱][@][📶][🏊]; [M]Ciutadella Vila Olímpica) Set in a sky-high tower looming above Port Olímpic, this is one of Barcelona's most fashionable hotels. It has more than 450 rooms with unbeatable views, and prices vary greatly according to size, position and time of year. Services range from enticing spa facilities to fine dining in Arola, run by the Michelin-starred Sergi Arola.

EUROSTARS GRAND
MARINA HOTEL   HOTEL €€

Map p302 ([✆]902 932424; www.grandmarinahotel. com; Moll de Barcelona; r €240-350; [✱][@][📶][🏊]; [M]Drassanes) Housed in the World Trade Center, the Grand Marina has a maritime flavour that continues into the rooms, with lots of polished timber touches and hydro-massage bathtubs. Some rooms on either side of the building offer splendid views of the city, port and open sea. The rooftop gym and outdoor pool have equally enticing views.

MARINA VIEW   B&B €€

Map p302 ([✆]678 854456; www.marinaview bcn.com; Passeig de Colom; d with/without view €139/116, tr €165/136; [✱][📶]; [M]Drassanes) In an excellent location near both the old town and the waterfront, this Irish-run B&B has six airy, comfortably furnished rooms, some with small balconies sporting sun-lit views over the marina. The welcome is genuinely warm, and Paddy, the owner, has loads of tips on neighbourhood eateries and how to make the most of your visit. Phoning ahead is recommended.

HOTEL DEL MAR   HOTEL €€

Map p302 ([✆]93 319 30 47; www.gargallo-hotels. com; Pla del Palau 19; s/d €113/130; [✱][@][📶]; [M]Barceloneta) The nicely modernised Sea Hotel is strategically placed between Port Vell and El Born. Some of the rooms in this historic building have balconies with water-

front views. You're in a fairly peaceful spot but no more than 10 minutes' walk from the beaches and seafood of La Barceloneta, and the bars and mayhem of El Born.

HOTEL 54   HOTEL €€

Map p302 ([✆]93 225 00 54; www.hotel54bar celoneta.com; Passeig de Joan de Borbó 54; s/d €140/150; [✱][@][📶]; [M]Barceloneta) This place is all about location. Modern rooms, with dark tile floors and designer bathrooms, are sought after for the marina and sunset views. Other rooms look out over the lanes of La Barceloneta. You can also sit on the roof terrace and enjoy the harbour views.

HOTEL MARINA FOLCH   HOTEL €

Map p302 ([✆]93 310 37 09; www.hotelmarinafolch bcn.com; Carrer del Mar 16; s/d/tr €45/65/85; [✱][📶]; [M]Barceloneta) Simple digs above a busy seafood restaurant, this hotel has just one teeny single and nine doubles of varying sizes and quality. The best are those with small balconies facing out towards the marina. The rooms are basic but well maintained, and the location is unbeatable, just a couple of minutes from the beach.

EQUITY POINT SEA HOSTEL   HOSTEL €

Map p302 ([✆]93 231 20 45; www.equity-point.com; Plaça del Mar 1-4; dm €19-28; [✱][@][📶]; [🚇]17, 39, 57 or 64, [M]Barceloneta) Perched near the sea in a rather ugly high-rise is this busy backpackers' hostel. Rooms are basic, cramped and noisy (bring earplugs) but you will not find a room closer to the beach. It organises activities such as bike tours (and hire). You pay extra for lockers, sheets and towels.

HOTEL ME   HOTEL €€

Map p304 ([✆]902 144440; www.me-barcelona. com; Carrer de Pere IV 272-286; r €185-255; [P][✱][@][📶][🏊]; [M]Poblenou) This daring, slim tower, designed by Dominique Perrault, is made from two filigree slabs of glass. It overlooks Jean Nouvel's Parc del Centre del Poblenou and offers designer digs. Whites, creams and reds dominate the decor. Rooms come in an array of sizes and comfort levels, with possible city or sea views. The 6th-floor Angels & Kings Club can get quite lively.

POBLENOU BED & BREAKFAST   HOTEL €€

Map p304 ([✆]93 221 26 01; www.hostalpoble nou.com; Carrer del Taulat 30; s €60, d €80-120; [✱][@][📶]; [M]Llacuna) Experience life in this colourful working-class neighbourhood, just back from the beach and increasingly home to a diverse population of loft-inhabiting gentrifiers. The 1930s house, with its high ceilings and beautiful tile floors, has a handful of rooms, each a little different and all with a fresh feel, light colours, comfortable beds and, occasionally, a little balcony.

🛏 L'Eixample

It comes as little surprise that this extensive bourgeois bastion should also be home to the greatest range of hotels in most classes. The grid avenues house some of the city's classic hotels and a long list of decent midrange places.

HOTEL PRAKTIK   HOTEL €€

Map p310 (📞93 343 66 90; www.hotelpraktikrambla.com; Rambla de Catalunya 27; r from €80-170; ❄@🛜; ⓂPasseig de Gràcia) This Modernista gem hides a gorgeous little boutique number. While the high ceilings and the bulk of the original tile floors have been maintained, the 43 rooms have daring ceramic touches, spot lighting and contemporary art. There is a chilled reading area and deck-style lounge terrace. The handy location on a tree-lined boulevard is an added plus.

HOTEL MAJÈSTIC   HOTEL €€€

Map p310 (📞93 488 17 17; www.hotelmajestic.es; Passeig de Gràcia 68; d from €410; P❄@🛜🏊; ⓂPasseig de Gràcia) This sprawling, central option has the charm of one of the great European hotels. The rooftop pool is great for views and relaxing, or you can pamper yourself in the spa after a workout in the gym. The standard rooms (no singles) are smallish but comfortable and with marble bathrooms.

MANDARIN ORIENTAL   DESIGN HOTEL €€€

Map p310 (📞93 151 88 88; www.mandarinoriental.com; Passeig de Gràcia 38; d from €375; P❄@🛜🏊; ⓂPasseig de Gràcia) At this imposing former bank, 98 rooms combine contemporary designer style with subtle Eastern touches. Straight lines, lots of white and muted colours dominate the look. Many of the standard rooms (no smaller than 32 sq metres) have luxurious tubs and all overlook either Passeig de Gràcia or an interior sculpted garden.

HOTEL OMM   DESIGN HOTEL €€€

Map p310 (📞93 445 40 00; www.hotelomm.es; Carrer de Rosselló 265; d from €360; P❄@🏊;

ⓂDiagonal) Design meets plain zany here, where the balconies look like strips of skin peeled back from the shiny hotel surface. The idea would no doubt have appealed to Dalí. In the foyer, a sprawling, minimalist and popular bar opens before you. Light, clear tones dominate in the ultramodern rooms, of which there are several categories.

HOTEL HISPANOS SIETE SUIZA   HOTEL €€€

Map p306 (📞93 208 20 51; www.hispanos7suiza.com; Carrer de Sicilia 255; r 2-5 people €200-260; P❄@🛜; ⓂSagrada Família) Within spitting distance of the towering madness that is La Sagrada Família is this original lodging option. Wander in past seven vintage Hispano-Suiza cars to one of several apartments, which generally have two double rooms with separate bathrooms (note the super showers!), a lounge, kitchen, washer-drier and terrace.

COMTES DE BARCELONA   HOTEL €€

Map p310 (📞93 445 00 00; www.condesdebarcelona.com; Passeig de Gràcia 73-75; s/d €177/260; P❄@🛜🏊; ⓂPasseig de Gràcia) The most attractive half of the Comtes (Condes) de Barcelona occupies the 1890s Modernista Casa Enric Batlló. Across the road stands a more modern extension. Clean, designer lines dominate inside each, with luxurious rooms, hardwood floors and architectural touches reminiscent of the Modernista exterior. The rooftop pool is a great place to relax after a hard day's sightseeing.

HOTEL SIXTYTWO   DESIGN HOTEL €€

Map p310 (📞93 272 41 80; www.sixtytwohotel.com/en; Passeig de Gràcia 62; d €170-265; P❄@🛜; ⓂPasseig de Gràcia) This 21st-century designer setting, housed in a well-preserved 1930s edifice, boasts Bang & Olufsen TVs and expansive, softly backlit beds. Inside the block is a pretty Japanese garden; you can also opt for a massage in your room. All rooms enjoy designer features (and Etro bath products) but the more tempting (and dearer) ones have balconies or little private terraces.

FIVE ROOMS   BOUTIQUE HOTEL €€

Map p310 (📞93 342 78 80; www.thefiverooms.com; Carrer de Pau Claris 72; s/d from €115/135, apt from €175; ❄@🛜; ⓂUrquinaona) Like they say, there are five rooms (standard rooms and suites) in this 1st-floor flat virtually on the border between L'Eixample and the old centre of town. Each is different and features include broad, firm beds, stretches of exposed brick wall, restored mosaic tiles and minimalist decor. There are also two apartments.

ST MORITZ HOTEL
HOTEL €€

Map p310 (☎93 481 73 50; www.hcchotels.com; Carrer de la Diputació 262bis; s/d €180/195; P❄@☎; MPasseig de Gràcia) This upmarket hotel, set in a late-19th-century building, has 91 fully equipped rooms and boasts an elegant restaurant, terrace bar and small gym. Some of the bigger rooms, with marble bathrooms, even have their own exercise bikes. You can dine in the modest terrace garden.

SUITES AVENUE
APARTMENT €€

Map p310 (☎93 487 41 59; www.derbyhotels.es; Passeig de Gràcia 83; apt from €192; P❄@☎☒; MDiagonal) Fancy apartment-style living is the name of the game in this apart-hotel. Self-contained little apartments with own kitchen and access to a terrace, gym and pool (not to mention the mini-museum of Hindu and Buddhist art) lie behind the daring facade by Japanese architect Toyo Ito.

HOTEL ASTORIA
HOTEL €€

Map p310 (☎93 209 83 11; www.derbyhotels.es; Carrer de Paris 203; s/d from €130/140; P❄@☎☒; MDiagonal) Nicely situated a short walk from Passeig de Gràcia, this three-star hotel is equally well placed for long nights out in the restaurants, bars and clubs of adjacent Carrer d'Aribau. Room decor and types vary wildly. The hotel has its own mini gym and a display of art by Catalan painter Ricard Opisso.

HOTEL CONSTANZA
BOUTIQUE HOTEL €€

Map p310 (☎93 270 19 10; www.hotelconstanza. com; Carrer del Bruc 33; s/d €130/150; ❄@; MGirona or Urquinaona) This boutique beauty has stolen the hearts of many a visitor to Barcelona. Design touches abound, and little details like flowers in the bathroom add charm. Suites and studios are further options. The terrace is a nice spot to relax for a while, looking over the rooftops of the L'Eixample.

MARKET HOTEL
BOUTIQUE HOTEL €€

Map p306 (☎93 325 12 05; www.forkandpillow. com; Passatge de Sant Antoni Abad 10; s €110, d €120-130, ste €145 ; ❄@; MSant Antoni) Attractively located in a renovated building along a narrow lane just north of the grand old Sant Antoni market (now shut for renovation), this place has an air of simple chic. Room de-

cor is a pleasing combination of white, dark nut browns, light timber and reds.

HOTEL D'UXELLES
HOTEL €€

Map p310 (☎93 265 25 60; http://hostaldux elleshotelbarcelona.priorguest.com; Gran Via de les Corts Catalanes 688; s/d €90/109; ❄@; MTetuan) A charming simplicity pervades the rooms here. Wrought-iron bedsteads are overshadowed by flowing drapes. Room decor varies, with a vaguely Andalucian flavour in the bathrooms. Some rooms have little terraces (€16 extra). Get a back room if you can, as Gran Via is noisy.

HOSTAL GOYA
HOSTAL €€

Map p310 (☎93 302 25 65; www.hostalgoya. com; Carrer de Pau Claris 74; s €70, d €96-113; ❄; MPasseig de Gràcia) The Goya is a modestly priced gem on the chichi side of L'Eixample. Rooms have a light colour scheme that varies from room to room. In the bathrooms, the original mosaic floors have largely been retained, combined with contemporary design features. The more expensive doubles have a balcony.

HOSTAL CENTRAL
HOSTAL €€

Map p310 (☎93 245 19 81; www.hostalcentralbar celona.com; Carrer de la Disputació 346; s/d/tr €50/85/106; ❄☎; MTetuan) In a pretty early-20th-century apartment building you'll find 13 renovated rooms (most with own bathroom). They are not excessively big but are pleasant and clean.

HOSTAL OLIVA
HOSTAL €€

Map p310 (☎93 488 01 62; www.hostaloliva. com; Passeig de Gràcia 32; s/d without bathroom €38/66, d with bathroom €85; ❄☎; MPasseig de Gràcia) A picturesque antique lift wheezes its way up to this 4th-floor *hostal*, a terrific, reliable cheapie in one of the city's most expensive neighbourhoods. Some of the single rooms can barely fit a bed but the doubles are big enough, light and airy (some with tiled floors, others with parquet and dark old wardrobes).

FASHION HOUSE
B&B €€

Map p310 (☎637 904 044; www.bcnfashionhouse. com; Carrer del Bruc 13; s/d/tr without bathroom €55/80/125; MUrquinaona) The name is a little silly but this typical, broad 1st-floor L'Eixample flat contains eight rooms of varying size done in tasteful style, with 4.5m-high ceilings, parquet floors and, in some cases, a little balcony onto the street.

Bathrooms are located along the broad corridor, one for every two rooms.

HOSTAL CÈNTRIC
HOSTAL €€

Map p306 (☑93 426 75 73; www.hostalcentric. com; Carrer de Casanova 13; s €47-72, d €65-99; ❄@; MUrgell) The *hostal*, in a good central location just beyond the old town, has rooms starting from basics with shared bathroom and ranging to renovated rooms with private bathroom facilities and air-con. Midrange ones are similar, but a little older and without air-con.

SOMNIO HOSTEL
HOSTEL €€

Map p310 (☑93 272 53 08; www.somniohostels. com; Carrer de la Diputació 251; dm €25, s/d without bathroom €44/78, d with bathroom €87; ➲❄@🛜; MPasseig de Gràcia) A crisp, tranquil hostel with 10 rooms (two of them six-bed dorms and all with a simple white and light-blue paint job), Somnio is nicely located in the thick of things in L'Eixample and a short walk from the old town. Rain showers and thick flex mattresses are nice features in these 2nd-floor digs.

HOSTAL MUNTANER
HOSTAL €

Map p306 (☑93 410 94 74; www.hostalmun taner.com; Carrer de Muntaner 175; s/d €40/75, s/d without bathroom €25/40; ℗❄; MHospital Clínic) Within a five-block walk of Passeig de Gràcia and Diagonal, this is a busy residential location surrounded by restaurants and bars (especially along nearby Carrer d'Aribau, a block away). Crisp, simple rooms are comfy and light. Be aware of traffic noise at the front of the house; a room deeper inside will guarantee tranquillity.

🛏 Gràcia

Staying up in Gràcia takes you out of the mainstream tourist areas and gives you a more authentic feel for the town. All the touristy bits are never far away by metro and the restaurant and bar life in Gràcia is great on its own.

HOTEL CASA FUSTER
DESIGN HOTEL €€€

Map p312 (☑93 255 30 00, 902 202345; www. hotelcasafuster.com; Passeig de Gràcia 132; s/d from €300/330; ℗➲❄@🛜; MDiagonal) This sumptuous Modernista mansion, built in 1908–11, is one of Barcelona's most luxurious hotels. Standard rooms are plush, if small. Period features have been restored at considerable cost and complemented

---

GAY BARCELONA

Barcelona has a few excellent gay-friendly options, one in the heart of the old city and fairly simple, another a full design explosion in the heart of the 'Gaixample'. You could start a room search at **Gay Apartments Barcelona** (www.gayapartment barcelona.com).

➡ **Hotel Axel** (Map p310; ☑93 323 93 93; www.axelhotels.com; Carrer d'Aribau 33; r from €142; ❄@🛜; MUniversitat) Favoured by a mixed fashion and gay set, Axel occupies a sleek corner block and offers modern touches in its 105 designer rooms. A subtle, light colour scheme, plasma TVs and (in the double rooms) king-sized beds are just some of the pluses. The hotel was completely overhauled in 2010. Take a break in the rooftop pool, the Finnish sauna or the spa bath. The rooftop Skybar is open for cocktails from May to September.

➡ **Hotel California** (Map p292; ☑93 317 77 66; www.hotelcaliforniabcn.com; Carrer d'en Rauric 14; s/d €70/120; ❄@🛜; MLiceu) This (gay) friendly and central hotel has 31 straightforward but fastidiously sparkling-clean rooms, with light, neutral colours, satellite plasma TV and good-sized beds. Double glazing helps ensure a good night's sleep, given the modest prices, the rooms have surprising details such as hairdryers. Meet new friends in the bustling breakfast room and avail yourself of room service 24 hours a day.

➡ **Casa de Billy Barcelona** (Map p310; ☑93 426 30 48; www.casabillybarcelona.com; Gran Via de les Corts Catalanes 420 ; d €70-120; @; MRocafort) Set in a rambling apartment, a stone's throw from the Gaixample bars, this is an intriguing, gay-friendly stop. The rooms are largely decorated in flamboyant art deco style and guests may use the kitchen. There is a two-night-minimum policy.

with hydro-massage tubs, plasma TVs and king-size beds. The rooftop terrace (with pool) offers spectacular views. The Café Vienés, once a meeting place for Barcelona intellectuals, hosts excellent jazz nights.

APARTHOTEL SILVER
HOTEL €€

(☎93 218 91 00; www.hotelsilver.com; Carrer de Bretón de los Herreros 26; s/d €99/123; ❄@☎; MFontana) There are no fewer than five types of rooms here, from chintzy, tiny basic rooms to the very spacious 'superior rooms'. Aim for the better ones. All come with a kitchenette and some have a terrace or balcony. There is a little garden too. Booking online is great for discounts.

🛏 La Zona Alta

Except for a certain business clientele, this mostly residential area is a little too far from the action for most people. Several exceptional places are well worth considering if being in the centre of things is not a priority.

ABAC BARCELONA
LUXURY HOTEL €€€

Map p314 (☎93 319 66 01; www.abacbarcelona.com; Avinguda Tibidabo 1; d from €280; ❄@☎≋; ℝFGC Avinguda Tibidabo) This uber-stylish new addition to Barcelona receives high marks for its beautifully designed rooms, kitted out with Bang & Olufsen TVs, rainfall showerheads, Jacuzzi tubs with aromatherapy and luxury bed linens. A lovely spa and one of the city's best restaurants (with two Michelin stars) add to the appeal.

HOTEL REY JUAN CARLOS I
HOTEL €€

Map p314 (☎93 364 40 40; www.hrjuancarlos.com; Avinguda Diagonal 661-671; d from €130; P❄@☎≋; MZona Universitària) Like an ultramodern lighthouse at this southwest gateway to the city, the glass towers of this luxury mega-hotel hold more than 430 spacious rooms, most with stunning views. Extensive gardens, once part of the farmhouse that stood here until well into the 20th century, surround the hotel. The nearby Metro can take you to central Barcelona in around 20 minutes.

HOTEL TURÓ DE VILANA
DESIGN HOTEL €€

Map p314 (☎93 434 03 63; www.turodevilana.com; Carrer de Vilana 7; s/d from €87/97; ❄@☎; ℝFGC Les Tres Torres, ☒64) This bright designer hotel is set in the charming residen-

tial hood of Sarrià. Its 20 rooms feature hardwood floors, a warm colour scheme, marble bathrooms and plenty of natural light. There's not a lot to do in the immediate vicinity, but it's an attractive option for those who like the idea of dipping in and out of central Barcelona.

HOTEL ANGLÍ
HOTEL €€

Map p314 (☎93 206 99 44; www.eurostarshotels.com; Carrer d'Anglí 60; d from €135; ❄@☎≋; ℝSarrià) Hotel Anglí is a comfortable business stay. Glass dominates the three-storey design and the semi-transparent tower is lit up in various hues at night. Huge firm beds are set in rooms where floor-to-ceiling windows and expanses of mirrors add to the sense of light. The buffet breakfast is good and from the rooftop pool you can contemplate the Collserola hills.

HOTEL MEDIUM PRISMA
HOTEL €

Map p316 (☎93 439 42 07; www.mediumhoteles.com; Avinguda Josep Tarradellas 119; d from €70; ❄☎; MEntença) Part of a chain of inexpensive Spanish hotels, the Medium Prisma has helpful staff and clean and well-maintained rooms, although they're little on the small side (thin walls are also a minus). It's set on a busy boulevard with a handful of decent dining options nearby but it's a fair stroll (10 minutes) to the nearest metro station.

HOTEL CONFORTGOLF
HOTEL €€

Map p316 (☎93 238 68 28; www.bestwestern.es; Travessera de Gràcia 72; s/d €90/120; ❄@☎; ℝFGC Gràcia) This small 36-room hotel, run by Best Western, has friendly, efficient staff and a few unusual touches, including a small rooftop golfing area. Although it's not in the most central locale, it's still near some uptown bars and restaurants. Rooms don't bubble over with character, but they're neat, modern and spacious.

ALBERG MARE DE DÉU
DE MONTSERRAT
HOSTEL €

(☎93 210 51 51; www.xanascat.cat; Passeig de la Mare de Déu del Coll 41-51; dm €22; @; ☒28 or 92, MVallcarca) This 167-bed hostel is 4km north of Barcelona's city centre. The main building is a magnificent former mansion with a Mudéjar-style lobby. Most rooms sleep six and the common areas are extensive and relaxed. The hostel's website provides details of other hostels in Barcelona and wider Catalonia.

⌂ Montjuïc, Sants & El Poble Sec

Montjuïc and its surrounding suburbs are good areas for the cash-strapped. There are several options strung out along and near the El Poble Sec side of Avinguda del Paral.lel, as well as near the train station in Sants.

TOP CHOICE HOTEL AC MIRAMAR   HOTEL €€€

Map p318 (☏902 292293, 93 281 16 00; www. ac-hotels.com; Plaça de Carlos Ibáñez 3; r €330-495; ❄ ⚲ ☎; ⌨50) Welcome to the only hotel on the hill, a designer five-star job. Local architect Oscar Tusquets took the shell of a building created for the 1929 World Fair and later the Barcelona HQ of Spanish national TV (1959–83), and created this olive-green block where all rooms have broad balconies and views over the port, city or park. The modern rooms feature neutral decor, with deep browns, creams and beiges dominating the colour scheme.

URBAN SUITES   HOTEL, APARTMENT €€

Map p318 (☏93 201 51 64; www.theurbansuites. com; Carrer de Sant Nicolau 1-3; ste from €170; ⓟ ❄ @ ☎; ⓜSants Estació) Directed largely at the trade-fair crowd, this contemporary spot with 16 suites and four apartments makes for a convenient and comfortable home away from home. You get a bedroom, living room and kitchen, DVD player and free wi-fi, and the configuration is good for families. Prices fluctuate enomously according to demand.

MELON DISTRICT   HOSTEL €

Map p318 (☏93 329 96 67; www.melondistrict. com; Avinguda del Paral.lel 101; s €55-65, d €60-70; ⓟ ❄ @ ☎; ⓜParal.lel) Whiter than white seems to be the policy in this student residence: where the only coloured objects are the green plastic chairs. Erasmus folks and international students are attracted to this hostel-style spot, where you can stay the night or book in for a year. There are meeting lounges, kitchen facilities, a cafe and a laundrette on the premises.

HOSTEL MAMBO TANGO   HOSTEL €

Map p318 (☏93 442 51 64; www.hostelmambotan go.com; Carrer del Poeta Cabanyes 23; dm €26; @ ☎; ⓜParal.lel) A fun international hostel, the Mambo Tango has basic dorms (sleeping from six to 10 people) and a welcoming, somewhat chaotic atmosphere. This playful vibe is reflected in the kooky colour scheme in the bathrooms. Advice on what to do and where to go out is always on hand.

Understand Barcelona

Barcelona Today

There's no denying Barcelona faces enormous challenges. Declining house prices, rising foreclosures and the looming threat of financial insolvency dominate the headlines, while ongoing protests lash out against the austerity measures. Against this dour backdrop, the city continues to attract record numbers of visitors, with tourism contributing to 15% of its GDP. Meanwhile, the city that fueled the imaginations of Gaudí, Miró and Picasso is still a font of innovation in the realms of urban planning, architecture and sustainability.

Best on Film

All about my Mother (director Pedro Almodóvar, 1999) One of Almodóvar's best-loved films is full of plot twists and dark humour, complete with transsexual prostitutes and doe-eyed nuns.

Vicky Cristina Barcelona (director Woody Allen, 2008) Allen gives Barcelona the *Manhattan* treatment, showing a city of startling beauty and neuroticism.

L'Auberge Espagnol (director Cédric Klapisch, 2002) Warmly told coming-of-age story about a mishmash of foreign-exchange students thrown together in Barcelona.

Barcelona (director Whit Stillman, 1994) A sharp and witty romantic comedy about two Americans living in Barcelona during the end of the Cold War.

Best in Print

Barcelona (Robert Hughes, 1992) Witty and passionate study of 2000 years of history.

Shadow of the Wind (Carlos Ruiz Zafón, 2001) Page-turning mystery set in post-civil-war Barcelona.

Homage to Catalonia (George Orwell, 1938) Classic account of the early days of the Spanish Civil War.

Economic Woes

In 2012, the Spanish economy slipped into recession for its second time in three years. Unemployment levels in the city have risen above 20% (slightly lower than Spain's nearly 24%). Meanwhile austerity measures prescribed by bureaucrats – slashing budgets, raising taxes and freezing public sector pay – have done nothing to alleviate the hardship.

Anger at the labour reforms and dramatic spending cuts has led to nationwide strikes, with tens of thousands marching in the streets of Barcelona in 2012 (joining millions of protesting Spaniards nationwide). In the city there's much gloom over the future – particularly among those under age 25, half of whom remain without work.

Reinventing Neighbourhoods

The financial crisis has stalled some projects like Norman Foster's dramatic (some would say psychedelic) €250 million redesign of the Camp Nou football stadium. Yet the city has pushed ahead on other major developments. Ongoing expansion work continues on the Metro, with plans for new stations (including one out to the airport) and overall accessibility, greatly improving travel options for those with limited mobility.

New buildings like the Filmoteca de Catalunya with exhibition space and cinemas have added to the city's creative credibility; the film centre is the latest in a series of other major art spaces (including the Richard Meier–designed Macba and the cutting-edge CCCB) that have contributed to the ongoing revitalisation of El Raval. Other key developments in this once down-and-out neighbourhood include the reopening of Palau Güell and the refurbishing of the Museu Marítim.

Out in Poble Nou, the city envisions a new centre of activity, with the construction of a design museum along with other new buildings and abundant green

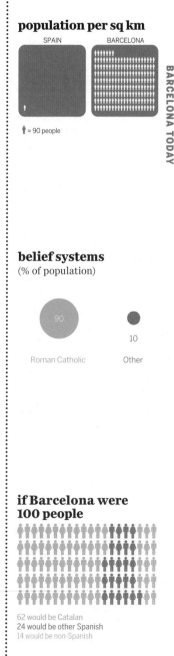

space. This development is part of a continuing scheme to transform the formerly industrial landscape of Poble Nou into a business district for high-tech companies. Christened 22@ *(vint-i-dos arroba)*, the 200-hectare area has indeed become a centre for innovation and design, and some of the city's best new architecture – like Zaha Hadid's wild Torre Espiral (Spiral Tower) – is happening here.

Sustainable Initiatives

The first Smart City Expo and World Congress was held in Barcelona in 2011 to discuss urban planning, the environment and a host of other increasingly important urban issues. Barcelona was chosen as the host city because of intelligent strategies in the urban landscape. Since 2000, the city has required all new buildings to install solar panels to provide most of their hot water. Its massive solar panel near the Parc del Fòrum is the largest of any city in Europe. In the realm of wind energy, Catalonia announced plans to quintuple wind capacity by 2020.

Barcelona's shared bike program, Bicing, launched in 2007, has helped reduce traffic on the road. Some 120,000 subscribers use the service – a dramatic increase from the previous decade. Bicycles aren't the only way Barcelona is reducing its carbon footprint: the city aims to be a leader in the realm of electric vehicles and has set up more than 200 charging stations.

No Smoke, No Bull

Other ways the air is getting a little cleaner: Spain's strict antismoking ban went into effect in 2011. Bars, restaurants and nightclubs are now smoke-free, as is Camp Nou. Speaking of bans, in 2012 Catalonia officially outlawed bullfighting, becoming the first region in mainland Spain to prohibit the practice.

A Catalan Nation

Sensitivity over regional identity is never far from Spanish political debates, particularly as public perception has been that Catalonia makes substantial financial contributions to the state but often gets a proportionally tiny piece of the pie. Perhaps angered by this, Barcelona staged a symbolic referendum on Catalan independence in 2011. Scarcely more than 20% of eligible voters turned out, although 90% of them voted in favour of independence.

Food Frontiers

Barcelona's pioneering approach to cuisine continues. Ferran Adrià, the mastermind behind molecular gastronomy, has opened a new restaurant in the city. Food, culture, design – it's boom days in Barcelona – though of course the economy says otherwise. But regardless of financial forecasts, most *barcelonins* couldn't imagine living anywhere else.

BARCELONA TODAY

population per sq km

SPAIN   BARCELONA

👤 ≈ 90 people

belief systems
(% of population)

90
Roman Catholic

10
Other

if Barcelona were 100 people

62 would be Catalan
24 would be other Spanish
14 would be non-Spanish

History

The layered settlement of Barcelona has seen waves of immigrants and conquerors over its 2000-plus years of existence, including Romans, Visigoths, Franks and later Catalans. Barcelona has seen its fortunes rise and fall over the years – from the golden era of princely power in the 14th century to dark days of civil war and the Franco era. A fierce independent streak has always run through Barcelona, which has often put it into conflict with the Kingdom of Castilla – an antagonism that continues to the present, with a desire for more autonomy (full independence say some Catalans) from Spain.

ANCIENT TRIBES, ROMANS, VISIGOTHS & FRANKS

In 1991 the remains of 25 corpses, dating from 4000 BC, were found in Carrer de Sant Pau in El Raval. In those days, much of El Raval was a bay and the hillock (Mont Tàber) next to Plaça de Sant Jaume may have been home to a Neolithic settlement.

Stone-age peoples from the Pyrenees were probably the first on the scene, followed much later (in the 3rd century BC) by the Iberian Laietani, who built a settlement on present-day Montjuïc. Little is known of this tribe, aside from the fact that they minted their own coins. Barcelona's recorded history really begins with the Romans when Barcino (much later Barcelona) was founded in the reign of Caesar Augustus.

The heart of the Roman settlement lay within what would later become the medieval city – now known as the Barri Gòtic. The temple was raised on Mont Tàber. Remains of city walls, temple pillars and graves all attest to what would eventually become a busy and lively town. The Latin poet Ausonius paints a picture of contented prosperity – Barcino lived well off the agricultural produce in its hinterland and from fishing. Oysters, in particular, appeared regularly on the Roman menu in ancient times. Wine, olive oil and *garum* (a rather tart fish paste and favourite staple of the Romans) were all produced and consumed in abundance.

As the Roman Empire wobbled, Hispania (as the Iberian Peninsula was known to the Romans) felt the effects. It is no coincidence that the bulk of Barcelona's Roman walls, vestiges of which remain today, went up in the 4th century AD. Marauding Franks, followed by Romanised Visigoths and other tribes, wrought death and destruction on the city; successive waves of invaders flooded across the country like great Atlantic rollers.

TIMELINE	c 4000 BC	218 BC	15 BC
	A Neolithic settlement may have thrived around the present-day Plaça de Sant Jaume at this time, as indicated by Jasper implements discovered around Carrer del Paradís.	In a move to block supplies to the Carthaginian general Hannibal, Roman troops under Scipio land at Empúries, found Tarraco (Tarragona) and take control of the Catalan coast.	Caesar Augustus grants the town of Barcino, possibly established under his auspices, the rather long-winded title of Colonia Julia Augusta Faventia Paterna Barcino.

In 711 the Muslim general Tariq landed an expeditionary force at present-day Gibraltar (Arabic for Tariq's Mountain). He had no trouble sweeping across the peninsula all the way into France, where he and his army were only brought to a halt in 732 by the Franks at Poitiers.

Barcelona fell under Muslim sway but they seem not to have been overly impressed with their prize. The town is mentioned in Arabic chronicles but it seems the Muslims resigned themselves early on to setting up a defensive line along the Riu Ebro to the south. Louis the Pious, the future Frankish ruler, retook Barcelona from them in 801.

The *comtes* (counts) installed here as Louis' lieutenants hailed from local tribes roaming on the periphery of the Frankish empire. Barcelona was a frontier town in what was known as the Frankish or Spanish March – a rough-and-ready buffer zone south of the Pyrenees.

A HAIRY BEGINNING

The March was under nominal Frankish control but the real power lay with local potentates who ranged across the territory. One of these rulers went by the curious name of Guifré el Pelós, or Wilfred the Hairy. This was not a reference to uneven shaving habits: according to legend, old Guifré had hair in parts most people do not (exactly which parts was never specified!). He and his brothers gained control of most of the Catalan counties by 878 and Guifré entered the folk mythology of Catalonia. If Catalonia can be called a nation, then its 'father' was the hirsute Guifré. He founded a dynasty that lasted nearly five centuries and developed almost independently from the Reconquista wars that were playing out in the rest of Iberia.

A POWER MARRIAGE & MEDITERRANEAN EMPIRE

The counts of Barcelona gradually expanded their territory south and in 1137 Ramon Berenguer IV, the Count of Barcelona, married Petronilla, heir to the throne of neighbouring Aragón, thus creating a joint state that set the scene for Catalonia's golden age.

In the following centuries the regime became a flourishing merchant empire, seizing Valencia and the Balearic Islands from the Moors, and later taking territories as far flung as Sardinia, Sicily and parts of Greece.

THE RISE OF PARLIAMENT

In 1249 Jaume I authorised the election of a committee of key citizens to advise his officials. The idea developed and, by 1274, the *Consell dels*

Barcelona's first patron saint, Santa Eulàlia (290-304), was martyred for her faith during the persecutory reign of Diocletian. Her death involved 13 tortures (one for each year of her life), including being rolled in a glass-filled barrel, having her breasts cut off, and crucifixion. Some paintings depict her holding a tray containing her cut-off breasts.

Although dating from much earlier, Catalan people, initially hailing from the plains and mountains north of Barcelona, were first mentioned in the 12th century. Catalan is closely related to the *langue d'oc*, the post-Latin lingua franca of southern France – of which Provençal is about the only barely surviving reminder.

AD 415	718	801	878
Visigoths under Athaulf, with captured Roman empress Galla Placidia as his wife, make Barcino their capital. With several interruptions, it remains so until the 6th century.	Only seven years after the Muslim invasion of Spain launched from Morocco at Gibraltar, Barcelona falls to Tariq's mostly Arab and Berber troops on their blitzkrieg march north into France.	After a year-long siege, the son of Charlemagne and future Frankish king Louis the Pious wrests Barcelona from Muslims and establishes the Spanish March under local counts.	The last count named by a disintegrating Frankish Empire, Wilfred the Hairy consolidates power throughout Catalonia and founds a long-lasting dynasty with his capital in Barcelona.

Cent Jurats (Council of the Hundred Sworn-In) formed an electoral college from which an executive body of five *consellers* (councillors) was nominated to run city affairs.

In 1283 the Corts Catalanes met for the first time. This new legislative council for Catalonia was made up of representatives of the nobility, clergy and high-class merchants to form a counterweight to regal power. Its home was, and remains, the Palau de la Generalitat.

Meanwhile, Barcelona's trading wealth paid for the great Gothic buildings that bejewel the city to this day. La Catedral, the Capella Reial de Santa Àgata and the churches of Santa Maria del Pi and Santa Maria del Mar were all built within the city's boundaries during the late 13th or early 14th centuries. King Pere III (1336–87) later created the breathtaking Reials Drassanes (Royal Shipyards) and also extended the city walls yet again, this time to include the El Raval area to the west.

According to a medieval legend, Barcelona was founded by Hercules himself. Although versions differ, all tell of nine '*barcas*' (boats), one of which separates from the others in a storm, and is piloted by Hercules to a beautiful spot on the coast where he founds a city, naming it Barca Nona (ninth boat).

DECLINE & CASTILIAN DOMINATION

Preserving the empire began to exhaust Catalonia. Sea wars with Genoa, resistance in Sardinia, the rise of the Ottoman Empire and the loss of the gold trade all drained the city's coffers. Commerce collapsed. The Black Death and famines killed about half of Catalonia's population in the 14th century. Barcelona's Jewish population suffered a pogrom in 1391.

After the last of Guifré el Pelós' dynasty, Martí I, died heirless in 1410, Barcelona saw its star diminish, when Catalonia effectively became part of the Castilian state, under the rule of Fernando from the Aragonese throne and Isabel, queen of Castilla.

Impoverished and disaffected by ever-growing financial demands from the crown, Catalonia revolted in the 17th century in the Guerra dels Segadors (Reapers' War; 1640–52) and declared itself to be an independent 'republic' under French protection. The countryside and towns were devastated, and Barcelona was finally besieged into submission.

WAR OF THE SPANISH SUCCESSION

Although Catalonia had only limited autonomy in the late 1600s, things grew worse at the turn of the 18th century when it supported the wrong side in the War of the Spanish Succession. Barcelona, under the auspices of British-backed archduke Charles of Austria, fell after an 18-month siege on 11 September 1714 to the forces of Bourbon king Philip V, who established a unitary Castilian state.

Angered at Catalonia's perceived treachery, the new king abolished the Generalitat, leveled a whole district of medieval Barcelona to build

985	1060	1137	1225–29
Al-Mansur (the Victorious) rampages across Catalan territory and devastates Barcelona in a lightning campaign. Much of the population is taken as slaves to Córdoba.	Some 200 years before the Magna Carta, Count Ramon Berenguer I approves the 'Usatges de Barcelona', a bill of rights establishing all free men equal before the law.	Count Ramon Berenguer IV is betrothed to one-year-old Petronilla, daughter of the king of Aragón, creating a new combined state that would be known as the Corona de Aragón.	At age 18, Jaume I takes command; four years later he conquers Muslim-held Mallorca, the first of several dazzling conquests that lead him to be called El Conqueridor (the Conqueror).

TRAGEDY IN EL CALL

Tucked away in the Barri Gòtic, the narrow medieval lanes of El Call were once home to a thriving Jewish population. Jews arrived to Roman Barcino as early as the 2nd century AD and in later centuries were instrumental in bringing wealth to the city's coffers. Catalonian Jews worked as merchants, scholars, cartographers and teachers. By the 11th century, as many as 4000 Jews lived in El Call.

Despite the civic contributions made by Jews, during the 13th century a wave of anti-Semitism swept through Catalonia (and other parts of Europe). In 1243 Jaume I isolated El Call from the rest of the town, and required all Jews to wear identifying badges. When famine struck in the 1330s followed by plague in 1348, it left a wake of devastation, with thousands dead. Trying to make sense of the Black Death, many residents blamed the Jews – for poisoning the wells, sacrificing babies and other grotesque imaginings. Hundreds were tortured to 'confess' their crimes. The harassment continued through the following decades.

The anti-Semitism peaked in 1391 when a frenzied mob tore through El Call, looting and destroying private homes and murdering hundreds of Jews – perhaps as many as 1000. El Call never recovered, and most of the remaining Jews fled the city. What little Jewish life remained was further crushed in 1492, when the crown issued an edict expelling all Jews from Spain.

a huge fort (the Ciutadella) to watch over the city, and banned writing and teaching in Catalan. What was left of Catalonia's possessions were farmed out to the great powers.

A NEW BOOM

After the initial shock, Barcelona found the Bourbon rulers to be comparatively light-handed in their treatment of the city. The big break came in 1778, when the ban on trade with the Spanish American colonies was lifted. In Barcelona itself, growth was modest but sustained. Small-scale manufacturing provided employment and profit. Wages were rising and the city fathers even had a stab at town planning, creating the grid-based workers' district of La Barceloneta.

Before the industrial revolution, based initially on the cotton trade with America, could really get underway, Barcelona and the rest of Spain had to go through a little more pain. A French revolutionary army was launched Spain's way (1793–95) with limited success, but when Napoleon turned his attentions to the country in 1808 it was another story. Barcelona and Catalonia suffered along with the rest of the country until the French were expelled in 1814.

In Catalonian folklore, the idea for the Catalan flag – alternating red-and-yellow bars – was born when, during a battle, King Louis the Pious dipped four fingers into the wound of a dying Wilfred the Hairy, and ran them across Wilfred's golden shield. Never mind that Louis died long before Wilfred was born!

1283	1323	1348	1383
The Corts Catalanes, a legislative council for Catalonia, meets for the first time and begins to curtail unlimited powers of sovereigns in favour of nobles and the powerful trading class.	Catalan forces land in Sardinia and launch a campaign of conquest that would only end in 1409. Their fiercest enemy was Eleonora de Arborea, a Sardinian Joan of Arc.	Plague devastates Barcelona. More than 25% of the city's population dies. Further waves of the Black Death, a plague of locusts in 1358 and an earthquake in 1373 deal further blows.	After 50 or so years of frenzied construction the massive Santa Maria del Mar rises above the Ribera. It is one of many Gothic architectural gems completed in the 14th century.

By the 1830s, Barcelona was beginning to ride on a feel-good factor that would last for most of the century. Wine, cork and iron industries developed. From the mid-1830s onwards, steamships were launched off the slipways. In 1848 Spain's first railway line was opened between Barcelona and Mataró.

A DRAMATIC REDESIGN

Creeping industrialisation and prosperity for the business class did not work out so well down the line. Working-class families lived in increasingly putrid and cramped conditions. Poor nutrition, bad sanitation and disease were the norm in workers' districts, and riots, predictably, resulted. As a rule they were put down with little ceremony – the 1842 rising was bombarded into submission from the Montjuïc castle.

In 1869 a plan to expand the city was begun. Ildefons Cerdà designed L'Eixample (the Enlargement) as a grid, broken up with gardens and parks and grafted onto the old city, beginning at Plaça de Catalunya. The plan was revolutionary. Until then it had been illegal to build in the plains between Barcelona and Gràcia, the area being a military zone. As industrialisation got underway this building ban also forced the concentration of factories in Barcelona itself (especially in La Barceloneta) and surrounding towns like Gràcia, Sant Martí, Sants and Sant Andreu (all of which were subsequently swallowed up by the burgeoning city).

L'Eixample became (and to some extent remains) the most sought-after chunk of real estate in Barcelona – but the parks were mostly sacrificed to an insatiable demand for housing and undisguised land speculation. The flourishing bourgeoisie paid for lavish, ostentatious buildings, many of them in the unique, Modernista style.

There seemed to be no stopping this town. In 1888 it hosted a Universal Exhibition. Although the exhibition attracted more than two million visitors, it did not generate the international attention some had hoped for.

Still, changing the cityscape had become habitual in modern Barcelona. La Rambla de Catalunya and Avinguda del Paral.lel were both slammed through in 1888. The Mirador de Colom and Arc de Triomf, rather odd monuments in some respects (Columbus had little to do with Barcelona and tangible triumphs were in short supply), also were built that year.

A 19TH-CENTURY RENAISSANCE

Barcelona was comparatively peaceful for most of the second half of the 19th century but far from politically inert. The relative calm and grow

Justice in feudal days was a little rough by modern standards. As prescribed in a 1060 bill: 'In regard to women, let the rulers render justice by cutting off their noses, lips, ears and breasts, and by burning them at the stake if necessary.'

1387	1469	1478	1640–52
During the reign of Juan I, Barcelona hosted its first bullfight, according to the city's historical archive. It isn't until the 19th century, however, that bullfighting gains widespread popularity.	Isabel, heir to the Castilian throne, marries Aragonese heir Fernando, uniting two of Spain's most powerful monarchies and effectively subjugating Catalonia to the Castilian state.	Isabel and Fernando, the Reyes Católicos (Catholic Monarchs), stir up religious bigotry and establish the Spanish Inquisition that will see thousands killed until it's finally abolished in 1834.	Catalan peasants, angered at having to quarter Castilian troops during the Thirty Years War, declare their independence under French protection. Spain eventually crushes the rebellion.

ing wealth that came with commercial success helped revive interest in all things Catalan.

La Renaixença (Renaissance) reflected the feeling in Barcelona of renewed self-confidence. Politicians and academics increasingly studied and demanded the return of former Catalan institutions and legal systems. The Catalan language was readopted by the middle and upper classes and new Catalan literature emerged as well.

In 1892 the *Unió Catalanista* (Catalanist Union) demanded the re-establishment of the Corts in a document known as the *Bases de Manresa*. In 1906 the suppression of Catalan news-sheets was greeted by the formation of *Solidaritat Catalana* (Catalan Solidarity, a nationalist movement). It attracted a broad band of Catalans, not all of them nationalists.

Perhaps the most dynamic expression of the Catalan Renaissance occurred in the world of art. Barcelona was the home of Modernisme, Catalan Art Nouveau. While the rest of Spain stagnated, Barcelona was a hotbed of artistic activity, an avant-garde base with close links to Paris. The young Picasso spread his artistic wings here and drank in the artists' hangout Els Quatre Gats.

An unpleasant wake up call came with Spain's short, futile war with the US in 1898, in which it lost not only its entire navy, but its last colonies (Cuba, Puerto Rico and the Philippines). The blow to Barcelona's trade was enormous.

MAYHEM

Barcelona's proletariat was growing fast. The total population grew from 115,000 in 1800 to over 500,000 by 1900 and over one million by 1930 – boosted, in the early 19th century, by poor immigrants from rural Catalonia and, later, from other regions of Spain. All this made Barcelona ripe for unrest.

The city became a swirling vortex of anarchists, Republicans, bourgeois regionalists, gangsters, police terrorists and hired *pistoleros* (gunmen). One anarchist bomb at the Liceu opera house on La Rambla in the 1890s killed 20 people. Anarchists were also blamed for the *Setmana Tràgica* (Tragic Week) in July 1909 when, following a military call-up for Spanish campaigns in Morocco, rampaging mobs wrecked 70 religious buildings and workers were shot on the street in reprisal.

In the post-WWI slump, unionism took hold. This movement was led by the anarchist *Confederación Nacional del Trabajo* (CNT), or National Workers' Confederation, which embraced 80% of the city's workers. During a wave of strikes in 1919 and 1920, employers hired assassins

Many Gothic masterpieces were built in the mid-14th century, a time of great suffering in Barcelona. When a wheat crop failed in 1333, the resulting famine killed 10,000 people (a quarter of the city's population). In the 1340s, plague devastated the city, killing four of its five counsellors along with many others.

1714	1770	1808
Barcelona loses all autonomy after surrendering to the Bourbon king, Felipe V, on 11 September at the end of the War of the Spanish Succession.	A freak hurricane strikes Barcelona, causing considerable damage. Among other things, the winds destroy more than 200 of the city's 1500 gaslight street lamps.	In the Battle of Bruc, Catalan militiamen defeat occupying Napoleonic units, yet Barcelona, Figueres and the coast remain under French control until Napoleon's retreat in 1814.

RICHARD CUMMINS / LONELY PLANET IMAGES ©

Siege of Barcelona monument

A CATALONIAN SUBMARINE

It could have been the Spanish Navy's V2, a late-19th-century secret weapon. Narcis Monturiol i Estarriol (1819–85), part-time publisher and all-round utopian, was fascinated by the sea. In 1859, he launched a wooden, fish-shaped submarine, the *Ictíneo*, in Barcelona. Air shortages made only brief dives possible but Monturiol became an overnight celebrity. He received, however, not a jot of funding.

Undeterred, he sank himself further into debt by designing *Ictíneo II*. This was a first. It was 17m long, its screws were steam driven and Monturiol had devised a system for renewing the oxygen inside the vessel. It was trialled in 1864 but again attracted no finance. Four years later, the vessel was broken up for scrap.

If the Spaniards had had a few of these when they faced the US Navy off Cuba and in the Philippines in 1898, perhaps things might have turned out differently!

to eliminate union leaders. The 1920s dictator General Miguel Primo de Rivera opposed bourgeois-Catalan nationalism and working-class radicalism, banning the CNT and even closing Barcelona football club, a potent symbol of Catalanism. But he did support the staging of a second world fair in Barcelona, the Montjuïc World Exhibition of 1929.

Rivera's repression only succeeded in uniting, after his fall in 1930, Catalonia's radical elements. Within days of the formation of Spain's Second Republic in 1931, leftist Catalan nationalists of the ERC *(Esquerra Republicana de Catalunya)*, led by Francesc Macià and Lluís Companys, proclaimed Catalonia a republic within an imaginary 'Iberian Federation'. Madrid pressured them into accepting unitary Spanish statehood, but after the leftist Popular Front victory in the February 1936 national elections, Catalonia briefly won genuine autonomy. Companys, its president, carried out land reforms and planned an alternative Barcelona Olympics to the official 1936 games in Nazi Berlin.

But things were racing out of control. The left and the right across Spain were shaping up for a showdown.

> Ever at the vanguard, Barcelona had the first daily newspaper printed in Spain, its first cinema, public phone and airline (to Majorca). It also built the world's second metropolitan railroad (London was first).

THE CIVIL WAR

On 17 July 1936, an army uprising in Morocco kick-started the Spanish Civil War. Barcelona's army garrison attempted to take the city for General Franco but was defeated by anarchists and police loyal to the government.

Franco's Nationalist forces quickly took hold of most of southern and western Spain; Galicia and Navarra in the north were also his. Most of the east and industrialised north stood with Madrid. Initial rapid

1869	1873	1888
Ildefons Cerdà designs L'Eixample (the Enlargement) district with wide boulevards and a grid-like pattern. Modernista architects of the day showcase their creations here.	Antoni Gaudí, 21 years old and in Barcelona since 1869, enrols in architecture school, from which he graduates five years later, having already designed the street lamps in Plaça Reial.	Showcasing the grand Modernista touches of recent years (including L'Eixample), Barcelona hosts Spain's first International Exposition, held in the manicured new Parc de la Ciutadella.

Arc de Triomf

NEIL SETCHFIELD / LONELY PLANET IMAGES ©

advances on Madrid were stifled and the two sides settled in for almost three years of misery.

For nearly a year, Barcelona was run by anarchists and the Trotskyist militia of the *Partido Obrero de Unificación Marxista* (POUM; the Marxist Unification Workers' Party), with Companys president only in name. Factory owners and rightists fled the city. Unions took over factories and public services, hotels and mansions became hospitals and schools, everyone wore workers' clothes (in something of a foretaste of what would later happen in Mao's China), bars and cafes were collectivised, trams and taxis were painted red and black (the colours of the anarchists) and one-way streets were ignored as they were seen to be part of the old system.

The anarchists were a disparate lot ranging from gentle idealists to hardliners who drew up death lists, held kangaroo courts, shot priests, monks and nuns (over 1200 of whom were killed in Barcelona province during the civil war), and also burnt and wrecked churches – which is why so many of Barcelona's churches are today oddly plain inside. They in turn were shunted aside by the communists (directed by Stalin from Moscow) after a bloody internecine battle in Barcelona that left 1500 dead in May 1937.

Barcelona became the Republicans' national capital in autumn 1937. The Republican defeat in the Battle of the Ebro in southern Catalonia in summer 1938 left Barcelona undefended. Republican resistance crumbled, in part due to exhaustion, in part due to disunity. In 1938 Catalan nationalists started negotiating separately with the Nationalists. Indeed, the last resistance put up in Barcelona was by some 2000 soldiers of the Fifth Regiment that had fought so long in Madrid! The city fell on 25 January 1939.

Films set in Franco's Spain

Pan's Labyrinth (2006)

The Spirit of the Beehive (1973)

¡Bienvenido, Mr Marshall! (Welcome, Mr Marshall!; 1952)

Las 13 Rosas (The 13 Roses; 2007)

OCCUPATION

That first year of occupation was a strange hiatus before the onset of the full machinery of oppression. Within two weeks of the city's fall, a dozen cinemas were in operation and the following month Hollywood comedies were being shown between rounds of Nationalist propaganda. The people were even encouraged to dance the *sardana*, Catalonia's national dance, in public (the Nationalists thought such folkloric generosity might endear them to the people of Barcelona).

On the other hand, the city presented an exhausted picture. The Metro was running but there were no buses (they had all been used on the front). Virtually all the animals in the city zoo had died of starvation or wounds. There were frequent blackouts, and would be for years.

1895	1898	July 1909	1914
Málaga-born Pablo Picasso, 13, arrives in Barcelona with his family. His art-teacher father gets a job in the Escola de Belles Artes, where Pablo enrols as a pupil.	Spain loses its entire navy and last remaining colonies (the Philippines, Cuba and Puerto Rico) in two hopeless campaigns against the USA, dealing a heavy blow to Barcelona businesses.	After a call for reserve troops to fight in Morocco, *barcelonins* riot, destroying city property. Over 100 are reportedly killed in what's now known as *Setmana Tràgica* (Tragic Week).	The Mancomunitat de Catalunya, a first timid attempt at self-rule (restricted largely to administrative matters) and headed by Catalan nationalist Enric Prat de la Riba, is created in April.

DEATH FROM THE SKIES

It made little difference to Benito Mussolini, General Franco's overbearing Fascist comrade-in-arms, that Barcelona possessed few military targets worthy of note beyond its port and railway, or that it had been declared an open city precisely to avoid its destruction.

Italian bombers based in Mallorca (joined towards the end of the war by Germany's terrifying Junkers JU87 Stuka dive-bombers) carried out a trial run for the horrors that would rain down on Europe in WWII. They conducted air raids on the largely defenceless city (only three Italian planes were brought down over Barcelona in the entire war) regularly from 16 March 1937 to 24 January 1939, a day before Nationalist troops marched in. Mussolini ordered the raids with or without Franco's blessing, which the latter often withheld, realising that indiscriminate bombing of civilians would hardly boost his popularity. Indeed, Franco prohibited attacks on urban centres in March 1938, after three days of relentless raids that cost almost 1000 lives, but the Italians paid no heed. By the end of the war, almost 3000 *barcelonins* had been killed, with 7000 wounded and 1800 buildings destroyed.

In a radio broadcast on 18 June 1940, as the Battle of Britain began, Winston Churchill declared: 'I do not underrate the severity of the ordeal which lies before us but I believe our countrymen will show themselves capable of standing up to it like the brave men of Barcelona.' He might have added women and children, who together formed the bulk of the bombers' victims.

Historical Reads

Barcelona (Robert Hughes)

Barcelona - A Thousand Years of the City's Past (Felipe Fernández Armesto)

Homage to Catalonia (George Orwell)

Homage to Barcelona (Colm Tóibín)

By 1940, with WWII raging across Europe, Franco had his regime more firmly in place and things turned darker for many. Catalan Francoists led the way in rounding up victims and up to 35,000 people were shot in purges. At the same time, small bands of resistance fighters continued to harry the Nationalists in the Pyrenees through much of the 1940s. Lluís Companys was arrested in France by the Gestapo in August 1940, handed over to Franco, and shot on 15 October on Montjuïc. He is reputed to have died with the words '*Visca Catalunya!*' ('Long live Catalonia!') on his lips.

The executions continued into the 1950s. Most people accepted the situation and tried to get on with living, while some leapt at opportunities, occupying flats abandoned by 'Reds' who had been forced to flee. Speculators and industrialists allied with Franco were able to earn a lucrative income, but the majority of *barcelonins* were affected by nationwide poverty.

LIFE UNDER FRANCO

Franco had already abolished the Generalitat in 1938. Companys was succeeded as the head of the Catalan government-in-exile in Mexico

July 1936	March 1938	1939	1940
General Franco launches the Spanish Civil War in Morocco. General Goded leads army units to take Barcelona for Franco but is defeated by left-wing militia, workers and loyalist police.	In just three days of day-and-night air raids on Barcelona carried out by Fascist Italian bombers based in Franco-controlled Mallorca, 979 people are killed and 1500 wounded.	On 26 January, the first of Franco's troops, and Italian tanks, roll into Barcelona from Tibidabo and parade down Avinguda Diagonal. Thousands flee for the French border.	Hitler's henchman and chief of the SS, Heinrich Himmler, visits Barcelona, stays at the Ritz, enjoys a folkloric show at Poble Espanyol and has his wallet stolen.

by Josep Irla and, in 1954, by the charismatic Josep Tarradellas, who remained its head until after Franco's demise.

Franco, meanwhile, embarked on a programme of Castilianisation. He banned public use of Catalan and had all town, village and street names rendered in Spanish (Castilian). Book publishing in Catalan was allowed from the mid-1940s, but education, radio, TV and the daily press remained in Spanish.

In Barcelona, the Francoist Josep Maria de Porcioles became mayor in 1957, a post he held until 1973. That same year, he obtained for the city a 'municipal charter' that expanded the mayor's authority and the city's capacity to raise and spend taxes, manage urban development and, ultimately, widen the city's metropolitan limits to absorb neighbouring territory. He was responsible for such monstrosities as the concrete municipal buildings on Plaça de Sant Miquel in the Barri Gòtic. His rule marked a grey time for Barcelona.

By the 1950s, opposition to Franco had turned to peaceful mass protests and strikes. In 1960, an audience at the city's Palau de la Música Catalana concert hall sang a banned Catalan anthem in front of Franco. The ringleaders included a young Catholic banker, Jordi Pujol, who would later rise to pre-eminence in the post-Franco era. For his singing effort he wound up in jail for a short time.

Under Franco a flood of 1.5 million immigrants from poorer parts of Spain, chiefly Andalucía, Extremadura and the northwest, poured into Catalonia (750,000 of them to Barcelona) in the 1950s and '60s looking for work. Many lived in appalling conditions. While some made the effort to learn Catalan and integrate as fully as possible into local society, the majority came to form Spanish-speaking pockets in the poorer working-class districts of the city and in a ring of satellite towns. Even today, the atmosphere in many of these towns is more Andalucian than Catalan. Catalan nationalists will tell you it was all part of a Francoist plot to undermine the Catalan identity.

History Sites

Museu d'Història de Barcelona (p74)

Museu d'Història de Catalunya (p121)

Via Sepulcral Romana (p78)

Museu Marítim (p120)

HISTORY THE ROAD TO RECOVERY

THE ROAD TO RECOVERY

Two years after Franco's death in 1975, Josep Tarradellas was invited to Madrid to hammer out the Catalan part of a regional autonomy policy. Eighteen days later, King Juan Carlos I decreed the re-establishment of the Generalitat and recognised Josep Tarradellas as its president. Twenty years after his stint in Franco's jails, Pujol was elected president of Catalonia in 1980; these were the first free regional elections since before the civil war. A wily antagonist of the central authorities in Madrid, he waged a quarter-century war of attrition, eking out greater

1957	1980	1992	2010
The Francoist Josep Maria de Porcioles becomes mayor of Barcelona and remains in charge until 1973. He presides over a willy-nilly building spree in the city.	Right-wing Catalan nationalist Jordi Pujol is elected president of the resurrected Catalan regional government at the head of the CiU coalition; he remains in power without interruption until 2003.	Barcelona is catapulted to the world stage when it hosts the Olympic Games. In preparation, the city undergoes a radical renovation program whose momentum continues today.	Hot on the heels of their victory in the European football championship in 2008, Spain defeats Holland in the World Cup held in South Africa, its first-ever World Cup title.

fiscal and policy autonomy and vigorously promoting a re-Catalanisation programme, with uneven success.

Politics aside, the big event in post-Franco Barcelona was the successful 1992 Olympics, planned under the guidance of the popular Socialist mayor, Pasqual Maragall. The Games spurred a burst of public works and brought new life to areas such as Montjuïc, where the major events were held. The once-shabby waterfront was transformed with promenades, beaches, marinas, restaurants, leisure attractions and new housing.

After the turn of the millennium, Barcelona continued to invest in urban renewal, with ambitious projects such as the 22@hi-tech zone in the once-industrial El Poblenou district, the major development around new trade fair grounds between the city and the airport, and the glimmering Diagonal Mar waterfront development around the Parc del Fòrum at the northeast tip of the city.

THE CATALAN–SPANISH DIVIDE

Pujol remained in power until 2003, when he stepped down and was succeeded by the former socialist mayor of Barcelona, Pasqual Maragall. Maragall's principal achievement was reaching agreement between various parties on a new autonomy statute *(Estatut)*. Since the demise of Franco, Spain has devolved considerable powers to the regions, which are officially known as *comunidades autónomas* (autonomous communities). Catalans approved the new Estatut in a referendum in 2006, but within months the right wing Partido Popular (warning of the 'Balkanistation' or break-up of Spain) launched an appeal in the Constitutional Court against the Estatut, which it claimed grants too much autonomy.

After four years of wrangling, in 2010 the court delivered a verdict, ruling that 14 of the articles were unconstitutional – including areas of language, taxes, the judiciary and self-recognition as a 'nation'. Catalans converged on the streets en masse to protest the decision, which was widely hailed as one more blow to relations between Barcelona and Madrid.

Barcelona nearly staged the Olimpíada Popular (People's Olympiad) in 1936, an alternative to the Olympics that was being held in fascist Germany. Around 6000 athletes from 23 countries registered. However, the civil war erupted just before the start. Some athletes who arrived stayed on and joined militias to help defend the republic.

January 2012	March 2012	2026	
After a parliamentary vote in 2010, bullfighting is banned in Catalonia. It is the first region in mainland Spain to outlaw the practice (the Canary Islands banned it in 1991).	With 23% unemployment nationwide, thousands take to the streets in Barcelona (and other cities) to protest the conservative government's spending cuts and tax increases.	Builders aim to finish La Sagrada Família on the centenary of the death of its creator Gaudí (1852–1926), which is over 140 years after its construction began.	

CHRISTOPHER GROENHOUT / LPI ©

La Sagrada Família

Gothic Architecture

Barcelona's first great building boom came at the height of the Middle Ages, when its great Gothic churches, mansions and shipyards were raised, together creating what survives to this day as one of the most extensive Gothic quarters in Europe. Most of these architectural treasures lie within the boundaries of Ciutat Vella but a few examples can be found beyond, notably the Museu-Monestir de Pedralbes in Sarrià.

HISTORICAL ROOTS

This soaring style took off in France in the 12th century and spread across Europe. Its emergence coincided with Jaume I's march into Valencia and the annexation of Mallorca and Ibiza, accompanied by the rise and rise of a trading class and a burgeoning mercantile empire. The enormous cost of building the grand new monuments could thus be covered by the steady increase in the city's wealth.

Perhaps the single greatest building spurt came under Pere III (1319-1387). This is odd in a sense because, as Dickens might have observed, it was not only the best of times, but also the worst. By the mid-14th century, when Pere III was in command, Barcelona had been pushed to the ropes by a series of disasters: famine, repeated plagues and pogroms.

Maybe he didn't notice. He built, or began to build, much of La Catedral, the Drassanes, the Llotja stock exchange, the Saló del Tinell, the Casa de la Ciutat (which now houses the town hall) and numerous lesser buildings, not to mention part of the city walls. The churches of Santa Maria del Pi and Santa Maria del Mar were completed by the end of the 14th century.

ARCHITECTURAL FEATUES

The style of architecture reflected the development of building techniques. The introduction of buttresses, flying buttresses and ribbed vaulting in ceilings allowed engineers to raise edifices that were loftier and seemingly lighter than ever before. The pointed arch became standard and great rose windows were the source of light inside these enormous spaces.

Think about the hovels that labourers on such projects lived in and the primitive nature of building materials available, and you get an idea of the awe such churches, once completed, must have inspired. They were not built in a day. It took more than 160 years, a fairly typical time frame, to finish La Catedral, although its facade was not erected until the 19th century. Its rival, the Església de Santa Maria del Mar, was one for the record books, taking only 59 years to build.

Gothic Masterpieces

La Catedral (Barri Gòtic)

Església de Santa Maria del Mar (La Ribera)

Església de Santa Maria del Pi (Barri Gòtic)

Saló del Tinell (in Museu d'Història de Barcelona, Barri Gòtic)

The Drassanes (Museu Marítim, Baceloneta)

OH HOW AWFULLY GOTHIC!

The lofty Gothic buildings of medieval Europe inspire awe in their modern visitors. But as early as the 16th century, when Renaissance artists and architects turned to the clean lines of classical antiquity for inspiration, all things medieval looked crude, rough and, well, frankly barbarian, just like the ancient Germanic tribes of Goths that had stormed across Europe centuries before. To label something Gothic became the ultimate insult. This attitude spread across Europe. In Barcelona, many private homes built in Gothic style would get a baroque makeover later, but thankfully most of the major monuments were left alone. Not until the 19th century did this extraordinary heritage again awaken admiration, to such an extent that in some north European countries in particular it led to a wave of Gothic revival building.

CATALAN GOTHIC

Catalan Gothic did not follow the same course as the style typical of northern Europe. Decoration here tends to be more sparing and the most obvious defining characteristic is the triumph of breadth over height. While northern European cathedrals reach for the sky, Catalan Gothic has a tendency to push to the sides, stretching its vaulting design to the limit.

The Saló del Tinell, with a parade of 15m arches (among the largest ever built without reinforcement) holding up the roof, is a perfect example of Catalan Gothic. Another is the present home of the Museu Marítim, the Drassanes, Barcelona's medieval shipyards. In their churches, too, the Catalans opted for a more robust shape and lateral space – step into the Església de Santa Maria del Mar or the Església de Santa Maria del Pi and you'll soon get the idea.

Another notable departure from what you might have come to expect of Gothic north of the Pyrenees is the lack of spires and pinnacles. Bell towers tend to terminate in a flat or nearly flat roof. Occasional exceptions prove the rule – the main facade of Barcelona's Catedral, with its three gnarled and knobbly spires, does vaguely resemble the outline that confronts you in cathedrals in Chartres or Cologne. But then it was a 19th-century addition, admittedly to a medieval design.

Catalonia's vast 14th-century mercantile empire fueled Barcelona's boom. All manner of goods flowed to and from Sardinia, Flanders, North Africa and other places, with Catalan Jews carrying out much of this trade. The later pogroms, Inquisition and expulsion of Jews had devastating financial consequences and helped reduce Barcelona to penury.

LATE GOTHIC

Gothic had a longer use-by date in Barcelona than in many other European centres. By the early 15th century, the Generalitat still didn't have a home worthy of its name, and architect Marc Safont set to work on the present building on Plaça de Sant Jaume. Even renovations carried out a century later were largely in the Gothic tradition, although some Renaissance elements eventually snuck in – the facade on Plaça de Sant Jaume is a rather disappointing result.

Carrer de Montcada, in La Ribera, was the result of a late-medieval act of town planning. Eventually, mansions belonging to the moneyed classes of 15th- and 16th-century Barcelona were erected along it. Many now house museums and art galleries. Although these former mansions appear forbidding on the outside, their interiors often reveal another world, of pleasing courtyards and decorated external staircases. They mostly went through a gentle baroque makeover in later years.

Antoni Gaudí & the Modernistas

Barcelona's architectural gift to the world was Modernisme, a flamboyant Catalan creation that erupted in the late 19th and early 20th centuries. Modernisme was personified by the visionary work of Antoni Gaudí, a giant in the world of architecture. His dynamic and utterly imaginative creations, along with works by Josep Puig i Cadafalch and Lluís Domènech i Montaner have filled Barcelona with dozens of masterpieces – including one iconic church that has become very nearly synonymous with the city.

A BLANK CANVAS

In the 1850s, a rapidly growing city fuelled by industrialisation meant notoriously crowded conditions in the narrow streets of the Ciutat Vella, Barcelona's old quarter. It was time to break down the medieval walls and dramatically expand the city. In 1869, the architect Ildefons Cerdà was chosen to design a new district, which would be called L'Eixample (the Enlargement).

He drew wide boulevards on a gridlike layout, and envisioned neighbourhoods with plenty of green space – an objective that city planners unfortunately overruled amid the rampant land speculation of the day. With a blank slate before them, and abundant interest from upper class residents eager to custom-design a new home, architects were much in demand. What developers could not have predicted was the calibre of those architects.

ANTONI GAUDÍ

Leading the way was Antoni Gaudí. Born in Reus to a long line of coppersmiths, Gaudí was initially trained in metalwork. In childhood he suffered from poor health, including rheumatism, and became an early adopter of a vegetarian diet. He was not a promising student. When he obtained his architecture degree in 1878, the school's headmaster is reputed to have said, 'Who knows if we have given a diploma to a nutcase or a genius. Time will tell.'

The Book of Nature

As a young man, what most delighted Gaudí was being outdoors, and he became fascinated by the plants, animals and geology beyond his door. This deep admiration for the natural world would heavily influence his designs. 'This tree is my teacher,' he once said. 'Everything comes from the book of nature.' Throughout his work, he sought to emulate the harmony he observed in the natural world, eschewing the straight line and favouring curvaceous forms and more organic shapes.

The spiral of a nautilus shell can be seen in staircases and ceiling details, tight buds of flowers in chimney pots and roof ornamentation, while undulating arches evoke a cavern, overlapping roof tiles mimic the scales of an armadillo and flowing walls resemble waves on the sea. Tree branches, spider webs, stalactites, honeycombs, starfish, mushrooms, shimmering beetle wings and many other elements from nature – all were part of the Gaudian vernacular.

A Catholic & Catalan

Gaudí was a devout Catholic and a Catalan nationalist. In addition to nature, he drew inspiration from Catalonia's great medieval churches and took pride in utilising the building materials of the countryside: clay, stone and timber. In contrast to his architecture, Gaudí lived a simple life, and was not averse to knocking on doors, literally begging for money to help fund construction on the cathedral.

As Gaudí became more adventurous he appeared as a lone wolf. With age he became almost exclusively motivated by stark religious conviction and devoted much of the latter part of his life to what remains Barcelona's call sign – the unfinished La Sagrada Família. He died in 1926, struck down by a streetcar while taking his daily walk to the Sant Felip Neri church. Wearing ragged clothes with empty pockets – save for an orange peel – Gaudí was initially taken for a beggar and taken to a nearby hospital where he was left in a pauper's ward; he died two days later. Thousands attended his funeral, in a half-mile procession to La Sagrada Família where he was buried in the crypt.

Much like his work in progress, La Sagrada Família, Gaudí's story is far from over. In March 2000 the Vatican decided to proceed with the examination of the case for canonising him and pilgrims already stop by the crypt to pay him homage. One of the key sculptors at work on the church, the Japanese Etsuro Sotoo, converted to Catholicism because of his passion for Gaudí.

One person unimpressed by Sagrada Família was British writer George Orwell, who described it as 'one of the most hideous buildings in the world'. After passing through Barcelona during the Spanish Civil War, he later wrote, 'I think the Anarchists showed bad taste in not blowing it up.'

GEORGE ORWELL

Gaudí's Creations

The architect's work is an earthy appeal to sinewy movement, but often with a dreamlike or surreal quality. The private apartment house Casa Batlló is a fine example in which all appears a riot of the unnaturally natural – or the naturally unnatural. Not only are straight lines eliminated, but the lines between real and unreal, sober and dream-drunk, good sense and play are all blurred. Depending on how you look at the facade, you might see St George (one of Barcelona's patron saints) defeating a dragon, a magnificent and shimmering fish (a symbol of Mediterranean peoples) or elements of an effusive Carnaval parade.

Gaudí seems to have particularly enjoyed himself with rooftops. At Palau Güell he created all sorts of fantastical, multicoloured tile figures as chimney pots, resembling oversized budlike trees that seem straight out of Alice in Wonderland – or perhaps Dr Seuss.

La Sagrada Família

Gaudí's masterpiece was La Sagrada Família (begun in 1882), and in it you can see the culminating vision of many ideas developed over the years. Its massive scale evokes the grandeur of Catalonia's Gothic cathedrals, while organic elements foreground its harmony with nature.

The Nativity Facade, the only one Gaudí completed in his lifetime, contains dozens of species of plants, while turtles hold up two of the major columns. Inside, massive helicoidal columns lean like great tree trunks at dynamic angles, branching off as they join the roof and create clusters of leaves. Magnificent stained-glass windows create a play of vivid colours – fiery reds and golds and deep blues and greens; others are left translucent to symbolise purity.

The church is rife with symbols that tangibly express Gaudí's Catholic faith through architecture: 18 bell towers symbolise Jesus, the Virgin Mary, the four evangelists and the 12 apostles. Three facades cover Jesus' life, death and resurrection. Even its location is expressive: the Nativity Facade faces east where the sun rises; the Passion Facade, depicting Christ's death, faces west where the sun sets.

DOMÈNECH I MONTANER

Although overshadowed by Gaudí, Lluís Domènech i Montaner (1849–1923) was one of the great masters of Modernisme. He was a widely travelled man of prodigious intellect, with knowledge in everything from mineralogy to medieval heraldry, and he was an architectural professor, a prolific writer and a nationalist politician. The question of Catalan identity and how to create a national architecture consumed Domènech i Montaner, who designed more than a dozen large-scale works in his lifetime.

The exuberant, steel-framed Palau de la Música Catalana is one of his masterpieces. Adorning the facade are elaborate Gothic-style windows, floral designs (Domènech i Montaner also studied botany) and sculptures depicting characters from Catalan folklore and the music world as well as everyday citizens of Barcelona. Inside, the hall leaves visitors dazzled with delicate floral-covered colonnades, radiant stained-glass walls and ceiling and a rolling, sculpture-packed proscenium referencing the epics of musical lore.

His other great masterpiece is the Hospital de la Santa Creu i de Sant Pau, with sparkling mosaics on the facade and a stained-glass skylight that fills the vestibule with golden light (like Matisse, Domènech i Montaner believed in the therapeutic powers of colour). Its floral decoration, abundant use of sculpture and intricately detailed domes create a remarkable sense of structural beauty.

PUIG I CADAFALCH

Like Domènech i Montaner, Josep Puig i Cadafalch (1867–1956) was a polymath; he was an archaeologist, an expert in Romanesque art and one of Catalonia's most prolific architects. As a politician – and later president of the Mancomunitat de Catalunya (Commonwealth of Catalonia) – he was instrumental in shaping the Catalan nationalist movement.

One of his many Modernista gems is the Casa Amatller, a rather dramatic contrast to Gaudí's Casa Batlló next door. Here the straight line is very much in evidence, as is the foreign influence (the gables are borrowed from the Dutch). Blended with playful Gothic-style sculpture, Puig i Cadafalch has designed a house of startling beauty and invention.

Other important works by Puig i Cadafalch include the Casa Martí (better known as Els Quatre Gats), which was one of Barcelona's first Modernista-style buildings (from 1896), with Gothic window details and whimsical wrought-iron sculpture. He was also adept at industrial design as evidenced by the Fàbrica Casaramona, an imposing brick edifice that looks more like a medieval fortress than a factory. Today it houses the excellent museum CaixaForum.

The unusual warrior-like chimneys at La Pedrera are said to have inspired George Lucas' costume designers, who modelled the figure of Darth Vader and the imperial storm troopers on the unusual (otherworldly?) structures.

GEORGE LUCAS

ANTONI GAUDÍ & THE MODERNISTAS DOMÈNECH I MONTANER

MODERNISME & CATALAN IDENTITY

Modernisme did not appear in isolation in Barcelona. To the British and French the style was art nouveau; to the Italians, Lo Stile Liberty; the Germans called it Jugendstil (Youth Style); and the Austrians, Sezession (Secession). Its vitality and rebelliousness can be summed up in those epithets: modern, new, liberty, youth and secession. A key uniting element was the sensuous curve, implying movement, lightness and vitality. It touched painting, sculpture and the decorative arts, as well as architecture. This leitmotif informed much art nouveau thinking, in part inspired by long-standing tenets of Japanese art.

There is something misleading about the name Modernisme. It suggests 'out with the old, in with the new'. In a sense, nothing could be further from the truth. From Gaudí down, Modernista architects looked to the past for inspiration. Gothic, Islamic and Renaissance design all had something to offer. At its most playful, Modernisme was able to intelligently flout the rule books of these styles and create exciting new creations.

Aesthetics aside, the political associations are significant, as Modernisme became a means of expression for Catalan identity. It barely touched the rest of Spain; where it did, one frequently finds the involvement of Catalan architects.

As many as 2000 buildings in Barcelona and throughout Catalonia display Modernista traces. Everything from rich bourgeois mansion blocks to churches, from hospitals to factories, went up in this 'style', a word too constraining to adequately describe the flamboyant breadth of eclecticism inherent in it.

MATERIALS & DECORATIONS

The Arabs invented the ancient technique of *trencadís*, but Gaudí was the first architect to revive it. The procedure involves taking ceramic tiles or fragments of broken pottery or glass and creating a mosaic-like sheath on roofs, ceilings, chimneys, benches, sculptures or any other surface.

Modernista architects relied on the skills of artisans that have now been all but relegated to history. There were no concrete pours (contrary to what is being done at La Sagrada Família today). Stone, unclad brick, exposed iron and steel frames, and copious use of stained glass and ceramics in decoration, were all features of the new style – and indeed it is often in the decor that Modernisme is at its most flamboyant.

The craftsmen required for these tasks were the heirs of the guild masters and had absorbed centuries of know-how about just what could and could not be done with these materials. Forged iron and steel were newcomers to the scene, but the approach to learning how they could be used was not dissimilar to that adopted for more traditional materials. Gaudí, in particular, relied on these old skills and even ran schools in La Sagrada Família workshops to keep them alive.

Iron came into its own in this period. Nowhere is this more evident than in Barcelona's great covered markets: Mercat de la Boqueria, Mercat de Sant Antoni and Mercat de la Llibertat, just to name the main ones. Their grand metallic vaults not only provided shade over the produce, but were a proclamation of Barcelona's dynamism and the success of 'ignoble' materials in grand building.

The Rome-trained sculptor Eusebi Arnau (1864–1934) was one of the most popular figures called upon to decorate Barcelona's Modernista piles. The appearance of the Hospital de la Santa Creu i de Sant Pau is one of his legacies and he also had a hand in the Palau de la Música Catalana and Casa Amatller.

Olympic & Contemporary Architecture

Barcelona's latest architectural revolution began in the 1980s. The appointment then of Oriol Bohigas, who was regarded as an elder statesman for architecture, as head of urban planning by the ruling Socialist party marked a new beginning. The city set about its biggest phase of renewal since the heady days of L'Eixample.

BARCELONA SINCE THE OLYMPIC GAMES

The biggest urban makeover in 100 years happened in the run-up to the 1992 Olympics, when more than 150 architects beavered away on almost 300 building and design projects. The city saw dramatic transformations, from the construction of huge arterial highways to the refurbishment of whole neighbourhoods in dire need of repair. In a rather crafty manoeuvre, the city government used national monies to fund urban improvements the capital would never normally have approved. Several kilometres of waterfront wasteland that included Port Vell was beautifully transformed into sparkling new beaches – suddenly Barcelona had prime beachfront real estate. The long road to resurrecting Montjuïc took off with the refurbishment of the Olympic stadium and the creation of landmarks like Santiago Calatrava's Torre Calatrava.

Post-1992, landmark buildings still went up in strategic spots, usually with the ulterior motive of trying to pull the surrounding area up by its bootstraps. One of the most emblematic of these projects is the gleaming white Museu d'Art Contemporani de Barcelona, better known as Macba, which opened in 1995. The museum was designed by Richard Meier and incorporates the characteristic elements for which the American architect is so well known – the geometric minimalism, the pervasive use of all-white with glass and steel – and remains much debated in architectural circles. '...Meier's building was unkind to the art, badly lit and spatially only barely coherent,' wrote the art critic Robert Hughes.

More widely hailed, the Teatre Nacional de Catalunya, which opened in 1996, is a splendid blend of the neoclassical with the modern. Framed by 26 columns with a single gabled roof and grand entrance steps, the theatre takes the form of a Greek temple, though its all-glass exterior gives it a light and open appearance.

Henry Cobb's World Trade Center, at the tip of a quay jutting out into the waters of Port Vell, has been overshadowed by Ricardo Bofill's new hotel, W Barcelona, whose spinnaker-like front looks out to sea from the south end of Barceloneta's beach strip.

One of the biggest projects of the last decade is Diagonal Mar. A whole district has been built in the northeast coastal corner of the city where before there was a void. High-rise apartments, waterfront office towers and

Best Contemporary Buildings

....

Torre Agbar (p122) (Barceloneta)

....

Teatre Nacional de Catalunya (p154) (L'Eixample)

....

Mercat de Santa Caterina (p108) (La Ribera)

....

W Barcelona (p217) (Barceloneta)

....

Santos Porta Fira Hotel (Llobregat)

....

Edificio Fòrum (Plaça de Llevant)

....

Les Arenes (Plaça d'Espanya)

ART ON THE STREETS

Barcelona hosts an array of street sculpture, from Miró's 1983 *Dona i Ocell*, in the park dedicated to the artist, to *Peix*, Frank Gehry's shimmering, bronze-coloured headless fish facing Port Olímpic. Halfway along La Rambla, at Plaça de la Boqueria, you can walk all over Miró's *Mosaïc de Miró*.

Picasso left an open-air mark with his design on the facade of the Col.legi Arqui-tectes opposite La Catedral in the Barri Gòtic. Other works include the Barcelona Head by Roy Lichtenstein at the Port Vell end of Via Laietana and Fernando Botero's tumescent *El Gat* on Rambla del Raval.

Wander down to the Barceloneta seaside for a gander at Rebecca Horn's 1992 trib-ute to the old shacks that used to line the waterfront. The precarious stack is called Homenatge a la Barceloneta (Tribute to La Barceloneta). A little further south is the 2003 Homenatge als Nedadors (Tribute to the Swimmers), a complex metallic rendi-tion of swimmers and divers in the water by Alfredo Lanz.

Heading a little further back in time, Antoni Tàpies in 1983 constructed Homenatge a Picasso on Passeig de Picasso; it's essentially a glass cube set in a pond and filled with, well, junk. Antoni Llena's David i Goliat, a massive sculpture of tubular and sheet iron, in the Parc de les Cascades near Port Olímpic's two skyscrapers, looks like an untidy kite inspired by Halloween. Beyond this, Avinguda d'Icària is lined by architect Enric Miralles' so-called *Pergoles* – bizarre, twisted metal contraptions.

And who is this pondersome creature sitting pretty at the end of Rambla de Cat-alunya? The statue of a thinking bull is simply called *Meditation*, but one wonders what Rodin would make of it.

One of the best known pieces of public art whimsy is Xavier Mariscal's *Gamba* (meaning prawn, although it is actually a crayfish) on Passeig de Colom. Stuck here in 1989 on the roof of the Gambrinus bar, when this strip was lined by popular designer bars, it has remained as a seafood symbol of the city (and was restored in 2004).

five-star hotels – among them the eye-catching Hotel Me (completed in 2008) by Dominique Perrault – mark this new district. The hovering blue, triangular Edifici Fòrum by Swiss architects Herzog & de Meuron is the most striking landmark here, along with a gigantic photovoltaic panel that provides some of the area's electricity. Much of the district was completed in 2004, though the area continues to evolve as new buildings are added to the mix.

The most prominent addition to the skyline came in 2005. The shim-mering, cucumber-shaped Torre Agbar is a product of French architect Jean Nouvel, emblematic of the city's desire to make the developing hi-tech zone of 22@ a reality.

Southwest, on the way to the airport, the new Fira M2 trade fair along Gran Via de les Corts Catalanes is now marked by red twisting twin landmark towers (one the Santos Porta Fira Hotel, the other offices) de-signed by Japanese star architect and confessed Gaudí fan Toyo Ito.

The heart of La Ribera got a fresh look with its brand-new Mercat de Santa Caterina. The market is quite a sight, with its wavy ceramic roof and tubular skeleton, designed by one of the most promising names in Catalan architecture until his premature death, Enric Miralles. Mi-ralles' Edifici de Gas Natural, a 100m glass tower near the waterfront in La Barceloneta, is extraordinary for its mirror-like surface and weirdly protruding adjunct buildings, which could be giant glass cliffs bursting from the main tower's flank.

No one longs for the pre-Olympic days when the waterfront was a dangerous and polluted waste-land. However, some old timers still bemoan the loss of its old rickety restaurant shacks, which sat on stilts over the water and served delectable if utterly unfussy seafood.

THE CITY TOMORROW

Big projects are slowly unfolding around the city, although the continuing economic crisis has slowed the pace of construction.The redevelopment of the Plaça de les Glòries Catalanes and surrounding area is one of latest projects underway, with the goal of revitalising the neighbourhood and making it a draw for tourism. The area will be transformed in a series of projects by MBM (Martorell, Bohigas & Mackey), which includes tearing down an unsightly elevated highway, moving major thoroughfares underground and adding new parks and and an underground train station. Its centerpiece will be the Disseny Hub (design museum), a daring project that incorporates sustainable features in its cantilevered, metal-sheathed building; vaguely futuristic, it will have a rather imposing, anvil-shaped presence over the new green space and small lake adjoining it. Further east, work on Zaha Hadid's dynamic Spiral Tower adds yet more futurism to the city, with hopes that cutting-edge architecture will help boost ongoing development in the 22@ zone.

Work proceeds apace in the Diagonal Mar/Fòrum area. The most significant new structure gracing the skyline there is a 24-storey whitewashed trapezoidal prism that serves as the headquarters for the national telephone company, Telefónica. Designed by Enric Massip-Bosch and dubbed the Torre ZeroZero, it has a deceivingly two-dimensional appearance upon initial approach. Shortly after its completion in 2011, the Torre was awarded the respected LEAF (Leading European Architects Forum) award for commercial building of the year.

Further away from the centre, in the long-neglected district of La Sagrera, construction of a major transport interchange for the Metro, buses and high-speed train from Madrid will be complemented by a characteristically out-there project from Frank Gehry, with five twisting steel and glass towers that will feature a large degree of solar energy self-sufficiency. Once complete, Sagrera will be the largest railway station in Spain.

In a rather thoughtful bit of recycling, British architect Lord Richard Rogers transformed the former Las Arenas bullring on Plaça d'Espanya into a singular, circular leisure complex, with shops, cinemas and more, which opened in 2011. He did so while still maintaining its red-brick, 19th-century Moorish-looking facade. Perhaps its best feature is the rooftop with 360-degree views from the open-air promenade and cafes and restaurants.

The increasingly dismal economic crisis, meanwhile, has put an end to some of the more extravagant projects. A new Barça president pulled the plug on Norman Foster's jaw-dropping makeover for Camp Nou Stadium. Foster, who in years past has kept to rather muted colour schemes, 'has begun designing buildings as if he's dropped acid,' Tom Dyckhoff wrote in the *Times* of London. Plans for the overhaul, which would have transformed the stadium into a kaleidoscopic, glow-in-the-dark sponge-cake have been shelved indefinitely.

The eminent British architect and town planner, Lord Richard Rogers, declared in 2000 that Barcelona was 'perhaps the most successful city in the world in terms of urban regeneration'.

OLYMPIC & CONTEMPORARY ARCHITECTURE THE CITY TOMORROW

Music & Dance

Barcelona's vibrant music and dance scene has been shaped by artists both traditional and cutting edge. From *Nova Cançó*, composed during the dark years of the dictatorship, to the hybridised Catalonian rumba to hands-in-the air rock ballads of the '70s and '80s, Barcelona's music evolves constantly. Today's groups continue to push musical boundaries, blending rhythms from all corners of the globe. In the realm of dance, flamenco is surprisingly popular, while the old-fashioned folk dance *sardana* has a small but growing number of followers.

Around the same time *Nova Cançó* singers were taking aim at the Franco regime, folk singers from Latin America were decrying their own corrupt military dictatorships. Songs by legendary artists like Victor Jara of Chile, Mercedes Sosa of Argentina and Chico Buarque of Brazil helped unite people in the fight against oppression.

CONTEMPORARY MUSIC

Nova Cançó

Curiously, it was probably the Franco repression that most helped foster a vigorous local music scene in Catalan. In the dark 1950s, the *Nova Cançó* (New Song) movement was born in the 1950s to resist linguistic oppression with music in Catalan (getting air time on the radio was long close to impossible), throwing up stars that in some cases won huge popularity throughout Spain, such as the Valencia-born Raimon.

More specifically loved in Catalonia as a Bob Dylan–style 1960s protest singer-songwriter was Lluís Llach, much of whose music was more or less anti-regime. Joan Manuel Serrat is another legendary figure. His appeal stretches from Barcelona to Buenos Aires. Born in the Poble Sec district, this poet-singer is equally at ease in Catalan and Spanish. He has repeatedly shown that record sales are not everything to him. In 1968 he refused to represent Spain at the Eurovision song contest if he were not allowed to sing in Catalan. Accused of being anti-Spanish, he was long banned from performing in Spain.

Rock Català

A specifically local strand of rock has emerged since the 1980s. *Rock Català* (Catalan rock) is not essentially different from rock anywhere else, except that it is sung in Catalan by local bands that appeal to local tastes. Among the most popular groups of years past include Sau, Els Pets, Lax'n Busto and the Valenciano band Obrint Pas.

LONGING FOR CUBA

The oldest musical tradition to have survived to some degree in Catalonia is that of the *havaneres* (from Havana) – nostalgic songs and melancholy sea shanties brought back from Cuba by Catalans who lived, sailed and traded there in the 19th century. Even after Spain lost Cuba in 1898, the *havanera* tradition (a mix of European and Cuban rhythms) continued. A magical opportunity to enjoy these songs is the *Cantada d'Havaneres* (www.havanerescalella.cat, in Catalan), an evening concert held in Calella de Palafrugell on the Costa Brava in early July. Otherwise, you may stumble across performances elsewhere along the coast or even in Barcelona, but there is no set program.

RETURN OF LA RUMBA

Back in the 1950s, a new sound mixing flamenco with salsa and other Latin sounds emerged in *gitano* (Roma people) circles in the bars of Gràcia and the Barri Gòtic. One of the founders of rumba Catalana was Antonio González, known as El Pescaílla (married to the flamenco star Lola Flores). Although he was well-known in town, the Matarò-born *gitano* Peret later took this eminently Barcelona style to a wider (eventually international) audience. By the end of the 1970s, however, rumba Catalana was running out of steam. Peret had turned to religion and El Pescaílla lived in Flores' shadow in Madrid. But Buenos Aires–born Javier Patricio 'Gato' Pérez discovered rumba in 1977 and gave it his own personal spin, bringing out several popular records, such as *Atalaya*, until the early 1980s. After Pérez, it seemed that rumba was dead. Not so fast! New rumba bands, often highly eclectic, have emerged in recent years. Papawa, Barrio Negro and El Tío Carlos are names to look out for. Others mix rumba with styles as diverse as reggae or ragga.

The Pinker Tones are a Barcelona duo that attained international success with an eclectic electronic mix of music, ranging from dizzy dance numbers to film soundtracks. Another Barcelona band with international ambitions and flavours is Macaco, a group that sings in different languages (Catalan, Spanish, English and Portuguese among others) and blends Latin rhythms and electronica in their rock anthems. When people talk about 'Raval sound' (after the name of the still somewhat seedy old town district), this is the kind of thing they mean.

Far greater success across Spain has gone to Estopa, a male rock duo from Cornellà, a satellite suburb of Barcelona. The guitar-wielding brothers sing a clean Spanish rock, occasionally with a vaguely flamenco flavour. Along the same vein, the Barcelona hit trio Pastora peddles a successful brand of Spanish pop, mixing electric sounds with a strong acoustic element.

Sabadell-born Albert Pla is one of the most controversial singer-songwriters on the national scene today and swings between his brand of forthright rock lyrics, stage and cinema.

Born in El Raval, Cabo San Roque is an even more experimental group, incorporating huge soundscapes, powerful rhythms and mechanical accents often using non-traditional John Cage-style instruments in their avant-garde performances. In one show, the five-person group shared the stage with a polyphonic washing machine powered by a bicycle chain.

Another key name in El Raval's scene is 08001 (which is Raval's postcode). This ever-evolving collective brings together musicians from all across the globe, fusing unusual sounds from hip-hop, flamenco, reggae and rock to styles from Morocco, West Africa, the Caribbean and beyond.

Top Albums

Techari, Ojos de Brujo

Verges 50, Lluís Llach

Wild Animals, Pinker Tones

Voràgine, 08001

Rey de la Rumba, Peret

La Diferencia, Albert Pla

X Anniversarium, Estopa

CLASSICAL, OPERA & BAROQUE

Spain's contribution to the world of classical music has been modest, but Catalonia has produced a few exceptional composers. Best known is Camprodon-born Isaac Albéniz (1860–1909), a gifted pianist who later turned his hand to composition. Among his best-remembered works is the *Iberia* cycle.

Montserrat Caballé is Barcelona's most successful voice. Born in Gràcia in 1933, the soprano made her debut in 1956 in Basel (Switzerland). Her hometown launch came four years later in the Gran Teatre del Liceu. In 1965, she performed to wild acclaim at New York's Carnegie

Hall and went on to become one of the world's finest 20th-century sopranos. Her daughter, Montserrat Martí, is also a singer and they occasionally appear together. Another fine Catalan soprano was Victoria de los Ángeles (1923–2005), while Catalonia's other world-class opera star is the renowned tenor Josep (José) Carreras.

Jordi Savall has assumed the task of rediscovering a European heritage in music that predates the era of the classical greats. He and his late wife, soprano Montserrat Figueras, have along with musicians from other countries been largely responsible for resuscitating the beauties of medieval, Renaissance and baroque music. In 1987, Savall founded La Capella Reial de Catalunya and two years later he formed the baroque orchestra Le Concert des Nations. You can sometimes catch their recitals in locations such as the Església de Santa Maria del Mar.

DANCE

Flamenco

For those who think that the passion of flamenco is the preserve of the south, think again. The *gitanos* (Roma people) get around, and some of the big names of the genre come from Catalonia. They were already in Catalonia long before the massive migrations from the south of the 1960s, but with these waves came an exponential growth in flamenco bars as Andalucians sought to recreate a little bit of home.

First and foremost, one of the greatest *bailaoras* (flamenco dancers) of all time, Carmen Amaya (1913–63) was born in what is now Port Olímpic. She danced to her father's guitar in the streets and bars around La Rambla in pre–civil war years. Much to the bemusement of purists from the south, not a few flamenco stars today have at least trained in flamenco schools in Barcelona – dancers Antonio Canales and Joaquín Cortés are among them. Other Catalan stars of flamenco include *cantaores* (singers) Juan Cortés Duquende and Miguel Poveda, a boy from Badalona. He took an original step in 2006 by releasing a flamenco album, *Desglaç*, in Catalan. Another interesting flamenco voice in Catalonia is Ginesa Ortega Cortés, actually born in France. She masters traditional genres ably but loves to experiment. In her 2002 album, *Por los Espejos del Agua* (Through the Water's Mirrors), she does a reggae version of flamenco and she has sung flamenco versions of songs by Joan Manuel Serrat and Billie Holiday.

An exciting combo formed in Barcelona in 1996 and which defies classification is the seven-man, one-woman group *Ojos de Brujo* (Wizard's Eyes), who meld flamenco and rumba with rap, ragga and electronic music.

Sardana

The Catalan dance *par excellence* is the *sardana,* whose roots lie in the far northern Empordà region of Catalonia. Compared with flamenco, it is sober indeed but not unlike a lot of other Mediterranean folk dances.

The dancers hold hands in a circle and wait for the 10 or so musicians to begin. The performance starts with the piping of the *flabiol,* a little wooden flute. When the other musicians join in, the dancers start – a series of steps to the right, one back and then the same to the left. As the music 'heats up' the steps become more complex, the leaps are higher and the dancers lift their arms. Then they return to the initial steps and continue. If newcomers wish to join in, space is made for them as the dance continues and the whole thing proceeds in a more or less seamless fashion.

PAU CASALS

Born in Catalonia, Pau Casals (1876–1973) was one of the greatest cellists of the 20th century. Living in exile in southern France, he declared he would not play in public as long as the Western democracies continued to tolerate Franco's regime. In 1958, he was a candidate for the Nobel Peace Prize.

Catalan Cuisine

Barcelona has a celebrated food scene fuelled by a combination of world-class chefs, imaginative recipes, and magnificent ingredients fresh from farms and the sea. Catalan culinary masterminds like Ferran Adrià and Carles Abellán have become international icons, reinventing the world of haute cuisine, while classic old-world Catalan recipes continue to earn accolades in dining rooms and tapas bars across the city.

CULINARY ROOTS

The Romans didn't just bring straight roads, a large temple and a functional sewerage system to the little town of Barcino. They also brought with them their culinary habits, which included such fundamentals as olives and grapes. We can perhaps be grateful that another Roman favourite, *garum* (a kind of tart fish paste that could survive long sea voyages), did not survive the demise of the empire.

The country's long history of Muslim occupation is reflected in the use of spices such as saffron and cumin and, in desserts, the predominance of honeyed sweets, almonds and fruit. Other major sources of culinary inspiration were imports brought back from South America, where everyday staples such as potatoes, tomatoes and, of course, chocolate came from.

Books Exploring Catalan Cuisine

A Day at El Bulli (Ferran Adrià)

Catalan Cuisine (Colman Andrews)

The New Spanish Table (Anya von Bremzen)

A LAND OF IMMIGRANTS

Barcelona has long attracted migrants, at first from the rest of Spain and, since the 1990s, from all over the world. Thus, the city is jammed with Galician seafood restaurants and Basque tapas bars, and since the mid-1990s, foreign cuisines have landed – big time. While cheap and cheerful Chinese establishments have always been here, until the early 1990s, you could count the Japanese, Thai and Indian restaurants on the fingers of one hand.

Today Barcelona offers temptations from all corners of the globe. Suddenly *pizzarie,* sushi restaurants, tandoori temptations, Thai, Korean and kebabs are everywhere. The number of non-Spanish restaurants in Barcelona has more than quadrupled since the start of the 21st century.

If a waiter proposes 'pijama', it is not an invitation to head home for bed and jammies. It is rather a suggestion to try one of the country's most lurid desserts. It consists of peach slices, flan and two balls of ice cream (say strawberry and vanilla), all covered in whipped cream and chocolate topping!

THE CATALAN BOUNTY

At the heart of Catalan cooking is a diversity of products and traditions. Some dishes are referred to as *mar i muntanya* (surf and turf; a mix of seafood and meats), a term which perhaps best sums up the situation. Barcelona has always been enamoured of edible marine inhabitants (Roman annals suggests big, juicy local oysters were once a common item on ancient menus), while the Catalan hinterland, especially the Pyrenees, has long been the hearth of a much chunkier, heartier cooking tradition. From wintry mountain stews to an array of sausages and a general fondness for charcuterie and venison, the Catalan countryside contributes much to the Spanish dinner table. To these basic ingredients the Catalans add a rich array of sauces, betraying a strong French influence on their culinary habits.

The Basics

The basics are simple enough: bread and olive oil. And lots of garlic. No Catalan would eat a meal without bread, and olive oil seems to make its way into just about every dish. Catalans find it hard to understand why other people put butter on bread when *pa amb tomàquet/pan con tomate* (bread sliced then rubbed with tomato, olive oil, garlic and salt) is so much tastier!

There are many local brands of olive oil, but one of the best is Borges, which has been produced in Tàrrega, in Lleida province, since 1896. Spices, on the other hand, are generally noticeable by their absence. If you're told something is *picante* (spicy, hot) you can generally be sure it is little more than mild.

Seafood

Fish and seafood are major components of the region's cuisine. Only a fraction of Catalonia's needs are fished in Catalan waters: much of what ends up on Catalan tables comes from the Bay of Biscay, France, the UK and as far off as South Africa (cod in particular in the last case). In 1996 only about 15% of all produce on sale at Barcelona's main wholesale market (Mercabarna) was imported; in 2011, more than half of the fish came from abroad.

A Rice Base

Paella's main ingredient, rice, is grown not far from the city limits, in the Delta de l'Ebre area of southern Catalonia, and used widely. Mixed with fish from the Mediterranean and meat from the nearby mountains, Barcelona's concoctions are some of the best in Spain, save of course Valencia.

Gathering

Bolets (wild mushrooms) are a Catalan passion – people disappear into the forests in autumn to pick them. There are many, many types of *bolets*; the large succulent *rovellons* are a favourite. *Trompetas de la muerte* (trumpets of death) are a veritable delicacy and are generally available during summer and autumn. A trip to Mercat de la Boqueria in central Barcelona around October will reveal even more varieties.

Cheesemaking

The main centres of cheese production in Catalonia are La Seu d'Urgell, the Cerdanya district and the Pallars area in the northwest. Although some traditional cheeses are becoming less common, you can still come across things like *formatge de tupí* (goat's cheese soaked in olive oil) in produce markets and specialist cheese shops.

Italian-influenced Dishes

The Catalan version of pizza is *coca*, often made in the shape of a long, broad tongue. There are many variations on this theme, savoury and sweet. The former can come with tomato, onion, pepper and sometimes sardines. The sweet version, often almond based, is more common and is a standard item at many a *festa* (festival), such as Dìa de Sant Joan in June. Catalans also like pasta, and *canelons* (similar to Italian cannelloni) is a common dish.

Tapas

Instead of heading for a sit-down meal, some locals prefer to *tapear* or *ir de tapeo* (go on a tapas crawl; also known as *picar* or *pica-pica*). This

VEGETARIANS

Vegetarians, and especially vegans, can have a hard time in Spain, but in Barcelona a growing battery of vegetarian restaurants offers welcome relief. Sometimes, however, meat lurks in surprising places: some salads, for instance the *amanida catalana*, may contain popular 'vegetables' such as ham or tuna.

is the delightful business of standing around in bars and choosing from a range of tasty little titbits. They can stay in one place or move from one to another, and basically keep munching and drinking until they've had enough.

The origin of the *tapa* appears to lie in the old habit of serving drinks with a lid (*tapa*) on the glass, perhaps to keep out pesky bugs. The *tapa* might have been a piece of bread and at some point a couple of morsels on the *tapa* became par for the course – usually salty items bound to work up a greater thirst. In some bars you will still get a few olives or other free snacks with your beer, but since tapas were always more a southern Spanish thing, it is not overly common – in Barcelona, if you want something, you pay for it.

Since the mid-1990s the number of Basque tapas bars has increased exponentially.

NUEVA COCINA ESPAÑOLA

Avant-garde chefs have made Catalonia famous throughout the world for their food laboratories, their commitment to food as art and their crazy riffs on the themes of traditional local cooking.

What started as a bit of experimentation has spawned a food revolution, across Spain and to the great restaurant centres around the globe. One of the grandfathers of *nueva cocina española* is the highly imaginative Catalan chef Ferran Adrià, who in the late 1980s and 1990s began playing around with new methods of preparation in the kitchen.

He turned liquids and solid foods into foams, created 'ice cream' of classic ingredients by means of liquid nitrogen, freeze-dried foods to make concentrated powder versions and employed spherification to create unusual and artful creations. This alchemical cookery was later dubbed molecular gastronomy, and fueled a craze for invention, as more chefs studied Adrià's techniques and added their own embellishments.

No matter the term – Adrià actually prefers to describe his technique as 'deconstruction' – creativity is of paramount importance. Chefs of *nueva cocina* aim to create thought-provoking – while still flavourful – dishes. It's cooking as high art: as all that is familiar is transformed into something wondrous and new, and sometimes utterly surreal.

An example of this deconstruction in action is the transformation of the classic *tortilla española* (Spanish omelette). Take its three component parts – eggs, potatoes and onions – and prepare each separately while altering their traditional composition. Turn the potatoes into foam, make puree of the onions, and create a mousse-like sabayon of the eggs. Layer each component one on top of the other and garnish with crumbs of deep-fried potatoes; serve in a sherry glass, and voila, a radical new take on the *tortilla española.*

Diners may encounter olive oil 'caviar'; hot ice cream; a pina colada of coconut foam, dehydrated pineapple and rum gel that's served on a spoon; spherical olives (olive puree and herbs that provide a curious replica of the real thing); 'snow' made of gazpacho with anchovies; gellified parmesan turned into spaghetti; and potato-foam gnocchi with a consommé of roasted potato skin, whipped cream and sea-water-jelly butter ravioli.

El Bulli, rated one of the world's best restaurants before it closed in 2011, introduced the world to *nueva cocina española*. Yet despite the high price tag (prix fixe meals at €270 per person), El Bulli never made money. Instead, operating profits came solely from El Bulli–related products and lectures by chef Ferran Adrià.

Spanish Wine & Cava

Spain is a wine-drinking country and *vi/vino* (wine) accompanies all meals (except breakfast!). Spanish wine, whether *blanc/blanco* (white), *negre/tinto* (red) or *rosat/rosado* (rosé), tends to have quite a kick, in part because of the climate but also because of grape varieties and production methods. That said, the long-adhered-to policy of quantity over quality has given way to a subtler approach.

As in the other major EU wine-producing countries, there are two broad categories: table wine and quality wine.

On occasion you may be asked if you'd like a *chupito* (a little shot of liquor) to round off a meal. Popular and refreshing Spanish *chupitos* are *licor de manzana verde* (green apple liqueur) and *licor de melocotón* (peach liqueur), both transparent, chilled and with around 20% alcohol.

TABLE WINES

At the lower end of the market, you find everything from the basic *vi de taula/vino de mesa* (table wine) to *vi de la terra/vino de la tierra*, the latter being a mid-range wine from an officially delimited wine-producing area. An entirely drinkable bottle of table wine can easily enough be had for around €5 in supermarkets and from wine merchants (especially the old kind, a slowly dying breed, where they will fill your bottle from giant barrels). The same money in a restaurant won't get you far. Apart from *vi/vino de la casa* (house wine), which is commonly ordered at lunchtime by the litre or half-litre, you will pay an average of €10 to €15 for a reasonable bottle, and considerably more for something classier. You can also generally order wine by the *copa* (glass) in bars and restaurants, although the choice will be more limited.

QUALITY WINES

If an area meets certain strict standards, it receives DO (*denominación de origen*) status. Outstanding wine regions get DOC (*denominación de origen calificada*) status. In Catalonia, there are 12 DOs (appellations), including a regional one (DO Catalunya; www.do-catalunya.com) and a general one for *cava*. Some of the DOs cover little more than a few vineyards. Classifications are not always a guarantee of quality, and many drinkers of Spanish wine put more faith in the name and reputation of certain producers or areas than in the denomination labels.

Not generally available in bars is the acquired taste of *calimocho*, a mix of Tetra Pak red wine and Coke, beloved of penniless partying students across the country.

WINE REGIONS

The bulk of DO wines in Catalonia are made from grapes produced in the Penedès area, which pumps out almost two million hectolitres a year. The other DO winemaking zones (spread as far apart as the Empordà area around Figueres in the north and the Terra Alta around Gandesa in the southwest) have a combined output of about half that produced in Penedès. The wines of the El Priorat area, which tend to be dark, heavy reds, have been promoted to DOC status, an honour shared only with those of the Rioja (categorised as such since 1926). Drops from the neigh

---

SOMETHING GOOD BURNING

With Catalan impresarios making money hand over fist in sugar plantations in Cuba and other South American colonies from the late 18th century, it is hardly surprising they developed a taste for one of its by-products, *rom/ron* (rum). In 1818 the Pujol liquor company set up a rum distillery in Catalonia, and since then Ron Pujol has been one of the dominant local brands for this sweet firewater. Today it produces all sorts of rum and rum-based drinks, including the classic Ron Pujol (42% alcohol), Pujol & Grau (38%, a lighter, white rum) and Ron 1818, based on the original recipe made in the Antilles. Closer to the Brazilian *cachaça* is Cana Pujol (50%). But the great Catalan drink especially popular in summer festivals is *rom cremat* (burned rum), a sweet concoction made with cinnamon and lemon zest, that's set alight.

---

bouring Montsant area are frequently as good (or close) and considerably cheaper.

There is plenty to look out for beyond Penedès. Raïmat, in the Costers del Segre DO area of Lleida province, produces fine reds and a couple of notable whites. Good fortified wines come from around Tarragona and some nice fresh wines are also produced in the Empordà area in the north.

CAVA

The bulk of production in and around the Penedès area is white wine. Of these the best-known drop is *cava*, the regional version of champagne. The two big names in bubbly are Freixenet and Codorníu. Connoisseurs tend not to get too excited by these, however, preferring the output of smaller vintners. The main name in Penedès wine is Miguel Torres – one of its stalwart reds is Sangre de Toro.

SANGRIA

Sangria is a red-wine-and-fruit punch (usually with lemon, orange and cinnamon), sometimes laced with brandy. It's refreshing going down, but can leave you with a sore head. Indeed, the origins of the drink go back to the days when wine quality was not great and the vinegary taste needed a sweetener. Another version is *sangría de cava*, a punch made with sparkling white. *Tinto de verano* (summer red) is a mix of wine and Casera, which is a brand of *gaseosa*, similar to lemonade. It is both a means of sweetening tart table wine and avoiding lunchtime hangovers. As its name suggests, it is also popular as a refreshing summertime lunch tipple.

Most of the grapes grown in Catalonia are native to Spain and include White Macabeo, Garnacha and Xarel. lo (for whites), and Black Garnacha, Monastrell and Ull de Llebre (Hare's Eye) red varieties. Foreign varieties (such as chardonnay, riesling, chenin blanc, cabernet sauvignon, merlot and pinot noir) are also common.

FOOD & WINE PAIRINGS

➡ A glass of bubbly *cava* is extremely versatile, pairing nicely with a wide range of tapas dishes, especially mussels, shrimp, crab and other seafood. Another fine drop for tapas is light, slightly fruity *albarino* wine, which hails from northwest Spain.

➡ In Basque-style tapas bars, the drink of choice is *txacolí*, a slightly sparkling dry white wine produced in Basque country (and several other northern provinces). This is the perfect accompaniment to lighter seafood bites on offer, for example (try it with anchovies).

➡ Catalan rosés (called here *rosats*) tend to be deeper, darker and slightly more intense than other Spanish rosés. These go well with pork, seafood and paellas.

➡ Some excellent red wines are emerging from Catalonia, with DO regions Priorat and Montsant well worth seeking out. These complex and full-bodied wines tend to go well with meats – especially sausages and roast pork – as well as richer seafood dishes.

Survival Guide

Transport

GETTING TO BARCELONA

Most travellers enter Barcelona through El Prat airport. Some budget airlines use Girona-Costa Brava airport or Reus airport.

Flights from North America take about eight hours from the east coast (10 to 13 hours typically, with a stopover); from the west coast count on 13 or more hours including a stopover. Flights from London take around two hours; from Western Europe it's about two to three hours.

Travelling by train is a pricier but perhaps more romantic way of reaching Catalonia from other European cities. The overnight *trenhotel* takes 12 hours from Paris to Barcelona. Long-distance trains arrive in Estació Sants, about 2.5km west of La Rambla.

Long-haul buses arrive in Estació del Nord.

Websites that list competitive airfares include the following:

➡ www.kayak.com
➡ www.flightline.co.uk
➡ www.lastminute.com
➡ www.openjet.co.uk
➡ www.opodo.com
➡ www.orbitz.com
➡ www.planesimple.co.uk
➡ www.skyscanner.net
➡ www.travelocity.co.uk

Flights, tours and rail tickets can be booked online at lonelyplanet.com/bookings.

El Prat Airport

Barcelona's **El Prat airport** (☑902 404704; www.aena.es) lies 17km southwest of Plaça de Catalunya at El Prat de Llobregat. The airport has two main terminal buildings: the new T1 terminal and the older T2, itself divided into three terminal areas (A, B and C).

In T1, the main arrivals area is on the 1st floor (with separate areas for EU Schengen Area arrivals, non-EU international arrivals and the Barcelona-Madrid corridor). Boarding gates for departures are on the 1st and 3rd floors.

The main **tourist office** (☉9am-9pm) is on the ground floor of Terminal 2B. Others on the ground floor of Terminal 2A and in Terminal 1 operate the same hours. Lockers (which come in three sizes) can be found on the 1st floor of Terminal 1 and at the car park entrance opposite Terminal 2B. Lost-luggage offices can be found by the arrivals belts in Terminal 1 and on the arrivals floor in Terminals 2A and 2B.

Bus

The **A1 Aerobús** (☑93 415 60 20; www.aerobusbcn.com; one way €5.65; ☉30 to 40 minutes) runs from Terminal 1 to Plaça de Catalunya (single/return €5.65/9.75, 30 to 40 minutes depending on traffic) via Plaça d'Espanya, Gran Via de les Corts Catalanes (corner of Carrer del Comte d'Urgell) and Plaça de la Universitat every five to 10 minutes from 6.10am to 1.05am. It departs Plaça de Catalunya from 5.30am to 12.30am, stopping at the corner of Carrer de Sepúlveda and Carrer del Comte d'Urgell, and at Plaça d'Espanya.

The A2 Aerobús from Terminal 2 (stops outside terminal areas A, B and C) runs from 6am to 1am with a frequency of between 10 and 20 minutes and follows the same route as the A1.

Buy tickets on the bus or from agents at the bus stop. Considerably slower local buses (such as the No 46 to/from Plaça d'Espanya and a night bus, the N17, to/from Plaça de Catalunya) also serve Terminals 1 and 2.

Mon-Bus (www.monbus.cat) has regular direct buses (which originate in central Barcelona) between Terminal 1 only and Sitges (€2.90). In Sitges you can catch it at Avinguda de Vilanova 14. The trip takes about 35 minutes and runs hourly.

Alsa (☑902 422242; www.alsa.es) runs the Aerobús Rápid service several times daily from El Prat airport to various cities including Girona, Figueres, Lleida, Reus, and Tarragona. Fares range from €7.66/14.55 one-way/return to Tarragona up to €26.60/47.90 one way/return to Lleida.

Plana (☑977 35 44 45; www.empresaplana.es) has services between the airport and Reus, stopping at Tarragona, Port Aventura and other southwest coastal destinations nearby along the way.

CLIMATE CHANGE & TRAVEL

Every form of transport that relies on carbon-based fuel generates CO_2, the main cause of human-induced climate change. Modern travel is dependent on aeroplanes, which might use less fuel per kilometre per person than most cars but travel much greater distances. The altitude at which aircraft emit gases (including CO_2) and particles also contributes to their climate change impact. Many websites offer 'carbon calculators' that allow people to estimate the carbon emissions generated by their journey and, for those who wish to do so, to offset the impact of the greenhouse gases emitted with contributions to portfolios of climate-friendly initiatives throughout the world. Lonely Planet offsets the carbon footprint of all staff and author travel.

Train

Train operator Renfe runs the R2 Nord line every half an hour from the airport (from 5.42am to 11.38pm) via several stops to Barcelona's main train station, **Estació Sants** (Plaça dels Països Catalans; Sants Estació), and Passeig de Gràcia in central Barcelona, after which it heads northwest out of the city. The first service from Passeig de Gràcia leaves at 5.08am and the last at 11.07pm, and about five minutes later from Estació Sants. The trip between the airport and Passeig de Gràcia takes 25 minutes. A one-way ticket costs €3.60 (unless you have a multiride ticket for Barcelona public transport).

The airport railway station is about a five-minute walk from Terminal 2. Regular shuttle buses run from the station and Terminal 2 to Terminal 1 – allow for an extra 15 to 20 minutes.

Taxi

A taxi between either terminal and the city centre – about a half-hour ride depending on traffic – costs €20 to €26. Fares and charges are posted inside the passenger side of the taxi – make sure the meter is used.

Girona–Costa Brava Airport

Girona-Costa Brava airport (902 404704; www.aena.es) is 12km south of Girona and 92km northeast of Barcelona. You'll find a tourist office, ATMs and lost-luggage desks on the ground floor.

➡ **Train** (www.renfe.com) Regular services run between Girona and Barcelona (€7.50 to €10, around 1 1/2 hours).

➡ **Bus Sagalés** (902 130014; www.sagales.com) runs hourly bus services from Girona-Costa Brava airport to Girona's main bus/train station (€2.60, 30 minutes) in connection with flights. The same company runs direct **Barcelona Bus** (902 130014; www.barcelonabus.com) services to/from **Estació del Nord** (902 260606; www.barcelonanord.com; Carrer d'Ali Bei 80; Arc de Triomf) bus station in Barcelona (one way/return €15/25, 70 minutes). For greater flexibility at greater cost, check out www.resorthoppa.com. It puts on minibuses to destinations around the region, including Barcelona.

➡ **Taxi** A ride into Girona from the airport costs €20 to €26. To Barcelona you would pay around €140.

Reus Airport

Reus airport (902 404704; www.aena.es) is 13km west of Tarragona and 108km southwest of Barcelona. The tourist office and lost luggage desks are in the main terminal building.

➡ **Bus Hispano-Igualadina** (902 292900; www.igualadina.net; Estació Sants & Plaça de la Reina Maria Cristina) services run between Reus airport and **Estació d'Autobusos de Sants** (Carrer de Viriat; Sants Estació) to meet flights (€14.50/25 one-way/return, 2 hours). Local bus 50 (www.reustransport.cat) serves central Reus (€2.40, 20 minutes) and other buses run to local coastal destinations.

Estació Sants

The main train station in Barcelona is **Estació Sants** (Plaça dels Països Catalans; Sants Estació), located 2.5km west of La Rambla. Direct overnight trains from Paris, Geneva, Milan and Zurich arrive here. From here it's a short Metro ride to the Ciutat Vella or L'Eixample.

Estació Sants has a tourist office, a telephone and fax office, currency exchange booths open between 8am and 10pm, ATMs and left-luggage lockers.

Estació del Nord

Long-distance buses leave from **Estació del Nord** (902 260606; www.barcelonanord.com; Carrer d'Ali Bei 80; Arc de Triomf). A plethora of companies operates to different parts of Spain, although many come under the umbrella of **Alsa** (902 422242; www.alsa.es). For other

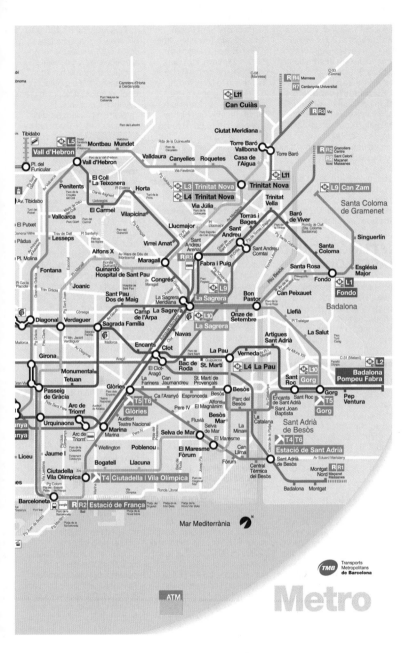

Mar Mediterrània

Transports
Metropolitans
de Barcelona

Metro

companies, ask at the bus station. There are frequent services to Madrid, Valencia and Zaragoza (20 or more a day) and several daily departures to distant destinations such as Burgos, Santiago de Compostela and Seville.

Eurolines (www.eurolines. es), in conjunction with local carriers all over Europe, is the main international carrier. Its website provides links to national operators; it runs services across Europe and to Morocco from Estació del Nord, and Estació d'Autobuses de Sants, next to Estació Sants in Barcelona. Another carrier is **Linebús** (www.linebus.com).

GETTING AROUND BARCELONA

Barcelona has abundant options for getting around town. The excellent Metro can get you most places, with buses and trams filling in the gaps. Taxis are the best option late at night.

Metro

The easy-to-use **TMB Metro** (Map p260; ☑010; www.tmb. net) system has 11 numbered and colour-coded lines. It runs from 5am to midnight Sunday to Thursday and holidays, from 5am to 2am on Friday and days preceding holidays, and 24 hours on Saturday.

Ongoing work to expand the Metro continues on several lines. Lines 9 and 10 will eventually (2014 at the earliest) connect with the airport.

Suburban trains run by the **Ferrocarrils de la Generalitat de Catalunya** (FGC; ☑93 205 15 15; www.fgc.net) include a couple of useful city lines. All lines heading north from Plaça de Catalunya stop at Carrer de Provença and Gràcia. One of these lines (L7) goes to Tibidabo and another (L6 to Reina Elisenda) has a stop within spitting distance of the Monestir de Pedralbes.

Most trains from Plaça de Catalunya continue beyond Barcelona to Sant Cugat, Sabadell and Terrassa. Other FGC lines head west from Plaça d'Espanya, including one for Manresa that is handy for the trip to Montserrat.

Depending on the line, these trains run from about 5am (with only one or two services before 6am) to 11pm or midnight Sunday to Thursday, and from 5am to about 1am on Friday and Saturday.

Bus

Transports Metropolitans de Barcelona (TMB; ☑010; www.tmb.net) buses run along most city routes every few minutes from between 5am and 6.30am to between around 10pm and 11pm. Many routes pass through Plaça de Catalunya and/or Plaça de la Universitat. After 11pm, a reduced network of yellow *nitbusos* (night buses) runs until 3am or 5am. All *nitbus* routes pass through Plaça de Catalunya and most run every 30 to 45 minutes.

Taxi

Taxis charge €2.05 flag fall plus meter charges of €0.93 per kilometre (€1.18 from 8pm to 8am and all day on weekends). A further €3.10 is added for all trips to/from the airport, and €1 for luggage bigger than 55cm x 35cm x 35cm. The trip from Estació Sants to Plaça de Catalunya, about 3km, costs about €11. You can call a **taxi** (☑93 225 00 00) or flag them down in the streets. The call-out charge is €3.40 (€4.20 at night and on weekends). In many taxis it is possible to pay with a credit card and, if you have a local telephone number, you can join the T033 Ràdio Taxi service for booking taxis online (www. radiotaxi033.com, in Spanish). You can also book online at www.catalunyataxi.com.

General information is available on ☑010.

Taxi Amic (☑93 420 80 88; www.taxi-amic-adaptat. com) is a special taxi service for people with disabilities or difficult situations (such as transport of big objects). Book at least 24 hours in advance if possible.

Women passengers who feel safer with taxis driven by women can order one on the **Línea Rosa** (☑93 330 07 00).

Tram

TMB (☑902 193275; www. trambcn.com) runs three tram lines (T1, T2 and T3) into the suburbs of greater Barcelona from Plaça de Francesc Macià and are of limited interest to visitors. The T4 line runs from behind the zoo (near the Ciutadella Vila Olímpica Metro stop) to Sant Adrià via Glòries and the Fòrum. The T5 line runs from Glòries to Badalona (Gorg stop). The T6 runs between Badalona (Gorg) and Sant Adrià. All standard transport passes are valid. A more scenic option is *tramvia blau* (blue tram), which runs up to the foot of Tibidabo.

Bicycle

Over 180km of bike lanes have been laid out across the city, so it's possible to commute on two environmentally friendly wheels. A waterfront path runs northeast from Port Olímpic to Riu Besòs and scenic itineraries are mapped for cyclists in the Collserola parkland.

You can transport your bicycle on the Metro on weekdays (except between 7am and 9.30am or 5pm and 8.30pm). On weekends and holidays, and during July and August, there are no restrictions. You can use FGC trains to carry your bike at any time and Renfe's *rodalies* trains from 10am to 3pm on weekdays and all day on weekends and holidays.

TICKETS & TARGETES

The Metro, FGC trains, *rodalies/cercanías* (Renfe-run local trains) and buses come under one zoned-fare regime. All single-ride tickets within Zone 1 cost €2.

Targetes, multitrip transport tickets, are sold at all city-centre Metro stations. The prices listed below are for adults in Zone 1 (children under four years of age travel free):

➡ Targeta T-10 (€9.25) – 10 rides (each valid for 1¼ hours) on the Metro, buses, FGC trains and *rodalies*. You can change between Metro, FGC, *rodalies* and buses.

➡ Targeta T-DIA (€6.95) – unlimited travel on all transport for one day.

➡ Two-/three-/four-/ five-day tickets (€12.80/18.50/23.50/28) – unlimited travel on all transport except the Aerobús; buy them at Metro stations and tourist offices.

➡ T-Mes (€50) – 30 days' unlimited use of all public transport.

➡ Targeta T-50/30 (€37) – 50 trips within 30 days, valid on all transport.

➡ T-Trimestre (€135) – 90 days' unlimited use of all public transport.

Hire

Countless companies around town offer bicycles (and anything remotely resembling one: tandems, tricycle carts and more).

➡ **BarcelonaBiking.com**
(Map p292; ☎656 356300; www.barcelonabiking.com; Baixada de Sant Miquel 6; per hr/24hr €5/15; ⏱10am-8pm; ⓂJaume I or Liceu)

➡ **Barnabike** (Map p302; ☎93 269 02 04; www.barnabike.com; Carrer del Pas de Sota la Muralla 3; per 2hr/24hr €6/15; ⏱10am-9.30pm; ⓂBarceloneta)

➡ **Biciclot** (Map p302; ☎93 221 97 78; www.biciclot.net; Passeig Marítim de la Barceloneta 33; per hr/day €5.50/€18; ⏱10am-3pm Mon-Thu Mar-May & Sat-Sun & holidays Dec-Feb, closed Mon-Fri Oct-Feb, 10am-8pm all other times; ⓂCiutadella Vila Olímpica)

➡ **Bike Rental Barcelona**
(Map p292; ☎666 057655; www.bikerentalbarcelona. com; Carrer d'en Rauric 20; per 3hr/24hr from €9/16; ⏱10am-8pm; ⓂJaume I)

➡ **My Beautiful Parking**
(Map p292; ☎93 304 15 80; www.mybeautifulparking.com; Carrer de Cervantes 5; per 2hr/24hr €6/15; ⏱10am-8pm; ⓂJaume I or Liceu)

➡ **Un Cotxe Menys** (☎93 268 21 05; www.bicicletabarce

lona.com; Carrer de l'Esparteria 3; per hr/day/week €5/15/55; ⏱9am-7pm Easter-Nov, 11am-2pm Dec-Easter; ⓂJaume I)

Car & Motorcycle

With the convenience of public transport and the high price of parking in the city, it's unwise to drive in Barcelona. However, you may still want to hire a car for a road trip.

Hire

Avis, Europcar, National/Atesa and Hertz have desks at El Prat airport, Estació Sants and Estació del Nord. Rental outlets in Barcelona include the following:

Avis (☎902 110 275; www. avis.com; Carrer de Còrsega 293-295; ⓂDiagonal)

Cooltra (Map p302; ☎93 221 40 70; www.cooltra.com; Passeig de Joan de Borbó 80-84; ⓂBarceloneta) You can rent scooters here for around €35 (plus insurance). Cooltra also organises scooter tours.

Europcar (☎93 302 05 43; www.europcar.com; Gran Via de les Corts Catalanes 680; ⓂGirona)

Hertz (☎93 419 61 56; www. hertz.com; Carrer del Viriat 45; ⓂSants)

MondoRent (Map p302; ☎93 295 32 68; www.mondorent.

com; Passeig de Joan de Borbó 80-84; ⓂBarceloneta) A similar deal on scooter rental to Cooltra.

National/Atesa (☎93 323 07 01; www.atesa.es; Carrer de Muntaner 45; ⓂUniversitat)

Vanguard (☎93 439 38 80; www.vanguardrent.com; Carrer de Viladomat 297; ⓂEntença) For anything from a Fiat Seicento to an Alfa Romeo. It also rents out scooters.

TOURS

Barcelona offers a wide range of guided tour options: on foot and by bus, bicycle or scooter (p30). Boat tours of the harbour and beaches depart daily from the waterfront (p129).

Helicopter Tours

See **BCN Skytour** (☎93 224 07 10; www.cathelicopters. com; Heliport, Passeig de l'Escullera; 5-min/35-min tour per person €50/300; ⏱10am-7pm; ⓂDrassanes or Paral.lel) for a 800m high thrill that truly gives a bird's-eye view of the city. A 35-minute trip for €300 per person takes in Montserrat. Five-minute tasters cost €50 per person. It's easiest to get to the heliport by taxi.

264

Directory A–Z

Business Hours

Reviews in this guide won't list business hours unless they differ from the following standards.

➡ **Restaurants** lunch 1–4pm, dinner 8.30pm–midnight

➡ **Shops** 10am–2pm and 4–8pm Monday–Saturday

➡ **Department stores** 10am–10pm Monday–Saturday

➡ **Bars** 6pm–2am

➡ **Clubs** midnight–6am Thursday–Saturday

➡ **Banks** 8.30am–2pm Monday–Friday; some also 4–7pm Thursday or 9am–1pm Saturday

➡ **Museums and art galleries** opening hours vary considerably, but generally fall between 10am and 8pm (some shut for lunch from around 2pm–4pm). Many museums and galleries are closed all day on Mondays and from 2pm on Sundays.

Discount Cards

The **ISIC** (International Student Identity Card; www.isic.org) and the **European Youth Card** (www.euro26.org) are available from most national student organisations and allow discounted access to some sights. Students generally pay a little more than half of adult admission prices, as do chil-

dren aged under 12 and senior citizens (aged 65 and over) with appropriate ID.

Possession of a **Bus Turístic** (☎93 285 38 32; www.barcelonaturisme.com; day ticket adult/child €24/14; ⊙9am-8pm) ticket entitles you to discounts at some museums.

Articket (www.articketbcn.org) gives admission to the following key sites for €30 and is valid for six months. You can pick up the ticket at the tourist offices at Plaça de Catalunya, Plaça de Sant Jaume and Sants train station (p267).

➡ Museu Picasso

➡ Museu Nacional d'Art de Catalunya (MNAC)

➡ Macba (Museu d'Art Contemporani de Barcelona)

➡ Fundació Antoni Tàpies

➡ Centre de Cultura Contemporània de Barcelona (CCCB)

➡ Fundació Joan Miró

➡ La Pedrera

Arqueoticket is for those with a special interest in archaeology and ancient history. The ticket (€14) is available from participating museums and tourist offices. Admission includes:

➡ Museu Marítim

➡ Museu d'Història de la Ciutat

➡ Museu d'Arqueologia de Catalunya (MAC)

➡ Museu Egipci

PRACTICALITIES

➡ Currency: the euro (€)

➡ Smoking: banned in restaurants and bars

➡ Museu Barbier-Mueller d'Art Pre-Colombí

Barcelona Card (www.barcelonacard.com) is handy if you want to see lots in a limited time. It costs €29/35/40/47 (a little less for children aged four to 12) for two/three/four/five days. You get free transport (and 20% off the Aerobús), and discounted admission prices (up to 30% off) or free entry to many museums and other sights, as well as minor discounts on purchases at a small number of shops, restaurants and bars. The card is available at tourist offices and online (buying online saves you 10%).

The **Ruta del Modernisme** pack (p33) is well worth looking into; it allows you to visit Modernista sights at discounted rates.

Electricity

Spain uses 220V, 50Hz, like the rest of continental Europe.

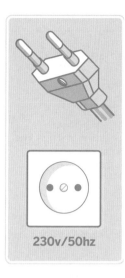

230v/50hz

Emergency

The following are the main emergency numbers:

Ambulance (☎061)

Catalan police (Mossos d'Esquadra; ☎088)

EU standard emergency number (☎112)

Fire brigade (Bombers; ☎080, 085)

Guardia Civil (civil guard; ☎062)

Guàrdia Urbana (local police; ☎092; La Rambla 43; MLiceu)

Policía Nacional (national police; ☎091)

Internet Access

Barcelona is full of internet centres. Some offer student rates and also sell cards for several hours' use at reduced rates. Look also for *Locutorios* (public phone centres), which often double as internet centres.

Bornet (Carrer de Barra Ferro 3; per hr/10hr €2.80/20; ☉10am-11pm Mon-Fri, 2pm-

11pm Sat, Sun & holidays; MJaume I) A cool little internet centre and art gallery.

Internet MSN (Carrer del Penedès 1; per min €0.02; ☉10am-midnight; MFontana)

Medical Services

All foreigners have the same right as Spaniards to emergency medical treatment in public hospitals. EU citizens are entitled to the full range of health-care services in public hospitals, but must present a European Health Insurance Card (enquire at your national health service) and may have to pay upfront.

Non-EU citizens have to pay for anything other than emergency treatment. Most travel-insurance policies include medical cover.

For minor health problems you can try any *farmàcia* (pharmacy), where pharmaceuticals tend to be sold more freely without prescription than in places such as the USA, Australia or the UK.

If your country has a consulate in Barcelona, its staff should be able to refer you to doctors who speak your language.

Hospitals include the following:

Hospital Clínic i Provincial (Carrer de Villarroel 170; MHospital Clínic)

WI-FI ACCESS

Many hotels offer their guests wi-fi access (not always for free). A growing array of city bars and restaurants are latching on to the service – look for the black-and-white wi-fi signs.

Places in this guide that offer wi-fi have the symbol 🛜.

Hospital Dos de Maig (Carrer del Dos de Maig 301; MSant Pau–Dos de Maig)

Some 24-hour pharmacies include the following:

Farmàcia Castells Soler (Passeig de Gràcia 90; MDiagonal)

Farmàcia Clapés (La Rambla 98; MLiceu)

Farmàcia Torres (www.farmaciaabierta24h.com; Carrer d'Aribau 62; ⓡFGC Provença)

Money
ATMS

Barcelona abounds with banks, many of which have ATMs. ATMs are also in plentiful supply around Plaça de Catalunya, Plaça de Sant Jaume (in the Barri Gòtic) and La Rambla.

Changing Money

You can change cash or travellers cheques in most major currencies without problems at virtually any bank or *bureau de change* (usually indicated by the word *canvi/cambio*).

The foreign-exchange offices that you see along La Rambla and elsewhere are open for longer hours than banks, but they generally offer poorer rates. Also, keep a sharp eye open for commissions at *bureaux de change*.

Credit Cards

Major cards such as Visa, MasterCard, Maestro and Cirrus are accepted throughout Spain. They can be used in many hotels, restaurants and shops. If your card is lost, stolen or swallowed by an ATM, you can telephone toll free to immediately stop its use:

Amex (☎902 375637)

Diners Club (☎900 801331)

MasterCard (☎900 971231)

Visa (☎900 991124)

PUBLIC HOLIDAYS

➡ **New Year's Day** (Any Nou/Año Nuevo) 1 January

➡ **Epiphany/Three Kings' Day** (Epifanía or El Dia dels Reis/Día de los Reyes Magos) 6 January

➡ **Good Friday** (Divendres Sant/Viernes Santo) March/April

➡ **Easter Monday** (Dilluns de Pasqua Florida) March/April

➡ **Labour Day** (Dia del Treball/Fiesta del Trabajo) 1 May

➡ **Day after Pentecost Sunday** (Dilluns de Pasqua Granda) May/June

➡ **Feast of St John the Baptist** (Dia de Sant Joan/Día de San Juan Bautista) 24 June

➡ **Feast of the Assumption** (L'Assumpció/La Asunción) 15 August

➡ **Catalonia's National Day** (Diada Nacional de Catalunya) 11 September

➡ **Festes de la Mercè** 24 September

➡ **Spanish National Day** (Festa de la Hispanitat/Día de la Hispanidad) 12 October

➡ **All Saints Day** (Dia de Tots Sants/Día de Todos los Santos) 1 November

➡ **Constitution Day** (Día de la Constitución) 6 December

➡ **Feast of the Immaculate Conception** (La Immaculada Concepció/La Inmaculada Concepción) 8 December

➡ **Christmas** (Nadal/Navidad) 25 December

➡ **Boxing Day/St Stephen's Day** (El Dia de Sant Esteve) 26 December

Travellers Cheques & Moneycards

Travellers cheques are far less convenient than simply using bank cards at ATMs. If you do opt for this old-school option, Amex and Visa are widely accepted brands. For lost cheques, call a **24-hour freephone number** (for Amex 900 810029, for Visa 900 948978).

The Travelex Cash Passport (www.travelex.com) and Thomas Cook Travel Moneycard (www.thomascook money.com) are prepaid cards. You can load funds onto them before you travel and use them like any card in ATMs, restaurants or shops worldwide.

Post

Correos is Spain's national postal service. Barcelona's **main post office** (Plaça d'Antoni López; ☺8.30am-9.30pm Mon-Fri, 8.30am-2pm Sat; Ⓜ Jaume I) is just opposite the northeast end of Port Vell at Plaça d'Antoni López. Another handy **post office branch** (Carrer d'Aragó 282; ☺8.30am-8.30pm Mon-Fri,

9.30am-1pm Sat; Ⓜ Passeig de Gràcia) lies just off Passeig de Gràcia at Carrer d'Aragó 282. Many other branches tend to open between 8.30am and 2.30pm Monday to Friday and from 9.30am to 1pm on Saturday.

Segells/sellos (stamps) are sold at most *estancos* (tobacconists' shops) and at post offices throughout the city.

Safe Travel

It cannot be stressed enough that newcomers to Barcelona must be on their guard. Petty theft is a problem in the city centre, on public transport and around main sights. Report thefts to the national police. You are unlikely to recover your goods but you will need to make this formal *denuncia* (police report) for insurance purposes. To avoid endless queues at the *comisaría* (police station), you can make the report by phone (☎90 210 21 12) in various languages. The following day you go to the station of your choice to pick

up and sign the report (for a list of *comisarías*, go to the website www.policia.es under 'Denuncias'). There's a handy (and busy) **police station** (☎088; Carrer Nou de la Rambla 80; Ⓜ Paral.lel) near La Rambla and you can also report petty crime online at www.policia.es/denuncias. You could also try the **Guàrdia Urbana** (local police; ☎092; La Rambla 43; Ⓜ Liceu).

Taxes & Refunds

Value-added tax, or VAT, is also known as IVA (*impuesto sobre el valor añadido,* pronounced 'EE-ba'). IVA is 8% on accommodation and restaurant prices and is usually – but not always – included in quoted prices. On most retail goods the IVA is 16%. IVA-free shopping is available in duty-free shops at all airports for people travelling between EU countries.

Non-EU residents are entitled to a refund of the 18% IVA (expected to rise to 20% in 2013) on purchases costing more than €90 from any shop, if the goods are taken out of the EU within three months. Ask the shop for a Cashback (or similar) refund form showing the price and IVA paid for each item and identifying the vendor and purchaser. Then present the form at the customs booth for IVA refunds when you depart from Spain (or elsewhere in the EU). You will need your passport and a boarding card that shows you are leaving the EU, and your luggage (so do this before checking in bags). The officer will stamp the invoice and you hand it in at a bank at the departure point to receive a reimbursement.

Telephones

Public telephones The ubiquitous blue payphones are easy to use for international and domestic calls. They accept coins, *tarjetas telefónicas* (phonecards) issued by the national phone company Telefónica and, in some cases, credit cards. *Tarjetas telefónicas* are sold at post offices and tobacconists.

Call centres A few *Locutorios*, which also double as internet centres, are scattered around El Raval (look around Carrer de Sant Pau and Carrer de l'Hospital). Check rates before making calls.

Making calls To call Barcelona from outside Spain, dial the international access code, followed by the code for Spain (34) and the full number (including Barcelona's area code, 93, which is an integral part of the number). To make an interna-

tional call, dial the international access code (00), country code, area code and number.

Mobile Phones
Mobile-phone numbers start with 6 or 7. Numbers starting with 900 are national toll-free numbers, while those starting with numbers between 901 and 905 come with varying conditions. A common one is 902, which is a national standard-rate number. In a similar category are numbers starting with 803, 806 and 807.

Spain uses GSM 900/1800, compatible with the rest of Europe and Australia but not with the North American GSM 1900 or the system used in Japan. If your phone is tri- or quadriband, you will probably be fine. You can buy SIM cards and prepaid call time in Spain for your own national mobile phone (provided what you own is a GSM, dual- or tri-band cellular phone and not code-blocked). You will need your passport to open any kind of mobile-phone account, prepaid or otherwise.

Time

Spain is one hour ahead of GMT/UTC during winter, and two hours ahead during daylight saving (the last Sunday in March to the last Sunday in October). Most other western European countries are on the same time as Spain year-round. The UK, Ireland and Portugal are one hour behind. Spaniards use the 24-hour clock for official business (timetables etc) but generally

switch to the 12-hour version in daily conversation.

Tourist Information

Several tourist offices operate in Barcelona. A couple of general information telephone numbers worth bearing in mind are ☎010 and ☎012. The first is for Barcelona and the other is for all Catalonia (run by the Generalitat). You sometimes strike English speakers, although for the most part operators are Catalan/Spanish bilingual. In addition to tourist offices, information booths operate at Estació del Nord bus station and at Portal de la Pau, at the foot of the Mirador de Colom at the port end of La Rambla. Others set up at various points in the city centre in summer.

Plaça de Catalunya (☎93 285 38 34; www.barcelonaturisme.com; underground at Plaça de Catalunya 17-S; ◷8.30am-8.30pm; Ⓜ Catalunya)

Plaça de Sant Jaume (☎93 285 38 32; Carrer de la Ciutat 2; ◷8.30am-8.30pm Mon-Fri, 9am-7pm Sat, 9am-2pm Sun & holidays; Ⓜ Jaume I)

Estació Sants (Estació Sants; ◷8am-8pm; 圓 Estació Sants)

El Prat Airport (El Prat Airport; El Prat Airport, Terminal 1 arrivals, Terminal 2B arrivals hall, Terminal 2A arrivals hall; ◷9am-9pm)

La Rambla Information Office (www.barcelonaturisme.com; La Rambla dels Estudis 115; ◷8.30am-8.30pm; Ⓜ Liceu)

Palau Robert Regional Tourist Office (☎93 238 80 91, from outside Catalonia 902 400012; www.gencat.net/probert; Passeig de Gràcia 107; ◷10am-8pm Mon-Sat, 10am-2.30pm Sun) Audiovisual

OPERATOR SERVICES

International operator for reverse-charge calls	☎1408
International directory enquiries	☎11825
Domestic operator for a domestic reverse-charge call (llamada por cobro revertido)	☎1409
National directory inquiries	☎11818

resources, a bookshop and a branch of Turisme Juvenil de Catalunya (for youth travel).

Travellers with Disabilities

Some hotels and public institutions have wheelchair access. All buses in Barcelona are wheelchair accessible and a growing number of Metro stations are theoretically wheelchair accessible (generally by lift, although there have been complaints that they are only any good for parents with prams). Lines 2, 9, 10 and 11 are completely adapted, as are the majority of stops on 1. In all, about 80% of stops have been adapted (you can check which ones by looking at a network map here: www.tmb.cat/en/transport-accessible). Ticket vending machines in Metro stations are adapted for the disabled and have Braille options for the blind.

Several taxi companies have adapted vehicles including **Taxi Amic** (☑93 420 80 88; www.taxi-amic-adaptat.com), Gestverd (93 303 09 09) and T033 Ràdio Taxi (93 303 09 09).

Most street crossings in central Barcelona are wheelchair-friendly.

For more information on what the city is doing to improve accessibility check out the council's *Accessible Barcelona Guide* in several languages (www.barcelona-access.com).

ONCE (☑93 325 92 00; Carrer de Sepúlveda 1; Ⓜ️Plaça d'Espanya) is a national organisation for the vision-impaired, which can help with information, including lists of places such as restaurants where Braille menus are provided.

Visas

Spain is one of 25 member countries of the Schengen Convention, under which 22 EU countries (all but Bulgaria, Cyprus, Ireland, Romania and the UK) plus Iceland, Norway and Switzerland have abolished checks at common borders.

EU nationals require only their ID cards to visit Spain. Nationals of many other countries, including Australia, Canada, Israel, Japan, New Zealand and the USA, do not require visas for tourist visits to Spain of up to 90 days. Non-EU nationals who are legal residents of one Schengen country do not require a visa to visit another Schengen country.

All non-EU nationals entering Spain for any reason other than tourism (such as study or work) should contact a Spanish consulate, as they may need a specific visa and will have to obtain work and/or residence permits. Citizens of countries not mentioned above should check with their Spanish consulate whether they need a visa.

Women Travellers

Think twice about going by yourself to isolated stretches of beach or down empty city streets at night. It's inadvisable for women to hitchhike – either alone or in pairs.

Topless bathing is OK on beaches in Catalonia and also at swimming pools. While skimpy clothing tends not to attract much attention in Barcelona and the coastal resorts, tastes in inland Catalonia tend to be somewhat conservative.

Ca la Dona (☑93 412 71 61; www.caladona.org; Carrer de Casp 38; Ⓜ️Catalunya) The nerve centre of the region's feminist movement, Ca la Dona (Women's Home) includes many diverse women's groups.

Centre Francesca Bonnemaison (☑93 268 42 18; www.bonnemaison-ccd.org; Carrer de Sant Pere més Baix 7; Ⓜ️Urquinaona) A women's cultural centre where groups put on expositions, stage theatre productions and carry out other cultural activities.

Institut Català de la Dona (☑93 495 16 00; www.gencat.net/icdona; Plaça de Pere Coromines1; Ⓜ️Liceu) It can direct you to information on marriage, divorce, rape/assault counselling and related issues. The hotline for assault victims is ☑90 090 01 20.

Language

Catalan (*català*) and Spanish (*español,* more precisely known as *castellano,* or Castilian) both have official-language status in Catalonia. Aranese (*aranés*), which is a dialect of Gascon, is also an official language in the Val d'Aran. In Barcelona, you'll hear as much Spanish as Catalan, so we've provided some Spanish as well as Catalan basics here to get you started.

Most Spanish sounds are pronounced the same as their English counterparts. If you follow our coloured pronunciation guides, you'll be understood. Note that the kh is a throaty sound (like the 'ch' in the Scottish *loch*), ly is pronounced as the 'lli' in 'million', ny as the 'ni' in 'onion', th is pronounced with a lisp, and r is strongly rolled. In our pronunciation guides, the stressed syllables are in italics.

Where necessary, masculine and feminine forms are given for the words and phrases in this chapter, separated by a slash and with the masculine form first, eg *perdido/a* (m/f). Where both polite and informal options are given, they are indicated by the abbreviations 'pol' and 'inf' respectively.

BASICS

Hello.	Hola.	o·la
Goodbye.	Adiós.	a·dyos
How are you?	¿Qué tal?	ke tal
Fine, thanks.	Bien, gracias.	byen gra·thyas
Excuse me.	Perdón.	per·don
Sorry.	Lo siento.	lo see·en·to
Yes./No.	Sí./No.	see/no

Please.	Por favor.	por fa·vor
Thank you.	Gracias.	gra·thyas
You're welcome.	De nada.	de na·da

My name is ...
Me llamo ... — me *lya·*mo ...

What's your name?
¿Cómo se llama Usted? — ko·mo se *lya·*ma oo·ste (pol)
¿Cómo te llamas? — ko·mo te *lya·*mas (inf)

Do you speak (English)?
¿Habla (inglés)? — a·bla (een·gles) (pol)
¿Hablas (inglés)? — a·blas (een·gles) (inf)

I (don't) understand.
Yo (no) entiendo. — yo (no) en·tyen·do

ACCOMMODATION

I'd like to book a room.
Quisiera reservar una habitación. — kee·sye·ra re·ser·var oo·na a·bee·ta·thyon

How much is it per night/person?
¿Cuánto cuesta por noche/persona? — kwan·to kwes·ta por no·che/per·so·na

Does it include breakfast?
¿Incluye el desayuno? — een·kloo·ye el de·sa·yoo·no

hotel	hotel	o·tel
guesthouse	pensión	pen·syon
youth hostel	albergue juvenil	al·ber·ge khoo·ve·neel

I'd like a ... room.	Quisiera una habitación ...	kee·sye·ra oo·na a·bee·ta·thyon ...
single	individual	een·dee·vee·dwal
double	doble	do·ble

air-con	aire acondicionado	ai·re a·kon·dee·thyo·na·do
bathroom	baño	ba·nyo
window	ventana	ven·ta·na

KEY PATTERNS

To get by in Spanish, mix and match these simple patterns with words of your choice:

When's (the next flight)?
¿Cuándo sale   kwan·do sa·le
(el próximo vuelo)?   (el prok·see·mo vwe·lo)

Where's (the station)?
¿Dónde está   don·de es·ta
(la estación)?   (la es·ta·thyon)

Where can I (buy a ticket)?
¿Dónde puedo   don·de pwe·do
(comprar   (kom·prar
un billete)?   oon bee·lye·te)

Do you have (a map)?
¿Tiene (un mapa)?   tye·ne (oon ma·pa)

Is there (a toilet)?
¿Hay (servicios)?   ai (ser·vee·thyos)

I'd like (a coffee).
Quisiera (un café).   kee·sye·ra (oon ka·fe)

I'd like (to hire a car).
Quisiera (alquilar   kee·sye·ra (al·kee·lar
un coche).   oon ko·che)

Can I (enter)?
¿Se puede (entrar)?   se pwe·de (en·trar)

Could you please (help me)?
¿Puede (ayudarme),   pwe·de (a·yoo·dar·me)
por favor?   por fa·vor

Do I have to (get a visa)?
¿Necesito   ne·the·see·to
(obtener   (ob·te·ner
un visado)?   oon vee·sa·do)

DIRECTIONS

Where's ...?
¿Dónde está ...?   don·de es·ta ...

What's the address?
¿Cuál es la dirección? kwal es la dee·rek·thyon

Could you please write it down?
¿Puede escribirlo,   pwe·de es·kree·beer·lo
por favor?   por fa·vor

Can you show me (on the map)?
¿Me lo puede indicar me lo pwe·de een·dee·kar
(en el mapa)?   (en el ma·pa)

at the corner	en la esquina	en la es·kee·na
at the traffic lights	en el semáforo	en el se·ma·fo·ro
behind	detrás de	de·tras de
far (away)	lejos	le·khos
in front of	enfrente de	en·fren·te de
left	izquierda	eeth·kyer·da
near	cerca	ther·ka
next to	al lado de	al la·do de
opposite	frente a	fren·te a
right	derecha	de·re·cha
straight ahead	todo recto	to·do rek·to

EATING & DRINKING

I'd like to   Quisiera   kee·sye·ra
book a table   reservar una   re·ser·var oo·na
for ...   mesa para ...   me·sa pa·ra ...

  (eight) o'clock las (ocho)   las (o·cho)

  (two) people   (dos)   (dos)
                       personas   per·so·nas

What would you recommend?
¿Qué recomienda?   ke re·ko·myen·da

What's in that dish?
¿Que lleva ese plato? ke lye·va e·se pla·to

I don't eat ...
No como ...   no ko·mo ...

Cheers!
¡Salud!   sa·loo

That was delicious!
¡Estaba buenísimo!   es·ta·ba bwe·nee·see·mo

Please bring the bill.
Por favor nos trae   por fa·vor nos tra·e
la cuenta.   la kwen·ta

Key Words

appetisers	aperitivos	a·pe·ree·tee·vos
bar	bar	bar
bottle	botella	bo·te·lya
bowl	bol	bol
breakfast	desayuno	de·sa·yoo·no
cafe	café	ka·fe
children's menu	menú infantil	me·noo een·fan·teel
(too/very) cold	(muy) frío	(mooy) free·o
dinner	cena	the·na
food	comida	ko·mee·da
fork	tenedor	te·ne·dor
glass	vaso	va·so
highchair	trona	tro·na
hot (warm)	caliente	ka·lyen·te
knife	cuchillo	koo·chee·lyo
lunch	comida	ko·mee·da
main course	segundo plato	se·goon·do pla·to
market	mercado	mer·ka·do
menu (in English)	menú (en inglés)	oon me·noo (en een·gles)

CATALAN

The recognition of Catalan as an official language in Spain is the end result of a regional government campaign that began when the province gained autonomy at the end of the 1970s. Until the Battle of Muret in 1213, Catalan territory extended across southern France, taking in Roussillon and reaching into the Provence. Catalan was spoken, or at least understood, throughout these territories and in what is now Catalonia and Andorra. In the couple of hundred years that followed, the Catalans spread their language south into Valencia, west into Aragón and east to the Balearic Islands. The language also reached Sicily and Naples, and the Sardinian town of Alghero is still a partly Catalan-speaking outpost today. Catalan is spoken by up to 10 million people in Spain.

In Barcelona you'll hear as much Spanish as Catalan. Your chances of coming across English speakers are also good. Elsewhere in the province, don't be surprised if you get replies in Catalan to your questions in Spanish. However, you'll find that most Catalans will happily speak to you in Spanish, especially once they realise you're a foreigner. This said, the following Catalan phrases might win you a few smiles and perhaps help you make some new friends.

Hello.	*Hola.*	**Monday**	*dilluns*
Goodbye.	*Adéu.*	**Tuesday**	*dimarts*
Yes.	*Sí.*	**Wednesday**	*dimecres*
No.	*No.*	**Thursday**	*dijous*
Please.	*Sisplau./Si us plau.*	**Friday**	*divendres*
Thank you (very much).	*(Moltes) gràcies.*	**Saturday**	*dissabte*
You're welcome.	*De res.*	**Sunday**	*diumenge*
Excuse me.	*Perdoni.*		
May I?/Do you mind?	*Puc?/Em permet?*	**1**	*un/una* (m/f)
I'm sorry.	*Ho sento./Perdoni.*	**2**	*dos/dues* (m/f)
		3	*tres*
What's your name?	*Com et dius?* (inf)	**4**	*quatre*
	Com es diu? (pol)	**5**	*cinc*
My name is ...	*Em dic ...*	**6**	*sis*
Where are you from?	*D'on ets?*	**7**	*set*
Do you speak English?	*Parla anglès?*	**8**	*vuit*
I understand.	*Ho entenc.*	**9**	*nou*
I don't understand.	*No ho entenc.*	**10**	*deu*
Could you speak in	*Pot parlar castellà*	**11**	*onze*
Castilian, please?	*sisplau?*	**12**	*dotze*
How do you say ... in	*Com es diu ... en*	**13**	*tretze*
Catalan?	*català?*	**14**	*catorze*
		15	*quinze*
I'm looking for ...	*Estic buscant ...*	**16**	*setze*
How do I get to ...?	*Com puc arribar a ...?*	**17**	*disset*
Turn left.	*Giri a mà esquerra.*	**18**	*divuit*
Turn right.	*Giri a mà dreta.*	**19**	*dinou*
near	*a prop de*	**20**	*vint*
far	*a lluny de*	**100**	*cent*

Signs	
Abierto	Open
Cerrado	Closed
Entrada	Entrance
Hombres	Men
Mujeres	Women
Prohibido	Prohibited
Salida	Exit
Servicios/Aseos	Toilets

plate	*plato*	*pla*·to
restaurant	*restaurante*	res·tow·*ran*·te
spoon	*cuchara*	koo·*cha*·ra
supermarket	*supermercado*	soo·per·mer·*ka*·do
vegetarian food	*comida vegetariana*	ko·*mee*·da ve·khe·ta·*rya*·na
with/without	*con/sin*	kon/seen

Meat & Fish

beef	*carne de vaca*	*kar*·ne de *va*·ka
chicken	*pollo*	*po*·lyo
duck	*pato*	*pa*·to
lamb	*cordero*	kor·*de*·ro
lobster	*langosta*	lan·*gos*·ta
pork	*cerdo*	*ther*·do
prawns	*camarones*	ka·ma·*ro*·nes
tuna	*atún*	a·*toon*
turkey	*pavo*	*pa*·vo
veal	*ternera*	ter·*ne*·ra

Fruit & Vegetables

apple	*manzana*	man·*tha*·na
apricot	*albaricoque*	al·ba·ree·*ko*·ke
artichoke	*alcachofa*	al·ka·*cho*·fa
asparagus	*espárragos*	es·*pa*·ra·gos
banana	*plátano*	*pla*·ta·no
beans	*judías*	khoo·*dee*·as
beetroot	*remolacha*	re·mo·*la*·cha
cabbage	*col*	kol
carrot	*zanahoria*	tha·na·o·*rya*
celery	*apio*	*a*·pyo
cherry	*cereza*	the·*re*·tha
corn	*maíz*	ma·*eeth*
cucumber	*pepino*	pe·*pee*·no
fruit	*fruta*	*froo*·ta
grape	*uvas*	*oo*·vas

lemon	*limón*	lee·*mon*
lentils	*lentejas*	len·*te*·khas
lettuce	*lechuga*	le·*choo*·ga
mushroom	*champiñón*	cham·pee·*nyon*
nuts	*nueces*	*nwe*·thes
onion	*cebolla*	the·*bo*·lya
orange	*naranja*	na·*ran*·kha
peach	*melocotón*	me·lo·ko·*ton*
peas	*guisantes*	gee·*san*·tes
(red/green) pepper	*pimiento (rojo/verde)*	pee·*myen*·to (*ro*·kho/*ver*·de)
pineapple	*piña*	*pee*·nya
plum	*ciruela*	theer·*we*·la
potato	*patata*	pa·*ta*·ta
pumpkin	*calabaza*	ka·la·*ba*·tha
spinach	*espinacas*	es·pee·*na*·kas
strawberry	*fresa*	*fre*·sa
tomato	*tomate*	to·*ma*·te
vegetable	*verdura*	ver·*doo*·ra
watermelon	*sandía*	san·*dee*·a

Other

bread	*pan*	pan
butter	*mantequilla*	man·te·*kee*·lya
cheese	*queso*	*ke*·so
egg	*huevo*	*we*·vo
honey	*miel*	myel
jam	*mermelada*	mer·me·*la*·da
oil	*aceite*	a·*they*·te
pasta	*pasta*	*pas*·ta
pepper	*pimienta*	pee·*myen*·ta
rice	*arroz*	a·*roth*
salt	*sal*	sal
sugar	*azúcar*	a·*thoo*·kar
vinegar	*vinagre*	vee·*na*·gre

Drinks

beer	*cerveza*	ther·*ve*·tha
coffee	*café*	ka·*fe*
(orange) juice	*zumo (de naranja)*	*thoo*·mo (de na·*ran*·kha)
milk	*leche*	*le*·che
tea	*té*	te
(mineral) water	*agua (mineral)*	*a*·gwa (mee·ne·*ral*)
(red) wine	*vino (tinto)*	*vee*·no (*teen*·to)
(white) wine	*vino (blanco)*	*vee*·no (*blan*·ko)

EMERGENCIES

Help!	*¡Socorro!*	so·ko·ro
Go away!	*¡Vete!*	ve·te
Call ...!	*¡Llame a ...!*	lya·me a ...
a doctor	*un médico*	oon me·dee·ko
the police	*la policía*	la po·lee·thee·a

I'm lost.
Estoy perdido/a. es·toy per·dee·do/a (m/f)

I had an accident.
He tenido un e te·nee·do oon
accidente. ak·thee·den·te

I'm ill.
Estoy enfermo/a. es·toy en·fer·mo/a (m/f)

It hurts here.
Me duele aquí. me dwe·le a·kee

I'm allergic to (antibiotics).
Soy alérgico/a a soy a·ler·khee·ko/a a
(los antibióticos). (los an·tee·byo·tee·kos) (m/f)

SHOPPING & SERVICES

I'd like to buy ...
Quisiera comprar ... kee·sye·ra kom·prar ...

I'm just looking.
Sólo estoy mirando. so·lo es·toy mee·ran·do

Can I look at it?
¿Puedo verlo? pwe·do ver·lo

I don't like it.
No me gusta. no me goos·ta

How much is it?
¿Cuánto cuesta? kwan·to kwes·ta

That's too expensive.
Es muy caro. es mooy ka·ro

Can you lower the price?
¿Podría bajar un po·dree·a ba·khar oon
poco el precio? po·ko el pre·thyo

There's a mistake in the bill.
Hay un error en ai oon e·ror en
la cuenta. la kwen·ta

ATM	*cajero*	ka·khe·ro
	automático	ow·to·ma·tee·ko
internet cafe	*cibercafé*	thee·ber·ka·fe
post office	*correos*	ko·re·os
tourist office	*oficina*	o·fee·thee·na
	de turismo	de too·rees·mo

TIME & DATES

What time is it?
¿Qué hora es? ke o·ra es

It's (10) o'clock.
Son (las diez). son (las dyeth)

Half past (one).
Es (la una) es (la oo·na)
y media. ee me·dya

morning	*mañana*	ma·nya·na
afternoon	*tarde*	tar·de
evening	*noche*	no·che
yesterday	*ayer*	a·yer
today	*hoy*	oy
tomorrow	*mañana*	ma·nya·na
Monday	*lunes*	loo·nes
Tuesday	*martes*	mar·tes
Wednesday	*miércoles*	myer·ko·les
Thursday	*jueves*	khwe·bes
Friday	*viernes*	vyer·nes
Saturday	*sábado*	sa·ba·do
Sunday	*domingo*	do·meen·go
January	*enero*	e·ne·ro
February	*febrero*	fe·bre·ro
March	*marzo*	mar·tho
April	*abril*	a·breel
May	*mayo*	ma·yo
June	*junio*	khoo·nyo
July	*julio*	khoo·lyo
August	*agosto*	a·gos·to
September	*septiembre*	sep·tyem·bre
October	*octubre*	ok·too·bre
November	*noviembre*	no·vyem·bre
December	*diciembre*	dee·thyem·bre

TRANSPORT

boat	*barco*	bar·ko
bus	*autobús*	ow·to·boos
plane	*avión*	a·vyon
train	*tren*	tren
first	*primer*	pree·mer
last	*último*	ool·tee·mo
next	*próximo*	prok·see·mo

Question Words

What?	*¿Qué?*	ke
When?	*¿Cuándo?*	kwan·do
Where?	*¿Dónde?*	don·de
Who?	*¿Quién?*	kyen
Why?	*¿Por qué?*	por ke

I want to go to ...
Quisiera ir a ... kee·sye·ra eer a ...

What time does it arrive/leave?
¿A qué hora llega/sale? a ke o·ra lye·ga/sa·le

Does it stop at ...?
¿Para en ...? pa·ra en ...

Can you tell me when we get to ...?
¿Puede avisarme pwe·de a·vee·sar·me
cuando lleguemos a ...? kwan·do lye·ge·mos a ...

What stop is this?
¿Cuál es esta parada? kwal es es·ta pa·ra·da

I want to get off here.
Quiero bajarme aquí. kye·ro ba·khar·me a·kee

a ... ticket	*un billete de ...*	oon bee·lye·te de ...
1st-class	*primera clase*	pree·me·ra kla·se
2nd-class	*segunda clase*	se·goon·da kla·se
one-way	*ida*	ee·da
return	*ida y vuelta*	ee·da ee vwel·ta
aisle seat	*asiento de pasillo*	a·syen·to de pa·see·lyo
cancelled	*cancelado*	kan·the·la·do
delayed	*retrasado*	re·tra·sa·do
platform	*plataforma*	pla·ta·for·ma
ticket office	*taquilla*	ta·kee·lya
timetable	*horario*	o·ra·ryo
train station	*estación de trenes*	es·ta·thyon de tre·nes
window seat	*asiento junto a la ventana*	a·syen·to khoon·to a la ven·ta·na
I'd like to hire a ...	*Quisiera alquilar ...*	kee·sye·ra al·kee·lar ...
bicycle	*una bicicleta*	oo·na bee·thee·kle·ta
car	*un coche*	oon ko·che
motorcycle	*una moto*	oo·na mo·to

Numbers

1	*uno*	oo·no
2	*dos*	dos
3	*tres*	tres
4	*cuatro*	kwa·tro
5	*cinco*	theen·ko
6	*seis*	seys
7	*siete*	sye·te
8	*ocho*	o·cho
9	*nueve*	nwe·ve
10	*diez*	dyeth
20	*veinte*	veyn·te
30	*treinta*	treyn·ta
40	*cuarenta*	kwa·ren·ta
50	*cincuenta*	theen·kwen·ta
60	*sesenta*	se·sen·ta
70	*setenta*	se·ten·ta
80	*ochenta*	o·chen·ta
90	*noventa*	no·ven·ta
100	*cien*	thyen
1000	*mil*	meel

diesel	*gasóleo*	ga·so·lyo
helmet	*casco*	kas·ko
mechanic	*mecánico*	me·ka·nee·ko
petrol/gas	*gasolina*	ga·so·lee·na
service station	*gasolinera*	ga·so·lee·ne·ra

(How long) Can I park here?
¿(Por cuánto tiempo) (por kwan·to tyem·po)
Puedo aparcar aquí? pwe·do a·par·kar a·kee

The car has broken down.
El coche se ha averiado. el ko·che se a a·ve·rya·do

I have a flat tyre.
Tengo un pinchazo. ten·go oon peen·cha·tho

I've run out of petrol.
Me he quedado sin gasolina. me e ke·da·do seen ga·so·lee·na

GLOSSARY

Items listed below are in Catalan/Spanish (Castilian) where they start with the same letter. Where the two terms start with different letters, or where only the Catalan or the Spanish term is provided, they are listed separately and marked (C) for Catalan or (S) for Spanish. If an entry is not marked at all, it is because it takes the same form in both languages.

ajuntament/ayuntamiento – town hall

artesonado (S) – Mudéjar wooden ceiling with interlaced beams leaving a pattern of spaces for decoration

avinguda (C) – avenue

barcelonin (C) – inhabitant/ native of Barcelona

Barcino – Roman name for Barcelona

barri/barrio – neighbourhood, quarter of Barcelona

caganer (C) – the crapper, a character appearing in Catalan nativity scenes

El Call (C) – the Jewish quarter in medieval Barcelona

capella/capilla – chapel

carrer/calle – street

casa – house

castellers (C) – human-castle builders

cercanías (S) – local trains serving Barcelona's airport, suburbs and some outlying towns

comte/conde – count

correfoc (C) – appearance of firework-spouting devils at festivals; literally 'fire runs'

església (C) – church

farmàcia/farmacia – pharmacy

festa/fiesta – festival, public holiday or party

FGC (C) – Ferrocarrils de la Generalitat de Catalunya; local trains operating alongside the Metro in Barcelona

fundació/fundació – foundation

garum – a spicy sauce made from fish entrails, found throughout the Roman Empire

gegants – huge figures paraded at *festes*

Generalitat (C) – Catalan regional government

guiri – foreigner (somewhat pejorative)

hostal – commercial establishment providing one- to three-star accommodation

iglesia (S) – church

IVA – *impost sobre el valor afegit/impuesto sobre el valor añadido*, or value-added tax

masia – Catalan country farmhouse

mercat/mercado – market

Modernisme (C) – the turn-of-the-19th-century artistic style, influenced by Art Nouveau, whose leading practitioner was Antoni Gaudí

Modernista – an exponent of Modernisme

Mudéjar (S) – a Muslim living under Christian rule in medieval Spain; also refers to their decorative style of architecture

palau (C) – palace

passatge (C) – laneway

pensió/pensión – commercial establishment providing one- to three-star accommodation

plaça/plaza – plaza

platja/playa – beach

Renaixença – rebirth of interest in Catalan literature, culture and language in the second half of the 19th century

rodalies (C) – see *cercanías*

saló (C) – hall

sardana – traditional Catalan folk dance

s/n (S) – *sin número* (without number)

tablao – restaurant where flamenco is performed

teatre – theatre

terrassa/terazza – terrace; often means a café or bar's outdoor tables

trencadís – a Modernista style of mosaic, created using broken tiles

turista – second class; economy class

Behind the Scenes

SEND US YOUR FEEDBACK

We love to hear from travellers – your comments keep us on our toes and help make our books better. Our well-travelled team reads every word on what you loved or loathed about this book. Although we cannot reply individually to postal submissions, we always guarantee that your feedback goes straight to the appropriate authors, in time for the next edition. Each person who sends us information is thanked in the next edition – the most useful submissions are rewarded with a selection of digital PDF chapters.

Visit **lonelyplanet.com/contact** to submit your updates and suggestions or to ask for help. Our award-winning website also features inspirational travel stories, news and discussions.

Note: We may edit, reproduce and incorporate your comments in Lonely Planet products such as guidebooks, websites and digital products, so let us know if you don't want your comments reproduced or your name acknowledged. For a copy of our privacy policy visit lonelyplanet.com/privacy.

OUR READERS

Many thanks to the travellers who used the last edition and wrote to us with helpful hints, useful advice and interesting anecdotes:

Badong Abesamis, David van Dam, Marcus Durham, Nicole Efron, Steve Groves, Vega Iodice, Gareth McGowan, Selin Tessa Ozalp, Björn Somell, Steve Tallantyre, Francis Vanoverschelde, Daniëlle Wolbers

AUTHOR THANKS

Regis St Louis

I'm grateful for all the great advice from locals, expats and tourism staff. In particular, I'd like to thank Eric Mills, Sol Polo, Maria Asuncion Guardia, Margherita Bergamo Meneghini, Meritxell Checa Esteban and friends, Carine Ferry and friends, Laura of Runner Bean, and Diego in Barri Gòtic. Thanks also go to my editors Dora Whitaker and Angela Tinson, to co-author Vesna for tips on the road and Anna for her keen eye for getaways. Finally, big hugs to my family for their continued support.

Anna Kaminski

On the road, thanks to my long-suffering flatmates Pedrito and Andrea, to Dawn for submitting to my relentless schedule like a trooper, to everyone who's cooked for me along the way, to all the helpful tourist office staff (particularly in Girona), and to the lady in that bookshop in Tarragona for procuring for me a Catalonia road atlas that seems to be rarer than gold dust. Finally, a huge thank you to Dora for this assignment, and to Regis and Vesna for all their hard work.

Vesna Maric

Thanks go to Rafael, as always, for all the help, support and fun. *Hvala* to my mother and sister for babysitting help. Big thanks to my lovely Frida for being such a great traveller. Great thanks to Dora Whitaker and Regis St Louis – it was a pleasure to work with you. Most fervent thanks of all go to David Carroll and the dedicated SPP team in Melbourne for their tireless support and middle-of-the-night emails when technology was being uncooperative.

ACKNOWLEDGMENTS

Cover photograph: Font Màgica at night, Palau Nacional, Montjuïc, David Noton/Alamy. Barcelona Metro map © Ferrocarril Metropolita de Barcelona, S.A. Tots els drets reservats. Ilustrations pp136-7, pp186-7 by Javier Zarracina.

THIS BOOK

This 8th edition of Lonely Planet's *Barcelona* guidebook was researched and written by Regis St Louis, Anna Kaminski and Vesna Maric. The previous seven editions were written by Damien Simonis. This guidebook was commissioned in Lonely Planet's London office, and produced by the following:

Commissioning Editor Dora Whitaker

Coordinating Editor Mardi O'Connor

Coordinating Cartographer Alex Leung

Coordinating Layout Designer Jacqui Saunders

Managing Editors Barbara Delissen, Angela Tinson

Managing Cartographers Shahara Ahmed, Adrian Persoglia

Managing Layout Designer Jane Hart

Assisting Editors Laura Gibb, Elizabeth Harvey, Kate Morgan, Joanne Newell, Charlotte Orr

Cover Research Naomi Parker

Internal Image Research Louise Byrnes

Illustrator Javier Zarracina

Language Content Branislava Vladisavljevic

Thanks to Dan Austin, Imogen Bannister, Laura Crawford, Ryan Evans, Tobias Gattineau, Jouve India, Asha Ioculari, Sophie Marozeau, Kate McDonell, Andrea McGinniss, Annelies Mertens, Trent Paton, Averil Robertson, Silvia Rosas, Amanda Sierp, Fiona Siseman, Rob Townsend, Gerard Walker

BEHIND THE SCENES

Index

See also separate subindexes for:

✗ EATING P286

🍷 DRINKING & NIGHTLIFE P287

☆ ENTERTAINMENT P287

🛍 SHOPPING P288

🏃 SPORTS & ACTIVITIES P288

🛏 SLEEPING P288

Sights 000
Map Pages **000**
Photo Pages **000**

✕ EATING

🛍 SHOPPING

🏃 SPORTS & ACTIVITIES

🛏 SLEEPING

Barcelona Maps

Map Legend

Sights
- Beach
- Buddhist
- Castle
- Christian
- Hindu
- Islamic
- Jewish
- Monument
- Museum/Gallery
- Ruin
- Winery/Vineyard
- Zoo
- Other Sight

Eating
- Eating

Drinking & Nightlife
- Drinking & Nightlife
- Cafe

Entertainment
- Entertainment

Shopping
- Shopping

Sleeping
- Sleeping
- Camping

Sports & Activities
- Diving/Snorkelling
- Canoeing/Kayaking
- Skiing
- Surfing
- Swimming/Pool
- Walking
- Windsurfing
- Other Sports & Activities

Information
- Post Office
- Tourist Information

Transport
- Airport
- Border Crossing
- Bus
- Cable Car/Funicular
- Cycling
- Ferry
- Metro
- Monorail
- Parking
- S-Bahn
- Taxi
- Train/Railway
- Tram
- Tube Station
- U-Bahn
- Other Transport

Routes
- Tollway
- Freeway
- Primary
- Secondary
- Tertiary
- Lane
- Unsealed Road
- Plaza/Mall
- Steps
- Tunnel
- Pedestrian Overpass
- Walking Tour
- Walking Tour Detour
- Path

Boundaries
- International
- State/Province
- Disputed
- Regional/Suburb
- Marine Park
- Cliff
- Wall

Geographic
- Hut/Shelter
- Lighthouse
- Lookout
- Mountain/Volcano
- Oasis
- Park
- Pass
- Picnic Area
- Waterfall

Hydrography
- River/Creek
- Intermittent River
- Swamp/Mangrove
- Reef
- Canal
- Water
- Dry/Salt/Intermittent Lake
- Glacier

Areas
- Beach/Desert
- Cemetery (Christian)
- Cemetery (Other)
- Park/Forest
- Sportsground
- Sight (Building)
- Top Sight (Building)

MAP INDEX

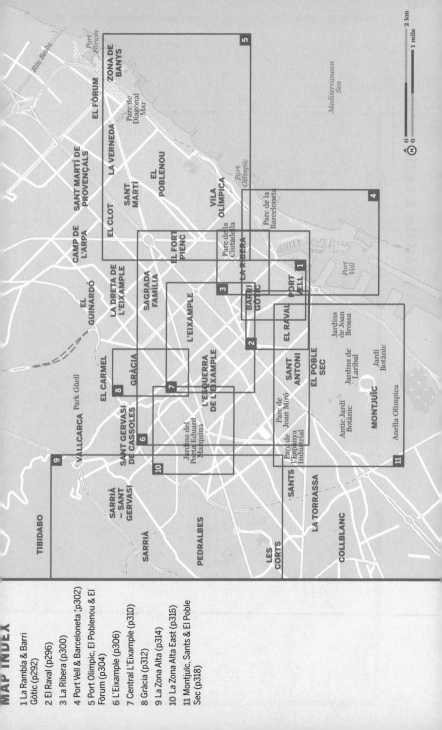

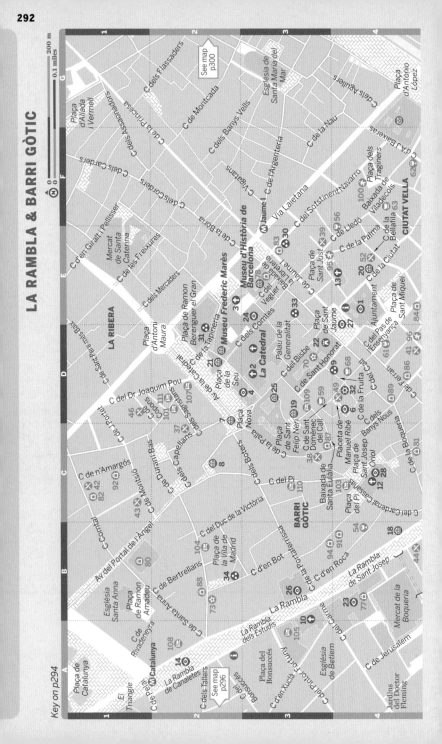

LA RAMBLA & BARRI GÒTIC

Key on p294

See map p300

See map p296

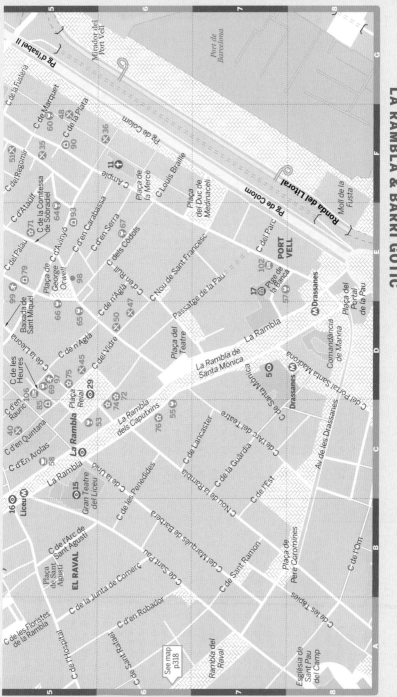

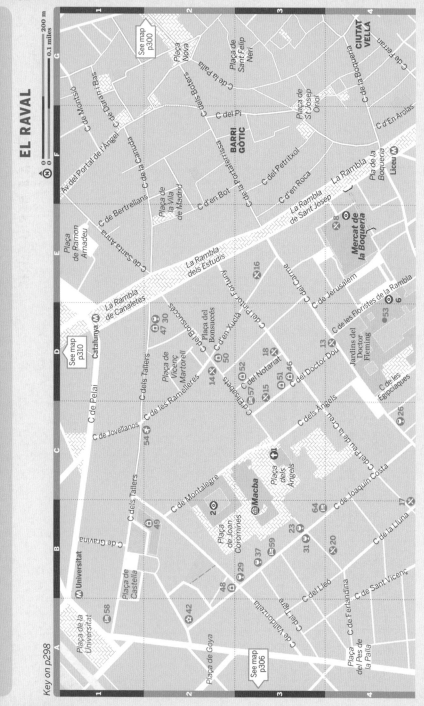

EL RAVAL

Key on p298

See map p300

See map p310

See map p306

BARRI GÒTIC

CIUTAT VELLA

Macba

Mercat de la Boqueria

Plaça de la Universitat

Plaça de Castella

Plaça de Goya

Plaça de Joan Coromines

Plaça dels Àngels

Plaça de Vicenç Martorell

Plaça del Bonsuccés

Plaça de la Vila de Madrid

Plaça de Ramon Amadeu

Plaça Nova

Plaça de Sant Felip Neri

Plaça de St Josep Oriol

Plaça del Pes de la Palla

Jardins del Doctor Fleming

Pla de la Boqueria

La Rambla de Canaletes

La Rambla dels Estudis

La Rambla de Sant Josep

La Rambla

M Universitat

M Catalunya

M Liceu

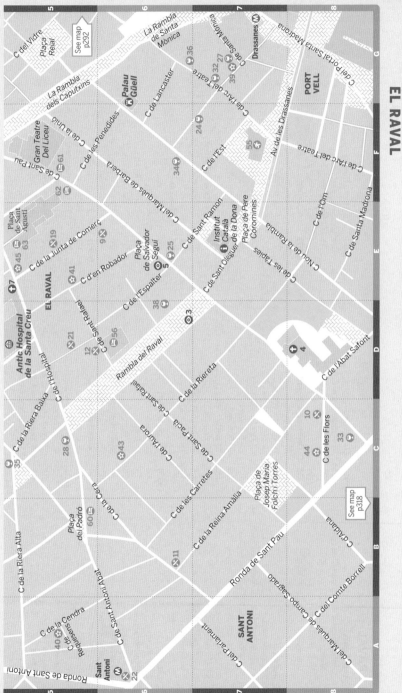

EL RAVAL

See map p292

La Rambla de Santa Mònica

Drassanes Ⓜ
C de Santa Mònica

C del Vidre
Plaça Reial

36 Ⓒ
32 Ⓒ 27 Ⓒ
39 Ⓒ
C de l'Arc del Teatre

La Rambla dels Caputxins

Palau Güell Ⓜ

C de Lancaster

PORT VELL
C del Portal Santa Madrona

La Rambla dels Caputxins

24 Ⓒ

C de l'Arc del Teatre

Av de les Drassanes

Gran Teatre Del Liceu Ⓜ
C de la Unió
C de Sant Pau
61 Ⓒ
C de les Penedides
34 Ⓒ
C de l'Est

55 Ⓒ

C de l'Om
C de Santa Madrona

62 Ⓒ

C del Marquès de Barberà

C de Sant Ramon
Institut Català ⓘ
Plaça de Pere Coromines

Plaça de Sant Agustí
45 Ⓒ 19 Ⓒ
63 Ⓒ
C de la Junta de Comerç
9 Ⓒ
Plaça de Salvador Seguí
25 Ⓒ
C de Sant Oleguer
C de Sant Ramon

7 Ⓒ
41 Ⓒ
EL RAVAL
C d'en Robador
5 Ⓒ

C de les Tàpies
C Nou de la Rambla

Antic Hospital de la Santa Creu

C de l'Espalter
38 Ⓒ

21 Ⓒ
12 Ⓒ 56 Ⓒ
3 Ⓒ

C de l'Abat Safont
4 Ⓒ

Rambla del Raval

C de la Riera Baixa
C de l'Hospital

C de Sant Rafael

C de la Riereta

35 Ⓒ
28 Ⓒ

C de l'Aurora

C de Sant Pacià
C de Sant Rafael

10 Ⓒ
33 Ⓒ
C de les Flors
44 Ⓒ

43 Ⓒ

C de les Carretes

Plaça de Josep Maria Folch i Torres

See map p318

C de la Riera Alta

Plaça del Padró
60 Ⓒ
C de la Cera

C de la Reina Amàlia

C d'Aldana

C del Marquès de Campo Sagrado
C del Comte Borrell

40 Ⓒ
C de la Cendra
C de Requesens
C de Sant Antoni Abat

11 Ⓒ

SANT ANTONI

C del Parlament

Ronda de Sant Pau

Sant Antoni Ⓜ
22 Ⓒ
Ronda de Sant Antoni

EL RAVAL *Map on p296*

LA RIBERA

Key on p299

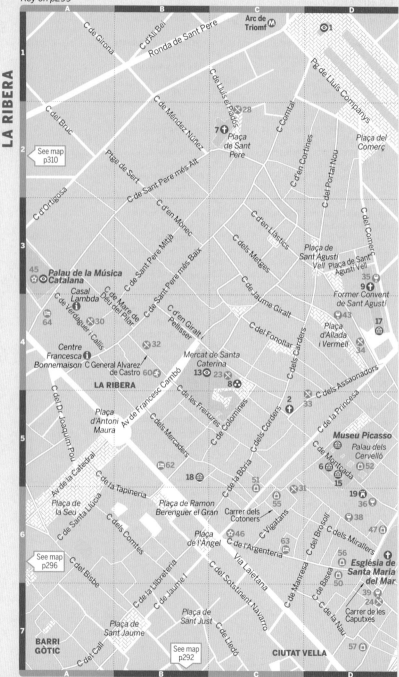

LA RIBERA

See map
p310

C de Girona
C d'Alí Bei
Ronda de Sant Pere
Arc de Triomf
1

C del Bruc
C de Méndez Núñez
C de Lluís el Piadós
28
7
Plaça de Sant Pere
C Comtal
Pg de Lluís Companys
Plaça del Comerç

Ptge de Sert
C de Sant Pere més Alt
C d'en Cortines
C del Portal Nou
C del Comerç

C d'Ortigosa
C d'en Monec
C d'en Llàstics
Plaça de Sant Agustí Vell
Plaça de Sant Agustí Vell

45
Palau de la Música Catalana
Casal Lambda
C de Verdaguer i Callís
C de Mare de Déu del Pilar
C de Sant Pere Mitjà
C de Sant Pere més Baix
C dels Metges
C de Jaume Giralt
9
Former Convent de Sant Agustí
35
43
17

64
30
C d'en Giralt i Pellisser
C del Fonollar
Plaça d'Allada i Vermell
34

Centre Francesca Bonnemaison
32
C General Alvarez de Castro
60
Mercat de Santa Caterina
13 23
C dels Carders
C dels Assaonadors

LA RIBERA
Av de Francesc Cambó
8
C de les Freixures
C de Colomines
C dels Corders
2
33
C de la Princesa

Plaça d'Antoni Maura
C dels Mercaders
Museu Picasso
Palau dels Cervelló
6
52
15
C de Montcada

62
C de la Bòria
18
51
55
31
19
36
38
47

C de la Tapineria
Plaça de Ramon Berenguer el Gran
Carrer dels Cotoners
C Vigatans
63
C de Manresa
C dels Mirallers
56

Plaça de la Seu
C de Santa Llúcia
C dels Comtes
Plaça de l'Àngel
46
C de l'Argenteria
Via Laietana
50
Església de Santa Maria del Mar

C del Dr Joaquim Pou
Av de la Catedral

See map
p296

C del Bisbe
C de la Llibreteria
C de Jaume I
C del Sotstinent Navarro
C de la Nau
C de Basea
C de Bro-solí
39
24
Carrer de les Caputxes

Plaça de Sant Jaume
Plaça de Sant Just
C de Lledó
57

BARRI GÒTIC
C del Call

Plaça de Sant Jaume

See map
p292

CIUTAT VELLA

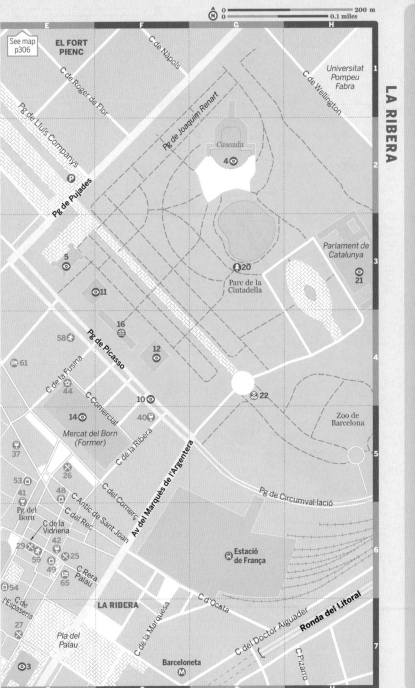

LA RIBERA

200 m
0.1 miles

See map
p306

EL FORT
PIENC

C de Nàpois

C de Roger de Flor

Universitat
Pompeu
Fabra

C de Wellington

Pg de Lluís Companys

Pg de Joaquim Renart

Cascada

4

Pg de Pujades

Parlament de
Catalunya

5

20

21

11

Parc de la
Ciutadella

58

16

Pg de Picasso

12

61

C de la Fusina

44

C Comercial

10

14

40

Mercat del Born
(Former)

C de la Ribera

Zoo de
Barcelona

37

26

Pg de Circumval·lació

53

41

48

C Antic de Sant Joan

C del Comerç

Av del Marquès de l'Argentera

Pg del
Born

C del Rec

29

42

59

25

49

C de la
Vidrieria

C Rera
Palau

65

Estació
de França

54

C de
l'Espaseria

LA RIBERA

C de la Marquesa

C d'Ocata

Ronda del Litoral

27

Pla del
Palau

C del Doctor Aiguader

C Pizarro

3

Barceloneta

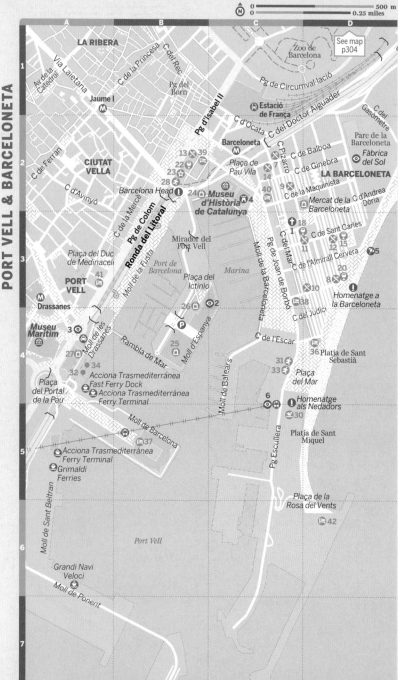

PORT VELL & BARCELONETA

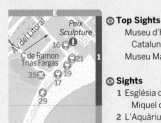

PORT VELL & BARCELONETA

PORT OLIMPIC, EL POBLENOU & EL FÒRUM

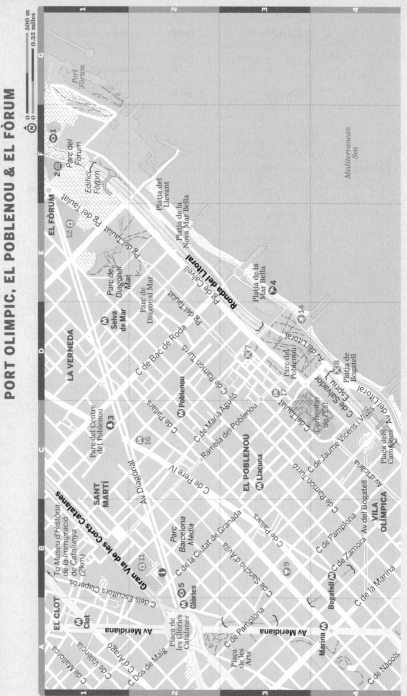

0 500 m
0 0.25 miles

Mediterranean Sea

EL FÒRUM

Port Fòrum
Parc del Fòrum
Edifici Fòrum

Platja del Llevant
Platja de la Nova Mar Bella

Parc de Diagonal Mar
Parc de Diagonal Mar
Pg de del Taulat

LA VERNEDA

Selva de Mar

Platja de la Mar Bella

Ronda del Litoral
Pg de Calvell
Pg del Taulat

C de Bac de Roda
C de Ramon Turró
Av del Litoral

Parc del Centre del Poblenou

Poblenou

C de Palais
C de Marià Aguiló
Rambla del Poblenou

Parc del Poblenou
Cementiri del Est
C de Salvador Espriu

Platja de Bogatell
Platja del Litoral

SANT MARTÍ

Av Diagonal
C de Pere IV

EL POBLENOU

Llacuna

C de Ramon Turró

Plaça dels Campions

Parc Barcelona Mèdia

C de la Ciutat de Granada
C de Palais
C de Pamplona

C de Jaume Vicens i Vives

Av d'Icària

VILA OLÍMPICA

EL CLOT

Clot

Gran Via de les Corts Catalanes

To Museu d'Història de la Immigració de Catalunya (2km)

C dels Escultors Claperós
C de Sancho d'Àvila

Av Meridiana

Bogatell
C de Zamora
Av del Bogatell

C de Mallorca
C de València
C d'Aragó
C Dos de Maig

Plaça de les Glòries Catalanes
Glòries

Plaça de les Arts

C de Pamplona

Av Meridiana

Marina
C de la Marina
C de Nàpols

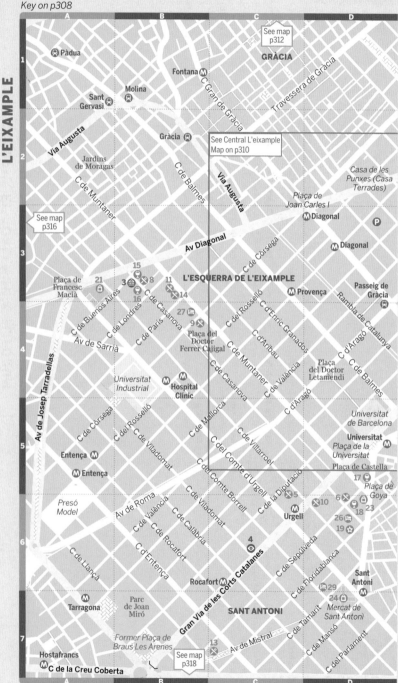

Key on p308

L'EIXAMPLE

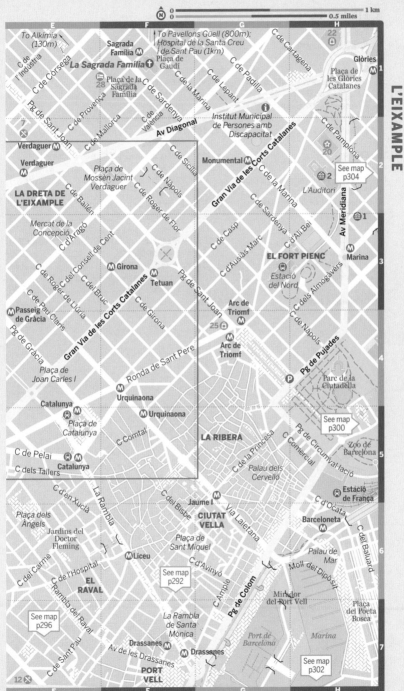

To Alkímia (130m)

To Pavellons Güell (800m); Hospital de la Santa Creu i de Sant Pau (1km)

Sagrada Família

La Sagrada Família

Plaça de Gaudí

C de l'Indústria

C de Còrsega

28

Plaça de la Sagrada Família

C de Sardenya

C de la Marina

C de Lepant

C de Padilla

C de Cartagena

22

Glòries

Plaça de les Glòries Catalanes

Pg de Sant Joan

C de Provença

C de Mallorca

C de València

Av Diagonal

Institut Municipal de Persones amb Discapacitat

C de Pamplona

Verdaguer

Verdaguer

LA DRETA DE L'EIXAMPLE

Plaça de Mossèn Jacint Verdaguer

C de Bailén

C de Nàpols

C de Sicília

C de Roger de Flor

Monumental

Gran Via de les Corts Catalanes

C de la Marina

20

See map p304

2

L'Auditori

Mercat de la Concepció

C d'Aragó

C del Consell de Cent

C de Casp

C de Sardenya

1

C de Roger de Llúria

C del Bruc

Girona

Tetuan

C d'Ausiàs Marc

C d'Alí Bei

EL FORT PIENC

Marina

C de Pau Claris

Passeig de Gràcia

Gran Via de les Corts Catalanes

C de Girona

Pg de Sant Joan

Estació del Nord

C dels Almogàvers

C de Nàpols

3

Pg de Gràcia

Arc de Triomf

25

Arc de Triomf

Pg de Pujades

Plaça de Joan Carles I

Ronda de Sant Pere

Parc de la Ciutadella

P

4

Catalunya

Urquinaona

Urquinaona

See map p300

Catalunya

Plaça de Catalunya

C Comtal

LA RIBERA

Pg de Circumval·lació

Pg de Circumval·lació

Zoo de Barcelona

5

C de Pelai

C dels Tallers

Catalunya

C de la Princesa

C Comercial

Palau dels Cervelló

Plaça dels Àngels

C d'en Xuclà

La Rambla

C del Bisbe

Jaume I

Via Laietana

CIUTAT VELLA

Barceloneta

Estació de França

C d'Ocata

C del Ballard

Jardins del Doctor Fleming

C del Carme

C de l'Hospital

Liceu

C d'Avinyó

Plaça de Sant Miquel

See map p292

Palau de Mar

Moll del Dipòsit

6

EL RAVAL

Rambla del Raval

See map p296

C Ample

Pg de Colom

Mirador del Port Vell

Plaça del Poeta Boscà

La Rambla de Santa Mònica

Marina

7

C de Sant Pau

Av de les Drassanes

Drassanes

Drassanes

PORT VELL

Port de Barcelona

See map p302

12

L'EIXAMPLE *Map on p306*

CENTRAL L'EIXAMPLE *Map on p310*

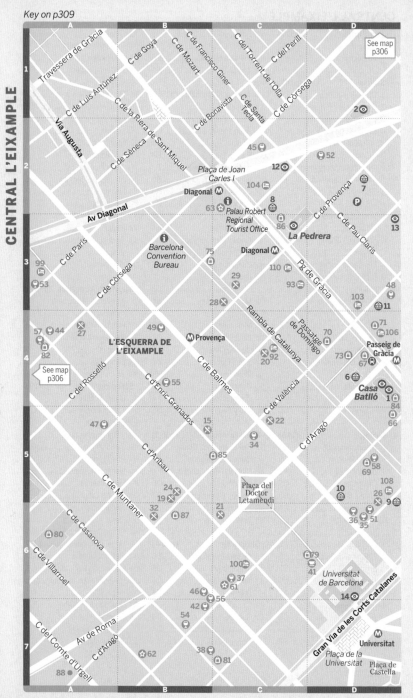

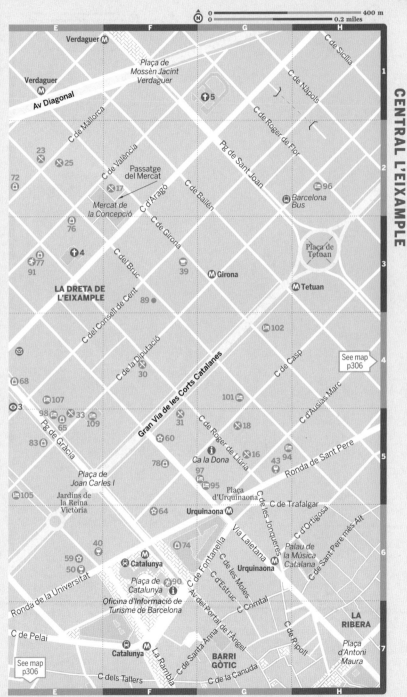

0   400 m
0   0.2 miles

Verdaguer Ⓜ

Plaça de
Mossèn Jacint
Verdaguer

Verdaguer
Ⓜ

Av Diagonal

C de Sicília

C de Nàpols

✝5

C de Roger de Flor

C de Mallorca

Pg de Sant Joan

23

✕25

C de València

Passatge
del Mercat

72
🔒

✕17

C d'Aragó

C de Bailèn

Mercat de
la Concepció

C de Girona

🛍96

Barcelona
Bus

76

Plaça de
Tetuan

🔒77
91

✝4

C del Bruc

39

Ⓜ Girona

Ⓜ Tetuan

LA DRETA DE
L'EIXAMPLE

C del Consell de Cent

89 ●

🛍102

✉

C de la Diputació

C de Casp

See map
p306

🔒68

30

👁3

🛍107

Gran Via de les Corts Catalanes

101🛍

98 ✕33
65 109

C de Roger de Llúria

31

✕18

C d'Ausias Marc

Pg de Gràcia

83🔒

✿60

78🔒

Ca la Dona

ℹ

✕16

43 94

Ronda de Sant Pere

97

🛍95

Plaça de
Joan Carles I

Plaça
d'Urquinaona

C de Trafalgar

🛍105

Jardins de
la Reina
Victòria

✿64

Ⓜ Urquinaona

C de les Jonqueres

C d'Ortigosa

C de Sant Pere més Alt

40

Via Laietana

Palau de
la Música
Catalana

59✿

🔒74

Ⓜ Urquinaona

50🛍

Ⓡ Catalunya

C de Fontanella

C de les Moles

Ronda de la Universitat

Plaça de
Catalunya

✿90

ℹ

C d'Estruc

C Comtal

LA
RIBERA

Oficina d'Informació de
Turisme de Barcelona

Av del Portal de l'Àngel

C de Ripoll

Plaça
d'Antoni
Maura

C de Pelai

Ⓜ Catalunya

La Rambla

C de Santa Anna

BARRI
GÒTIC

See map
p306

C dels Tallers

C de la Canuda

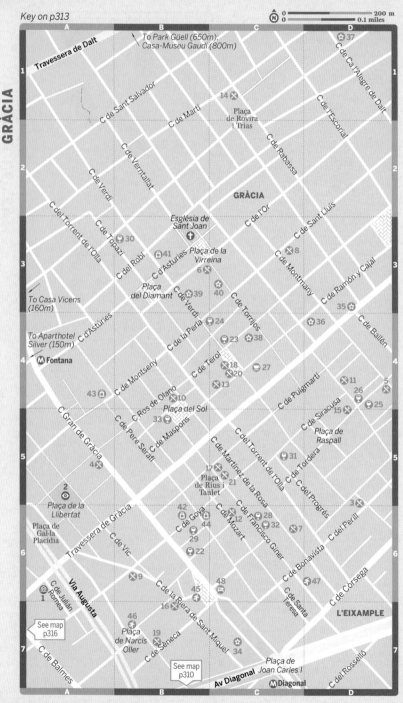

Key on p313

0 — 200 m
0 — 0.1 miles

Travessera de Dalt

To Park Güell (650m);
Casa-Museu Gaudí (800m)

C de Ca l'Alegre de Dalt

C de Sant Salvador

C de Martí

Plaça
de Rovira
i Trias

C de l'Escorial

C de Rabassa

C de Verntallat

C de Verdi

GRÀCIA

C del Torrent de l'Olla

C de Topazi

C de l'Or

C de Sant Lluís

Església de
Sant Joan

C del Robí

C d'Astúries

Plaça de la
Virreina

C de Montmany

C de Ramón y Cajal

To Casa Vicens
(160m)

Plaça
del Diamant

C de Verdi

C de Torrijos

C de Bailèn

C d'Astúries

C de la Perla

To Aparthotel
Silver (150m)

Fontana

C de Montseny

C de Terol

C de Puigmartí

C Ros de Olano

Plaça del Sol

C de Siracusa

C Gran de Gràcia

C de Pere Serafí

C de Maspons

C del Torrent de l'Olla

Plaça de
Raspall

C de Tordera

C del Progrés

2

Plaça de la
Llibertat

C de Martínez de la Rosa

Plaça
de Rius i
Taulet

Plaça de
Gal·la
Placídia

Travessera de Gràcia

C de Vic

C de Goya

C de Mozart

C de Francisco Giner

C del Perill

C de Bonavista

C de Còrsega

C de Julián
Romea

1

Via Augusta

C de la Riera de Sant Miquel

C de Santa
Teresa

L'EIXAMPLE

See map
p316

C de Balmes

Plaça
de Narcís
Oller

C de Sèneca

See map
p310

Plaça de
Joan Carles I

Av Diagonal

Diagonal

C del Rosselló

GRÀCIA *Map on p312*

GRÀCIA

LA ZONA ALTA

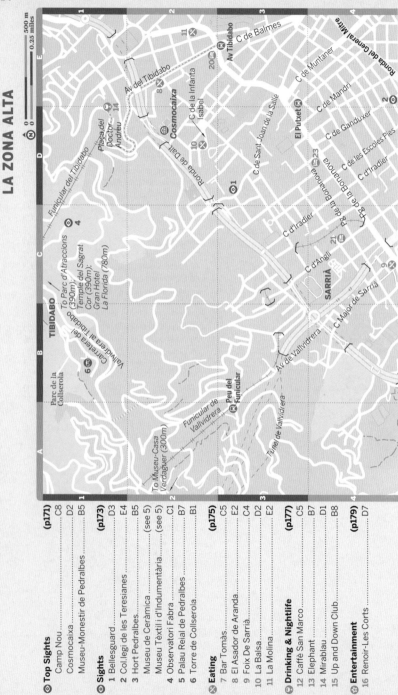

0   500 m
0   0.25 miles

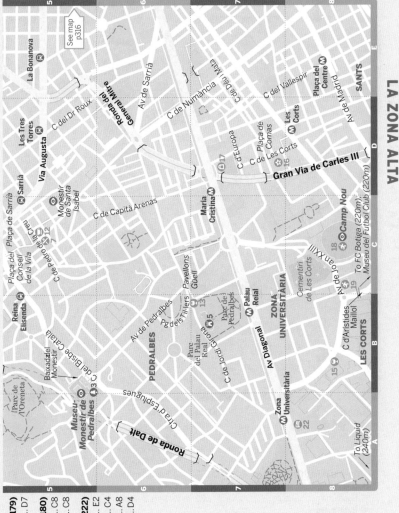

See map p316

Gran Via de Carles III

LA ZONA ALTA EAST

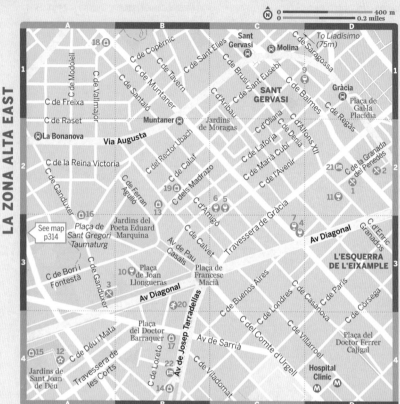

MONTJUÏC, SANTS & EL POBLE SEC *Map on p318*

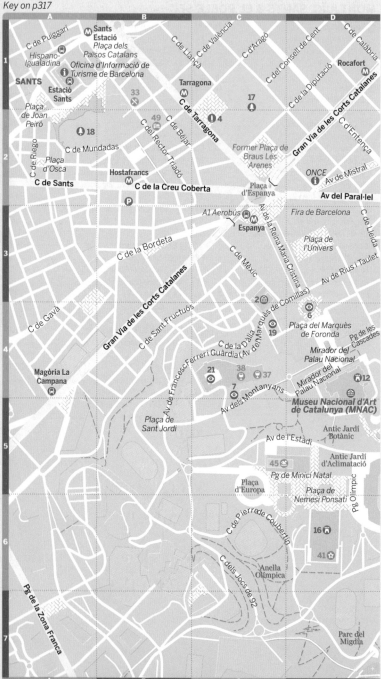

Key on p317

MONTJUÏC, SANTS & EL POBLE SEC

SANTS

Sants Estació
Plaça dels Països Catalans
Oficina d'Informació de Turisme de Barcelona

C de Puiggarí
Hispano-Igualadina
Estació Sants
Plaça de Joan Peiró
33
49
18
C de Riego
Plaça d'Osca
C de Mundadas
Hostafrancs
C de Sants
C del Rector Triadó
C de la Creu Coberta
C de Béjar
C de Llança
C de València
C de Tarragona
Tarragona
4
C d'Aragó
C del Consell de Cent
17
Rocafort
C de la Diputació
C d'Entença
Gran Via de les Corts Catalanes
Former Plaça de Braus Les Arenes
Plaça d'Espanya
ONCE
Av de Mistral
Av del Paral·lel

A1 Aerobús
Espanya
Fira de Barcelona
C de Lleida
Plaça de l'Univers
Av de Rius i Taulet
C de la Bordeta
C de Mèxic
Av de la Reina Maria Cristina
Gran Via de les Corts Catalanes
C de Gavà
C de Sant Fructuós
2
19
Plaça del Marquès de Foronda
6
Av del Marquès de Comillas
Pg de les Cascades
C de la Dàlia
Mirador del Palau Nacional
Magòria La Campana
Av de Francesc Ferrer i Guàrdia
21
38
37
Mirador del Palau Nacional
12
7
Av dels Montanyans
Museu Nacional d'Art de Catalunya (MNAC)
Plaça de Sant Jordi
Av de l'Estadi
Antic Jardí Botànic
Antic Jardí d'Aclimatació
45
Pg de Minici Natal
Plaça d'Europa
Plaça de Nemesi Ponsati
Pg Olímpic
C de Pierre de Coubertin
16
41
C dels Jocs de 92
Anella Olímpica
Pg de la Zona Franca
Parc del Migdia

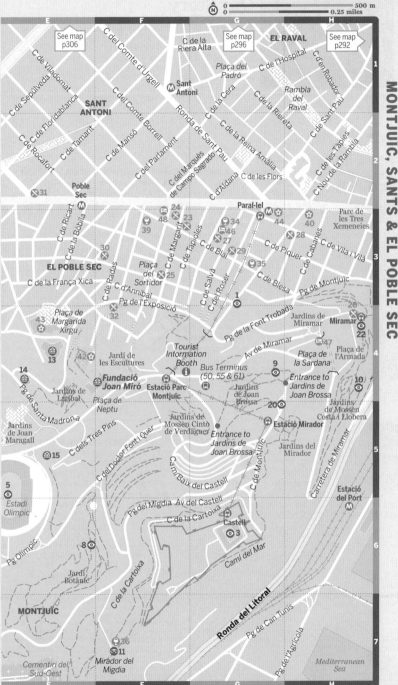

E F G H

See map p306

See map p296

See map p292

EL RAVAL

C del Comte d'Urgell

C de la Riera Alta

C de l'Hospital

C d'en Robador

C de Viladomat

Plaça del Padró

M Sant Antoni

C de la Cera

C de la Riereta

Rambla del Raval

C de Sant Pau

C de Sepúlveda

SANT ANTONI

C del Comte Borrell

Ronda de Sant Pau

C de la Reina Amàlia

C de les Tàpies

C de Floridablanca

C del Parlament

C de Marsó

C del Marquès de Campo Sagrado

C d'Aldana

C de les Flors

C Nou de la Rambla

C de Tamarit

C de Rocafort

🗙 31

Poble Sec M

Paral·lel M ⊕ 44 40

Parc de les Tres Xemeneies

C de Ricart

C de la Bòbila

🗙 24 23

48 39

🗙 34 46 27

28

C de Vila i Vilà

30 🗙

Plaça del Sortidor

C de Margarit

C de Tapioles

C de Blai

29

C de Piquer

C de Cabanes

35

EL POBLE SEC

25

C de Salvà

C de Blesa

Pg de Montjuïc

C de la França Xica

C de Radas

C d'Annibal

C del Roser

26

43

Plaça de Margarida Xirgu

Pg de l'Exposició

32

1

Jardins de Miramar

Miramar 22

13

42

Jardí de les Escultures

Tourist Information Booth i

Pg de la Font Trobada

Av de Miramar

47

Plaça de la Sardana

Plaça de l'Armada

14

Fundació Joan Miró

Estació Parc Montjuïc

Bus Terminus (50, 55 & 61)

9

Entrance to Jardins de Joan Brossa

10

Pg de Santa Madrona

Jardins de Laribal

Plaça de Neptú

Jardins de Joan Brossa

20

Jardins de Mossèn Costa i Llobera

Jardins de Joan Maragall

C dels Tres Pins

Jardins de Mossèn Cinto de Verdaguer

Estació Mirador

15

C del Doctor Font i Quer

Entrance to Jardins de Joan Brossa

Jardins del Mirador

Carretera de Miramar

5

Cami Baix del Castell

C de Montjuïc

Estació del Port M

Estadi Olímpic

Pg del Migdia Av del Castell

Pg Olímpic

C de la Cartoixa

Castell

8

3

6

Jardí Botànic

C de la Cartoixa

Cami del Mar

MONTJUÏC

Ronda del Litoral

Pg de Can Tunis

7

36 11

Mirador del Migdia

Pg de l'Agrícola

Mediterranean Sea

Cementiri del Sud-Oest

E F G H

0 ——— 500 m
0 ——— 0.25 miles

Our Story

A beat-up old car, a few dollars in the pocket and a sense of adventure. In 1972 that's all Tony and Maureen Wheeler needed for the trip of a lifetime – across Europe and Asia overland to Australia. It took several months, and at the end – broke but inspired – they sat at their kitchen table writing and stapling together their first travel guide, *Across Asia on the Cheap*. Within a week they'd sold 1500 copies. Lonely Planet was born.

Today, Lonely Planet has offices in Melbourne, London and Oakland, with more than 600 staff and writers. We share Tony's belief that 'a great guidebook should do three things: inform, educate and amuse'.

Our Writers

Regis St Louis

Coordinating Author; La Rambla & Barri Gòtic; Barceloneta & the Waterfront; Camp Nou, Pedralbes & La Zona Alta Regis first fell in love with Barcelona and Catalonia on a grand journey across Iberia in the late 1990s. Since then he has returned frequently, learning Spanish and a smattering of Catalan, and delving into the rich cultural history of this endlessly fascinating city. Favourite memories from his most recent trip include lingering over long seafood lunches with friends in Barceloneta, exploring hidden corners of La Zona Alta, catching evening concerts in the Ciutat Vella and feasting on perhaps the last *calçots* of the season. Regis is also the author of *Discover Barcelona*, and he has contributed to *Spain*, *Portugal* and dozens of other Lonely Planet titles. He lives in Brooklyn, New York. Regis also wrote the majority of the Plan Your Trip chapters, the Understand Barcelona and Survival Guide sections, and co-wrote the Sleeping chapter.

Read more about Regis at:
lonelyplanet.com/members/regisstlouis

Anna Kaminski

Day Trips Anna's love affair with Spain began with a Spanish course in Santander in 2001, and has continued unabated in spite of a severe bout of salmonella, prompting her to return to these shores time and time again. Having adopted Barcelona as her current home, she has particularly enjoyed exploring the incredibly diverse surrounding area, wandering the same landscapes as her favourite artist, Salvador Dalí, and widening her culinary horizons (not to mention her waistline) by sampling some of the best food in the country.

Vesna Maric

El Raval, La Ribera, La Sagrada Família & L'Eixample, Gràcia & Park Güell, Montjuïc Vesna is originally from Bosnia-Herzegovina; her love of all things Spanish started when she met her partner, Rafael, 10 years ago. She has since learned the language, explored the country and fallen in love with Barcelona over and over again, returning any time she has a chance. She loves the city's beaches, incredible food markets, architecture, great nightlife and fantastic Catalan cuisine. Vesna also wrote the What's New, With Kids, Entertainment and Shopping chapters and co-wrote the Sleeping chapter.

Published by Lonely Planet Publications Pty Ltd
ABN 36 005 607 983
8th edition – Nov 2012
ISBN 978 1 74220 021 7
© Lonely Planet 2012   Photographs © as indicated 2012
10 9 8 7 6 5 4 3 2 1
Printed in China